P9-DFF-519

Tonkin Gulf

Eugene G. Windchy

Tonkin Gulf

1971
Doubleday & Company, Inc.
Garden City, New York

Library of Congress Catalog Card Number 68–25593
Copyright © 1971 by Eugene G. Windchy
All Rights Reserved
Printed in the United States of America
First Edition

To my patient and beloved wife

Contents

A NOTE ON SOURCES

Most of the hitherto unrevealed information in this book I have obtained directly from the Navy men and ex-Navy men who were present in the Tonkin Gulf or involved with the Tonkin incidents in some way. I began interviewing these men in 1967. During four years of writing and research I came to know many of them fairly well, well enough to be impressed by their seriousness, their good nature, and their patriotism.

The interviews tended to be lengthy, sometimes stretching over a period of two or three days. Until late in 1967 I was able to record most of the interviews on tape. Then the Tonkin incidents became the subject of public controversy. That cauterized my sources for a while, and they never flowed so freely again. Even from the beginning some persons were apprehensive about discussing the Tonkin patrol. Few persons specified that they be anonymous; nonetheless, I have tended to make minimal use of attributed quotations. Many of the attributed quotations that do appear in this book I have taken from other published sources, chiefly newspaper articles and government documents.

Some persons who were at high levels of command in 1964 rejected my attempts to question or interview them. I regret not having been able to communicate directly with the former Secretary of Defense, Robert S. McNamara; the former Commander-in-Chief of the Pacific, Admiral Ulysses S. Grant Sharp; and the former Commander-in-Chief of the Pacific Fleet, Admiral Thomas H. Moorer (now Chairman of the Joint Chiefs of Staff).

The U. S. Defense Department did not encourage the writing of this book, but it did provide, following repeated requests, substantial

amounts of information. Official footdragging slowed my work considerably; yet official help did much to make it possible.

The government of North Vietnam provided no special assistance.
I was able to gather official North Vietnamese information only from
periodicals and radio broadcasts. Wherever used in this book, North
Vietnamese and other information of Communist origin is so
identified.

The speeches of Senator Wayne Morse were extremely useful, and
so were the published hearings of the Senate Foreign Relations Committee. Some of the initial leads for my research came from *I. F.
Stone's Weekly* (now a biweekly), which was consistently skeptical
of the Tonkin incidents. The Friends Committee on National Legis-
lation permitted me to examine their file of newspaper clippings.
The Associated Press photograph of the *Columbia Eagle* was flagged
by Charles H. Gill, Jr., who, seeing the picture in a suburban edition
of the Washington *Post,* wrote a letter about it to the editor.

To all who gave assistance, I offer my sincerest gratitude. In return, I have done my best to make every sentence in this book accurate and responsible.

GLOSSARY

Attack aircraft   A multiweapon plane intended primarily to destroy
  targets on the surface.
Black shoe   (Slang) A Navy officer who is not an aviator. Formerly
  only aviators wore brown shoes with the khaki uniform.
Bogey   Unidentified aircraft.
CIA   Central Intelligence Agency.
Conn   To direct the steersman. Responsibility for controlling the
  ship's movements.
Crusader   A supersonic jet interceptor aircraft built by Chance
  Vought; an F-8.
DD   A general purpose destroyer of conventional design.
DIA   Defense Intelligence Agency.
DMZ   Demilitarized Zone. The formerly neutral area between North

Vietnam and South Vietnam. The frequently unneutral area between North Korea and South Korea.

DRV   Democratic Republic of Vietnam; North Vietnam; NVN.

ECM   Electronic Countermeasure; a means of nullifying or misleading the enemy's electronic device—radio, radar, sonar, etc. ECM also refers to the monitoring and analysis of incoming waves, such as radar waves; thus "no ECM" can mean that no incoming radar has been detected.

ECCM   Electronic Counter-Countermeasure; a means of nullifying or misleading the enemy's ECM.

Golf time   The "zone time" applicable to the Tonkin Gulf, Indochinese peninsula, and that 15-degree segment of longitude; also known as Minus Seven because subtracting 7 hours from Golf time results in Greenwich Mean time (Zulu time). To convert Golf to Eastern Daylight time, subtract 11 hours; to convert Golf to Eastern Standard time, subtract 12 hours; to convert Golf to South Vietnamese civil time, *add* 1 hour. Golf time is the same as North Vietnamese civil time.

GQ   General Quarters; battle stations for all hands.

Gulf time   The time actually observed by U. S. Navy ships operating in the area of the Tonkin Gulf; usually the same as South Vietnamese civil time, though not in the case of Task Group 72.1.

Gunboat   A small surface vessel that carries guns as its primary armament.

Interceptor   An aircraft designed to combat other aircraft.

Light off   (Slang) Light; light up; turn on. Often heard in the past tense: lit off.

MAAG   Military Assistance Advisory Group; the ancestor of MACV. MAAG merged into MACV on May 15, 1964.

MACV   Military Assistance Command, Vietnam; U.S. forces in South Vietnam. Established in 1962.

MiG   A Russian warplane designed by Artem Mikoyan and Mikhail Gurevich, a design team famous for its subsonic and supersonic fighters.

Mosquito boat   (Slang) A torpedo boat.

Nasty boat   A fast gunboat which the U. S. Navy converted from the Norwegian torpedo boat of the same name.

NSA   National Security Agency.

NVN   North Vietnam.

Original ambush   In this book, the picture on *Maddox*'s radarscope at the time the ship went to General Quarters on the evening of August 4, 1964.

Phantom   A supersonic two-seated jet interceptor built by McDonnell Douglas; an F-4.

PT boat   A "patrol torpedo" boat used by the U. S. Navy during World War II. The wooden-hulled PT carried four torpedoes but proved more useful as a night scout and gunboat, according to recognized authorities.

Skunk   (Radar term) An unidentified surface blip.

Skyhawk   A light attack jet made by McDonnell Douglas; an A-4.

Skyraider   A propeller-driven attack plane made by Douglas Aircraft; an A-1, formerly designated AD; a Spad.

South Vietnamese time   An artificial zone or "civil time" 1 hour faster than Golf time and 1 hour faster than North Vietnamese civil time.

Spad   (Slang) A Skyraider; an A-1. "Spad" is an affectionate nickname inspired by the versatile, propeller driven French fighter plane of World War I, which was flown by Captain Eddie Rickenbacker and some other Allied aces.

Striker   (Slang) A Navy enlisted man studying for advancement to a new rating or specialty.

Supercarrier   A post-World War II aircraft carrier of more than 60,000 tons, now ranging up to 100,000 tons. With two flight decks, one angled away from the hull (a British innovation), the supercarrier can launch and recover planes at the same time.

Swatow   A type of fast gunboat. The Red Chinese converted Russian P-6 torpedo boats into "Swatow" gunboats and supplied a number of them to North Vietnam.

Tonkin spook   (Slang) A deceptive radar image ("phantom" or "ghost") found in the area of the Tonkin Gulf.

Torpedo boat   A small surface vessel, capable of high speed, which carries torpedoes as its principal armament, light guns as secondary armament.

Zone time   Time according to the 1-hour zones that correspond to 15-degree changes of longitude. Each of the 24 zones is designated alphabetically. Zone time bears only a rough relation to the civil time (or "standard time") established by local governmental authorities.

Prologue

The murky and endless jungle conflict in Southeast Asia represents the longest American war since the Revolution. It is one of the bloodiest of American wars, one of the most expensive, and by far the most frustrating; it may well prove the most damaging to American democracy. Some call it the first American war to be lost. Others insist that South Vietnam can yet be preserved as an independent, non-Communist state. In any event, those who wanted to get into the war have been looking for an honorable way out of it. As for those who opposed the war, they see no honor to be gained, whatever happens; they talk of a "moral disaster" and the "greatest tragedy of American history." To the people of Indochina, the war is more than a tragedy, more than a point of honor. It is a never-ending cataclysm, one of history's longest and most destructive armed conflicts.

How did the American people get into it? Few Americans wanted the war and even fewer expected it. The Vietnam War—or Indochina War—never has been officially declared, nor has it been generally understood. A democracy is not supposed to get into that kind of war, formerly the prerogative of kings. Yet the United States did get into it. As for how, the question has many answers. It has as many answers as there were steps along the way, most of them secret at the time they were taken. We could trace back more than thirty years American involvement with the Indochinese peninsula. Few Americans realize it, but for their country World War II began with a crisis over Vietnam.

In 1940 Western Europe fell to German conquest, and Imperial Japan took this opportunity to "station" troops in French Indochina.

A tropical area the size of Texas, the colonies of French Indochina included the present states of North Vietnam (Democratic Republic of Vietnam), South Vietnam (Republic of Vietnam), Laos, and Cambodia. "Indochina" is a misleading geographical expression that derives from India and China; the peninsula, of course, is neither, though it has been influenced by both. In 1940 the invading Japanese were interested in the northernmost part of Vietnam, specifically the province of Tonkin bordering on the Republic of China. Japan and China were at war, and through the Tonkinese port of Haiphong flowed most of China's life-giving trade with the United States. For years the mechanized might of Japan had been swallowed up by the vastness of the Asian continent. Now the militarists in Tokyo hoped to achieve victory through encirclement, blocking their enemy's last important route of supply. In response to this new aggression, President Franklin D. Roosevelt restricted the sale of American scrap iron, a move which inconvenienced but did not hamstring the ambitious islanders. Roosevelt's embargo did underline an important fact: those nations opposed to Germany and Japan controlled most of the world's raw materials.

For the benefit of Japan, French officials were permitted to continue administering the colonies of Indochina, extracting their resources in rubber, rice, and coal. The French loss of face, however, invited disorder, as did the "Asia for the Asiatics" propaganda of the Japanese. In the latter part of 1940, French soldiers dealt very severely with Vietnamese revolts, which had been endemic since the French conquered Vietnam in the nineteenth century. The Vietnamese were (and remain) the most vigorous and numerous of the Indochinese peoples.

In 1941 German armor drove deeply into the Soviet Union, and the Japanese generals looked on enviously, still bogged down in China. The Chinese now were getting most of their foreign supplies through a British colony, Burma. Increasingly the strategists in Tokyo were tempted to seize Burma and the rest of Southeast Asia, a rich prize in markets and raw materials. In preparation for these new conquests, the Japanese decided to build military bases in southern Vietnam. The French could not stop them. But how would the United States react? Except for some half-secret anti-submarine operations in the Atlantic, helping to maintain Britain's fragile line of supply, American power was not yet engaged in the European conflict. Indeed, the biggest ships of the U. S. Navy were based, threateningly, in the Pacific, at Pearl Harbor, Hawaii. Furthermore, the Japanese war machine was running chiefly on American oil

As he had done before, President Roosevelt demanded that the Japanese give up their war on the Asian continent. As before, the Japanese refused. (Imperial Japan considered that she had never lost a war, although, in fact, centuries before she had withdrawn from unsuccessful expeditions to China and Korea.) Now the American President took decisive steps. Quietly, he warned the Japanese to go no farther with their schemes of conquest. At the same time, Roosevelt arranged to cut off Japan's international supply of oil. The new embargo left the aggressor dependent on stockpiles of fuel. Something had to give. Within months came the earth-shaking attack on Pearl Harbor. A swift crippling of the U. S. Pacific Fleet was part of Tokyo's strategy for seizing the oil of Indonesia (then the Dutch East Indies). The Japanese had no intention of invading the United States, though it seemed that way at the time.

With the all-out help of the American people, the Allied powers recovered from their early setbacks, as happened previously in World War I.

By 1943 President Roosevelt was making specific plans for the postwar world, and somehow he had acquired a keen sense of responsibility for the people of Indochina. He was "terribly worried" about them; he felt they deserved something better than a continuation of French rule.[1] Roosevelt asked Generalissimo Chiang Kai-shek whether he wanted Indochina. The Chinese leader did not. The people there, he explained, were not Chinese and would not assimilate. The Generalissimo and the President then discussed the possibility of arranging self-government. Roosevelt suggested an international trusteeship. He thought that it would take a long time to educate the people of Indochina for self-government.

As matters turned out, the occupying Japanese provided steps toward self-government. With Germany in ruins and their own power ebbing away, the Japanese began to reconsider the advantages of anti-colonialism. Moreover, they noticed signs of rebelliousness among the French soldiers and administrators of Indochina. In the

---

[1] *The Public Papers and Addresses of Franklin D. Roosevelt,* compiled by Samuel I. Rosenman (New York: Harper and Brothers, 1950), page 562.

spring of 1945, the Japanese suddenly imprisoned the French and replaced them with native puppet regimes headed by native royalty—Vietnamese, Laotian, and Cambodian. The new French humiliation demonstrated once more that the white man was neither all-wise nor all-powerful.

Vietnam's chief executive was to be an anti-French nationalist by the name of Ngo Dinh Diem. At the last minute, however, the Japanese rejected him and picked out a man easier to deal with.

Meanwhile, the war was still going on, and American infiltrators were active in the hinterlands of Vietnam. Their job was to gather intelligence on the Japanese and to rescue shot-down American airmen, who were bombing the Japanese-controlled port facilities. The American infiltrators lived and worked with Communist-led, anti-French Vietnamese guerrillas. Like their Commander-in-Chief, the Americans sympathized with the local desire for independence, and, hoping to spur resistance to the Japanese, they gave material aid to the guerrillas—"notably Ho Chi Minh," according to a later Secretary of State.[2] The wispy, genial Ho impressed his American benefactors favorably, even though he and his men did little to bother the Japanese.

As World War II came to an end, far-reaching events took place in Vietnam, as elsewhere. By the Potsdam agreements, in which President Harry S Truman participated, the Chinese army was to disarm Japanese forces in northern Vietnam and keep order there temporarily while British troops did the same in southern Vietnam. Essentially, the Potsdam division of Vietnam continues today, as do the Allied divisions of Korea and Germany.

When the Chinese marched into Hanoi, huge, well-organized demonstrations welcomed them as allies in the recent war against Japan. In charge of a Vietnamese government was Ho Chi Minh, who already had displaced the Japanese puppet regime. The Japanese troops waited quietly for repatriation, while guarding the Bank of Indochina. The men loyal to Chiang Kai-shek did not like Communists, but they did not like the French, either, and they decided to regard Ho Chi Minh as a French problem. Besides, the Vietnamese leaders clearly were on good terms with American military officers

[2] Dean Acheson, *Present at the Creation* (New York: W. W. Norton, Inc., 1969), page 671.

in Hanoi, whose number included two generals from the U. S. South China Command. The Chinese put some anti-Communists into Ho's government. For the most part, Chiang's men were content to settle down to business as usual: extorting bribes and selling arms. On the international scene, the Generalissimo used his hold on northern Vietnam to bargain for the end of French treaty privileges in China.

The occupation of southern Vietnam did not go so smoothly. There, it might be said, the "First Indochina War" began. The British did not wish to promote the independence of Asian colonies, and they refused to deal with Ho Chi Minh's representatives in Saigon. Fighting broke out immediately. Far from disarming the Japanese, the British demanded that their erstwhile enemies help to keep order. For months, under British command, an international force of English, Indian, French, and Japanese troops tried to disarm the inhabitants of southern Vietnam.

Safe in Hanoi, under the protection of the Chinese Republic, Ho Chi Minh espoused the ideals of both Thomas Jefferson and Karl Marx. Nonetheless, he failed to obtain recognition from either the United States or the Soviet Union, which were competing for French favor in European politics. Not even the French Communist party, of which Ho was a founding member, supported the independence of Vietnam. The French government, however, recognized Hanoi in the spring of 1946, as the Chinese were about to withdraw.

A Paris-Hanoi agreement called for some French troops to enter northern Vietnam on a temporary basis (to be withdrawn in five annual installments), and for the Vietnamese people to determine their own future in free elections. There was no doubt that the Vietnamese, given the opportunity, would reject French rule. But the practical effect of the Paris-Hanoi agreement was to insure the safe entry of French troops into northern Vietnam, along with their heavy equipment. Soon the French High Commissioner for Indochina, Admiral Georges d'Argenlieu, felt strong enough to doublecross Hanoi. The admiral organized a separate state in southern Vietnam with its capital at Saigon, without benefit of free elections. Late in 1946 fighting broke out in the north, and a French warship, the cruiser *Suffren,* fired on Haiphong, killing from 6000 to 20,000 people. (The French estimate was 6000; the Vietnamese claimed 20,000 dead.) The torch of war then burned all over Vietnam, north as well as south.

The Hanoi government had time in which to raise a sizable army, but, lacking tanks and other heavy weapons, the Vietnamese soon were forced back into the hills. Ho and his men relied on the jungle for concealment and on the peasantry for information, food, and recruits. The French held the cities. On their side fought many "loyal" Vietnamese and European mercenaries, notably veterans of the German army. The French-led forces had plenty of firepower, but they seldom could find the enemy except when ambushed. The Communist-led guerrillas fought often enough and hard enough to make Vietnam a most unprofitable colony. The French continued the war largely for reasons of martial pride.

Over the years there have been many explanations for the war in Indochina. The French at first blamed it on machinations of the Japanese, of whom one or two thousand soldiers (according to French estimates) went over to the rebels. As late as 1947 French writers alleged that most of the Vietnamese people were loyal, that the Japanese stragglers had secret orders, and that Japanese commands sometimes could be heard over the din of battle. In private, French officials also blamed their troubles on the United States. The Americans, they said, persisted in sending arms to their old friend Ho Chi Minh. According to a distinguished and somewhat pro-French authority on Vietnam, the late Dr. Bernard B. Fall, secret American assistance to the guerrillas continued until 1947 and perhaps for some time thereafter.[3] Be that as it may, it is true that during the postwar period the United States exerted powerful diplomatic pressure on the European nations to free their colonies, as the United States freed the Philippines. It was the onset of the Cold War and the Red triumph in China that changed the American attitude toward Vietnam. Ho Chi Minh then was regarded as the tool of an international Communist conspiracy.

It was in 1949 or early 1950[4] that President Truman decided to help the French hang onto Vietnam, supporting "independence within the French Union." Massive assistance began in the latter part of 1950, following the North Korean invasion of South Korea—another consequence of divided occupation. By 1954, when the French

[3] *The Two Viet-Nams* (New York: Frederick A. Praeger, 1967), pages 71 and 469.

[4] U. S. Congress, Senate, Committee on Foreign Relations; *Supplemental Foreign Assistance;* Hearings, 89th Congress, 2nd Session (Washington: Government Printing Office, 1966), page 6.

effort collapsed, the United States was paying about 80 percent of the financial cost. As Senator J. William Fulbright has observed, this perhaps was the only time in history that the American people helped a European country maintain a colony.

Before quitting the struggle in Vietnam, the French sought direct American military assistance. Helping to plead their cause were some of President Dwight D. Eisenhower's top advisers, including the Vice-President, Richard M. Nixon, and the Chairman of the Joint Chiefs of Staff, Admiral Arthur W. Radford. But the leaders of the U. S. Army did not want a new land war in Asia, and neither did President Eisenhower. In his memoirs, Eisenhower remarked that the mass of the Vietnamese people "supported the enemy," and that every Indochina expert he could find thought that Ho Chi Minh could win a Vietnamese election, possibly with 80 percent of the vote.[5]

At a peace conference in Geneva, the big powers, including the United States and Red China, in 1954 recognized the independence of Vietnam, Laos, and Cambodia. Notwithstanding that fact, Vietnam again was divided in two, this time a little farther north than at Potsdam. Thus the French did not have to accept an immediate, total defeat. Again the division was supposed to be temporary; again free elections were planned. In two years a nationwide referendum was to reunite the northern and southern "zones." Until then the Vietnamese Communist troops, whether northern or southern in origin, were to regroup in the north; and the formerly pro-French troops, whether northern or southern in origin, were to regroup in the south.

Most observers assumed that the militarily victorious Ho Chi Minh would take over the whole of Vietnam sooner or later, one way or another. But the U. S. Government still hoped to prevent that. While Ho re-established his government in Hanoi, President Eisenhower installed in Saigon, as Premier of South Vietnam, the relatively obscure Ngo Dinh Diem, who had been living abroad since 1950. When in 1955 Ho Chi Minh asked about getting ready for the nationwide referendum, Premier Diem[6] rejected the whole plan. He explained

[5] *Mandate for Change* (New York: Doubleday, Inc., 1963), page 372.

[6] In Vietnam the family name is given first so that, properly, one would refer to "Premier Ngo" instead of "Premier Diem." But the Western practice, which will be followed in this text, is to use the given name in certain cases, especially those of South Vietnamese leaders.

to the world that free elections were not possible in North Vietnam, which would swamp the South with Communist votes. Diem then held an election within South Vietnam and became President with a claimed 98.2 percent of the ballots cast. In 1956, the year scheduled for nationwide referendum, South Vietnam's army and police began rounding up thousands of known Communists and their suspected sympathizers.

The Communist North was no paradise, either. Free elections were not held there, and a brutal collectivization of land inspired local revolts, especially in the poor, hardscrabble country around President Ho's birthplace. It has been estimated that from 10,000 to 50,000 people died in the Communist "land reform," which was not completed.[7]

By 1957 guerrilla warfare smoldered in South Vietnam, instigated or not by North Vietnam. The origin of the "Second Indochina War" was confused by the insistence of American officials that it did not exist, and by President Diem's ability to make violent enemies with no help from anybody. Diem's staunchest supporters were approximately 900,000 northerners who had chosen to live in the South; most of them, like Diem, were Catholic in religion. To the typical, non-Christian South Vietnamese, Diem was not an attractive or sympathetic leader. In economics he sided with the landlord more than with the tenant farmer. In politics he set the clock back five hundred years by abolishing the local election of village chiefs.[8] Diem preferred to rule the countryside with men of his own choosing, and the new guerrilla war began with the assassination of these appointees. By 1959 they were dying at the rate of ten per day; yet the Eisenhower administration thought that South Vietnam was making great strides, and it considered withdrawing the U.S. military advisory mission. The Pentagon was building a large, mechanized South Vietnamese military force in case North Vietnam should launch a Korean-style blitz over the border.

In actuality, a different kind of invasion was getting under way. The southern Communist troops who had regrouped in the North

[7] Joseph Buttinger, *Vietnam: A Dragon Embattled* (New York: Frederick A. Praeger, 1967), II, page 914. Fall, page 156. Buttinger estimated 10,000 to 15,000 dead. Fall estimated 50,000.

[8] Roger Hilsman, *To Move a Nation* (New York: Doubleday, Inc., 1967), page 418. Buttinger, page 945.

could not be expected to stay up there forever. They started to walk back home, carrying their weapons. In September of 1960 North Vietnamese support for these guerrillas became evident. A Communist party congress in Hanoi called for liberating South Vietnam from U.S. imperialism so as to achieve national unity, independence, and freedom.[9] By the end of 1960, according to the U. S. State Department, from 1800 to 4500 men had infiltrated into South Vietnam.[10] In the same year, the size of the full-time guerrilla force was estimated at 5000 men,[11] and the South Vietnamese army numbered 150,000.[12] In 1961, with the South Vietnamese army suffering reverses in the field, President John F. Kennedy began sending to Vietnam thousands of armed American "advisers."

Late in 1963 the unpopular President Diem died in a military coup. Within a few weeks, President Kennedy was the victim of an assassin's bullet. American policy in Vietnam then came under the direction of the former Vice-President, Lyndon B. Johnson.

As a senator, Lyndon Johnson in 1954 vehemently opposed direct American intervention in Vietnam, and during the presidential campaign of 1964 he took a strong stand against such proposals. Re-elected, however, President Johnson in 1965 plunged the United States into open warfare, not only in South Vietnam but, by air, in North Vietnam. The Johnson administration explained that North Vietnam was supplying and directing the Communist guerrillas in the South and that, increasingly, the Communist guerrillas were being joined by ethnic North Vietnamese. Red China, said the President, was spurring this "aggression from the north." As usual, Peking was loudly encouraging "wars of liberation" in the underdeveloped countries—that is, the non-Communist ones. The Chinese also had exploded an atomic bomb.

As legislative authority for war, President Johnson referred to the Tonkin Gulf resolution, a broadly worded document that the Congress had approved in the summer of 1964. The vote took place

[9] U. S. Department of State, Office of Public Services; *A Threat to the Peace;* Publication 7308 (Washington: Government Printing Office, 1961), I, page 14.

[10] U. S. Department of State, Office of Media Services; *Aggression from the North;* Publication 7839 (Washington: Government Printing Office, 1965), I, page 3.

[11] Hilsman, page 419.

[12] Admiral Harry D. Felt quoted in *Facts on File Yearbook,* 1960, page 211.

during a brief crisis that involved two perplexing naval incidents. On August 2, 1964, Communist torpedo boats, for no apparent reason, reportedly attacked an American destroyer. Two days later they attacked the same destroyer, plus another one accompanying her. Swiftly President Johnson ordered the Navy to strike back at North Vietnam from the air. At his request the Congress rapidly gave its assent to doing anything necessary to prevent further aggression. These critical events, both naval and legislative, took place within a single week. They were all but forgotten until 1965 when the nation went to war.

Whether it was proper to use the Tonkin Gulf resolution as authority for war eventually became the subject of bitter debate, and so did the naval action that stimulated its passage. Many persons came to doubt that the Johnson administration told the truth about what happened in the Tonkin Gulf; the Gulf itself has been termed the "birthplace of the credibility gap"—that great chasm of distrust which still separates the American people from their political leaders. Nevertheless, the Tonkin Gulf resolution—formally known as the Southeast Asia resolution—in 1970 helped to justify President Richard M. Nixon's invasion of Cambodia. In assailing the Cambodian venture, American doves recalled that President Nixon promised peace in the election campaign of 1968. Nixon retorted that the Cambodian "incursion" was necessary to that aim.

During the long slide into an expanding war, the American people seldom found it easy to understand what was happening, nor did most experts. Words differed from deeds. Doves turned into hawks, and hawks into doves. Looking backward, however, it can be seen that there was a particular time when the mystery was at its deepest, and the consequences of ignorance were the greatest.

That time was the first week of August 1964.

Tonkin Gulf

Chapter I

The Surface of the News

The morning of Sunday, August 2, 1964, was pleasantly warm, offering the promise of a fine day; and the nation was at peace. Then television and radio newscasters broke into the holiday calm with an important announcement: during the night, a ship of the U. S. Navy had been attacked on the high seas. The American vessel was a destroyer, the 3300-ton USS *Maddox*. The attackers were three torpedo boats. They belonged to—whom? The official announcement did not say. From the beginning, the naval events of this week were going to be more puzzling than any others since 1898 when, mysteriously, the USS *Maine* blew up in Havana harbor, precipitating the Spanish-American War.[1]

Judging from the location of what was called the *"Maddox* incident," the short-range torpedo craft ought to have been Communist. The fighting took place in the Tonkin Gulf (or Tonkin Bay), a little-known stretch of salt water almost entirely surrounded by Red territory. According to the officially reported latitude and longitude, the *Maddox* was attacked about 28 nautical miles from the coast of North

---

[1] The popular war cry was "Remember the *Maine!* To Hell with Spain," but the basic issue of the war was Cuban independence, which the American people favored, and President William McKinley did not actually accuse Spain of sinking the American battleship. He quoted the findings of a U. S. Navy Court of Inquiry, which said that the ship had been sunk by a mine placed by persons unknown. Spanish authorities contended that the explosion was internal and accidental, and recent American investigators have considered that not unlikely. See John E. Weems, *The Fate of the* Maine (New York: Holt, 1958), and the brief remarks in *Sea Power,* edited by E. B. Potter and Fleet Admiral Chester W. Nimitz (Englewood Cliffs, N.J.: Prentice-Hall, 1960).

Vietnam and 120 miles from the Red Chinese island of Hainan. Perhaps the attackers were North Vietnamese, although the notion of such a tiny country challenging the U. S. Navy sounded ridiculous.

The battle took place during the American night but during the Far Eastern day. Shortly after 4 P.M., local time, three torpedo boats launched a trio of deadly missiles, any one of which probably was capable of sinking the destroyer if it struck home. The *Maddox,* however, successfully dodged the feathery wakes. Somehow the ship also escaped damage from 37-millimeter shells fired by the enemy. The American sailors fought back with 5-inch guns, and Navy aircraft joined in their defense. Flying from the carrier *Ticonderoga,* four jet planes raked the torpedo boats with rocket missiles and cannon fire. The enemy gave up his attack.

One badly damaged torpedo boat lay motionless in the water. The other two, also damaged, retreated slowly. Retreated to where? The official announcement did not say. The American side, both ship and aircraft, came through the battle unscathed. Most baffling was the lack of any motive for an attack. The destroyer, far from land, was carrying out a "routine patrol in international waters." The attack was "unprovoked."

The official statement came from Pearl Harbor, headquarters of Admiral Ulysses S. Grant Sharp, Jr., Commander-in-Chief, Pacific (CINCPAC). (The news flash from Hawaii reminded many Americans of another surprise attack, more than twenty years before, which ended their days of global isolation.) Some newsmen interpreted the remote release as an attempt to cool off the crisis by treating it as a matter of regional—and therefore limited—consequence. To most journalists, however, getting the word from CINCPAC was more perplexing than ominous. They were familiar with—and annoyed by—the Johnson administration's habit of managing the news by centralizing spokesmen and reducing their number. Military information of any importance usually came from a few well-controlled offices in Washington. But now Hawaii was telling the world; and the news was not only important, it was sensational. Did President Johnson repose such extraordinary confidence in Admiral Sharp? Perhaps he did, but Sharp was not even in Hawaii. He was aboard an airplane, returning to headquarters from a visit to Bangkok and Saigon. Handing out the news at Pearl was Air Force Colonel Willis L. Helmantoler. Colonel Helmantoler didn't seem to know much about the naval action, even though it had happened some six hours before he announced it.

(In any event, the Honolulu release was no accident. The official statement was approved in Washington; transmitted to Hawaii; released there at 10:15 A.M., Eastern Daylight Time; and then released by the Pentagon, which *quoted* Hawaii. The roundabout procedure soft-pedaled the news to some extent; it also de-emphasized Washington's responsibility for what was said.)

In Washington reporters rushed to the White House, where they found top officials slipping in and out of the side door. The high-ranking officials, civilian and military, were keeping quiet. Nothing new was learned. The enemy, whoever he was, remained totally silent.

It was Sunday evening when the identity of the attackers became official: they were, after all, North Vietnamese. Again the information did not come from Washington. The Secretary of State, Dean Rusk, dropped the news in New York, where he had flown to keep a speaking engagement. In Hawaii somebody confirmed this statement, saying that the boats had been identified through photographs. There was talk about gun camera film from the fighter planes, but no pictures were released.

Admiral Sharp was not in his office at the critical time, but neither was he out of action. From his plane, an airborne command post, Sharp ordered that the Gulf patrol be continued and strengthened. Later, arriving in Honolulu, the wiry little admiral agreed with newsmen that the attack might reflect a change in Communist tactics. Somebody recalled that unarmed reconnaissance planes often had been shot at along Communist frontiers. Did the *Maddox*'s shooting back reflect any change in American tactics? "No," snapped the admiral. "We have always had a policy that if somebody shoots at us, we will shoot back at him. Our ships are always going to go where they need to be."

The Secretary of the Navy, Paul H. Nitze, was on a trip to Japan. There he told American newsmen that the U. S. Navy had been patrolling in the Tonkin Gulf for years and would continue to do so. The destroyer had "acquitted itself very well, indeed." Nitze sidestepped questions as to whether the ship ought to have chased the retreating boats in order to sink them. As time went on, Vietnam doves would raise embarrassing questions about the Tonkin Gulf, but the first hints of criticism came from the hawkish point of view.

Newsmen asked the State Department how much territorial water the North Vietnamese claimed. The Department sniffed that it had no record of any claim by that country, which the United States, anyway, did not recognize. The usual Communist claim was 12 miles, but the *Maddox* was reported to be more than 30 miles from shore. Somebody in the government explained that Communist countries have been known to assert sovereignty over huge gulfs and bays partially enclosed by their territory.

By Monday morning, August 3, the North Vietnamese still had said nothing. There had been no more shooting in the Gulf, and the nation breathed easily. Maybe the Communists had learned their lesson. The New York stock market declined very slightly, except for a little boost that Sunday's battle gave to the aircraft industry.

Congressmen of both parties heaped praise on the U. S. Navy; some talked of promoting the officers who gave the order to open fire. For many years, something strange had been going on in the jungles of Southeast Asia. It was good to get a Communist out in the open where the U. S. Navy could deal with him.

The Chairman of the Senate Armed Services Committee, Georgia Democrat Richard B. Russell, said there was no need for his Committee to investigate what had happened. Nevertheless, a few unanswered questions remained.

First of all, why would North Vietnam, boasting only a few hand-me-down mosquito boats, want to challenge the greatest maritime force in history, the U. S. Navy? Second, having made the challenge and lost, how did the damaged boats get away? One boat was left "not moving." Were there no survivors available for questioning? What finally happened to this boat? In Washington anonymous spokesmen used terms like "presumed sunk" and "almost certainly sunk." Why the uncertainty? The Navy reportedly patrolled the Gulf to "look for signs of unusual activity." Wasn't the battle on Sunday unusual? Why didn't the Navy know more about that?

Actually, such nagging questions took up very little space in the newspapers, which, sharing the mood of their readers, were delighted by the Navy's action. It was the other side that started a fight; it was our side that won; why complain?

Still, according to one news report, President Johnson, too, wondered why the Navy hadn't done a little more work on Sunday. Gathering his admirals, the President gave them a tongue-lashing. "You've got a whole fleet and all those airplanes," he exploded, "and you can't even sink three little old PT boats!" Of course, all 125 ships of the Seventh Fleet were not cruising in the Tonkin Gulf on Sunday, but a destroyer was there, and an aircraft carrier was close enough to send help. The red-faced admirals explained that, by the peacetime rules of engagement, naval forces were to shoot back if attacked, but they were not to pursue and destroy the attacker. The President soon fixed that.

At 11:30 A.M. Monday, Johnson read aloud to newsmen a statement on what he was doing about the North Vietnamese attack. The patrol in the Gulf, he said, would be doubled by adding another destroyer, and the two ships would have an air cover. If attacked again, the Navy not only would drive off the attackers but would destroy them as well. The usually talkative President refused to answer any questions.

Johnson said nothing about further action against North Vietnam. Evidently he intended to practice what the U. S. Government often preached—especially to nations of the Middle East—that retaliation violated international law, which requires the peaceful settlement of disputes. Secretary Rusk advised reporters that Sunday's action was sufficient. "The other side got a sting out of this," said he. "If they do it again, they'll get another sting." Newspapers generally praised the Johnson administration as showing the right mixture of firmness and restraint.

Predictably, the conservative New York *Daily News* took a potshot at the White House. "We're glad," sneered the *News,* "that President Johnson has dropped his great peacemaker pose long enough to order our naval forces in the area beefed up . . ." and went on to demand the bombing of North Vietnam, Laos, and Red China.

By a bizarre coincidence, the Republican presidential candidate, Senator Barry M. Goldwater, happened to be yachting in the Pacific on a converted torpedo boat. Hearing of the President's Monday morning statement, Goldwater hinted to the press that his own tough line on Vietnam was stiffening the administration's policy. But the senator wasn't convinced that the incident represented any big change in the offing. "Does it mean," he asked, "medium bombers are going to interdict supply lines?" Goldwater, a reserve major general in the Air Force, recommended bombing North Vietnam in order to win the guerrilla war in South Vietnam. Cynics called Goldwater the "Air Force's candidate for President." President Johnson discouraged talk of bombing North Vietnam. Soon to be nominated by the Democrats, Johnson would be the peace candidate.

There remained the big question of why North Vietnam chose to attack an American man-of-war. Hanoi was maintaining silence; and Washington officials, as the newspapers said over and over again, "refused to indulge in speculation." Some Washington officials, nevertheless, planted stories anonymously in "background briefings" and "off-the-record" interviews. Most of their explanations attributed some kind of elaborate plot to the Communist world. A few did not. From the spate of ideas thrown to eager newsmen, a number of theories emerged:

Trigger Happy Theory—Some local torpedo boat commander ordered the attack without proper authority.

Feint Theory—Red China ordered its puppet, North Vietnam, to make the attack in order to draw attention away from an imminent invasion of Taiwan, Korea, or Laos.

Confusion Theory—The North Vietnamese mistakenly thought the *Maddox* was involved with recent alleged South Vietnamese raids on their territory. The State Department denied that there were any American attacks on North Vietnam and had "no knowledge" of attacks by anybody else. (The Confusion Theory appealed greatly to certain analysts who mistakenly thought that Sunday's battle was fought in darkness—perhaps because of the delay in identifying the torpedo craft and because the battle took place during the night, American time.)

Propaganda Theory—State Department officials were inclined to think that the North Vietnamese were trying to spotlight the U. S. Navy's habit of snooping along their coastline. (But two days after the attack—Tuesday morning—Hanoi still was making no propaganda.)

Testing of the Will Theory—By attacking the *Maddox*, North Vietnam was trying to scare the United States into refusing further aid to the South Vietnamese government in its fight against Communist rebels.

Paper Tiger Theory—The Red Chinese and their North Vietnamese puppets wanted to prove that the decadent, capitalistic Americans were weak and could be defeated easily. (Perhaps the Reds were keeping silent because the attack had failed.)

Conference Table Theory—The Communists were trying to push the United States into negotiating a settlement on Vietnam. (Both Hanoi and Paris had called for a new Geneva Conference. Also favoring negotiations were the UN's Secretary General, U Thant, and, by some accounts, the Soviet Union. President Johnson rejected negotiations as a device to "ratify terror.")

In time for the morning papers, Thursday, August 6, the Defense Department released an Official Chronology of Sunday's battle. According to this more detailed report, the *Maddox,* as early as 12:30 P.M., local time, observed three torpedo boats approaching from the north while the American ship was 30 miles from the coast.[2] More than two hours later, at 2:40 P.M., the torpedo craft, closing at high speed, took on a hostile appearance. At 3:08 P.M. the destroyer reported that she was under attack. The ship opened fire with her 5-inch battery after three warning shots failed to slow down the attackers. Two boats closed to 5000 yards, firing two torpedoes, which the *Maddox* evaded. The missiles passed close to starboard. The third boat came closer still, suffered a direct hit from *Maddox*'s gunfire, and dropped a torpedo which was not seen to run. The boats fired machine guns at the destroyer. In return, aircraft dived on them as the *Maddox* continued in a southerly direction. The ship met another destroyer, the *C. Turner Joy,* and the two began patrolling together.

The careful reader might have noticed a few discrepancies in the official statements now available. According to the Official Chronology the battle started at 3:08 P.M., local time; but in Sunday's statement it had begun at 4:08 P.M. Apparently somebody was confused as to the time zone in which the battle took place. In the Official Chronology the enemy's boats had fired machine guns; in Sunday's

[2] The Chronology did not say whether it was using nautical miles or statute ("land") miles. When measuring distances at sea, this book will use nautical miles except when otherwise specified and except when, as above, official sources do not make clear which is involved. One nautical mile equals approximately 1.15 statute miles. Thus, according to the August 2 press release from CINCPAC, the *Maddox* was attacked 28 nautical miles or 32 statute miles from North Vietnamese territory (measuring from coastal islands to the position 19:40 North and 106:34 East).

statement they had fired 37-millimeter shells. (Navy men, however, often call automatic cannon "heavy machine guns.") As for the "C. Turner Joy," the Navy had no ship by that name. It did have a *Turner Joy,* bearing the slightly abridged name of the deceased Admiral C. Turner Joy. In all innocence, mistakes can be made.

Most puzzling of all, the Official Chronology was vague about who was going in what direction. The Chronology read as if *Maddox* were steaming southward the whole time, but it did not explicitly say so. The destroyer's southerly course and the patrol boats' southerly course were mentioned in different paragraphs, under different times. In its typed form, the Chronology ran on for more than a page, single-spaced. But with all of that information, the careful reader could not with confidence draw a diagram of what happened.

As the *Daily News* remarked, it did seem that the President was beefing up our forces in the South China Sea. On Tuesday morning, August 4, newspapers had reported the departure from Hong Kong of the supercarrier *Constellation.* Hong Kong newsmen thought the ship left rather suddenly, and there were tales of Shore Patrolmen grabbing sailors from their customary places of recreation. The Navy did not say where the carrier was going, but, as became known later, she headed for the Tonkin Gulf. Evidently the Navy did not subscribe to the Feint Theory.

The *Constellation*'s departure for the Gulf proved opportune. By 9 A.M., EDT, Tuesday, when the carrier was 12 hours at sea, the destroyers in the Gulf reported another Communist attack shaping up, this time in the darkening gloom after sunset. The *Maddox* and the *Turner Joy* were surrounded by radar contacts. Messages now streamed all over the high command circuits as admirals in Japan, Hawaii, Washington—and who could tell where else?—sat back to watch the second match in the Gulf series. This time the Navy had new rules and a bigger stake in the game. Two destroyers were in the pot, the carrier *Ticonderoga* backed them up, and the *Constellation* was on the way.

By 11 A.M., EDT, the destroyers reported that torpedoes and gunfire were being exchanged.

Win or lose, there were plans to be made. The Secretary of Defense, Robert S. McNamara, called the Joint Chiefs of Staff to his office. Secretary of State Rusk came over to join the military planners. Rusk had worked in the Defense establishment for many years, and he prided himself on a thorough knowledge of military affairs, especially in the Far East, where he had served in China during World War II. Before noon this group proceeded to the White House, joining men from other agencies. Newsmen noticed nothing unusual: there previously had been scheduled a meeting of the National Security Council to discuss trouble in the Mediterranean, where the Turks were threatening to bomb Cyprus.

But if newsmen noted nothing out of the ordinary, stock market speculators did. On Tuesday, August 4, the market, by the *Times* average, took its biggest one-day loss since the assassination of President Kennedy. Commentators attributed the drop to heavy selling by professional traders and to anxiety concerning the international situation. Even aircraft issues were weak. (Perhaps Pentagon market buffs triggered the decline. Rumors of the "Pentagon selling out"— if any—would spread like wildfire among brokers and traders.)

Officials at the White House agreed that the North Vietnamese should not go unpunished for their second attack. It was decided to retaliate by air, and there was some discussion concerning whether the strike ought to be made by South Vietnamese or American planes. According to the New York *Times,* President Johnson decided "unequivocally" that American aircraft would do the job.

Having made this decision, the President went to a previously scheduled luncheon with Rusk, McNamara, and McGeorge Bundy, the White House Assistant for National Security Affairs. (This was the beginning of the "Tuesday lunch," which, in later years, would plan bombing operations on a regular and detailed basis.) By early afternoon, when the lunch started, the shooting match in the Gulf was over. Again, there had been no damage to the American side. Two torpedo boats, at a minimum, were reported sunk. But the decision to retaliate already had been made.

Being light in Washington, it was still dark in the Gulf, and precise air strikes would have to wait for the planet to turn North Vietnam into the sun. The President and his advisers had all afternoon in which to make their plans. News media said later that, following lunch, more officials joined the elite planning group. They included George W. Ball, Undersecretary of State; John A. McCone, Director of the Central Intelligence Agency (CIA); and Richard Helms, a CIA man who later became Director. General Earle G. Wheeler, Chairman of the Joint Chiefs, was out of town until late in the afternoon. The newspapers said nothing about naval men at the White House meeting. Chief of Naval Operations was Admiral David L. McDonald, who was barely heard of all week.

The naval activist seemed to be "Oley" Sharp, out in Honolulu, who spent a lot of time talking to Washington on his gold telephone. McNamara asked him whether the two carriers had enough punch for the job at hand. "Hell, yes!" Sharp informed his civilian superior. The targets were to include certain North Vietnamese naval bases and an oil storage facility reportedly near one of them. The oil tanks, it was said, were thrown in to make sure the Communists knew we meant business. Untouched by the raids would be the North Vietnamese capital, Hanoi, and the major port of Haiphong with its international shipping.

Commentators later were to marvel at President Johnson's speed. They contrasted it with the long days of agony that preceded the Cuban missile confrontation—noting, however, that the Cuban crisis involved a much greater risk of nuclear war.

Having heard nothing about the new battle in the Tonkin Gulf, newspapers on Tuesday evening reported that the crisis was over. But even as they were hitting the stands up and down the eastern coast, the Pentagon—directly this time—announced the swirling night attack. Nothing was said about retaliation.

Meanwhile, at 6 P.M. members of the National Security Council began gathering at the White House to discuss and ratify the bombing plan.

That did not take long. By 6:45 P.M. the President had gathered together sixteen congressional leaders. Newspapers described this White House meeting as a "consultation," but it seemed more like a briefing. A panoply of high officials spoke to the lawmakers, presenting the views of Defense, State, and CIA. The attack was described as a probing operation directed by Red China. President Johnson outlined his plans brusquely, and the Democrats fell into line. Among Republicans, the key man was Everett M. Dirksen, the Senate Minority Leader. Dirksen waved his O.K. As a Goldwater supporter, he had to look tough.

President Johnson reminded the lawmakers of how President Truman and other Chief Executives had been forced to take military action without first securing a declaration of war. Sometimes that could not be helped. Tonight, however, this consultation was being held, and everybody agreed that strong action was necessary. Would the Congress show its support publicly? The Congress had passed resolutions, Johnson recalled, to back up President Eisenhower in the Taiwan Strait and in the Middle East. The legislators agreed that such a resolution would be a good idea. Before they left the White House, Johnson shook the hand of each, wringing from it an individual pledge of support.

Before and after the meeting, which lasted an hour and a half, officials of the Executive Branch stressed the need for absolute security. The enemy was not to know of the air raids until the planes were over their targets. The House Minority Leader, Charles A. Halleck, fearing that a possible leak might be blamed on his party, took care to remain above suspicion. "I hid out for a couple of hours," he later told the House, "and did not even answer the telephone when I finally got home."

The White House tried several times to reach Senator Goldwater, but the ship-to-shore telephone on his torpedo boat was not in good working order. After the senator was back on land, the President talked to him personally, and, at 10:07 P.M., obtained affirmation of his support.

It remained for the American people to be informed.

Television cameras and lights rolled into the Fish Room of the White House. At 11:35 P.M. the President stepped into the glare, and, speaking in grave tones, made the most awe-inspiring telecast since President Kennedy had announced the Cuban missile confrontation. Some Republicans had muttered that President Kennedy delayed his announcement with the forthcoming congressional elections in mind, but no such charge could be leveled against President Johnson, who was on the air within hours of the new attack in the Tonkin Gulf.

Since the air action was "now in execution," the President could not give details, but he described the raids as "limited and fitting." Johnson mentioned the meeting with congressional leaders. He said that they had promised swift passage of a resolution "making it clear that our government is united in its determination to take all necessary measures in support of freedom and in defense of peace in Southeast Asia." The President expressed his conviction that "firmness in the right is indispensable for peace."

During the Korean War, then called the Korean Conflict, American forces had been part of a United Nations army so that, technically, the raids on North Vietnam constituted the first American assault on Communist territory. The concept of sanctuary, which the Red Chinese had enjoyed in Manchuria—and UN forces had enjoyed in Japan—was dealt a heavy blow.

The raids were to be a surprise attack—what used to be called a "sneak attack"—by a large country on a small one. In weighing the opinions during the Cuban missile crisis, President Kennedy had specifically rejected such tactics. Deeming it repugnant, with overtones of Pearl Harbor, Kennedy chose a confrontation with the Soviet Union instead. However, Cuba had not made a sneak attack on us as the North Vietnamese now were said to have done. Johnson's raid would amount to retaliation for this attack.

Instead of saying "retaliation," however, the President used words like "positive reply" because, as mentioned earlier, retaliation violated international law. So far as domestic American law is concerned, most constitutional experts agree that limited military action is within the authority of the Commander-in-Chief when American forces are attacked. Many Presidents have exercised this authority, though what is "limited" has given rise to serious dispute.

The vast majority of Americans applauded President Johnson's firm and decisive action. To the extent that most people thought about it, the President's request of Congress for a resolution of support seemed a wise and prudent formality. The resolution would also serve as a warning to the Communists that the American people stand together against aggression.

According to news reports, Senator Goldwater did not even wait for the telecast before issuing a press release. Said the Republican candidate: "We cannot allow the American flag to be shot at anywhere on earth if we are to retain our respect and prestige."

Following the telecast, there occurred another scene of drama at the Pentagon, where Secretary McNamara, pointer in hand, held a midnight press conference. It was a rare privilege, as reporters thought at the time, to get briefed by the Secretary of Defense while American bombers made this historic raid. It demonstrated how confident was the new, computerized Pentagon, honeycombed as it was with secret gadgets and bristling with slide rules. Crank any problem into the Defense Department, and it would break down under rational, arithmetical attack. That was the general belief back in 1964. Yet, given the irrational behavior of Asian Communists, there was no telling what might happen next.

Secretary McNamara read a prepared statement. Aircraft from the *Ticonderoga* and *Constellation,* said he, already were making strikes on North Vietnamese torpedo boat bases and certain supporting facilities. He would not name the targets because—glancing at his watch—some of the raids were continuing.

The naval engagement, said McNamara, had lasted for hours. The North Vietnamese again attacked with torpedoes and gunfire. They even were so bold as to shine searchlights on the *Turner Joy.* Aircraft illuminated the battle area with flares and attacked the Communist craft, but the pilots were hampered by bad weather. Visibility was poor. McNamara thought the enemy numbered from three to six boats, including torpedo boats and gunboats. He would not say how many torpedoes had been detected.

Twice reporters asked how McNamara could be sure that two enemy boats sank. The Secretary chose to answer other questions. He expressed confidence that a boat sank on Sunday, too.

An imaginative reporter inquired, "Mr. Secretary, I am sure that there is no doubt in your mind that these PT boats came from, in fact, North Vietnam?"

"There is none," the Secretary assured him. "The radar made it quite clear that they were coming from North Vietnamese bases."

Somebody asked about prisoners. McNamara said that none were picked up after either engagement.

As in the case of Sunday's battle, there was an unnoticed discrepancy concerning the time the engagement started. The Pentagon's first announcement said that the second battle began at 10:30 P.M., local time in the Gulf. At the press conference, McNamara said 9:30 P.M.

Wednesday morning's papers were stuffed with far more news than they could digest. At the top of the front page, banner headlines celebrated the air raids; below, thinner streamers told of the treacherous attack in the dark.

Secretary McNamara had spent the night in the Pentagon, reportedly snatching only a few hours sleep between bulletins from Southeast Asia. At 9 A.M. he met again with the press. The raids, said McNamara, were very successful; they caught the North Vietnamese completely by surprise. The two carriers had launched sixty-four attack sorties that damaged or destroyed twenty-five torpedo boats and gunboats—half of the North Vietnamese navy. The aircraft also destroyed nearly all of fourteen oil storage tanks at the city of Vinh. The latter "supporting" facility contained approximately 10 percent of North Vietnam's oil supply. The raids, "basically one strike," continued for a period of four to five hours. Two airplanes were lost. One pilot, Lieutenant (jg) Richard C. Sather, was killed. The other pilot, Lieutenant (jg) Everett Alvarez, Jr., was captured. Both were twenty-six years old.

President Johnson called the raids "limited and fitting." Somebody in the State Department said, "If the bee stings, you go for the hive."

McNamara announced details of reinforcements being sent to Southeast Asia and the Western Pacific:

"First, an attack carrier group has been transferred from the First Fleet on the Pacific Coast to the Western Pacific. Secondly, interceptor and fighter bomber aircraft have been moved into South Vietnam. Thirdly, fighter bomber aircraft have been moved into Thailand. Fourthly, interceptor and fighter bomber squadrons have been transferred from the United States into advance bases in the Pacific. Fifthly, anti-submarine task force group has been moved into the South China Sea. And, finally, selected Army and Marine forces have been alerted and readied for employment."

We seemed to be getting loaded for bear or, more accurately, Chinese dragon. North Vietnam at that time had no effective air force—just propeller trainers—and no submarines. U.S. armed forces were preparing, then, for a possible showdown with Red China. Nor did McNamara give the entire story. To the astonishment of newsmen in Saigon, there came roaring into South Vietnam a large number of twin-engine B-57 jet bombers. One crashed near Saigon, killing two Air Force pilots. Three other B-57s were damaged in landing accidents.

Appearing on television, Secretary McNamara was asked to comment on the possibility of Soviet or Chinese intervention. "We are prepared for any action they might take," said the Defense Secretary.

The U. S. Congress, too, was moving into gear. On Wednesday morning Speaker John W. McCormack said he was certain the House would act quickly and probably unanimously in passing the resolution requested by the President. The Congress was not writing its own resolution. Senate Majority Leader Mike Mansfield expected to get a draft from the White House that afternoon. Minority Leader Dirksen was so much in a hurry that he hoped to avoid referring the matter to any committee. "Speed," he intoned, "is of the essence." The Democrats, however, decided to hold committee hearings on Thursday and to vote on Friday, August 7.

The careful reader of the press might well have gained the impression that some kind of formal warning to the Communists was needed. One conservative columnist interpreted the Tonkin attacks as a Red Chinese declaration of war on the United States. Another columnist, by reputation a close friend of the President, explained that the North Vietnamese, having no true understanding of sea power, believed that with fifty patrol craft they could take on the whole Seventh Fleet.

Though it was hardly noticed, Hanoi finally found its voice in time for Wednesday morning's newspapers. Drawing itself up to the full height of a pawn in the power struggle, the North Vietnamese capital asserted that on Sunday its patrol craft "took action and chased" the *Maddox* out of territorial water. As for the so-called "second attack," the U. S. Government *invented* that. "Sheer fabrication," scoffed Hanoi.

Hanoi's charge that the second battle was an American invention sounded so absurd that virtually nobody could take it seriously. Even the Russians didn't seem to believe it. Their propaganda machine accused the U. S. Navy of sinking two North Vietnamese craft in the night battle. The Chinese backed up Hanoi. Peking asserted that the attack was fictitious.

On the subject of air raids, Hanoi did nothing for its credibility by claiming five American planes shot down. The Red count later went up to eight.

On Wednesday, President Johnson flew to New York State, where he accepted an honorary degree from Syracuse University and, in return, delivered a fighting speech on Communist aggression. In later years Johnson would fall so far from youthful favor that he could not set foot on a university campus anywhere in the country. But on August 5, 1964, the scene at Syracuse was one of presidential triumph. Clothed in cap and gown, Johnson spoke facing a huge, white banner that proclaimed in foot-high letters: SYRACUSE LOVES LBJ.

The President bore down hard on every word, giving it its full, emotional weight; and he frequently was interrupted by tumultuous applause. "Aggression—deliberate, willful, and systematic aggression —has unmasked its face to the entire world," declaimed LBJ. "The world remembers—the world must never forget—that aggression unchallenged is aggression unleashed." This was the Munich analogy: Hitler could have been stopped in 1938 when his generals were hesitant, but France and Britain chose instead to negotiate at Munich a false "peace in our time." (Classical scholars in the audience might have been reminded of a different lesson: disaster befell ancient Athens when she sent an expedition to a far-off place, the Sicilian city of Syracuse.)

From his platform in Academe, Johnson gave notice that during an election year the United States did not become weak and indecisive. Even a few Republicans followed this lead, proclaiming that the Communists, not understanding the nature of free elections, mistook political debate for weakness and, for that reason, tended to make trouble in election years.

(Superficially, this might seem true. Cold War crises do tend to come in election years. But it was the citizens of Budapest that started the Hungarian crisis of 1956, not the Russians, though, of course, they were to blame for Hungary's subjugation to Communist dictatorship. As for the election year of 1960, it was the American dispatch of a U-2 aircraft that broke up the summit conference in Paris. The year 1962 was one of congressional elections, and Premier Nikita S. Khrushchev tried to plant missiles in Cuba. But President Kennedy's reaction was not weak or indecisive. As for 1964, the most vigorous dissent was on the side of the hawks, who called for bombing North Vietnam and for more leeway in the use of nuclear weapons. In short, in 1964 there was no valid reason for Hanoi to believe that an election would force the President of the United States to go soft on communism.)

There was in 1964 a little dovish dissent. In New York City a few hippies and weirdos demonstrated against American policy in Vietnam, claiming it was "aggressive." And in Europe, the press took issue with the U. S. Government. Most continental newspapers seemed to feel that the election campaign had engendered a tougher attitude in Washington, and that this rather than any provocation offered by the North Vietnamese, had resulted in the air raids. The British press, on the other hand, tended to support the United States. The prestigious Manchester *Guardian,* however, was skeptical. "Many people—not only Communists," said the *Guardian,* "will be tempted to suspect that the U.S. air attacks, and the great movement now proceeding of military power into Southeast Asia, had long been planned and required only a suitable occasion—easily manufactured—to set them off."

In Japan the normally docile Foreign Office privately expressed "shock" at the bombings. The Japanese government tried to gloss over this remark, but still said that it hoped the crisis would end soon. Postwar Japanese opinion, strongly pacifist, continued to be very suspicious of military adventures. The Japanese did not need Munich or Syracuse to provide historical analogies. They recalled how in the 1930s a few mysterious shooting incidents, involving Japanese and Chinese military personnel, expanded into full-scale warfare. The bigger the war became, the more the Imperial Army took control of the government in Tokyo; the more the army took control, the bigger the war became. Eventually the army's ambition led to Pearl Harbor and defeat. Now, in 1964, the Japanese public watched with apprehension as ships of the U. S. Seventh Fleet disappeared from the big naval base at Yokosuka.

In New York City the United Nations Security Council met on Wednesday to hear Ambassador Adlai E. Stevenson's complaint about North Vietnamese aggression in the Tonkin Gulf. The Russian delegate, Platon D. Morozov, wanted a day's postponement in order to get instructions from home, but after a few hours' delay the Security Council met anyway. Morozov declared that the American bombing of North Vietnam was "aggression." Stevenson said it was "self-defense." Morozov demanded that the North Vietnamese be permitted to tell their side of the story. In the end, both North Vietnam and South Vietnam were invited to appear, but North Vietnam refused. Hanoi regarded the UN as a capitalist tool for subverting the Geneva agreements of 1954. Peking saw it that way, too. The Russians ended up sandbagged by their inscrutable Asian allies.

Gone was the day when President Eisenhower's Secretary of State, John Foster Dulles, an ex-corporation lawyer, could regard international communism as one global enterprise controlled by a lofty holding company in Moscow. Now American officials viewed Peking as independent, but managing to retain control of North Vietnam which, as a loyal subsidiary, was trying to add South Vietnam to the corporate structure. Ambassador Stevenson explained the American objective in Southeast Asia: "We are in Southeast Asia to help our friends preserve their own opportunity to be free of imported terror, of alien assassination, managed by the North Vietnam Communists based in Hanoi and backed by the Chinese Communists from Peking." Yet, in later years, it became apparent that the North Vietnamese were skillful at playing off the Chinese against the Russians, drawing help from both sides of the Communist world.

By Thursday morning, August 6, no more shooting had been heard in the Tonkin Gulf, and American commentators lauded President Johnson's handling of the crisis. The Washington *Post* remarked on how the "impressive orchestration of American policies contrast revealingly with the fragmented and tardy reactions of the different Communist states."

On Thursday morning administration officials shuttled back and forth between the Senate and House committees that were to consider the proposed Southeast Asia resolution or, as it came to be known, the "Tonkin Gulf resolution." The principal witnesses were the Secretary of State, the Secretary of Defense, and the Chairman of the Joint Chiefs. In short order, all of the committees stamped their approval on the proposed resolution. The House Foreign Affairs Committee voted for it 29–0. (The House Armed Services Committee did not even convene—over the protest of at least one member.) Two Senate Committees, Foreign Relations and Armed Services, met jointly, and they approved the resolution by a combined vote of 31–1. The dissenter was a member of Foreign Relations: the Oregonian maverick Wayne L. Morse, once a Republican and now a Democrat. To the bewilderment of his colleagues, Morse denounced the resolution as an "unconstitutional, pre-dated declaration of war."

The hearings on Capitol Hill gave reporters an opportunity to catch General Wheeler and ask him about a disturbing report buried in a New York *Times* article of Tuesday, August 4. On page 2, at the very bottom of a long story on Southeast Asia, appeared this rather startling sentence: "It has been reported that the destroyers on patrol have sometimes collaborated with South Vietnamese hit-and-run raids on North Vietnamese port cities, though the destroyers themselves stay in international waters." If true, this not only could explain why the North Vietnamese made their attacks, but amounted to saying that the U. S. Navy was engaging in acts of war. Unfortunately, the *Times* did not give further details or cite the source of the report. Reporters asked General Wheeler whether the *Maddox* had convoyed South Vietnamese raiding craft. "There was no effort to assist South Vietnamese boats," said Wheeler. Newsmen still wondered whether there had been any South Vietnamese raids, assisted or not by the U. S. Navy, and at a press conference late Thursday afternoon asked Secretary McNamara whether he knew of any. McNamara said he did not. In this way the Defense Secretary and Chairman of the Joint Chiefs laid to rest once more the speculation aroused by the remarkable sentence exhumed from the *Times*.

Newsmen paid little attention to Wayne Morse who, as early as Wednesday, contended on the floor of the Senate that South Vietnamese raids did take place on the night of July 30–31. Morse claimed that American officials knew about the raids in advance, and said that they ought not to have scheduled *Maddox's* patrol when they did. The North Vietnamese, he argued, would assume that the destroyer was involved with the attacks on their territory. Morse kept up his drumfire of criticism, but on Thursday afternoon his information on the raids was contradicted by Senator Frank J. Lausche, Democrat of Ohio, who had attended the same secret briefings that Morse did (on Monday as well as Thursday morning). Lausche all but called Morse a liar when asserting that American officials knew nothing of any South Vietnamese raids. The two senators exchanged heated words.

Senator Morse attracted a little more attention from the news media with his argument that the proposed congressional resolution amounted to an "unconstitutional, pre-dated declaration of war." Following is the complete text of the resolution:

Joint Resolution to promote the maintenance of international peace and security in Southeast Asia

Whereas naval units of the Communist regime in Vietnam, in violation of the principles of the Charter of the United Nations and of international law, have deliberately and repeatedly attacked United States naval vessels lawfully present in international waters, and have thereby created a serious threat to international peace; and

Whereas these attacks are part of a deliberate and systematic campaign of aggression that the Communist regime in North Vietnam has been waging against its neighbors and the nations joined with them in the collective defense of their freedom; and

Whereas the United States is assisting the peoples of Southeast Asia to protect their freedom and has no territorial, military or political ambitions in that area, but desires only that these peoples should be left in peace to work out their own destinies in their own way: Now, therefore, be it.

Resolved by the Senate and House of Representatives of the United States of America in Congress assembled, That the Congress approves and supports the determination of the President, as Commander in Chief, to take all necessary measures to repel any armed attack against the forces of the United States and to prevent further aggression.

Sec. 2. The United States regards as vital to its national interest and to world peace the maintenance of international peace and security in Southeast Asia. Consonant with the Constitution of the United States and the Charter of the United Nations and in accordance with its obligations under the Southeast Asia Collective Defense Treaty, the United States is, therefore, prepared, as the President determines, to take all necessary steps, including the use of armed force, to assist any member or protocol state of the Southeast Asia Collective Defense Treaty requesting assistance in defense of its freedom.

Sec. 3. This resolution shall expire when the President shall determine that the peace and security of the area is reasonably assured by international conditions created by action of the United Nations or otherwise, except that it may be terminated earlier by concurrent resolution of the Congress.

As a former professor of law, Senator Morse objected to Section 2, which declared that ". . . the United States is, therefore, prepared, as the President determines, to take all necessary steps, including the use of armed force, to assist any member or protocol state of the Southeast Asia Collective Defense Treaty requesting assistance in defense of its freedom." Morse interpreted this as a grant of the war power by the Congress to the President, to be used whenever he saw fit. The administration said it was against going to war in Southeast Asia, but, argued Morse, what if the President, armed with the Tonkin Gulf resolution, changed his mind? How could the Congress stop him? It could not, said Morse. Agreeing with him was Senator Ernest Gruening, a Democrat from Alaska. Both senators, however, favored withdrawal of American aid from Vietnam, and, to many, that seemed to explain their contrary attitude.

Other lawmakers described the resolution as a demonstration of firmness needed to back up the President in the hour of crisis. This was the generation that had seen the folly of appeasement. These men were determined to apply the lesson of Munich to dealing with Hanoi and Peking. In 1962 the same lesson had been taught to Moscow, and, fortunately, the aftermath of the Cuban missile crisis brought improvement in American relations with the Soviet Union (it also, unfortunately, stimulated Russian naval construction).

Managing the bill on the floor of the Senate were Majority Leader Mansfield, Minority Leader Dirksen, and Foreign Relations Committee Chairman Fulbright. Besides Morse and Gruening, some other liberals were concerned about the broad wording of the resolution. It was from Fulbright that they wanted to hear, and the Arkansan intellectual, to his everlasting regret, ended up doing most of the talking for the President's bill. Fulbright assured his liberal friends that the resolution was calculated to bring peace, not war. As for the possibility of sending an army to Asia, that was the "last thing we want to do," Fulbright declared on Thursday afternoon. The senator must have remembered what Secretary Rusk said in the morning's secret hearing:

". . . I think a highly relevant factor here is that there are a billion and a half people of Asia, half of them in the Communist world and half of them in the free world. I don't see how we are going to get a long-range solution to this problem on the basis of our trying to go in there, into this vast mass of people, and try to do a job as Americans in lieu of Asians."[3]

On Thursday the Lower House didn't even discuss the Tonkin Gulf resolution, and the press showed little interest in the Senate's deliberations. Most people regarded the resolution as something of a bore, however desirable it might be as a formality. There were more exciting events. Senator Goldwater charged that President Johnson's order to bomb North Vietnam could have been interpreted by the

---

[3] U. S. Congress, Senate, Committee on Foreign Relations and Committee on Armed Services; *Southeast Asia Resolution;* Joint Hearing, 88th Congress, 2nd Session, August 6, 1964 (Washington: Government Printing Office, 1966), page 25.

Navy as authorizing the use of nuclear weapons. Denials and affirmations of this charge occupied a great deal of space in the press.

A few seasoned guardians of the public interest did write about the Tonkin Gulf resolution. One of them was the New York *Times'* chief political analyst, James Reston. In his column Friday morning, Reston asked whether the American role in Vietnam would continue to be one of merely providing arms and assistance or, perhaps, did the President now seek a resolution which would "authorize him to take any military measure he pleases . . . at the request of any Southeast Asian ally?" Reston, writing from Washington, cautioned "The official view here is that it is 'not helpful' to raise such questions when the United States must act together, but the President, as Commander-in-Chief, has the power to repel any sudden attack, as he did last weekend, and it may be wise to take a day or two to analyze where we are and where we are going."

If Reston seemed strangely dubious, the sixteen congressional leaders, already having pledged their support, could take heart from their local paper, the Washington *Post*. It complimented the "promptness" of Congress and condemned the "reckless and querulous dissent" of Senator Morse. Patiently, the newspaper explained that the Tonkin Gulf resolution pledged military action only to resist aggression against American forces. The *Post* reflected the prevailing liberal opinion more accurately than did the column written by James Reston. As for the conservative papers, far from opposing the resolution, they outdid each other in expressions of approval.

The smell of danger was still in the air. One of the big stories Friday morning was Secretary McNamara's statement that Red China probably would send combat aircraft to North Vietnam. From Manila came a report that Red China's submarine fleet was the fourth largest in the world.

The Congress acted swiftly and almost unanimously.

Just forty minutes after the bill was introduced on Friday morning, the House of Representatives voted for it 416–0. Speaking for the bill was Pennsylvania Democrat Thomas E. Morgan, Chairman of the Foreign Affairs Committee, who assured his colleagues:

"This is definitely not an advance declaration of war. The Committee has been assured by the Secretary of State that the constitutional prerogative of the Congress in this respect will continue to be scrupulously observed."

In the Lower House there could be no real debate since nobody opposed the bill. The only disagreement concerned other aspects of the Tonkin Gulf crisis. A few members complained that they were being kept in the dark with respect to American policy in Vietnam; one even hinted that the administration might not be telling the truth about the Tonkin Gulf. The most colorful exchange of views concerned the air raid. A Goldwater Republican from Texas, Ed Foreman, complained that, according to the Pentagon's Official Chronology, the American aircraft were *not* over their targets at the time the President spoke on television. Foreman termed the telecast "shooting from the lip" and "publicity-happy political irresponsibility." Other congressmen rose to defend the White House. According to official information, they said, the North Vietnamese definitely had been caught by surprise.

The Senate, having argued about the resolution Wednesday, Thursday, and all of Friday morning, wound up its consideration at 1:15 P.M. Friday. It passed the bill 88–2. The two negative votes, of course, were cast by Morse and Gruening. In the middle of the debate, Morse was chided for his long-winded opposition which, he was reminded, could only delay the bill, not stop it. "The resolution will pass," said Morse, "and those senators who vote for it will live to regret it." Morse put into the *Congressional Record* hundreds of telegrams supporting his position on Vietnam and opposing the Tonkin Gulf resolution.

The congressional action, finishing up in the early afternoon, was well in time for the evening newspapers, but they showed little interest. They headlined instead such news as the arrest in Georgia of four members of the Ku Klux Klan. Few readers could have guessed that the U. S. Congress had just passed a declaration of war—or what the State Department a few years later would call its "functional equivalent."

The same issue of the Washington *Evening Star* that reported passage of the Tonkin Gulf resolution carried a story that seemed to explain, at last, how the trouble started. A *Star* reporter, Richard Fryklund, heard from an unnamed official in the Defense Department that the South Vietnamese, as alleged by Radio Hanoi, actually *did* raid North Vietnamese territory just a couple of nights before the *Maddox* was first attacked. American advisers in Saigon knew about the raid in advance, said Fryklund, but they did not tell the Seventh Fleet. Consequently, when the *Maddox* approached the raided territory, a coastal island known as Hon Me, the ship encountered some junks "picking up the pieces," and suddenly three torpedo boats "tore out at 50 knots to slay the dragon." Fryklund decided that this misunderstanding was the key to the whole thing. "The rest is history," he concluded.

But it was the second attack that the administration believed to be evidence of premeditated, systematic aggression. What of that? By Saturday morning Murrey Marder of the Washington *Post* had a new slant. Officials now conceded, said Marder, that Tuesday's attack might have resulted from a North Vietnamese desire to repair bruised prestige after losing Sunday's battle. The Communists, he said, did not have time to cook up any elaborate plot—they had been taken unawares by the Gulf patrol, which was neither so frequent nor so regular as the public had been led to believe. Indeed, said Marder, a warship the size of a destroyer hadn't been there for "weeks," and the *Maddox* herself didn't show up until Friday, July 31.

Marder called this "new information." It was new to the public, certainly, but it ought not to have been new to the government. In the Los Angeles *Times,* Ted Sell observed that Defense officials previously "had professed ignorance," but now the "curtain parted slightly." What was the reason for all this secrecy? Nobody seemed to know. Nor did anybody say who provided the "new information."

If the curtain did part slightly, President Johnson yanked it shut again. Down in Texas at the LBJ Ranch, the President held a news conference on Saturday morning, August 8. Somebody asked for his opinion on why the North Vietnamese had attacked ships of the U. S. Navy. Johnson treated the question lightly, suggesting that the reporter ask officials in Hanoi about their motives. Impudently, the same question popped up again. Johnson replied stiffly, "I am unable to speak with any accuracy on the imaginations or motives they may have had in mind on what they did. It would be pure speculation, and I don't care to indulge in that."

That day the big news story was Turkey's bombing of Cyprus. The Turks made a point of using sixty-four aircraft, in imitation of the sixty-four American sorties against North Vietnam; to the UN, they presented a complaint reminiscent of Ambassador Stevenson's.

By Monday morning, August 10, President Johnson was back in Washington and ready to sign the Tonkin Gulf resolution. Surrounded by the Joint Chiefs and congressional leaders, the Chief Executive signed the historic document. "The position of the United States," he declared, "is stated plainly. To any armed attack upon our forces, we shall reply. To any in Southeast Asia who ask our help in defending their freedom, we shall give it."

Whether the American position was stated plainly or not later became the subject of bitter and prolonged controversy. But for the moment it seemed plain, and newspaper cartoonists took up the theme of deterring Red Chinese aggression by means of this crystal-clear warning. In one sketch, a lawmaker is holding up to the face of a scowling Mao Tse-tung a sheet of paper emblazoned, "U.S. Unity Behind LBJ." Mao's bald head, covered with mysterious Chinese writing, is labeled in English: "Communist Motives?" Says the lawmaker: "The important thing is that he understands what's in OUR mind."

In this time of crisis, as in others, not only the Congress but the people rallied around the Commander-in-Chief. In July a Louis Harris survey had reported 58 percent of Americans critical of the President's handling of Vietnam. After the air raids of August 5, the balance turned in Johnson's favor. Now 72 percent approved. Before the Tonkin Gulf crisis most people had thought that Johnson could handle Vietnam better than Goldwater; but the number who thought so was decreasing, and it had reached a new low of 59 percent. After the crisis, the number favoring Johnson zoomed up to 71 percent—better than ever for the President. As a political issue, Vietnam no longer worked for Goldwater. Newspapers commented on the political advantage of being in power.

The new view of Johnson and Vietnam focused sharply in a political cartoon. The tiny figure of a Southeast Asian huddled in the crook of the President's arm, supported by a great, bulging bicep. "Comfy?" asked the President, smiling benevolently.

Chapter II

The Consequences, 1964-65

In Washington, D.C., the Tonkin Gulf crisis ended sooner than in Saigon or Hanoi; indeed, it barely outlasted the congressional vote on the resolution requested by the President (CONGRESS BACKS LBJ; WAR FEARS EASE).

But even as the crisis was being deflated in Washington, it was still ballooning in Saigon. On Friday, August 7, the South Vietnamese Premier, Major General Nguyen Khanh, proclaimed a state of emergency, which empowered his government to ban strikes, prohibit demonstrations and meetings, censor the press, restrict travel, search homes, and throw into jail without trial any "dangerous people." Military courts were to execute "speculators harmful to the national economy"; there would be no appeal from these swift sentences of death. In justifying such Draconian measures, Premier Khanh related the Tonkin Gulf incidents to a dangerous military situation which, he said, had been building up in recent weeks. The naval action, according to Khanh, portended a Korean-style invasion from the North, backed by Red China. Already the Red Chinese had troops "stationed" in North Vietnam, he said, and promised to go visit the front, by which he meant the Demilitarized Zone between the two Vietnams. Khanh urged the North Vietnamese people to rise up and overthrow their dictatorial masters. "The coming weeks," he prophesied, "will decide the destiny of our entire people. We will not accept becoming a minor province of Red China."

Having tightened things up on the home front, the soldier-Premier, true to his word, flew up to the DMZ. Saturday, August 8, found him dressed in battle fatigues and riding in a jeep camouflaged with branches. Khanh soon encountered representatives of the press, who had flown after him from the capital. He asked them how things were in Saigon.

"Quiet," said one of the newsmen.

"Good," said the Premier. "Let us hope it stays that way."

Through field glasses Khanh peered northward across the Ben Hai River. A few thousand yards away, Communist troops were said to be moving around suspiciously. The Communists had some reason for concern, too: on the southern side of the river, bulldozers labored to uncover 155-millimeter howitzers. Khanh advised reporters that these guns could shoot a long way into North Vietnam. Visiting a bunker, the Premier grabbed a periscope and, with his goatee hanging under it, posed for the photographers. This scene of Churchillian resolve, in somber hues, made the cover of an American magazine.

Before the day was out, Premier Khanh finished his inspection of the front and proceeded to the city of Hué, where a Mercedes-Benz awaited him. In no time the gleaming black car was surrounded by a mob of students, one of whom jumped onto the hood. Using the Mercedes as a soapbox, the brash student denounced the Premier's "state of emergency" as no more than a pretext for seizing dictatorial powers. Khanh, protected by the bayonets of a nervous bodyguard, spoke in return. First of all, he emphasized, the present government —unlike previous governments—would tell the truth. Second, the new security measures were needed because Hanoi and Peking were looking for an excuse to invade the country openly. The torpedo boat attacks proved that, said Khanh. Finally, the security measures helped to prepare for the *Bac Tien* ("To the North") campaign. In recent weeks, Khanh had been beating the drums for some kind of action against North Vietnam, which, according to the Saigon government, was responsible for the Viet Cong insurgency in the South. "There can be no *Bac Tien*," the Premier remonstrated in Hué, "unless we start getting ready right now."

With loud cheers the students showed their satisfaction with Premier Khanh's explanation, reported the censored Saigon *Daily News*.

The citizens of Saigon, despite all of Premier Khanh's eloquence, refused to take the threat of invasion seriously. On Monday, August 10, the city held an air-raid drill; afterward, a city official complained that people stood around the first-aid teams "as if it were all a play."

The same official assured a meeting of two hundred civil defense leaders that more drills would be held so that residents of the capital could experience life in a "real atmosphere of emergency."

As Premier Khanh rattled the saber on land, the U. S. Navy was making a show of strength at sea. A large part of the Seventh Fleet gathered off the coast. At a press conference aboard the carrier *Ticonderoga,* newsmen heard that the Navy had orders to pursue, attack, and destroy any Chinese Communist vessel committing a hostile act in international waters. Said a staff officer: "The pattern is established for a United States response to Chinese aggression. If they come at us with broomsticks, we will break their broomsticks and destroy their capacity to make any more broomsticks."

Back in Washington, Henry Cabot Lodge, until recently U. S. Ambassador to South Vietnam, threw some more spice into the Chinese stew. On Monday, August 10, Lodge told reporters that Chinese Communist advisers were active among the Viet Cong. None had been taken prisoner, he said, but they had been "seen by agents" and "heard on the radio." (Our South Vietnamese allies were somewhat careless in making such reports. Later they "sighted" a Chinese submarine in a place where, according to official American investigators, there was barely enough water to cover a sunken rowboat.) Ambassador Lodge was quite sure that Hanoi took orders from Peking. The torpedo boat attacks, he said, must have been cleared with the Chinese. Ho Chi Minh, thought Lodge, certainly couldn't end the war in South Vietnam without Chinese permission. At President Johnson's request, the Republican politician-diplomat made a tour of West European capitals, where he again explained what was happening in Southeast Asia.

From Taiwan our Chinese Nationalist allies let it be known that a marshal of the Red Chinese Army had masterminded the torpedo boat attacks. To be sure, the attacks, failing as they did, bore no stamp of naval genius. Nevertheless, Taiwan's report gained little currency.

The new American Ambassador in Saigon was General Maxwell D. Taylor, formerly Chairman of the Joint Chiefs of Staff. Taylor, like his civilian superiors in Washington, thought the crisis was over but advised everybody to keep alert.

As the days passed, it became clear that whatever the naval incidents might have foreshadowed, mass invasion from the North was not included. There simply was no Communist build-up along the border. Expectations shifted to a wave of Viet Cong terror, said the press; but nothing more happened than the explosion of a "bicycle bomb" in the town of My Tho. By Wednesday, August 12, the Army of the Republic of Vietnam (ARVN) was taking the initiative with a search-and-destroy mission. A short distance north of Saigon, four regiments surrounded a reported Viet Cong concentration of one or two thousand men. Somehow only four guerrillas were found, all dead. An American helicopter pilot died, too, the victim of machine-gun fire in the landing area.

In military acumen Premier Khanh seems not to have rated very high. Before the Tonkin Gulf incidents, his impending overthrow had been rumored in Saigon; yet afterward, he was in power more firmly than ever before, so far as the ruling junta was concerned. On Sunday, August 16, the Military Revolutionary Council (junta) elevated the Premier to President of the Republic, with Khanh receiving 50 out of 58 posssible votes. The junta also promulgated a new governmental charter which, according to American reporters, gave the President "dictatorial" powers.

How did Nguyen Khanh achieve such a spectacular comeback, rising so rapidly in the esteem of his professional colleagues? This was not clear, but there certainly was a new atmosphere in Saigon, at least among high officials. Said Peter Grose of the New York *Times:* "America's retaliatory air strikes were heralded here with an enthusiasm bordering, in some quarters, on the delirious. For the Khanh government, they represented a direct American military engagement, which the Premier has been seeking in the hope of reducing the responsibilities of his own forces." The new dictatorial measures, said Grose, had long been under consideration "for whenever justification could be found," as a means of "solidifying" the Premier's shaky rule. The *Times* correspondent warned that Khanh now might try to maneuver the United States into taking over the war.

"American policy," said Grose, "remains unchanged: No military action outside the country can substitute for continued and unspectacular counterinsurgency efforts inside this country."

President Khanh's triumph proved to be a fragile one. Within a few days of his promotion, students and Buddhist monks started rioting against the new Republic, which they criticized as undemocratic. Several persons died in the melee. By August 28, Khanh had resigned as President. Turmoil, however, continued in the streets of Saigon as repeated attempts to establish a government failed. Thirty students were reported missing. Ambassador Taylor postponed a scheduled trip to Washington; and, said the press, he threatened to cut off American aid if General Khanh were not restored to power.

Chaos reigned until September 2 when General Khanh was restored as Premier (not President). The military and the Buddhists had made a deal: no rioting for two months while the junta got ready to establish a more democratic government (a deal that also would see President Johnson through the election campaign). The Buddhists demanded that certain Catholic military commanders leave the country, and a few were dispatched as ambassadors.

This brief résumé of what took place between August 28 and September 2 is a simplified version of events largely as reported by the Saigon *Daily News,* which missed a few issues during the tumult. The South Vietnamese paper treated the demonstrators more favorably than did the American press. Periodicals here, reflecting the official U.S. attitude, tended to sympathize with the junta and to print very complicated accounts of what was going on. The students appeared as pawns in a power struggle engineered by ambitious civilian politicians and fanatical Buddhists—neither of which "cared about" the war. A liberal writer complained that there was no way to find out what the people of South Vietnam really wanted. A conservative blamed the whole trouble on the softness of General Khanh, who rejected advice to fire on the demonstrators. There was a general feeling that so long as an Asian government was not Communist, everybody ought to be satisfied with it. The real problem was to eliminate "apathy" and get on with the war. A cartoon depicted the familiar South Vietnamese coolie, still wearing his conical hat, but now being towed through deep water by an American lifeguard. The South Vietnamese is fully conscious, his arms folded and his legs stretched stiffly out. Asks the lifeguard: "Could you manage to kick a little bit?"

During the political uproar, everybody forgot about the Tonkin Gulf crisis which, in South Vietnam, disappeared in the middle of August. But in North Vietnam a sense of urgency continued. For some time, Hanoi had been predicting air raids as a prelude to an invasion from the South. The August 5 attack seemed to confirm the worst Communist forebodings. The people of North Vietnam continued to dig bomb shelters and trenches. Their government obtained from Red China its first combat aircraft, a dozen or more subsonic jet fighters (MiG 15s and MiG 17s).[1] Later the Chinese reportedly supplied additional patrol craft in the form of Swatow gunboats.

The United States had been the first to regard the crisis as ended. Certain skeptics even wondered whether there ever had *been* any crisis. Peace groups circulated copies of the Washington newspaper articles written by Richard Fryklund and Murrey Marder, citing them as evidence that the Johnson administration provoked the clashes in order to justify a military build-up planned in advance. Why else would a destroyer have headed for what had become a combat zone?

A strange bedfellow for the peaceniks appeared in September. The *National Review* magazine, edited by the conservative William F. Buckley, Jr., wondered whatever happened to the crisis down in Southeast Asia. In an editorial titled, "Mystery in the Tonkin Gulf," the magazine asked, "How did an affair of such magnitude apparently evaporate without leading to any noticeable consequences on one side or the other?" Complaining that the U. S. Government still offered no explanation for the North Vietnamese attacks, the spokesman for the Far Right turned for enlightenment to its Far Left counterpart, the *Peking Review*. After reminding its readers that Communists were not to be trusted, the American magazine proceeded to quote from the August 14 issue of the Chinese periodical, which claimed that the night battle of August 4 had never occurred. The claim was based on two arguments: the torpedo boat, a high-speed, short-range weapon would have been unable to chase a pair of destroyers for several hours; and torpedo boats certainly would not have waited for American air cover to arrive before starting their attacks, as they did according to the U. S. Official Chronology.

[1] The newly arrived jets were photographed from the air on August 7. See Admiral Ulysses S. Grant Sharp and General William C. Westmoreland, *Report on the War in Vietnam* (U. S. Government Printing Office, 1969), page 13. Premier Khanh told the press on August 8 that combat jet aircraft were in North Vietnam, and he warned of possible "air strikes" without mentioning that the jets were fighters, not bombers. Asked about North Vietnamese jets on August 8, President Johnson refused to indulge in "speculation." On August 11 the Defense Department announced that North Vietnam had obtained MiG 15s and MiG 17s from Red China, twelve to fifteen in number.

The Fictitious Attack Theory, however, had already been dealt with by Murrey Marder in the Washington *Post*. At the end of the August 8 story referred to earlier, Marder wrote: "What is causing indignation to American officials . . . are suggestions being made by diplomats of several non-Communist countries at the United Nations and elsewhere, that Communist denials of any second attack are true. The idea that the United States concocted the story . . . officials said, is utterly fantastic."

Moving on to the subject of evidence, Marder reported: "While the United States cannot provide photographic evidence of the night attack, there is considerable courtroom evidence . . . that a searchlight on one of the U.S. destroyers was knocked out by small arms fire in Tuesday's night attack . . . that one of the destroyers attempted unsuccessfully to ram an attacking torpedo boat, and that a torpedo passed within 300 feet of one destroyer."

The *National Review*'s skepticism did not spread very far. The conservatives were too pro-military; and the liberals were too pro-Johnson. Among many opinion-makers, there was a virtual moratorium on criticism of the Johnson administration while candidate Goldwater remained a threat to the Republic. Goldwater frightened most people with his talk of bombing North Vietnam and his desire for more flexibility in the use of nuclear weapons. Besides, naval battles in the Tonkin Gulf were getting to be almost routine. On the night of September 18, two American destroyers reportedly shot their way out of another dangerous situation.

The Defense Department again claimed the destruction of two enemy vessels. Once more the Russian news agency, Tass, accused the U. S. Navy of bullying the North Vietnamese. Once more Hanoi said that no attack had taken place.

This time, less information became available than in August. The destroyers were not even named. "They," one read in the press, were engaged in a secret, U-2 type of mission, using advanced electronic equipment. But no matter how sophisticated, a ship needs a crew to run her, and one of the September sailors spilled the beans. Fireman James J. Kress wrote to his home in Dubuque, Iowa: "Dear Mom and Dad, In case you haven't heard the names of those destroyers that were attacked in the Tonkin Gulf last Friday night, they were the *R. S. Edwards* and the *Morton*. Yep, we were there all right!" Mrs. Kress took the letter to her local paper for use in the serviceman's column. To her surprise, it hit front pages all over the country.

The Kress incident was so amusing, and the facts remained so murky that the public developed no great curiosity about why August 5's hammer blow from the air failed to deter the North Vietnamese. Nor did the President order a new raid following the September incident. One rumor had it that the Pentagon wasn't sure whether a real attack had taken place—phony radar images might have tricked the destroyers. According to a later announcement, real boats definitely were there.

After the September excitement, commentators were slow to reexamine what happened in August, but they were not slow to reinterpret the Tonkin Gulf resolution. Almost without anybody being conscious of it, this hitherto innocent-looking document turned into a potential authorization for war. It happened by degrees.

As early as August, two small magazines, the liberal *New Republic* and the conservative *National Review,* termed the resolution a "blank check." Here was a step in the fateful direction, but neither magazine anticipated a change of policy that would call for cashing the check. Even the veteran analyst, Richard Rovere, writing for *The New Yorker,* assured his readers that he could find nobody in the State Department—nor even in the Pentagon—who was in favor of widening the war.

By the beginning of October, however, a few observers began to be suspicious of the administration's top policy planners. In the *Times* of October 2, James Reston and Max Frankel, writing separate articles, reported that the President's advisers were debating whether to increase American participation in the war. Why? Here was a real mystery. True, South Vietnam's political condition remained weak, but the military situation was said to be improving. Ambassador Taylor, a military expert of some renown, declared that the Communists were farther from victory than ever before; and President Johnson appeared to see no need for American troops. Johnson talked of how "we don't want our American boys to do the fighting for Asian boys."

On the other hand, William P. Bundy, Assistant Secretary of State for the Far East, gave a speech in Tokyo that sounded hawkish. Expanding the war, Bundy said, "could be forced upon us by the increased external pressure of the Communists, including a rising scale of infiltration." William Bundy's younger brother, McGeorge Bundy, was the President's foreign affairs aide.

In his column, James Reston deplored the ambiguity of American policy in Vietnam, and added these chilling words: "It is even possible now to hear officials of this Government talking casually about how easy it would be to 'provoke an incident' in the Gulf of Tonkin that would justify an attack on North Vietnam. . . ."

But surely we could depend on the White House to prevent such machinations. In his article, Max Frankel said that the President was rejecting suggestions to expand the war; he had, for example, reportedly refused to bomb North Vietnam following the September 18 incident. Responsible officials, wrote Frankel, believed that the President's caution was not merely a temporary attitude adopted to prevent further trouble before Election Day.

The two *Times* men did not seem to agree. Like Bundy and Johnson, they faced in different directions.

After reading the *Times* that morning, Senator Gaylord A. Nelson felt compelled to write a letter to the editor. The Wisconsin Democrat found the idea of provoking an incident "extremely disturbing," but he was even more concerned about reinterpreting the Tonkin Gulf resolution, which, he declared, did not authorize war. The Senate debate in August, said he, had clarified that very point.

Behind Nelson's letter to the editor lay the ironic story of how the Wisconsin liberal had tried to amend the resolution in order to prevent any possible misinterpretation, only to be foiled by Senator Fulbright. Nelson's amendment would have expressed clearly the Congress's intent to provide limited assistance to the South Vietnamese government, without directly involving American forces in the war. Senator Fulbright, however, wanted the resolution passed on schedule; and, noting the lack of time, he rejected Nelson's proposal.

"I do not object to it [the amendment] as a statement of policy," Fulbright said. "I believe it is an accurate reflection of what I believe is the President's policy, judging by his statements. That does not mean that as a practical matter I can accept the amendment. It would delay matters to do so. It would cause confusion and require a conference . . . I regret that I cannot do it, even though I do not at all disagree with the amendment as a general statement of policy."

The junior senator from Wisconsin still thought that his amendment was needed. But after uttering only a few words, his allotted time ran out. He had been able to get only ten minutes, which he borrowed from Senator Morse. After listening to Senator Fulbright, however, Nelson felt a clear record of "legislative intent" had been established. He decided to vote for the resolution.

Before the United States went to war in Vietnam, the Congress never voted on that specific question. In 1964 the question was too remote. In 1965 it was too close at hand. The nearest thing to a vote was a poll of senators taken by the Associated Press in December of 1964.

The AP survey came at a time of renewed and acute frustration with Vietnam. The military situation no longer appeared to improve, despite the best efforts of Ambassador Taylor; and the political situation again was in a mess. A civilian government had been set up in November, as promised by the junta; but that government was deposed in a coup of December. The new Premier, Air Force General Nguyen Cao Ky, a refugee from North Vietnam, was a "hot pilot" trained by the French. He was outspoken, a notorious ladies' man, and a flamboyant dresser (later to be nicknamed "Captain Midnight"). In short, General Ky didn't seem the type to win the confidence of the South Vietnamese rice farmer.

In view of these discouraging developments, the AP tracked down eighty-three members of the U. S. Senate and asked them what ought to be done. Only eight recommended the use of American military force of any kind. Ten favored immediate negotiations. Thirty-one wished to continue the present policy of sending arms and advice. Eight said that they had no idea of what to do. Senator Allen J. Ellender, Democrat of Louisiana, recommended withdrawal "without any ifs or ands." Agreeing with Ellender, of course, were Morse and Gruening. Senator Mansfield opposed expanding the war. Frank Church, Democrat of Idaho, "foresaw disaster ahead." He wanted to set up an international arrangement to be supervised by the United Nations. The other twenty-one senators expressed a variety of views without, however, recommending American military action.

At the turn of the year, only eight senators recommended war. Nevertheless, during the next seven or eight months, the nation shuffled into it, two steps forward and one step back. President Johnson called the tune. When opposed by members of the Congress, he reminded them of the Tonkin Gulf resolution, which authorized "all necessary steps, including the use of armed force." Johnson kept a frayed copy of the resolution in his coat pocket, and he literally waved it under the noses of his critics.

It can be said for the President that he consulted frequently with senators and congressmen. He sought their advice, and they gave it to him. But when they could not suggest any sure means of saving South Vietnam from communism, Johnson went ahead with the Pentagon's "contingency plans," which existed in abundance and seemed ready for instant implementation. Public opinion, as expressed in the polls, supported the President. The people had rejected Goldwater; but they were brought around to his point of view in approving strong action by the President. The Congress went along, too. Dealt with individually and in small groups, the lawmakers were awed by the White House and by such convincing speakers as McNamara and Rusk. Some, according to a news magazine, feared "reprisals" if they opposed the President. Others supported what they hoped would be a limited escalation designed to improve the anti-Communist negotiating position.

Until American forces had been irrevocably committed to the conflict, there was no time when everybody could see that the nation was going to go to war. As late as February 4, 1965, President Johnson appeared to reaffirm the old policy of helping the South Vietnamese to help themselves. The bombing of North Vietnam started three days later. At first the raids were a tit-for-tat retaliation for Viet Cong attacks on American bases in South Vietnam. The air campaign soon became a regular operation, but, it seemed, air power could be turned off as easily as it was turned on. Next, however, came a gradual build-up of American troop strength. The first units landed as guards for American bases. After 3500 Marines took up residence at Da Nang, Secretary Rusk reassured everybody that U.S. ground troops were not needed in combat. Besides, he explained, there would be a "problem about foreign troops undertaking the kind of pacification effort that is required in South Vietnam." This, it seemed, alluded to the racial complication of Americans fighting Asians.

Nevertheless, more troops filtered in. Newspaper photographs began to show them leaping out of helicopters, armed to the teeth, searching for Viet Cong. Officials said that this amounted to "aggressive patrolling" around their bases. By the end of May, some 50,000 American military personnel were in South Vietnam, and a U.S. spokesman informed the press that two North Vietnamese battalions had joined forces with the Viet Cong—a North Vietnamese battalion numbered 500 men. There was talk of increasing the American count to 70,000.

Was the United States getting into a ground war in Asia?

The Vice-President, Hubert H. Humphrey, didn't seem to think so. On June 4, he was interviewed by Jack Bell of the Associated Press:

Q. You said we'd have to win on the ground. Do you mean with our ground forces?

A. No. I mean that while I do support the bombing . . . that ultimately this conflict will have to be won in South Vietnam.

Unimpressed, the New York *Times* buried this story on an inside page. Up front, the *Times* bannered an anonymous hint from Saigon, where somebody said of U.S. troops: "The time will come when they will play their role."

Other news stories told of an imminent Communist offensive and of how American soldiers increasingly exchanged fire with the enemy. The natural excitement of war tingled across the land.

Reporters in Washington tried to find out what was going on. Cornered by them on June 8, the State Department's Press Officer, Robert J. McCloskey, let the cat out of the bag. In "recent weeks," said he, General Westmoreland had received authority to use American troops as "combat support" when needed and if the South Vietnamese government asked for them. In such a case, McCloskey explained, the Americans would fight "shoulder to shoulder" with their allies, although, of course, under American officers. Plans for coordination were being worked out, he said.

Evening newspapers played this big (GIs GET COMBAT ROLE), and on the next morning a debate flared in the Senate. Jacob K. Javits, Republican from New York, predicted a "massive, bogdown land struggle." Strangely, Javits recommended that the President ask for a resolution *authorizing* this struggle. The Congress would comply, thought Javits, and a new, specific resolution would help to forestall dissent. That would suit the President too well, objected the anti-war Senator George D. Aiken, Republican of Vermont. Such a resolution, said Aiken, would take Johnson "off the hook." A fledgling warhawk, Gale W. McGee, Democrat from Wyoming, also attacked Javits's proposal, arguing that a new resolution was not needed. There was "nothing new," declared McGee, in sending "extra manpower" to South Vietnam. Nobody in either House of Congress suggested a resolution prohibiting the commitment of ground troops.[2]

The Senate debate became academic, it seemed, as the administration began stuffing Robert McCloskey's cat back into the bag. The White House Press Secretary, George E. Reedy, issued a written statement which evening newspapers interpreted as a contradiction of McCloskey's oral statement. The morning papers were less sure. If one examined Reedy's statement carefully, the first part of it seemed to contradict McCloskey, but the last part seemed to agree with him. Left out, incidentally, was the idea of fighting "shoulder to shoulder" with South Vietnamese troops.

The Viet Cong responded promptly to the widely publicized turn of events. According to their spokesman, the National Liberation Front now felt free to call on North Vietnam for volunteers.

Was the U. S. Government now waging a war declared by two press agents? It was. The President did not add any clarification until late in July, and the weeks in between filled with tension as the administration apparently conducted an agonizing reappraisal of the situation in Vietnam. Ambassador Taylor flew back to Washington. Secretary McNamara flew out to Saigon. On McNamara's return, there began what the *Times* called a "series of highly publicized secret meetings." Authoritative sources disclosed that the President would have to send 300,000 troops to South Vietnam; that he would have to call up the reserves; and that he might have to ask for a war tax.

It was Wednesday, July 28, when the President chose to appear on television to make an important announcement. At midday—not prime time—Johnson explained to the American people "why we are

[2] So far as I have been able to determine, the most active opposition in the Lower House was put up by twenty-eight relatively youthful Democrats who signed a petition circulated by Benjamin S. Rosenthal of New York. Rosenthal's petition asked the Foreign Affairs Committee to hold public hearings on Vietnam. This move was squelched by the seniority system. The Chairman of the Foreign Affairs Committee, Thomas E. Morgan of Pennsylvania, refused to hold any hearings.

in Vietnam." A "Midwestern woman," he said, had asked that question in a letter. The President on previous occasions had tried to answer the same question "dozens of times and more in practically every state in this Union." Now, patiently, he tried to answer it again. He outlined the nation's goals in Vietnam. He remarked that the conflict was a "different kind of war" but, nonetheless, "really war."

Editorial writers examined the speech microscopically. They noted the phrase "really war" and decided that the nation was at war. To bolster this conclusion, some newspapers quoted from the editorials of other newspapers. Surely there have been few times in history when the fact of war was so difficult to divine.

Meanwhile, the front page news had been in the letdown. The President did not call up the reserves; only 125,000 men were scheduled to serve in Vietnam; and the President did not ask for a special tax. Apparently, it would be a comfortable, guns-and-butter war.

Cynical reporters—of whom there were many—asked the President's new Press Secretary, the Reverend Bill Moyers, whether the weeks of rumor and tension had not been calculated for psychological effect. Such an assumption, said Moyers, would not only be capriciousness of the worst kind, but hypocrisy that could play havoc with the confidence of the people in their government. Still, as the New York *Herald Tribune* noted, the letdown came as a surprise, and President Johnson had a liking for surprises.

On the day of the telecast, the state governors were having their annual conference; and, by an overwhelming vote, they adopted a resolution supporting the President. There were only two dissenters, both Republican: George Romney of Michigan and Mark Hatfield of Oregon. After a dramatic meeting with the President, Romney changed his mind (in 1968 he was to dash his presidential chances by declaring that he had been "brainwashed"). Among governors, then, the only holdout was Mark Hatfield, later to become Senator Hatfield.

President Johnson now had everything that he could hope for in the way of domestic support—except one thing: a congressional vote specifically authorizing a land war in Asia.

Chapter III

A Most Serious Matter

The first attempt to repeal the Tonkin Gulf resolution came in the spring of 1966, just seven months after ground troops formally entered the war. The attempt was sponsored by Senator Wayne Morse, a man of principle; and it failed, as everybody knew it would. Morse's stab at repeal was notable for the fact that one of the few voting with him was J. William Fulbright, Chairman of the Foreign Relations Committee—the senator who in 1964 did the most to get the resolution passed. Once a pillar of the Establishment, the soft-spoken scholar from Arkansas now was at odds with his party and with his President.

Fulbright's real break with the Johnson administration began with an issue separate from Vietnam: the Dominican intervention. In the spring of 1965, the Vietnamese problem was temporarily overshadowed by a revolt in the Dominican Republic and President Johnson's hasty dispatch of armed forces in that direction. Thus, as U.S. military units were trickling into Vietnam, Fulbright and his committee were faced the other way, trying to figure out what was happening closer to home. Certain official reports turned out to be false. Outstanding among these were two from President Johnson, who on June 17 said that several hundred persons had had their heads cut off and that bullets were flying into the window of the U. S. Embassy. To protect American lives, said Johnson, troops were urgently needed. This explanation was plausible when the first 405 Marines landed. But by the time 30,000 armed Americans had reached the scene, it was clear that the U. S. Government meant to discourage the revolt; and, proudly, President Johnson averred that he would not allow a Communist government to be set up anywhere in the hemisphere. But were the Dominican rebels Communist? They appeared to be fighting for their duly elected President, Juan D. Bosch, who had been ousted by the current military government. Of course, there had to be some Communists among the rebels, but were they in control? Reports were extremely confusing. After the island quieted down, Washington officials congratulated each other that "another Cuba" had been prevented.

The Foreign Relations Committee investigated the Dominican affair in great detail, and the chairman delivered a report on the floor of the Senate, apparently speaking for most members of the committee. Fulbright said that the intervention had been unnecessary and unwise. Furthermore, he believed that the Congress had been misled concerning the facts of the revolt, the amount of Communist influence, and, worst of all, the purpose of sending troops. Senator Fulbright presented his views in September of 1965. From that time onward, he found himself in a running feud with the administration of his own party. The Johnson men showed their displeasure in many ways, especially by planting anti-Fulbright articles in the press.

Undeterred, Fulbright continued to examine the Johnsonian foreign policy, next turning his attention to Vietnam. Again the senator did not like what he found. During the first half of 1965, the senator had supported what he hoped would be a moderate escalation with the aim of bringing about a negotiated settlement of the war. But as the number of American troops in Vietnam continued to grow, Fulbright saw that the President's aim was military victory—an aim that the senator thought unrealistic.

Since the Dominican fracas—if not earlier—Fulbright had lost his influence at the White House, and so early in 1966 he took the Vietnam problem to the people. The Foreign Relations Committee conducted hearings that millions of Americans watched on television, fascinated and amazed. There, in public view, famous and respected men argued the merits of a war in which the nation was already engaged. The committee invited Secretary Rusk and General Taylor to defend the war. Speaking against it were Lieutenant General James M. Gavin, the ex-paratrooper now chairman of an industrial research firm, and former Ambassador George F. Kennan, a distinguished writer of diplomatic history and one of the government's original experts on the Cold War.

Secretary Rusk emphasized the need to "keep our word" to the people of South Vietnam. Both he and General Taylor stressed the favorable progress of military operations, and this line of argument was aided by reports of new victories in the field. Taylor thought the war would continue to go well if we could "avoid weakness on the home front." (At this Senator Morse exploded, calling Taylor a "militarist.") The opposing witnesses, General Gavin and Ambassador Kennan, argued that the strategic value of Vietnam did not justify a major military effort. To limit the number of troops involved, Gavin recommended a defensive strategy of holding "enclaves" along the coast. Sending an army big enough to win, said he, risked Chinese intervention and the reopening of the front in Korea. (This nightmare was to disturb President Johnson two years later when the North Koreans captured the USS *Pueblo*. The Pentagon wanted to retaliate or take the ship back by force. "Don't do it," said Johnson. "I don't want another war.")

On balance, the formidable debating talent of Secretary Rusk carried the Vietnam hearings for the administration. With quiet force, Rusk asked Fulbright whether he couldn't find something wrong with Ho Chi Minh. Rusk, however, could not prevent the "Fulbright hearings" from planting seeds of doubt. The hawk and dove confrontation had begun.

Senator Fulbright admitted publicly that he had been wrong in supporting the Tonkin Gulf resolution, and in turning down what he now saw as Senator Nelson's well-conceived amendment. Admission of error, always rare in the nation's capital, was virtually unheard of during the Johnson administration. Reporters, savoring the unique experience, asked Fulbright over and over again whether it was true that he had made a mistake. On a television program, the irritated senator snapped back: "Yes, I made a mistake. I said so myself, and I guess I'll have to keep on saying it from now on." Fulbright did indeed have to keep saying it because the subject continued to come up in connection with the growing disaster in Vietnam. Even as late as 1970 ex-President Johnson threw the old error back at him, saying the resolution was "misnamed." "It was a shame," explained the former President, "somebody didn't think of calling it the 'Fulbright resolution' . . . because Senator Fulbright introduced it . . . He passed it." His voice full of anger, Johnson almost shouted, "Don't tell me a Rhodes scholar didn't understand everything in that resolution!"

It is true that from the beginning Senator Fulbright knew the potential power contained in the resolution submitted to Congress. When on August 7, 1964, he explained to Senator Nelson the bill's intent and what he understood to be the President's policy, Fulbright, anxious to get the resolution passed on time, neglected to mention his realization that it *might* be used to authorize war. This realization was made clear—to the few senators present—on the day before, August 6, when Senator John Sherman Cooper asked how the resolution affected the SEATO (Southeast Asia Treaty Organization) treaty. Fulbright replied that the resolution could be used to implement the treaty, which obligates the United States to help South Vietnam, among other states, to resist aggression. Under certain circumstances, if one were to put the SEATO treaty together with the Tonkin Gulf resolution, the two documents, like the halves of a secret message, would spell "war." Only a few lawmakers noticed the potentially explosive combination, but Senator Fulbright was one of them. Apparently the senator's basic error was to believe that the President would not change his policy on Vietnam unless provoked to do so by a Korean-style invasion from the North.

For his part, President Johnson never admitted changing the policy on Vietnam. He pointed out that President Eisenhower and President Kennedy had also wanted a free and independent South Vietnam. Eisenhower and Kennedy, however, did not pledge to go to war in order to protect Saigon from the Viet Cong. It would be more accurate to say that the *goal* of a non-Communist South Vietnam remained the same while the *policy*—that is, the means of achieving the goal—changed radically.

Tired of the doves and their complaints, President Johnson dared them to repeal the congressional resolution which they had come to detest. Senator Morse, an advocate of withdrawal from Vietnam, took up the challenge.

To most observers, this was madness. What would be the effect of taking away the President's authority to wage war when, at that time, 230,000 men were waging it? Would a vote for repeal not be an unforgivable failure to support the drafted young men fighting in Vietnam? Besides, the President said that he could "carry out our commitments" in Vietnam even without the resolution. The repeal, it was felt, could not pass; and in the upcoming vote the White House saw an opportunity to win a mandate from the Senate—or at least the appearance of one. Just before the vote, which took place on March 1, 1966, Press Secretary Moyers announced that the President regarded it as a test of support. If senators wanted to "reverse" the Tonkin Gulf resolution "because of a change of heart," they ought to vote for repeal. Otherwise, said the Reverend Moyers, they ought to vote against repeal.

Few senators favored repeal. The proposal was crushed by a vote of 92–5.

The five doves were all Democrats: Wayne Morse of Oregon, Ernest Gruening of Alaska, J. William Fulbright of Arkansas, Eugene J. McCarthy of Minnesota, and Stephen M. Young of Ohio. Five years later, only Fulbright would remain in the Senate. Voting against Morse were not only the hawks, confident of military victory, but also the dovishly inclined, who thought it unwise to repudiate the Commander-in-Chief in time of war.

Like General Custer at Little Big Horn, Senator Fulbright had gotten trapped into a disastrous battle against overwhelming odds. These were hard days for a dove in Washington. Pressure came even from the State Department, which let dovish senators know that they were being kept under surveillance—to see what contacts they might have with foreigners. But Fulbright, once a star halfback at the University of Arkansas, was only beginning to fight.

A few days after Morse's quixotic proposal bit the dust, Fulbright received an interesting letter from a retired naval officer, Rear Admiral Arnold E. True. Writing from his ranch in California, True wanted to get more information on the Tonkin Gulf incidents. It seemed to him that the administration's description of them could not be correct. The admiral wrote with the authority of considerable experience. An Annapolis graduate of 1920, True during his naval career spent eight years on destroyers, commanding them singly, in division, and in squadron. One of his ships, the USS *Hammann,* was torpedoed by a Japanese submarine while trying to salvage the carrier *Yorktown* at the Battle of Midway. True was rescued four hours after the explosion, more dead than alive; he had been supporting in the water two seamen who already had perished. True retired from the service after World War II. He joined the Quakers and began taking part in their peace activities.

At the time the admiral wrote to Senator Fulbright, he did not know any more about the Tonkin Gulf incidents than what had appeared in the newspapers. What he had read, he could not understand. The Official Chronology of the August 2 incident told of "warning shots" fired by the *Maddox;* and Ambassador Stevenson stated to the UN that *Maddox* "in accordance with naval practice, fired three warning shots across the bows of the approaching vessels." But the Official Chronology, said True, indicated that the boats approached from behind the destroyers. It would be impossible, he said, to fire "over the bow" of a vessel to the rear. Moreover, said True, there is no provision in international law for firing warning shots at another man-of-war. "As commander of a man-of-war," wrote the admiral, "I would consider any such shots as hostile and would not only be justified but required by Navy regulations to retaliate."

True knew what he was talking about. He not only was a qualified destroyer commander but had written the Navy's *Revised Destroyer Tactical Manual.*

Senator Fulbright, who had steamrollered the Tonkin Gulf resolution through the Senate, must have found Admiral True's comments very disturbing. The Tonkin Gulf began to sound like the Dominican Republic all over again: wild stories followed by military action. On the other hand, True might have misunderstood the rather vague Official Chronology. Elsewhere, as at the August 6 secret hearings, administration officials stated plainly that the North Vietnamese fired first in both attacks. The *Maddox,* they said, shot back in self-defense. Nevertheless, Fulbright renewed his interest in the naval incidents. Before long, he began referring to them as "allegedly unprovoked."

Reporters tried in vain to make Fulbright explain his riddling references to the Tonkin Gulf. But in the open hearing of May 9, 1966, Fulbright, complaining to Rusk about how the resolution was being implemented, used strong words on the subject of the naval incidents: ". . . there have come to my attention suggestions that the whole affair was very questionable as to the character. . . . It is very easy to inflame anybody, particularly in the middle of a campaign for a presidential election, by stating that there has been an attack on the high seas on one of our ships. That was the whole purpose of that resolution. Certainly everyone agrees we ought to repel an unprovoked, deliberate attack upon our ships on the high seas where they had a right to be. Any suggestion at the time that this might have been a deliberate provocation on our part to invite the incident or that we had been inside the territorial waters of North Vietnam . . . was brushed aside in the emotions that naturally arose from an allegation by the administration that this was a deliberate and unprovoked attack upon our ships . . ."

The Chairman of the Foreign Relations Committee seemed to be implying that the U. S. Navy provoked the Tonkin Gulf incidents, which, in turn, persuaded the Congress to sign hastily—and without realizing it—a blank check thrust upon them by the President. These were ugly implications, indeed, but Fulbright's words lighted no great fires of controversy, just as, some eighteen months earlier, James Reston's column on provoking incidents had attracted little attention.

One man did catch a few sparks. Senator Milward C. Simpson, the Wyoming Republican, took the floor of the Senate and challenged Fulbright to substantiate his doubts. Simpson was seriously disturbed by the implication of "chicanery on the part of the Democratic administration during an election year." He himself was "inclined to accept the White House version" of the incidents but was quite willing to acknowledge that "utter candor is not a hallmark of this administration."

While speaking, Senator Simpson received from Fulbright a note that invited him to read the top secret transcript of a recent Foreign Relations Committee meeting with representatives of the Defense Department. In the course of the meeting that was concerned with the downing by Red China of an American airplane, the conversation had turned to the Tonkin Gulf incidents of 1964. The transcript never has been fully disclosed. In one part of it, however, a Pentagon representative testified that the USS *Maddox* at times had penetrated the 12-mile limit claimed by North Vietnam, though not the 3-mile limit recognized by the United States. This much Fulbright knew in 1964, as the result of secret briefings, but at the time he had dismissed territorial violations as justification for the attack. Now, putting together information from various sources, he began to see a different picture. The Pentagon official who had testified was John T. McNaughton, then Assistant Secretary of Defense for International Security Affairs. (A year later, in 1967, McNaughton died in a plane crash shortly after being designated Secretary of the Navy.)

In the spring of 1966 suspicions of a Tonkin Gulf plot began to be whispered in Washington. The political and military advantages were obvious. The reported attacks inspired the passage of a "blank check" resolution, which gave the President a free hand in Southeast Asia; they provided cause for a substantial military build-up in South Vietnam; and they provided an excuse for the first bombing of North Vietnam. The bombing not only "broke the ice" but gave the North Vietnamese an object lesson in the meaning of air power. Politically, these events had the effect of propping up the shaky regime of Premier Khanh, and, for President Johnson, they converted the Vietnam issue from an election liability into an election asset.

Publicly, Senator Fulbright produced no evidence to substantiate his doubts, and since nobody made a definite charge of deliberate wrongdoing, the subject of the Tonkin Gulf went into limbo for a year and a half. In July of 1967 the Associated Press distributed a third anniversary review of the Tonkin incidents, for which Tom Stewart and several other AP men had tracked down veterans of the *Maddox* and *Turner Joy*. On balance, the article contributed evidence for the two attacks having actually occurred, although pointing out serious misrepresentations of fact by officials of the Johnson administration. Few major newspapers bothered to print the story. None in Washington did.

Meanwhile, Admiral True, the Quaker pacifist, was finding out what it meant to buck the government. On December 27, 1966, Rear Admiral John E. Clark, Commandant of the 12th Naval District, sent True a letter, inviting him to the San Francisco office for a talk. When they met, Clark warned True that Washington was "getting restless." True had better "stop" or the consequences would be unpleasant. The commandant read aloud paragraph F-2016 of a Navy regulation dealing with public affairs: "No member of the Naval Service will utter any public statement reflecting adversely on, or belittling the role of, any other branch of the Armed Forces, the Department of Defense, or the foreign policy of the United States." Unless True cleared his speeches with the Department of the Navy, his next meeting with Admiral Clark might not be so "pleasant." The retired admiral gained the distinct impression that he was being threatened with a court-martial. Considering the activities of other retired officers, it would appear that if one wishes to "nuke the Chinks" or "hit Russia first," this is quite all right to urge upon the electorate. But if one speaks in favor of non-violence—and perhaps writes a letter to Washington—this reflects adversely on the nation's foreign policy and is a punishable offense. I have known retired military personnel who believe that "political activity" can jeopardize the pensions that they served twenty or thirty years to earn.

Admiral True was not intimidated. Rather than give up his right to criticize the government's foreign policy, he fought back by reporting the threat to Senator Fulbright. The senator went to bat for him. Without mentioning any names, Fulbright asked Secretary of the Navy Nitze whether paragraph F-2016 applied to retired personnel. Months went by. At last, on May 10, 1967, Nitze replied that the regulation *had been* interpreted in such a way; "subsequently," he said, ". . . we have been advised by the office of the Secretary of Defense that it was not intended . . ." The decision to exclude retired personnel reportedly was made by Deputy Secretary Cyrus R. Vance. As it stands, the nation's constantly increasing number of pensioned veterans, whether they know it or not, are permitted to exercise their right of free speech. Evidently this right would cease to exist if it were not for stubborn lawmakers like Senator Fulbright. Still, there are hazards in speaking out. After the Navy stopped threatening Admiral True, the Army started keeping tabs on him—as a "potential cause for civil disturbance." That is the basis for the Army's "political intelligence" effort within the United States. As one of the ugly outgrowths of the war, the Army has been employing more than a thousand agents to investigate such persons as Admiral True, anti-war people in show business, and a number of Democratic politicians. (In the news articles on this subject, I've never noticed the name of a Republican politician under investigation, even though some Republicans are more anti-war than certain of the Democrats being kept under surveillance.)

In the summer of 1967 new information impelled Senator Fulbright to launch an active investigation of the Tonkin Gulf incidents. Part of the information came from the AP story mentioned earlier. Part came from a Navy commander on duty at the Pentagon. An officer of more than twenty-five years' service, the commander at first wrote anonymously to the senator's office. Later he met secretly with Fulbright. Something had been worrying the commander and he wanted to get it off his chest. In 1964 he said the decision to bomb North Vietnam had been based on contradictory reports from the

Tonkin Gulf. The commander advised Fulbright on what reports to look for, providing accurate and specific data. Belatedly, Fulbright also decided to take Senator Morse's advice and seek the ships' logs. With the diligent application of pressure, Fulbright and his staff eventually were able to pry loose a large body of documents from their safekeeping at the Pentagon.

Like Admiral True, the helpful commander did not benefit from his public-spirited action. He now had something new to get off his chest; reportedly he went to his supervisor and told all. In a few days the senator's informant found himself hospitalized for psychiatric observation. He remained there for a month, convinced that the observation was taking too long and that his psychiatrist was under pressure to declare him unfit. Two medical boards finally decided that the commander, though moderately afflicted with anxiety, was, nevertheless, fit for duty. The Navy noted that this officer had earlier sought help from civilian psychiatrists, and that he was having marital difficulties. Senator Fulbright thought the hospitalization represented a threat to other officers who might be tempted to give him information. Happily for the senator, however, the troubled commander was replaced by another well-informed, letter-writing source in the Pentagon.

The Tonkin Gulf question, like a periodic comet, flashed back into public view in December of 1967. The propelling force was a young ex-Navy officer living in Connecticut. Former Lieutenant (jg) John W. White wrote a letter to the New Haven *Register* in which he expressed doubt that the August 4 attack actually took place. White ended his letter with the sort of statement that lights fires of controversy: "I maintain," said he, "that President Johnson, Secretary McNamara, and the Joint Chiefs of Staff gave false information to Congress in their report about U.S. destroyers being attacked in the Gulf of Tonkin."

What did the ex-lieutenant know about it? At the time of the naval action, he was far from the Tonkin Gulf. He was aboard a seaplane tender, the USS *Pine Island,* near Okinawa. Like the anonymous commander, however, White had access to radio messages on the high command circuit. In his letter, White wrote: "I recall clearly the confusing radio messages sent at that time by the destroyers—confusing because the destroyers themselves were not certain that they were being attacked." Later the *Maddox* visited Long Beach,

California, and Lieutenant White happened to be there. He bumped into a chief petty officer who, said White, was the *Maddox*'s chief sonarman. The expert soundman did not believe that any torpedoes had been fired at his ship. During the so-called "attack," the chief told Lieutenant White, he sent nothing but negative reports to the bridge. White concluded, "My naval experience as an anti-submarine warfare officer makes it clear that a chief sonarman's judgment in such a situation is more reliable than that of anyone else on the ship, including the commanding officer . . . in this case his judgment was that there was no attack."

The letter became a national sensation. The press reported that White was making a trip to Washington to see Senator Fulbright. At the same time, it became known that the Foreign Relations Committee already had initiated a quiet investigation of the reported naval action.

Another bombshell concerned the original preparation of the Tonkin Gulf resolution. The Foreign Relations Committee announced that William P. Bundy, who in the fall of 1964 had made the hawkish speech in Tokyo, had started writing the controversial resolution *before* the naval incidents occurred. Bundy explained that he had done this as a matter of normal contingency planning, anticipating that "things might take a more drastic turn at any time."[1] The effect of these disclosures was to deepen suspicion of the whole affair.

Remarked the Washington *Evening Star:* "The suggestion in some anti-administration circles is that the Tonkin incident was either a fraud or was a small matter seized upon by the administration, which was looking for an excuse to get the Tonkin resolution through Congress, thereby giving the President a free hand."

Understandably annoyed, the administration took steps to bolster its position. The Defense Department reasserted the truth of the two attacks. It said that even Hanoi admitted the first one; as for the second, there was plenty of courtroom evidence, including visual sightings from both surface ships and aircraft. When I asked about

[1] Testimony of September 20, 1966, to the Foreign Relations Committee. An unofficial report leaked to CBS in November of 1967 (see the Washington *Post* of November 10). The Committee decided on December 15, 1967, to release the exact text.

Lieutenant White's "chief sonarman," the Defense Department replied that there was no chief aboard the *Maddox*. The soundman on duty aboard the *Maddox,* said the Pentagon, reported numerous detections of torpedoes fired at the destroyers. Radarmen, added a written statement, tracked fast, small craft closing in. For the first time the Defense Department released photographs of the daytime incident of August 2. Though grainy, two pictures definitely showed fast-moving boats with shells exploding around them. The long-secret photographs made dramatic additions to television news coverage of the Tonkin Gulf controversy. They convinced everybody that "a battle" had taken place. From the angle of view, one could see that the pictures were not taken by gun cameras aboard fighter planes— the kind of photographs mentioned in 1964—but by a photographer aboard the *Maddox.*

For a while the controversy died down except for a few hints of revelations to come. The Foreign Relations Committee, it was learned, had prepared a secret report analyzing what happened in the Tonkin Gulf and how these events were evaluated in Washington. The report was prepared by the committee's staff under the direction of William Bader, an ex-Navy officer. It was said to be a "best seller" among senators. They were not permitted, however, to take it from the room in which the document was kept, usually locked in a safe. (The committee did not want the administration to accuse it of leaking classified information.) The closely guarded report convinced even some hawkish senators that the Tonkin Gulf incidents deserved further investigation. Secretary McNamara by now was planning to leave the Defense Department, but he agreed to meet with the committee. The confrontation was scheduled for February 20, 1968. It would not be open to the public.

The senators, armed with their secret analysis of the Pentagon's own documents, grilled Secretary McNamara for a full working day. For once the Legislative Branch had kept a secret well. Even McNamara complained of not knowing what was in the report. Nevertheless, the immediate result of the closed hearing was favorable to the Johnson administration.

McNamara lunched with the President that day and, before returning to Capitol Hill, released to the press a 21-page statement well calculated to buttress faith in the "second attack." In the statement McNamara admitted that there was doubt about many of the torpedoes detected by sonar during the night engagement, but he listed eighteen eyewitnesses to the attack; and he cited other previously secret evidence, including advance intelligence on the intentions of the North Vietnamese. Nothing was said, however, about the knocked-out searchlight reported by Murrey Marder in August 1964 as "courtroom evidence" for the second attack. At the end of the statement, McNamara described as "monstrous" any insinuation that the government had induced the August 4 incident in order to take retaliatory action. He closed with the following indignant words, reminiscent of Marder's anonymous source back in 1964:

"I find it inconceivable that any one even remotely familiar with our society and system of government could suspect the existence of a conspiracy which would include almost, if not all, the entire chain of military command in the Pacific, the Chairman of the Joint Chiefs of Staff, the Joint Chiefs, the Secretary of Defense, and his chief civilian assistants, the Secretary of State and the President of the United States."

As usual, the administration managed to dominate the news, and Fulbright was furious. "Everything related to the Tonkin incidents is 'secret' except that which the Pentagon deems should be made public," the senator fumed. "This, I believe, deceives the American people." In the battle for men's minds, the committee had several disadvantages, one of which was that it could not by itself decide what military information should be secret and what should not.

After the hearing was over, the administration and the committee reached agreement on publishing most of what had been said. The Defense Department combed through the material, striking out certain items, and returned the "sanitized" transcript on Friday night, February 23. The Pentagon's publicity men assured the White House that the senators could not possibly check the transcript and get it printed in time for release to Sunday newspapers. (The voluminous Sunday papers represent the best opportunity for the reporting of complex and bulky material. Monday papers, being thin with advertising, are the worst. Government agencies, therefore, when forced to reveal embarrassing information, often choose to release it late Saturday night.)

To the Pentagon's chagrin in this case both the Legislative Branch and the Government Printing Office moved with unwonted dispatch. Well before Sunday editions went to press, a 110-page pamphlet was available.[2] Newspapers were intrigued by the testimony. A few, notably the Washington *Post,* printed a great deal of it.

Again, however, the administration did not come off badly. The press emphasized tidbits of freshly revealed classified information. Losing out were the more complicated questions of provocation: Was the *Maddox* on a "routine patrol"? Did the administration have sufficient evidence of attack before ordering the air raids? The subject was becoming too big and too involved for the casual reader to comprehend. Fulbright said he was "far from convinced" of the August 4 attack, but men who were there seemed convinced. Were they not supposed to fire their guns? The eminent Senator John Sherman Cooper said he believed in the attack. Cooper and several other lawmakers thought that the administration had "overreacted." How important was that?

The doughty Senator Morse continued the anti-administration struggle. On the Senate floor he made three speeches in which, acting on his own responsibility, he revealed much of the secret information available to the committee. In his rasping, tireless voice, the former law professor declared that the United States provoked the Tonkin Gulf incidents. He branded his country a "constructive aggressor." As usual, the senior senator from Oregon, who failed of re-election that year, sounded pretty far out.

But in the autumn of the next year, 1969, a curious change of opinion took place. Drawing heavily on the text of the 1968 hearing and some interviews with sailors, Joseph Goulden, a former newspaperman, published a book entitled *Truth Is the First Casualty*[3] that persuasively summarized the case against an August 4 attack. Goulden himself seemed to think the battle was some kind of mistake skillfully covered up. He disagreed with the contention that the August 4 incident was a "manufactured lie" or the "product of a plot of the White House and the military." The book attracted little notice among the general public, but it had a profound effect on many opinion leaders. Editorial writers, columnists, and some politicians now began referring to the night battle as a "fraud" or "non-existent."

[2] U. S. Congress, Senate, Committee on Foreign Relations; *The Gulf of Tonkin, The 1964 Incidents;* Hearing, 90th Congress, 2nd Session, February 20, 1968 (Washington: Government Printing Office, 1968).

[3] Rand McNally.

Chapter IV

De Soto Patrol

When the destroyer *Maddox* got into her shooting scrape of Sunday, August 2, she was not on a routine patrol—at least not on what most civilians or even most Navy men would think of as a routine patrol.

Before her Tonkin Gulf assignment, one of the *Maddox*'s regular assignments was "plane guarding" for aircraft carriers, which entails trailing the carrier in order to pick up any pilots who might crash on the hazardous take-off or landing. Another routine task was looking for submarines, of any nationality—the Navy likes to know where the competition is and what kind of equipment it is using. During the spring and early summer of 1964, the *Maddox* sailed out of Yokosuka, Japan, with a number of other destroyers and a carrier, as part of a "hunter-killer team" engaged in anti-submarine exercises. Numbered DD 731, *Maddox* was a general purpose destroyer of World War II vintage. She was getting creaky but, with care, remained in good health.

Until midsummer the *Maddox* and her crew enjoyed what the Navy would consider an ordinary, routine cruise in the western Pacific. Then the big secret began to leak. The ship was going on an independent patrol.

First to be informed were the *Maddox*'s captain, Commander Herbert L. Ogier (pronounced Ozh' ur), and the executive officer, Lieutenant Commander Dempster M. Jackson. For security's sake, Ogier and Jackson would have preferred to say nothing about the new assignment until after the ship had left port. But there were preparations to make which would involve others. Hence, the secret had to be shared a little farther. Ogier and Jackson chose carefully those individuals who, at this stage, had a "need to know." This select group learned that their ship was getting a special job in a remote area, a place that probably nobody aboard had ever seen. The place was the Tonkin Gulf—that water between North Vietnam and Hainan —and the job was the De Soto patrol—a kind of coastal reconnaissance, named in honor of Hernando de Soto, the sixteenth-century conquistador who, while seeking gold, discovered the Mississippi River. The De Soto patrol was a monthly visit to the great rim of Communist Asia. Instead of gold, the modern explorers sought only information; their collecting devices were not shields and swords but fragile lenses and delicate electronic sensors. The basic purpose of the patrol would have been understood well enough by Hernando de Soto: it was to investigate the potential enemy.

But the *Maddox* was an old-fashioned destroyer, not a "sophisticated spy ship," to use a newspaper term of later years. How would the old sea dog learn new tricks? The De Soto responsibility was a temporary one, rotated among destroyers of the Seventh Fleet. There were not many special requirements. The ship would take aboard some extra men and some extra equipment. As for her own crew, only a small number of men would need special training, and that would not be too difficult. The training would not even begin until the ship was under way, so that nothing about the assignment could leak out ashore. This was a real hush-hush patrol. *Nobody* should know anything that he didn't *need* to know. That was the first principle of security.

On her way to the Tonkin Gulf, the *Maddox* would stop at Taiwan, where most of the extra men would come aboard. Also at Taiwan, the ship would take aboard a big "black box" (a term generally used for any piece of mysterious equipment, particularly an unfamiliar electronic device) known officially as the COMVAN. That was as much as anybody could or would say about the box. Neither the somewhat impatient captain nor the gruff executive officer were men of whom one would ask a lot of unnecessary questions.

In addition to carrying the COMVAN, the ship would be required to perform the following:

Collect information on water depths and temperature, navigational lights and buoys, currents, tides, and other subjects of hydrographic interest;

Observe junk traffic for signs of military activity, such as weapons, unusually large numbers of young men aboard, and concentrations of junks in excess of 300;

Identify types of radar transmitters, plot their locations, estimate effective ranges, and record their emissions;

Photograph the coastline, with especial attention to prominent landmarks, military installations, and new construction;

Conduct radarscope photography.

While never stated, the function of the COMVAN and its special detachment of men would be to eavesdrop on Communist radio communications. At the 1968 hearing, senators charged that the *Maddox,* far from being on a routine patrol, was outfitted for electronic surveillance—was, in fact, an electronic "spy ship." Secretary McNamara denied it. The COMVAN was aboard, said he, in order to protect the ship, meaning apparently that if the Communists were to broadcast a plan to attack the American destroyer, the COMVAN was there to pick it up and give warning.

What, then, was the purpose of the patrol? Senator Fulbright wanted to know.

The ship's primary task, explained McNamara, was to search for infiltrators who might be traveling by boat from North Vietnam to South Vietnam. The chief purpose, said the Secretary, was certainly not electronic surveillance. Except for the radio eavesdropping, the ship's work was to be done with "regularly installed" equipment.

Perhaps, even with his twenty-five security clearances, the Secretary of Defense was one of those who did not "need to know" what the *Maddox* was doing in the Tonkin Gulf. As it happened, before the ship left Japan, she was to obtain the following special equipment and special personnel: Automatic Pulse Analyzer[1] with a special KD-2 camera (for analyzing and recording radar waves); a radarscope camera with a trained operator; optical cameras with telescopic lenses and a trained operator; and secret reference publications, including charts of the Tonkin Gulf, reports of previous

---

[1] A device that displays on a scope the "fingerprint" of an incoming radar wave. The type of radar and its purpose—surface search, air search, missile guidance—can be determined from the characteristics of the wave: its frequency, rate of pulse, duration of pulse, and width of beam. Air search radar, for example, uses a lower frequency than surface search radar. Aircraft can and must be detected from a great distance, and the lower frequency gives more carrying power.

De Soto patrols, and data on known Communist equipment, such as radar transmitters.

Charts of the Tonkin Gulf took some time to locate. Everything else was readily available except for the radarscope camera and its operator. Apparently they were not standard for De Soto patrol. Navy headquarters at Yokosuka had no radarscope photographer; and casting about for one resulted in outsiders being informed of the *Maddox*'s assignment. Rather than risk any more breaches of security, the skipper reported the difficulty to higher command; it then was arranged for the *Maddox* to pick up a radarscope photographer and his equipment in Taiwan. Later events suggested what this curious pastime, photographing the radarscope, had to do with the Tonkin Gulf.

As the *Maddox* prepared to leave port, the crew could not help but notice that something unusual was happening. Mysterious packages came aboard. Few officers seemed to have a clue as to what was going on, and they would say nothing. Next, the Division Commodore and his staff arrived, along with their personal belongings—as if they planned to stay for a while. *Maddox* belonged to Destroyer Division 192 commanded by Commodore John J. Herrick, a captain in rank. The Division staff included an operations officer, medical officer, chaplain, an engineer, and a few enlisted men specializing in communications. The arrival of Herrick and his men kicked off a game of musical cabins. Herrick bumped Ogier, and Ogier bumped Executive Officer Jackson, who opted out of the game rather than bump the ship's operations officer, Lieutenant William S. Buehler. Buehler's cabin was full of steam pipes, and the voyage would be hot enough. Jackson decided to sleep topside in the motor whaleboat near the bridge.

To many of *Maddox*'s crew, the most interesting new arrival came not from Division but from Commander of Naval Forces, Japan (COMNAV, Japan). He was a photographer's mate, 2nd class, rigged with the shiny tools of his profession: three 35-millimeter cameras and a selection of telescopic lenses. The ship's amateur photographers, loaded down with expensive equipment purchased in Japan and Hong Kong, looked forward to some good shooting.

With a sense of adventure but no fanfare, men of the *Maddox* slipped out of Yokosuka harbor on Thursday, July 23. The other three ships of Destroyer Division 192 stayed behind. Wherever the

Maddox was going, she was going alone. The ship glided through the oily water of the coast and, reaching the blue sea, turned to starboard; amateur navigators struck Siberia off their list of probable destinations. All day the ship plunged southward at 20 knots. If the commodore were going to the tropics, why take an old tub like the *Maddox,* the crew wondered. His own ship, the USS *Berkeley,* was air conditioned. The *Maddox* was not.

The *Berkeley* was bigger, too, but the older destroyer was roomy enough. Commander Jackson, stretched out in the cool of the whaleboat, belied the fact that the *Maddox* offered plenty of bunks. In time of peace, the ship was authorized a complement of fourteen officers and 260 men, which totalled forty-eight bodies fewer than the wartime allowance of twenty-two officers and three hundred men. The ship, therefore, could accommodate not only the Division staff but the men of the COMVAN and a few others who were scheduled to come aboard.

After a three-day journey, the green slopes of Taiwan broke the horizon. There was the offshore stronghold of Generalissimo Chiang Kai-shek, whom the U. S. Government recognized as the ruler of China. The *Maddox* docked at the northern tip of the island, at the naval base of Keelung. The ship eased up beside another old destroyer, whose profile showed a peculiar lump between the stacks: a rectangular box the size of a moving van. This was the COMVAN or "black box," which turned out to be haze gray, the regulation color for Navy ships. The destroyer alongside had just finished her turn at De Soto patrol. She had cruised way up north in the Sea of Okhotsk—which sailors call the Sea of Oshkosh—a great, squarish body of water between the Russian peninsula of Kamchatka and the mainland of Siberia.

A dockside crane lifted the COMVAN from the other ship and set it down between the two stacks of the *Maddox,* thus stamping her with the mark of De Soto patrol. Like most secret operations overseas, this one took place within the bored view of countless foreigners. Milling around on the pier were the usual gang of Chinese dock wallopers and skilled workmen without whose services the U. S. Navy could not function. *Maddox* personnel speculated on which Chinese laborer would tap out the message to Peking: DD 731 JUST GOT THE BOX.

With the exception of the ship's radarmen, most of the *Maddox's* crew enjoyed liberty at Keelung. Having started their special training, the radarmen now were "in the know," and for that reason restricted to the ship. The assistant operations officer, Lieutenant (jg) Daley Evans, greatly impressed by the importance of the De Soto patrol, initiated the radarmen with a dramatic lecture. Whatever Evans might have said about the mission, the *Maddox*'s subsequent adventures were to justify almost any stretch of the lieutenant's imagination.

Commodore Herrick debarked at Keelung to meet with officers of the Patrol Force, Taiwan Defense Command, whose responsibility it was to manage the De Soto project. The De Soto patrol had begun in 1962, the same year that Rear Admiral Robert A. MacPherson took over the Patrol Force. Herrick, however, did not meet Admiral MacPherson, who was up in Okinawa with his flagship, a seaplane tender. MacPherson's staff briefed the commodore.

As Commander of the Patrol Force, Admiral MacPherson reported to the Seventh Fleet Commander, Vice Admiral Roy L. ("Royal") Johnson, who, as the *Maddox* left Yokosuka, was completing a visit to Saigon aboard his flagship, the missile cruiser *Oklahoma City*. The Seventh Fleet Commander paid his respects to the new U. S. Ambassador, General Taylor, and reportedly asked whether the Navy couldn't play a bigger role in Southeast Asian affairs. (According to a Radio Hanoi broadcast of June 12, Admiral MacPherson already had visited Saigon on June 8 aboard the seaplane tender *Currituck*.)

Back from liberty, the *Maddox*'s crewmen inspected the strange gray box, but from a slight distance. The door was locked, and next to it stood the unfamiliar figure of an armed Marine. With the box came a Navy lieutenant, five Marines, and ten sailors. The sailors were rated as communications technicians or CTs for short, so that the term COMVAN seemed to stand for communications van. The CTs called it simply the van. Considering the aura of mystery, the term "black box" still seemed appropriate, even if the box were painted a light gray. (Still more appropriate would have been the term "black chamber," the old appellation for a well-guarded office devoted to codebreaking.)

As senators came to suspect, the *Maddox*, before she entered the Gulf, was outfitted as what the press now calls a "spy ship." On a small scale, the *Maddox* would do the kind of work in the Tonkin

Gulf that the USS *Liberty* did off the coast of Sinai in 1967—when she was attacked by Israeli aircraft and torpedo boats—and the USS *Pueblo* did off the coast of North Korea in 1968—when she was captured by a North Korean subchaser and torpedo boats. All of these ships were mobile collection points for the vast electronic intelligence industry supervised by the ultrasecret National Security Agency (NSA). In 1964 few people had heard of NSA, although its headquarters at Fort George G. Meade, Maryland, measured twice the size of the CIA building at Langley, Virginia.

Whether electronic intelligence ships actually engage in espionage is a matter of opinion and circumstance. Like a spy, the *Pueblo* tried to disguise her identity. She did not fly the American flag, and, despite the proliferation of weird antennae, she made an effort to look like a cargo carrier. So that the ship would not look like a naval vessel, few men were allowed topside; those who were wore civilian clothes or a mixture of civilian-naval attire. When the North Koreans challenged the *Pueblo,* she gave up on the cargo cover and hoisted the hydrographic survey signal. Just before the North Koreans boarded the ship, the skipper, Commander Lloyd M. Bucher, finally took off a tassled white ski cap and replaced it with regulation Navy headgear. Bucher now is convinced that the North Koreans believed the *Pueblo* to be a South Korean vessel planning a commando raid (in retaliation for a raid attempted by the North Koreans two days before).[2] While attempting to disguise herself, the *Pueblo* also seems to have intruded on North Korea's claimed 12-mile territorial sea, though not at the time of her capture. The ship's own records showed that she often went closer to land than 12 miles. The *Pueblo*'s navigator says that his records were inaccurate; this and other testimony at the Court of Inquiry indicates that, at best, the navigator often did not know exactly where he was.[3]

From the North Korean point of view, the *Pueblo* definitely engaged in espionage, but this was not true from the American point of view because, whatever she did, the ship did not intrude on the

[2] Commander Lloyd M. Bucher, *Bucher: My Story* (New York: Doubleday, Inc., 1970), page 405.

[3] The transcript of the inquiry has not been published in full. The Defense Department allowed me to read the daily summaries prepared for the press and kept on file at the Pentagon.

3-mile territorial sea then recognized by the U. S. Government. The destroyer *Maddox* did enter—and deliberately—what the North Vietnamese considered to be their territorial water, and the legality of that will be discussed later. But the *Maddox* made no attempt to disguise her identity. She flew the American flag, and her crew wore regulation uniform at all times. The North Vietnamese recognized the *Maddox* as a ship of the U. S. Navy. The destroyer, therefore, did not engage in espionage. She did engage in reconnaissance, including radio eavesdropping. Whether the reconnaissance was legal or illegal depends on one's opinion as to the legal width of North Vietnam's territorial sea; the reconnaissance, in any case, was not espionage.

Both the *Pueblo* and the *Maddox* collected electronic intelligence, and, rather than "spy ship," the Navy prefers the term "elint ship" for this type of vessel, elint standing for ELectronic INTelligence.

Elint is part of a broader activity sometimes called "electronic warfare," which includes both intelligence and security work. Its objectives are two-sided: not only to read the other fellow's messages, for example, but to keep him from reading ours. Thus, while the elint people are breaking codes, the security people are busy inventing new ones to replace those of ours that might be wearing thin. Additional electronic challenges include how to evade the other fellow's radar and keep him from evading ours; how to deceive his missile guidance and keep him from deceiving ours; how to find his submarines and keep him from finding ours. An attempt to deceive or render useless the other fellow's electronic gadget is called an electronic countermeasure (ECM for short). We could, for example, transmit a false electronic blip in order to confuse the other fellow's radar. To screen out our false blip, he then might vary the rate of his radar pulse. That would be an electronic counter-countermeasure (ECCM). Almost every such trick can be nullified or improved upon. The job of the technological warrior is to get ahead of the game and stay there.[4]

The United States has an impressive record in electronic warfare, going all the way back to the early days of the electric telegraph, which was invented in 1835 by an American sculptor and painter,

---

[4] *Electronic News* of January 22, 1968, offers a brief survey of developments in ECM and ECCM.

Samuel F. B. Morse. During the Civil War, Union cryptanalysts often broke Southern codes more easily than the Southerners did. With the invention of radio, codebreaking became a large-scale activity because it was now so easy to intercept the enemy's messages—it was no longer necessary to tap a telegraph wire or intercept a messenger. In World War I the British did important work in cryptanalysis, and in World War II American codebreakers played a vital role. The crucial Battle of Midway was a victory for intelligence, according to General George C. Marshall and Admiral Chester W. Nimitz. By knowing in advance the Japanese plan of attack, the remnants of the U. S. Pacific Fleet were able to turn the tide of the war, instead of being wiped out, as the enemy had planned.

Both NSA and CIA grew out of the Pearl Harbor catastrophe of 1941, which in part represented a failure of intelligence. The armed forces had plenty of indications that the Japanese would make an attack somewhere. Even the FBI gave warning. But the various items of intelligence were not properly coordinated or evaluated. For example, Army and Navy officers in Hawaii heard that Japanese diplomats were destroying most of their codes, but they did not fully grasp the meaning of this classic event. Nor did Washington spell it out for them. Back in the capital, the Army's Chief of Far Eastern Intelligence, Colonel Rufus S. Bratton, sensing keenly the imminence of war, tried to make sure that the Pacific Fleet was ready and alert. Bratton's counterpart in Naval Intelligence assured him that the fleet was ready for action; indeed, said the naval officer, the fleet was *at sea* or *going to sea*. But in fact, the fleet tied up in port for the weekend—as usual; and the Japanese knew it—as usual. (It was not only Naval Intelligence that erred. The admiral in charge of War Plans "assumed" the fleet was at sea. As for the Chief of Naval Operations, Admiral Harold S. Stark, he seems to have known where the fleet was, though his testimony on "that particular detail" was rather fuzzy.)[5] After the war the awesome power of the atomic bomb made it clear that the nation would have to take better precautions against

---

[5] U. S. Congress, Joint Committee on the Investigation of the Pearl Harbor Attack; *Pearl Harbor Attack;* Hearings, 79th Congress, 1st Session (Washington: Government Printing Office, 1946), 39 Parts. See the testimony of Admiral Stark on page 2153 of Part 5 and page 1087 of Part 23; Admiral Turner on pages 1972–73, Part 4; Captain McCollum on page 3437, Part 8; Colonel Bratton on pages 4580–81, Part 9.

the possibility of surprise attack. Hoping to prevent the ultimate tragedy, Congress established two agencies for coordinating intelligence. They were the Central Intelligence Agency, specializing in the traditional forms of espionage, and the National Security Agency (at first called the Armed Forces Security Agency), specializing in certain esoteric technologies such as codebreaking and secret ink.

Over the years the two coordinating agencies have burgeoned into tremendous empires, each carrying out its own operations. NSA, however, has continued to serve the needs of military intelligence while the CIA has gone off into political intelligence and certain kinds of direct action, largely paramilitary. It is reported that the CIA's "operational side" now has nine overseas employees to every one on the "intelligence-gathering side."[6] By 1961 Secretary McNamara thought it necessary to create the Defense Intelligence Agency (DIA), under his own control, to do what the CIA originally was supposed to do. Since then the problem has been to coordinate not only the intelligence services of the traditional armed forces, but, on top of them, the multifarious activities of the NSA, CIA, and DIA. A succession of Presidents have dealt with the problem through committees connected to the White House staff and the National Security Council.[7] As in the case of Pearl Harbor, crossed wires and misjudgment resulted in the tragic fiascoes of the U-2, the *Liberty,* and the *Pueblo.*

Considering all of the trouble and risk involved, the citizen must wonder whether the intelligence game is worth the candle. Do these dangerous and expensive activities help to prevent war? Or do they bring war closer? Certainly the lessons of experience point to excessive risk in the short-range monitoring done by "ferret" aircraft and ships. Communist nations are notoriously sensitive about their borders. Add to that idiosyncrasy the American passion for data-collecting, and the result is a highly explosive combination.

[6] Colonel L. Fletcher Prouty, "The Secret Team," *Washington Monthly* (May, 1970), page 19. Now retired from the Air Force, Colonel Prouty served for years as the Joint Chiefs' liaison man to the CIA.

[7] Chiefly, supervision is supposed to come from an offshoot of the National Security Council known as the U. S. Intelligence Board, which is chaired permanently by the Director of the CIA. Also involved is a somewhat informal group recently going by the name of the "Forty Committee." Compare Colonel Prouty's description of how clandestine operations are directed by the CIA in cooperation with the White House staff.

In the case of the *Liberty*, the attackers were not even Communist. But thirty-four Americans died, and for a time the world trembled on the brink of nuclear holocaust. The Pentagon at first thought that the suddenly silent elint vessel had been attacked by the Russians. Fortunately, the torpedoed ship did not sink, and after regaining electrical power she informed Washington that her attackers were Israeli. Israeli aircraft and torpedo boats apparently mistook the *Liberty* for an Egyptian vessel. As Secretary McNamara said later, "Thank goodness our carrier commanders did not launch immediately against the Soviet forces who were operating in the Med [Mediterranean] at the time."[8] Thus the *Liberty*'s patrol tested severely the knife-edged balance of terror on which the nuclear age depends. Furthermore, there was no reason to continue the patrol beyond the outbreak of war—if that long. The Joint Chiefs had tried to move the ship, but their messages were lost and misrouted.

To military authorities, the Six-Day War demonstrated the value of electronic intelligence. The quick success of the Israeli onslaught required control of the air, which depended on a surprise attack designed to catch the Arab air forces on the ground. The element of surprise, in turn, depended on a thorough knowledge of the Arab defenses, including knowledge of the Arab radar screen.

The craft of intelligence no doubt will continue to be practiced so long as independent nations make war to settle their disputes. Perhaps its practitioners, however, could be persuaded to consider the ancient motto of the physician *Primum non nocere*—"First, do no harm."

The USS *Maddox*, with her special equipment and special personnel, remained a Navy ship but became a receptor for both DIA and NSA. (The Navy's full-time elint men work closely with DIA and NSA; sometimes they are stationed at NSA facilities, including Fort George G. Meade.) The COMVAN men came to the *Maddox* from elint stations spotted around the Pacific. Two of the box personnel, including the Navy lieutenant in command, were stationed regularly on Taiwan. The others flew in from more distant locations. Some, at least, had volunteered for the patrol in order to get away from humdrum desk work and experience life in the real, shipboard

---

[8] "Meet the Press" television program; February 4, 1968.

Navy—which they called the "basic Navy." Mentally, this was an elite group. They had been selected for elint work because of high scores in general intelligence, in the use of numbers, or in the use of words.

After spending a night in Taiwan's pleasure-ridden capital, the COMVAN men boarded a special bus for Keelung. In less than an hour they found their new home, the USS *Maddox*. She was not a large destroyer but a sufficiently salty-looking one, an old *Sumner* class vessel of 3300 tons,[9] built in 1944. Destroyers have grown steadily in tonnage and length, as ships do; and the *Sumner* vessels, though imposing at first, soon became known as "short hulls." The short-hulled *Maddox,* 376½ feet in length, had not been modernized like most of the Navy's older ships. The modernization process largely amounts to removing guns in order to make space for missiles and electronic equipment. The *Maddox* carried what had become an unusually large number of guns—six of 5-inch bore and four of 3-inch. The observant newcomer might also have noticed a freshly painted E awarded for exceptional skill in using these old-fashioned weapons. In short, if the *Maddox* had any special qualification for an independent patrol, it appeared to be a superior ability to aim and deliver explosive shells.

The superstitious newcomer would have been better off not to ask when the destroyer had left her home port. *Maddox* departed Long Beach, California, on Friday, March 13. She was, according to scuttlebutt, the thirteenth vessel to steam out of harbor that day.

Former Captain Herrick has given somewhat differing explanations for why he chose *Maddox* for De Soto patrol from among the four destroyers available to him in DesDiv 192. Herrick at first told me and at least one other writer that he selected *Maddox* because of her guns, her demonstrated skill in firing them, and certain other advantages. He had originally planned to take the *Picking,* another old ship of somewhat less firepower. Learning, however, that the Tonkin Gulf would be his destination, Herrick, sensing an extra element of risk, switched to the better-gunned *Maddox*. This is what I heard in 1967 before the Tonkin Gulf incidents became contro-

---

[9] In this book, tonnages of U. S. Navy ships are given as "full load" except when otherwise specified. By the more artificial "standard load" measurement, the *Maddox* was 2200 tons.

versial. More recently Herrick advised me that the real reason for taking the *Maddox* was that the *Picking* had no place for the COMVAN except on the fantail, where it would have masked the aftermost 5-inch gun. When Herrick and I had our first conversation, the COMVAN was supposed to be secret, and the former captain could not say anything about it.

What about the 431-foot *Berkeley?* Only three years old, the commodore's flagship was a comfortable, air-conditioned, guided missile armed destroyer of 4500 tons. Would not the newer ship, DDG 15, have been ideal for an independent patrol in the tropics? One can think of two major reasons for not taking the *Berkeley*. First, her armament would not have been adequate. The Navy's surface-to-surface tactical missile, Regulus, had been washed out by an Eisenhower economy wave; consequently, the *Berkeley*'s missiles could be guided only against aircraft and submarines, of which the North Vietnamese had neither (except for training planes). The North Vietnamese did have plenty of torpedo boats and gunboats, against which the $34,000,000 *Berkeley*, having only two guns, could not give a very good account of herself. As a second possible reason for not using the *Berkeley*, the ship might have been pre-empted for some other job in the South China Sea. As early as August 4, if not sooner, men of the *Maddox* heard that *Berkeley* was at the edge of the Tonkin Gulf, relaying messages for the commodore.

Still another factor in Herrick's final selection of the *Maddox* might have been his longstanding friendship with Captain Ogier. More than ten years before, the two had shared an office at the Naval Academy as instructors of marine engineering. Reunited in DesDiv 192, the old friends became "liberty buddies."

Both Herrick and Ogier were graduates of the Naval Academy, Herrick in 1943 and Ogier in 1944. Their years at the Academy overlapped, but the two did not know each other at that time, perhaps because of their different interests. Jack Herrick, a quiet young man from Warren, Minnesota, was a builder of ship models. Herbie Ogier, from nearby Baltimore, had been a high school swimming star. At the Academy his time was crowded with sports and social activities.

Each of the two ensigns began his naval career aboard an old-fashioned battlewagon, witnessing the twilight of the big guns. Though he graduated a year later, Ensign Ogier got into combat first. Aboard the *California,* one of the younger ships resurrected from the mud of Pearl Harbor, Ogier took part in the gigantic ship-to-ship battle at Surigao Strait in the Philippines. Herrick's ship, the ancient *New York*, bogged down in training assignments and repair problems. She was not present at Surigao, but with Herrick aboard, the relic of World War I lobbed 14-inch shells at the islands of Iwo Jima and Okinawa. Both the *California* and *New York* drew kamikaze attack. Herrick and Ogier escaped injury.

After the war, both officers continued in the surface Navy. During the Korean War, Herrick commanded a rocket firing ship, *Des Plaines River*, which directed its unguided missiles at Communist installations ashore.

Lieutenant Ogier missed the Korean War entirely. After finishing his teaching assignment at the Academy, he embarked on a series of cruises in the Mediterranean, first aboard a cargo ship, then on a *Sumner*-type destroyer. It was in 1962 that Ogier took command of the *Maddox;* by 1964 he ought to have been very familiar with this type of vessel. He was scheduled for transfer following the De Soto patrol.

Except that each officer was an experienced destroyerman, neither Herrick nor Ogier seems to have offered any special qualifications for the De Soto patrol. Their service records, indeed, were notably lacking in what the Navy considers "special qualifications." Neither had undertaken postgraduate education at the Naval War College or similar school, nor had either one any experience in submarines or in the air. The two were strictly destroyermen in a Navy largely dominated by airmen. By 1964 each had achieved the rank typically appropriate for members of his class at the Academy. In the Navy register, however, both now stood in the bottom half of their Academy class, with respect to precedence in consideration for promotion.[10] From the career standpoint, Herrick, as the commander of a destroyer division, was holding down a good job; so was Ogier as the captain of a ship. But Ogier was slated next for a staff job—a less certain mark of favor.

In personality, Herrick was still the quiet, careful type, easy to get along with, studious in appearance. Ogier, more impulsive, inclined

[10] *Navy and Marine Corps Register, 1964;* House Documents, Volume 24; 88th Congress, 2nd Session, 1964. Each officer's "lineal number" determines when he will be considered for promotion—the smaller the number, the sooner.

to sarcasm, was known as a demanding skipper. His motto for the ship: Proved Readiness. At the time of the Tonkin Gulf patrol, Ogier was forty-one years of age; Herrick had just turned forty-four. Herrick had a wife and four children, Ogier a wife and three children. Mrs. Ogier was French, a vocalist from Nice.

Something seems to have persuaded Commodore Herrick that the Tonkin Gulf would be a risky place to visit. Possibly he was worried by the same factors, mostly secret, that concerned the Joint Chiefs of Staff when they heard about the De Soto plan, which had to be submitted to them for approval. While the Joint Chiefs did approve the August patrol, in so doing they sent a cautionary message to CINCPACFLT (Admiral Thomas H. Moorer, Commander-in-Chief of the Pacific Fleet). CINCPACFLT ranked just below CINCPAC (Admiral Sharp, who commanded not only the Pacific Fleet but also Army and Air Force units in the Pacific area).

The Joint Chiefs' message to Admiral Moorer read:

A. LAST DE SOTO PATROL TO GULF OF TONKIN WAS MADE IN MARCH. WEATHER AT THAT TIME GREATLY PRECLUDED VISUAL INTELLIGENCE COLLECTION.

B. U.S. HAS STEPPED UP ASSISTANCE TO RVN [Republic of Vietnam] INCLUDING STATIONING OF CVA TG [the aircraft carrier *Ticonderoga*] AT MOUTH OF GULF OF TONKIN.

C. THERE HAVE BEEN CONSIDERABLE ARTICLES IN NEWS MEDIA DISCUSSING POSSIBILITY OF ACTION AGAINST NVN [North Vietnam].

D. ACTIVITY IN 34-A OPERATIONS HAS INCREASED.[11]

Spelled out, the message meant that since it had rained in March, the De Soto men could not see whether the natives were friendly or what new weapons they might have acquired. (Observation was probably limited by a peculiar kind of Tonkin Gulf weather called the "crachin," a prolonged spell of light rain accompanied by fog or low-lying clouds, which occurs at any time from December through April.) The presence of the *Ticonderoga* at their doorstep might well be making the North Vietnamese nervous, and the visit of the *Maddox* be interpreted in consequence as part of the attack on the North which the South Vietnamese had been loudly threatening. Furthermore, since increasingly gunboats were landing spies and com-

[11] Senator Morse's speech of February 29, 1968.

mandos in North Vietnam, *Maddox* might be thought to be engaged in this activity.

In short, the message seems to have been a warning that the *Maddox* was liable to get shot at. This much American officials knew even *before* the *Maddox* started her "routine patrol." North Vietnamese motives, therefore, were not so inscrutable as the American people were led to believe.

Senator Morse quoted the Joint Chiefs' message in his speech of February 29, 1968, after the second Tonkin Gulf hearing. The message had been censored from the hearing transcript.

Morse told his colleagues that the Foreign Relations Committee investigators had had a hard time trying to find out what "34-A" stood for. They were finally told that the term referred to clandestine activity by South Vietnamese gunboats. No wonder the Defense Department was reluctant to talk about 34-A. At the hearing of August 6, 1964, when the Tonkin Gulf resolution was being considered, Secretary McNamara had told the senators:

"Our Navy played absolutely no part in, was not associated with, was not aware of, any South Vietnamese action, if there were any. I want to make that very clear to you."

The Navy, in fact, was very much involved with "South Vietnamese action." The Navy provided the gunboats and had something to say about what would be done with them. At the 1968 hearing, senators threw this information at McNamara. Unperturbed, he explained that by the term "Navy" he had meant the *Maddox*. It was Commodore Herrick, he said, who did not know about the gunboat operations. After a lengthy argument, McNamara admitted that there was "an ambiguity" in his statement of August 6, 1964.

The war in Vietnam hinged on that "ambiguity," among others.

How much Commodore Herrick knew about the 34-A operations when he was in the Tonkin Gulf never became clear; the Foreign Relations Committee never invited him to testify. Herrick did know the term "34-A"; and in a later chapter evidence will be offered that he recognized the gunboats when he saw them.

During the briefing on Taiwan, Herrick expressed the opinion that the *Maddox* was liable to run into trouble. Always cautious, the commodore suggested that plans be made to deal with that possibility. MacPherson's staff, however, brushed aside these fears: other destroyers had been to the Gulf, and the place was so friendly that fishermen waved to the American sailors. Apparently the commodore and the Joint Chiefs, the two ends of the chain of command, were at odds with the middle. "Don't sweat the North Vietnamese," was the word from Taiwan. As viewed by Herrick's immediate superiors, this would be a routine patrol.

Chapter V

War in Peace

Having docked at Keelung on Sunday, July 26, the *Maddox* was ready to cast off on Tuesday, July 28. The ship was in a festive mood, with the black box and its curious menagerie added to the variety of guests already on board. But those who expected a picture-taking cruise were soon disappointed. At sea, all private cameras were confiscated —a most unusual event, even in wartime. There would be little frivolity on this patrol. Official photographers would take what pictures might be needed (and somebody would bootleg a few).

Missing when the *Maddox* cast off were the radarscope photographer, apparently as difficult to obtain on Taiwan as he had been in Japan; and representatives of the Military Assistance Command, Vietnam (MACV). The MACV men were to have joined the ship at Keelung in order to provide operational guidance during the patrol. A new plan called for taking them aboard, along with the radarscope photographer, at the edge of the Tonkin Gulf. There would be a transfer at sea. The ship would not call at any port until the patrol was over, not even to refuel.

Evidently higher command wanted *Maddox* to arrive in the Gulf completely by surprise. Among the special security measures was Emission Control, Condition One (EMCON One). This meant that on her way to the Gulf, the ship was to emit no radio or radar waves that would make it possible for Communist direction finders to plot her course. In addition, the ship steered far from Red territory, avoiding the direct route through the Strait of Taiwan. *Maddox* dropped to the south instead, keeping the big island between her and the Chinese mainland, as if she planned to visit the Philippines.

The destroyermen got a good look at Taiwan's eastern side. Like the other side, it bristled with fortifications.

Below Taiwan the destroyer took a dogleg to the right, starting a 650-mile trek through the South China Sea. This was open water, far from land. The *Maddox* encountered no other ships. Whether by design or accident, the destroyer was sailing in what climatologists call a "typical typhoon track."

During the month of July, this part of the South China Sea usually is swept by one or two typhoons (1.7 on the average). The American warship, however, sailed in a placid, empty sea.

Most of the COMVAN men blended easily into the ship's company. They attracted little notice except for the Marines, who were distinguishable by their green fatigue uniforms. Even after the patrol was over many of the ship's regular crew thought the box was inhabited solely by Marines. Perhaps this should be taken as a compliment to the communications technicians, who were heavily indoctrinated with the need for security, rather than as evidence of the Marine Corps's traditional flair for publicity.

To the destroyermen, the COMVAN represented an enigma; and to men of the COMVAN, the ship offered her puzzling aspects, too. Immediately the newcomers discovered something peculiar: the ship's clocks were running fast. Aboard *Maddox* all manner of timepiece was ticking to Japan time—one hour faster than Taiwan time and two hours faster than zone time in the Tonkin Gulf. So as not to miss any meals, the COMVAN borrowed an extra clock from the ship and set it to Japan time. Men in the box supposed that the ship kept Japan time because she planned to return there shortly (although Navy ships generally keep local time wherever they happen to be). An officer of the ship gave me a different explanation: *Maddox,* according to him, adhered to the time prescribed for De Soto patrols—all of which kept Japan time. He supposed that having every ship keep the same time simplified the record-keeping for Admiral MacPherson up in Okinawa.[1] In short, the box and the ship each thought the other responsible for the odd method of keeping time. The Mystery of the Clocks will be heard of again.

---

[1] MacPherson's regular headquarters were not on the Japanese island but Taiwan. On the other hand, the zone in which Japan is located was central to the De Soto patrol area.

On the afternoon of Thursday, July 30, the destroyer curved down around the eastern side of Hainan; at nightfall she was slipping under the southern shore of the big island, toward the Gulf of Tonkin. The ship still was keeping a tight EMCON One. Security, however, did not prevent the use of passive equipment—radio and radar receivers —and so radarmen glued themselves to the ECM equipment, hoping to collect a Chinese "fingerprint" on the Automatic Pulse Analyzer. Something wiggled on the scope, and the KD-2 snapped its picture. The radarmen supposed that the incoming waves emanated from Hainan, but, unfortunately, the ship's old direction finder could not handle the frequency. Hence nobody could be sure of where the radar was coming from. This was the first of many disappointments in store for the fledgling elint men.

The presumably Chinese radar did not necessarily detect the *Maddox*. Radar waves carry much farther than their effective echoing range.

The *Maddox*'s radarmen worked in a crowded compartment that the Navy calls a Combat Information Center (CIC). CIC was a major naval innovation of World War II, when it started out as the radar shack. During the early part of the war, Navy ships made little use of radar, partly because the officers had no confidence in it. But the equipment improved, and so did the skill of the men using it. Radar began to assume great importance. Naval officers found it convenient to make decisions near the source of radar information; and as other electronic gadgets came along, it made sense to put them all in the same compartment. In 1943 this compartment became formally known as the Combat Information Center. One of CIC's more interesting gadgets is the Dead Reckoning Tracer (DRT), a big table that shows the ship's position by means of a moving spot of light. The moving apparatus, called the "bug," creeps along a scroll of paper, and the DRT man plots around it information concerning other ships and submarines. The DRT man also draws torpedo tracks when need be. Aircraft are not marked on the scroll. They are drawn on a vertical plastic board nearby.

Depending on the nature of the problem at hand, and whether it is night or day, CIC and the bridge alternate as the decision-making center of the ship. In the *Maddox*'s generation of destroyer, the captain often stations himself on the bridge while the executive officer supervises CIC. World War II ships put CIC some distance abaft and below the bridge so that the enemy could not eliminate the whole top staff with one shot. More recent ships put CIC just behind the bridge and on the same level so that the captain can walk back and forth. In the atomic age, a little separation did not seem to make much difference. Besides, superstructures now were being made of aluminum, a light metal that protects the crew from weather and not much else.

While the *Maddox* passed under Hainan, the professional elint men with the box tried out their equipment, too. The destroyermen could see that the COMVAN amounted to a workroom for the men that came with it. The communications technicians worked in shifts there, around the clock. But how could they do any communicating? The box had no transmitting antenna. It merely plugged into the *Maddox*'s "long wire," a receiving aerial. The COMVAN acquired a new nickname: the "mad box."

In a way, the box was getting mad. Shortly after leaving Keelung, the air-conditioning unit broke down. The men inside now felt much closer to the basic Navy.

Emerging from under Hainan, the destroyer glided silently into the Tonkin Gulf. In darkness the ship drew behind her the brilliant, phosphorescent wake characteristic of tropical waters. Toward midnight, local time, flashes of another kind spelled trouble up along the coast of North Vietnam. Gunfire in two locations marked an escalation of the 34-A project. Hitherto, the "secret" operations (secret to the American people, not to the North Vietnamese) consisted of landing spies and commandos on the Communist shore, most of whom were caught before long. The night of July 30–31 marked something new. Instead of merely dropping some black-faced interlopers, naval vessels from South Vietnam landed shellfire on military targets. Here was a direct bombardment from the sea. Perhaps the Joint Chiefs had such a possibility in mind when they warned (or reminded) CINCPACFLT: ACTIVITY IN 34-A OPERATIONS HAS INCREASED.

The 34-A craft were fast gunboats known by a variety of unofficial names. At higher command some Navy men called them the "black boats," although, like the *Maddox*'s COMVAN, they were painted a light gray. Recently a new shipment of gunboats had arrived in South Vietnam. According to an unofficial report, they came in the LSD 7, which would have been the *Oak Hill,* a "parent ship" for small craft. The boats were based at Da Nang, a major airport and seaport about 90 miles south of the Demilitarized Zone.

On the afternoon of Thursday, July 30, four gunboats left Da Nang to make a round-trip journey of more than 500 miles up into the Gulf and back. Under the cover of darkness, one pair peeled off and headed slowly for the island of Hon Ngu; the others continued halfway up the coast and timed an almost simultaneous approach to the island of Hon Me. (In the Vietnamese language, *hon* is associated with islands.) Both islands lay close to the mainland. Hon Ngu guards the mouth of the Ca River, which leads to the port city of Vinh (population: 44,000). Near Vinh, it will be recalled, stood the oil tanks to be demolished by air attack on Wednesday, August 5. It was in the vicinity of Hon Me that the *Maddox*'s battle of Sunday, August 2, took place.

It never has been explained satisfactorily what the gunboat raids were intended to accomplish. In 1964 Secretary McNamara said he did not know of any such raids; but at the 1968 hearing, he admitted that they had taken place and he talked of shelling points associated with infiltration. In 1964 unofficial sources talked of landing commandos who were to dynamite radar stations. There also have been rumors of destroying communication facilities. Senator Morse, in his speech of February 29, 1968, defied security regulations to make public the following information from the Defense Department:

"Two of the patrol craft arrived off of Hon Me island at 12:21 A.M. local time[2] on the 31st of July. Because of enemy fire, the plan to lead an attack was aborted. The target, however, was taken under fire with 57-millimeter recoilless rifle fire as well as 40- and 20-millimeter weapons. The two other patrol craft proceeded at the same time to the eastern end of Hon Ngu island, arriving at approximately the same time as the first group arrived at Hon Me. During the ensuing bombardment of the island, a series of explosions started on the beach. The raiders left these two islands after at least 30 min-

[2] Radio Hanoi said the raids occurred approximately one hour earlier. Senator Morse's "local time" seems to have been South Vietnamese time, an artificial zone (equivalent to Taiwan time) that runs one hour faster than North Vietnamese time. The shooting started about 40 minutes after the rising of a half-moon, a fact that casts some doubt on the intention to sneak spies or commandos ashore.

utes and returned south to Da Nang, arriving at approximately 10
A.M. local time on the 31st of July . . ."

As for the nationality of the attacking craft, Senator Morse, relying on information from the Defense Department, said that they had
been supplied to South Vietnam by the United States. Radio Hanoi
called them "ships of the Americans and their henchmen." The North
Vietnamese, for that matter, did not even grant that South Vietnam
had a government. Hanoi referred to the Saigon regime as the "Southern administration" and regarded it as a tool of American foreign
policy.

Even though admitting at the 1968 hearing that the U. S. Government was not ignorant of the gunboat operations, Secretary Mc-
Namara tried to pretend that U.S. officials were not involved with
them. Senators, however, knew of continuing references to 34-A in
the Navy's communications concerning the Tonkin Gulf, and as they
pressed their inquiry, McNamara kept shifting his position, as can
be seen from the following excerpts from the Secretary's statements
at the 1968 hearing (italics mine).

Page 20: ". . . *we* were informed of the nature of the operations
but *we* did not participate in them and *we* did not command them."

Page 30: ". . . the *Navy* played no part in, and was not associated with these *South Vietnamese* actions."

Page 98: "I do not believe that the MAAG [Military Assistance
Advisory Group] officer was *in charge* of 34 operations. I think it
was a *MACV liaison officer*."

It seems that McNamara finally blurted out the truth.

Who was this MACV officer? Was he, in fact, a military officer?
William Bader of the committee's staff objected to the use of the
term "officer." Referring to a telegram under discussion, Bader
pointed out that it used the term "MACV representative." Senator
Albert Gore, Democrat of Tennessee, then asked McNamara what
the MACV man would be if not a military officer. In the published
text of the hearing, it appears that the Defense Secretary never answered that question. For whatever reason, at least a few of those
present were left with the impression that the "MACV representative" was an employee of the Central Intelligence Agency. It was the
CIA that usually managed the kind of "secret," that is, *deniable,*
operation in which the gunboats were engaged.

In sum, the 34-A boats were American-directed even though they were manned in whole or in part by South Vietnamese personnel. A Navy man familiar with Da Nang told me that he often saw South Vietnamese on the boats. Another officer advised me that, according to what he had heard, the boats never left port without Americans on them—"to make sure of what they would do."

Where was the destroyer *Maddox* at the time of the gunboat raids? Not many people aboard a ship know exactly where she is even in daylight, much less after dark. The results of my interviews suggest that the ship probably was still under Hainan or making her way across the Gulf toward the DMZ. But the Foreign Relations Committee had access to official records, and it elicited from Secretary McNamara a statement that the ship was "at least 130 miles to the southeast" of the raided areas. If we take the more southerly of the two targets, Hon Ngu, and measure exactly 130 miles directly to the southeast, we come to a location just five miles north-northeast of Tiger Island, a North Vietnamese possession near the DMZ. Tiger Island (*Con Co* in Vietnamese) marks the entrance to the Gulf on the coastal route north from South Vietnam. It was to be the first place visited by *Maddox* on her patrol. The island serves the North Vietnamese as an observation post, and if *Maddox* were in that vicinity, even at night, the Communists should have known it. Oddly, none of their public statements have indicated that they did see the ship around Tiger Island, even in the daytime.

Men who were aboard the *Maddox* recall very clearly that after sunrise on Friday, July 31, they were in the open sea somewhere between Hainan and North Vietnam, and that the destroyer was making a rendezvous with a fuel ship, the oiler *Ashtabula*. (Navy oilers are named for rivers.) Small by comparison, the *Maddox* pulled alongside the 25,000-ton oiler. Umbilicals hooked the two vessels as they steamed due west in the general direction of Tiger Island. About 9 A.M. the pair was 75 miles from North Vietnam when a startling image appeared on the northern horizon—the distinctive silhouettes of fast-approaching torpedo craft. In this area, close to the carrier *Ticonderoga,* there ought to have been no danger of hostile action; indeed, the water around here was so friendly that the Navy called it "Yankee Station." Nevertheless, hooked to the *Ashtabula,* it was no time to get caught by surprise.

The operations officers, Buehler and Evans, grabbed intelligence books and tried to match what they saw approaching them with what the Navy knew about Communist patrol craft. No luck. Within minutes, however, Commodore Herrick made his way to the bridge and solved the problem.

"Those are friendly," said the commodore. "They're Nasty class patrol boats."

As they closed in, the strange craft were seen to carry no torpedo tubes. They had been converted from torpedo boats to gunboats. Two of the rakish craft passed nearby, with one darting at the oiler. Then all sped off to the south. Eyewitnesses counted from two to five. The most authoritative sources report three.

The strange gray boats flew no flag. What were they doing in the Tonkin Gulf? Nobody aboard the *Maddox* seemed to know. The destroyermen suspected that the mysterious craft were on the way back from some kind of swashbuckling adventure up north; and, in fact, the adventure was more colorful than they supposed. These were the gunboats which had been raiding the islands of Hon Me and Hon Ngu. (What happened to the fourth boat I do not know. If *Maddox* saw only three, as seems to have been the case, the fourth must have taken a different route—perhaps a more direct route?)

If men of the *Maddox* were baffled by them, what were the North Vietnamese to make of these unmarked marauders? Even if sighted by daylight, the raiders showed no marks of nationality. Yet there could be no doubt as to who had paid for the fancy craft: the U.S.A.

How much Commodore Herrick knew about 34-A operations is a moot point. Since Herrick, later in the patrol, used the term "34-A" in correspondence, Secretary McNamara had to admit at the 1968 hearing that Herrick knew *that* much. But Herrick didn't know any more than the term itself, said McNamara, and to prove this unlikely contention, he asserted that Herrick on July 31 *mistook 34-A vessels for Soviet P-6 torpedo boats* (a few of which were in North Vietnamese possession). McNamara made that statement five times during the hearing, and nobody questioned it. Evidently the committee's investigation had turned up similar information—perhaps a message reporting Soviet-designed torpedo craft.

What kind of sighting report the *Maddox* sent to higher command I do not know. Several men, however, were on the bridge when Commodore Herrick identified the gunboats as "friendly," and nobody from the ship recalls mistaking the tubeless gunboats for torpedo boats. One officer volunteered the further information that only two of the boats were of the Nasty type. The third, he remembered, was a converted aluminum PT of the kind that the U. S. Navy experimented with during the 1950s (World War II PT boats were made of wood). Yet the Foreign Relations Committee accepted as fact the *Maddox*'s identification of 34-A vessels as Soviet-made P-6 torpedo craft. Something was radically wrong somewhere; indeed, this is one of the most curious discrepancies in the whole Tonkin Gulf story.

In 1964 the presence of fast gunboats in South Vietnam was a closely held secret; and in a way it has remained so even after the 1968 hearing. Even the 1970–71 edition of *Jane's Fighting Ships* did not report Nasty boats in South Vietnam, although the Saigon government usually seeks publicity for its naval acquisitions, large and small. The Nasty boat itself was not a secret in 1964. The Norwegian manufacturer advertised it for sale, and the 1964–65 edition of *Jane's* reported the purchase of Nasty craft by the U. S. Navy. More recently it has been disclosed that the Navy bought these Norwegian boats for use by special forces working in Vietnam with the CIA.[3] The Navy has SEAL—SEa, Air, Land—teams that are the equivalent of the Army's Green Berets. It seems possible, therefore, that the South Vietnamese *did not really acquire* the Nasty boats, whether or not Secretary McNamara thought they did.

The CIA and the Pentagon have developed a very intimate working relationship in military and paramilitary operations. In some ways the CIA has become so involved with the armed forces that it has become indistinguishable from them. Some military units are given directions by CIA personnel; some units are infiltrated by CIA personnel in military uniform; and some units actually are commanded by CIA men impersonating military officers. Even the Defense Department can lose track of which units are really military and which belong in whole or in part to the "spooks." Many a GI has served in one of these ghostly outfits without realizing it. On occasion a foul-up of some kind will blow the cover, as when a spooky requisition floats up through channels and no bona fide military commander recognizes an obligation to honor it. In general, however, the CIA finds these units very convenient for obtaining large amounts of military equipment not authorized in its appropriated budget. This

[3] Colonel L. Fletcher Prouty, "The Secret Team," *Washington Monthly* (May 1970), page 17.

in turn permits the agency to carry out paramilitary operations authorized—theoretically, anyway—by the President's national security staff.

It might be inferred that the U. S. Navy bought gunboats from Norway in order to camouflage their identity, but that was not the case. As usual, the Navy simply did not have suitable small craft when they were wanted for combat; in its infatuation with big ships, the organization had not changed since the days of the "battleship complex." (Even President Franklin D. Roosevelt could not persuade the Navy to build a fleet of small subchasers to counter the growing threat of German U-boats. Later the desperate Battle of the Atlantic caused Roosevelt to lament, "The Navy couldn't see any vessel under a thousand tons.") It was in 1962 that American naval men discovered a need for shallow water craft to be used in anti-guerrilla operations, patrolling coastlines and rivers. The Nasty boats, fast and seaworthy, performed well in NATO exercises, and so the Navy started buying them. The mahogany-built craft carried four torpedo tubes—of no use against guerrillas—for which the Navy substituted extra guns and electronic equipment. The conversion to gunboats saved some weight, increasing the top speed from 43 to 45 knots.

Even before men of the *Maddox* saw the "black boats," they had plenty of reason to believe that their assignment was far from routine. Now they knew that in this neighborhood something real was happening—not just the usual war games. Was the *Maddox* not involved? At best the situation was like stepping into a house when the husband and wife are having a quarrel. One could hardly hope to stay out of trouble.

Not far away—within radar range on Friday morning—cruised the *Ticonderoga* and a couple of destroyers. The nearness of the friendly Task Group, however, was less reassuring if one considered what it was up to. The *Ticonderoga* was not just steaming around aimlessly, waiting to lend the De Soto ship a hand. She was engaged with combat operations in Laos. Over in the Royal Kingdom, beyond Vietnam, Communist-led Pathet Lao guerrillas were troubling the "neutralist" government of Prince Souvanna Phouma; and in May of 1964 (as was announced at the time) unarmed Navy aircraft began flying reconnaissance in support of the Royal Lao Army.

These planes flew from carriers that took turns cruising at Yankee Station. They concentrated their search in the southern part of Laos adjacent to South Vietnam. The northern part, next to North Vietnam, was already being taken care of by the CIA, which had its own "Laotian" air force up there (not announced at the time). Of course, to the Pathet Lao one American plane was much like another. They shot indiscriminately at Navy and CIA planes alike, and very quickly two of the Navy planes were shot down. In retaliation Navy aircraft raided Pathet Lao positions. This reportedly shocked Prince Souvanna Phouma, who thought that the Navy planes would never carry arms. But the reconnaissance flights continued, and so did the shooting.

At first the Navy and the CIA tried not to notice each other, but this proved to be impractical. Thinking to rescue a downed Navy pilot, a CIA man set down his helicopter beside a Pathet Lao decoy, and, for his effort, died with a bullet between his eyes. After that the two fighting organizations got together to work out recognition signals and to find out more about each other's appearance and equipment. The "intelligence agency" and the Seventh Fleet now were allied in the perpetual, desultory war in Laos. The American commitment kept growing, as it did in Vietnam; but five years passed before the U. S. Senate investigated Laos and, apparently, was astonished to find Americans engaged there in combat. (Somebody ought to have added up how much the Congress had spent on "fact-finding" tours abroad since 1964.)

While he was in office, President Johnson became well known for the zeal with which he supervised the details of military operations. During the bombing campaign directed against North Vietnam, President Johnson's aides described him as "our foremost target planner." As early as 1964, according to columnists Rowland Evans and Robert Novak, Johnson "personally supervised" some "very secret air operations in Laos."[4] Did the President also take a personal interest in the *Maddox*'s patrol? Some persons familiar with the Defense establishment advised me, without hesitation, that it would have been "unthinkable" for a Navy ship to have entered the Tonkin Gulf in the summer of 1964 without permission from "the

---

[4] *Lyndon B. Johnson: The Exercise of Power* (New York: New American Library, 1966), page 533.

White House." This would mean permission from the White House staff if not from the President himself.

I queried the Defense Department on what was the highest level of command at which the *Maddox*'s patrol was approved. The official reply came back that this question was beyond the Navy's purview (odd for a routine patrol!), even though I had submitted the question not to the Navy but to the Office of the Assistant Secretary of Defense for Public Affairs. The "spy ship" operations of later years were reported to have been approved by one or more of the intelligence committees connected to the White House, and the unsuccessful U-2 flight of 1960 was approved at the White House level. It seems likely, therefore, that the patrol of the *Maddox* was approved by a member of the White House staff, if not by the President himself.

On Friday morning, July 31, as the unmarked gunboats sped off to the south, the *Ashtabula* continued to fill *Maddox*'s bunkers. The short-hulled *Maddox* was also "short-legged," the engineer's term for a ship's inability to get very far on one fueling. *Maddox* usually refueled every three or four days. Since the Gulf patrol was to last ten days, the destroyermen were concerned about running out of fuel in sight of Communist territory. Even at the fuel-saving speed of 10 knots, the ship in ten days would exhaust 90 percent of her rated capacity. Should the destroyer get into some kind of scrape toward the end of her patrol, maneuvering at high speed could burn up her last drops of oil. *Maddox*'s officers wanted to make the patrol in two sorties, refueling in between, but despite their objection they were ordered to do the job in a single round trip. The engineers, therefore, meticulously filled their bunkers to the brim, achieving 103 percent of the rated capacity, by using some of the air space provided for heat expansion—*Ashtabula*'s oil already had swelled in the tropical heat.

Besides oil, the men of the *Maddox* received another delivery. Hovering noisily, a helicopter from the *Ticonderoga* lowered on a rope the long-sought radarscope photographer and his equipment. For all his rarity, this specialist turned out to be a 3rd class radarman.

Commodore Herrick had expected the MACV representatives to come aboard at Yankee Station, but again they failed to appear. It now must have been clear to the commodore that, for whatever reason, nobody from MACV was going to accompany the *Maddox* into the Tonkin Gulf.

MACV's apparent lack of interest in the North Vietnamese coast was odd for several reasons. MACV men had accompanied the March patrol, and recently no less a personage than Admiral Sharp had authorized consultation between MACV and De Soto ships assigned to the Tonkin Gulf. On July 10, 1964, CINCPAC (Admiral Sharp) had sent the following message to CINCPACFLT (Admiral Moorer):

THE COMMANDER IN CHIEF OF THE U.S. FORCES IN PACIFIC AUTHORIZES HIS FLEET UNITS INVOLVED IN THE DE SOTO PATROL TO CONTACT COMMANDER, UNITED STATES MILITARY ASSISTANCE VIETNAM FOR ANY ADDITIONAL INTELLIGENCE REQUIRED FOR PREVENTION OF MUTUAL INTERFERENCE WITH 34-A OPERATIONS AND SUCH COMMUNICATIONS ARRANGEMENTS AS MAY BE DESIRED.

Admiral Sharp wanted to prevent "mutual interference" between the gunboats and the destroyers. He also authorized consultation with MACV, and suggested setting up a channel of communications. In speculating on what kind of interference might worry the admiral, it is easy to imagine that the destroyer's presence could interfere with intended gunboat activities. Suppose, for example, that gunboats planned to visit Hon Me at 11 P.M. on a certain night. The appearance of *Maddox* looming up in the dark at 10 P.M. would alert the island's defenders, who would still be nervously fingering their weapons at 11 P.M. A regular channel of communication between *Maddox* and MACV could prove useful in many ways. As an intelligence ship, the *Maddox* needed to know as much as possible about what was happening in the area of her patrol. Conversely, the 34-A men could benefit from *Maddox*'s leisurely, daytime observations—though, in that case, the destroyer would be participating in an act of war.

A week after Sharp sent his message, Admiral Moorer issued orders outlining the patrol and stating that operational guidance would be provided by MACV. But the MACV men did not appear. Why?

At the 1968 hearing Secretary McNamara was eager to explain. "They were invited," he said, "but they didn't believe that this was a patrol connected with their activities, and they saw no reason, therefore, to participate in it. They participated, I believe, on board the third patrol [in March], and found that they got so little out of it they didn't want to take the time to participate in a fourth, and therefore, were not on board that patrol." That MACV, from its huge staff, could not spare anybody to examine by day the places the gunboats were raiding by night may seem wildly implausible, like some other of McNamara's statements; but, in fact, it is difficult to exaggerate the U. S. Government's lack of curiosity in assessing the value of an expensive project. Furthermore, most U.S. officials in those days thought the real war was in South Vietnam; as for the slight amount of damage being inflicted up north by the gunboats, perhaps aerial reconnaissance was considered sufficient.

For some reason MACV did not want to put anybody on board the *Maddox,* but MACV still was part of Admiral Sharp's far-flung Pacific command, and the admiral wanted to prevent interference between the destroyer and the gunboats. How was that to be done? Again Secretary McNamara had a ready explanation. CINCPACFLT and MACV, said he, decided to handle the liaison *themselves.* By this plan, Admiral Moorer would transmit the *Maddox's* itinerary to MACV, and MACV would try to keep the gunboats away from where the destroyer was going. The Defense Secretary gave senators these details:

". . . CINCPAC Fleet advised MACV that they would make every effort to give him thirty-six hours' notice of changes in the time schedule of the patrol at certain points in order to allow MACV to change the suggestion that he might make regarding location of 34-A attacks. MACV came back and said that they had worked out with the South Vietnamese adjustments to assure that 34-A operations would prevent interference with the patrols."

Here was a delicate arrangement, indeed—peace hanging by a thread. Its success depended on the *Maddox* sticking to her planned itinerary and being, at all times, exactly where Admiral Moorer, 6000 miles away, thought she was. Did anybody tell *Maddox* that her precise movements were a matter of such consequence? Later events do not suggest that anybody did.

The plan certainly could not have been designed for efficiency. Commodore Herrick could have kept in touch with MACV by radio. What was the advantage of trading messages between Honolulu and Saigon, with Herrick out of the loop? To inquiring senators McNamara stressed a negative advantage: the indirect arrangement kept the commodore ignorant and therefore pure. If Herrick didn't know about the gunboat plans, he could not assist them. That being the case, no fair-minded Communist could associate the *Maddox* with nocturnal attacks on his territory. Ergo, any Communist attack on the destroyer was unprovoked. At best, one might describe this line of reasoning as laughable. Were the North Vietnamese supposed to have read the commodore's mind and found it lacking all knowledge of the gunboats, which, in fact, he saw on Friday morning?

The supervision of this "routine patrol" was plainly taking place at a very high level of command. Officers of the *Maddox* thought they were working for Admiral MacPherson, but his function, the more one learns about it, seems to have been very insubstantial.

Secretary McNamara didn't say when the high-level liaison went into operation. Whatever one thinks of it, the plan certainly was not working as advertised on the morning of Friday, July 31. Otherwise Buehler and Evans wouldn't have been rummaging through intelligence books trying to identify fast boats on the horizon. At this time was somebody really trying to keep the gunboats away from *Maddox?* Or was somebody trying to bring them together?

With the arrival of the radarscope photographer, *Maddox* had taken on everybody who was coming aboard. By radio the ship reported to Taiwan the acquisition of the 3rd class radarman and the non-arrival of the MACV representatives. Taiwan made no reply. After refueling, the old short hull proceeded on to the west, aiming for the North Vietnamese coast.

Chapter VI

Sindbad

In the armed forces of the United States, the enlisted man is thought to perform best when he understands why a thing has to be done rather than merely what has to be done. Since leaving Japan, most of the *Maddox*'s crew had heard nothing but rumors, and so, as the ship reached the Tonkin Gulf, Captain Ogier prepared an announcement to be read over the public address system. It was characteristic of Ogier that he seldom used the intercom himself. On this occasion, he put down on paper a few words in longhand and gave them to an ensign to read. Some three hundred officers and men paused in their work to hear a youthful voice tell them where they were and what they were doing:

"The ship is proceeding into the Gulf of Tonkin in order to collect hydrographic and oceanographic information. To the west is the coast of North Vietnam, and to the east is the island of Hainan, belonging to Communist China. We have a right to enter the Gulf since at all times we will be in international waters. We will leave the Gulf around 9 August. Keep alert and conserve fresh water. The ship's daily routine will be carried out."

Most of the crew had never heard of the Tonkin Gulf. Maps were suddenly in demand.

The announcement ought to have reassured the men who were to sound the bottom and chart navigational aids. In the beginning, they had understood that the purpose of the patrol was to do a job for the Hydrographic Office, but, with the arrival of black box, they had begun to have doubts. The announcement said nothing about the box; and nothing about the new activities in CIC. The men in

CIC sensed that their work was just as confidential—and therefore as important—as they had been led to believe. Men of the COMVAN must have been amused by the announcement. The destroyer, they knew, was their taxicab.

The charm of the "need to know" game is that everybody thinks *he* has the big secret, or at least a major portion of it. But after the patrol, even Commodore Herrick was heard to remark: "There was a lot going on that *I* didn't know about."

The captain's instructions to "keep alert" and "conserve fresh water" were coupled together as of equal importance, because water rationing would be a serious matter. The tropical sun was so hot that a man could blister his arm by resting it on an unshaded piece of metal. The greatest luxury aboard ship was to take a lukewarm shower, but the men would be permitted only two very brief ones a day—the bather was to get in, get wet, turn off the water, apply soap, rinse quickly, and stop holding up the line. It would not be a comfortable cruise.

A part of keeping alert involved fetching ammunition from the magazines and loading the ready racks under the 5-inch guns. The gunners stocked a mixture of shell types and fuzes, including nighttime illumination rounds, known as "star shells." Since jostling can damage shells in the ready racks, filling them is not an ordinary procedure; it is reserved for danger zones. As another instance of extra alertness, the gunners began to take turns manning around the clock one of the forward 5-inch gun mounts. Two guns protruded from each of three 5-inch "mounts," or what the landlubber would call "turrets," a term the Navy reserves for the more elaborate and heavily armored gunhousings of larger warships.

Some critics of the Navy's role in the Tonkin Gulf have referred to the *Maddox* as a "heavily armored destroyer," but that is a contradiction in terms. A destroyer is supposed to sacrifice the weight of armor for an increase in speed. The *Maddox* carried little or no armor even where it was most needed. The 5-inch guns were shielded to some extent, but the 3-inchers stood in open, tublike enclosures, not even protected from rain. Yet the sacrifice of armor no longer guarantees exceptional speed: destroyers have tended to lose ground in that respect, while bigger warships, with brute horsepower, have increased their speed. The *Maddox* was designed to make 36 knots, a speed achieved by the HMS *Swift,* a British destroyer, back in

1907. In 1964, following twenty years of service, the *Maddox* could barely wheeze up to 34 knots and did so at her peril; but she still was faster than some later models. The destroyer type of vessel originally was designed to chase torpedo boats—it was, in fact, a "torpedo boat destroyer." But the perfection of the submarine—a submersible torpedo boat—presented a much greater threat to the world's navies and merchant shipping, so that the destroyer began to sacrifice speed for anti-submarine gear and greater cruising range. At present the oil-powered destroyer cannot keep up with the nuclear-powered aircraft carrier, and the slower "destroyer escort" is outdistanced by the nuclear submarine.

While patrolling in the Tonkin Gulf, the *Maddox* was to check in every hour by radio with the *Ticonderoga*. The destroyer's radio code name was Sindbad, the carrier's Jehovah. Colorful code names are used in military communications because they are easy to hear and to remember. They also spice up the daily routine. They are not supposed to suggest anything about the mission, but they often do. Like his namesake, the modern Sindbad would explore remote places and improvise his way out of some tough spots. Jehovah, in good time, would succor him.

On Friday morning the *Maddox* made her first landfall since Taiwan. Mountains rippled the horizon, sloping downward from South Vietnam into North Vietnam. Sailors also made out the low, green hump of Tiger Island, some 13 miles closer than the mainland shore. Here was Communist territory.

To *Maddox* the island was Checkpoint Alfa (*sic*), the first place to be inspected on the Gulf patrol. (Alfa is the phonetic word established by the International Code for the letter "A." Some other phonetic words that will appear: Bravo, Charlie, Delta, Golf, Uniform, and Xray.) The *Maddox* would follow a pre-planned "track" through the Gulf, loitering for specified periods of time in specified areas. In the neighborhood of each checkpoint, the ship would be free to circle around, make figure eights, or nose up to whatever looked interesting, so long as she kept within "international waters."

Friday was clear, a good day for the telescopic photographer to polish up his lenses and get to work. No doubt he photographed the conspicuous watchtower on Tiger Island, and perhaps some electronic equipment. In 1965 when the island was bombed and shelled intensively, U.S. military authorities identified it as a radar station.

Chief Quartermaster Murray T. McRae, in charge of the hydrographic survey, broke out his charts and looked around for navigational aids. Given the patrol's snail-like pace, it didn't matter that the ship lacked the Navy's newer and faster fathometer, a sonar instrument for measuring underwater depth. McRae grumbled that the Gulf already had been sounded so thoroughly by the French, the British, the Japanese, and, no doubt, by other Americans, that the "bottom was wore out." But the Navy wanted it done again, and so the readings were taken and charted.

As a north-reaching arm of the South China Sea, the Tonkin Gulf is deeper in the south, where the arm connects to the body, than in the north, where it tapers into finger-like islands clutching at marshes and mud flats. Off Tiger Island the *Maddox* sounded depths of 150 to 180 feet, the deepest water she would find along the coast. Midway between Tiger Island and Hainan, the bottom drops to about 350 feet; the Navy, however, was interested in a narrow strip along North Vietnamese territory.

As originally planned, the patrol required *Maddox* to cruise along the western coast all the way up to the head of the Gulf, where the Indochinese peninsula joins the mainland of Red China. The ship was to continue along the Chinese coast, sailing farther from land, and circle the Red Chinese island of Wei-chou. East of Wei-chou lies the sandy peninsula of Lei-chou Pan-tao, separated by a narrow channel from Hainan to the south. The Strait of Hainan narrows at one point to 10 miles; the whole of it is claimed as territorial water by Red China—and also by Nationalist China. *Maddox* was not to attempt to pass through the strait but was to leave the Gulf the way she came in, through the broad opening to the south. On the return trip, the plan called for revisiting briefly each of the previous checkpoints. Apparently the ship was to do little or no inspection of Hainan. As the patrol turned out, *Maddox* made most of the planned checkpoints, but did not get as far as Chinese territory.

Judging by previous events, the guidelines given Commodore Herrick on how close to approach land were bound to provoke the North Vietnamese, who were in the habit of protesting when any non-Communist naval vessels came closer than 12 miles. The *Maddox*, nevertheless, was permitted to patrol up to eight miles from the mainland and up to four miles from islands. (Why the difference? The territorial limit would be the same in both cases. Moreover, because of the gunboat raids, islands ought to have been quite as sensitive as the mainland, if not more so.) At the 1968 hearing, senators asked Secretary McNamara why the guidelines went closer than 12 miles. He explained that the U. S. Government did not know of any 12-mile claim in the case of North Vietnam; therefore, said McNamara, the government "believed" that the territorial zone amounted only to 3 miles, as it did in the days of French rule.

So far as I have been able to learn, it is true that North Vietnam prior to the *Maddox*'s patrol had not publicly claimed a 12-mile territorial zone. It is not true, however, that the U. S. Government "believed" in a 3-mile claim. Probably because of the protests mentioned above, the Defense Department and the State Department for two years prior to *Maddox*'s patrol had been using a map that showed a 12-mile claim; and on August 8, 1964, the Deputy Secretary of Defense, Cyrus Vance, told the world by Voice of America broadcast that *he* thought the North Vietnamese claimed 12 miles. These facts were not known to senators at the 1968 hearing, and Secretary McNamara was able to get away with his explanation even though the lawmakers, highly skeptical, returned repeatedly to the subject with various questions.

On coastal patrols, the U. S. Navy often violated Chinese territorial water.[1] The *Maddox* however, was instructed to respect Peking's 12-mile zone, and to add a 3-mile cushion in order to prevent misunderstanding. (The Navy assumes that its navigation is perfect, but it has less confidence in the calculations of foreigners.)

In telling his men that the *Maddox* would remain within "international waters," Captain Ogier was giving them the *official truth* as he knew it. The statement was officially correct because the U. S. Government did not *recognize* any territorial water claim beyond three miles. Relying on the advice of government officials, the news media in 1964 routinely referred to the 3-mile zone as the "legal" and "traditional" one. The 12-mile claim was regarded as a Communist quirk—an illegal and somewhat preposterous nuisance.

---

[1] Radio Peking announced hundreds of such violations, and the U. S. Government admitted the practice in 1969 at the time of the *Pueblo* Court of Inquiry. For years elint ships intruded on Red Chinese and North Korean territorial waters, although, according to Washington officials, such guidelines were rescinded before the *Pueblo*'s cruise of January 1968.

Somebody ought to have known better, and certain government officials did know better. For a long time, the sanctity of the 3-mile limit, though powerfully supported by the British and American navies, had been fighting a losing battle.

Some experts say that the 3-mile zone never did have enough international support to achieve the status of international law (which requires near-unanimity); others say that the point is debatable. The United States first claimed 3 miles in 1793, with Secretary of State Thomas Jefferson noting that this was as *little* as that claimed by any European country. Jefferson intended the 3-mile zone to be temporary; he expected his country to extend the margin as it grew more powerful. His expectation was not fulfilled. In 1900 the United States still adhered to the 3-mile zone while most other countries were making larger claims. In 1909 Czarist Russia asserted control over a 12-mile sea; this Imperial ambition, like many others, was later upheld by the Soviet Union. After World War II, most, but not all, of the new Communist states claimed 12-mile territorial zones; and many of the new, non-Communist countries emerging from colonial domination also staked out 12-mile claims. By the time of *Maddox*'s cruise in 1964, 12-mile outnumbered 3-mile claims and miscellaneous large claims—4 miles, 15 kilometers, even 200 miles —continued to proliferate. (In 1970 the U. S. State Department proposed that the world standardize on a 12-mile territorial sea. One must hope that the American attempt to compromise did not come too late, as did earlier proposals for establishing a 6-mile limit.)

At the 1968 hearing, the Defense Secretary stressed the point that the *Maddox* was not *required* to approach North Vietnamese territory as closely as she was *permitted* to approach it. Obviously, however, the value of the ship's observations would be increased by getting as close to shore as possible, and no destroyer commander would want to look "chicken" in the eyes of his superiors—who, in this case, included Admiral MacPherson, Admiral Johnson, Admiral Moorer, and Admiral Sharp, plus the Joint Chiefs of Staff.

As the *Maddox* began her lone patrol, conversation on the bridge turned to the tactical situation. The North Vietnamese were known to have approximately fifty patrol craft, including perhaps sixteen torpedo boats. The Red Chinese had similar patrol craft plus submarines and jet airplanes. If it came to an all-out fight, one of the tacticians speculated, the *Maddox* by herself could not withstand either power. "What's the matter?" Captain Ogier asked. "Are you afraid to die?" Ogier could have meant the question as a joke, but it was taken more as a reprimand.

The ship remained until late Friday night in the vicinity of Tiger Island. After dark the crew watched flares to the west, soaring over the Demilitarized Zone. One of the COMVAN men said that flares were fired by both sides in order to discourage infiltration.

In darkness the fuel-conscious destroyer plodded 80 miles into the Gulf, following the northwesterly slant of the coastline. Before sunrise electric lights glimmered off the port bow. Daybreak revealed their location on the cliffs of Mui Ron (*Mui* means "cape"). In this area was Checkpoint Bravo; the ship would loiter for a while. Looking as if they had rolled into the sea from the cape were a few stony islets; men of the *Maddox* were intrigued by the biggest one: Hon Son Duong. Convex on one side and falling steeply on the other, it reminded Chief Quartermaster McRae of a heeled over, sunken battleship. Commander Jackson agreed. "That's what we'll call it," he said. "The 'sunken battleship.'" The Vietnamese name was too hard to pronounce.

Naval Intelligence told of guns up on Mui Ron, but the cliffs were too high—754 feet—to afford easy inspection of the emplacement. The Vietnamese gunners, if they were up there, had the better view. They could spot a warship more than 30 miles away; and evidently the Communists did keep an eye on *Maddox*. In October of 1964 Hanoi published a map showing, roughly, the destroyer's course. The map alleged that the ship passed only 5½ miles from Mui Ron. I repeatedly requested the Defense Department for its version of the course, and, at last, it came through with an Official Diagram—very simplified in nature and slightly irregular in scale. The U. S. Official Diagram showed *Maddox* patrolling 10.3 miles from Mui Ron.

On Saturday morning the destroyer reversed course, steaming slowly back toward Alfa as if to get a look at what had been missed during the night. About 10 miles south of Mui Ron the ship found Mui Doc, a broader, greener cape not so high as Mui Ron. A pagoda stared down at the destroyermen. They must have observed, too, certain defensive facilities to be discussed later. Beyond the cape, a pair of wooden peaks rose to about 3400 feet.

South of Mui Doc the coast was low and flat. Most of the American sailors could see nothing but dark mountains in the extreme distance.

Those who could view the shoreline were a few officers and men responsible for navigation and the collection of intelligence. They were stationed on the ship's higher points of vantage, and they enjoyed the use of powerful optics. A man standing on the bridge of a destroyer, some 40 feet above the waterline, commands a view of nearly eight miles to the sea horizon. From just above the bridge, he can see a little farther. *Maddox*'s 8-mile guideline, therefore, was just close enough to allow inspection of the mainland from sea level to mountain tip. South of Mui Doc the shoreline consisted mostly of white beaches backed by rows of dazzling dunes. Beyond the dunes lay rice paddies, largely hidden from the sea; and an occasional hill lifted into view, a pagoda or a Catholic church. A fishing village dotted the shore every mile or two, but sizable towns were few. From north to south, *Maddox* passed by the coastal towns of Ron and Quang Khe (both less than 10,000 population), and Dong Hoi (30,000 or more).

If most of the American sailors could see little of the mainland, they could enjoy watching islands and fishing craft. Junks and sampans bobbed in all directions, mostly to landward. How does a junk differ from a sampan? It's a matter of size, according to the Navy, which defines a junk as big enough to stand a water buffalo athwartships. The men counting small craft were guided by that definition, though each might have had his own notion of how much space a water buffalo requires.

Many of the small craft were rigged with tall, wing-shaped sails, brown and tan in color, well-worn and patched. The boats looked like other wooden craft that the Americans had seen in the Orient; the Vietnamese fishing craft, however, is distinguished by its "basket bottom" woven of bamboo. The resin-treated bamboo wards off attack by wood worms and other troublesome mites of the sea; also, flexing like a rubber ball, the basket bottom helps to keep the boat from getting stuck in mud or sand.

Whole families rode aboard the fishing craft. The Americans tried waving at them but nobody waved back, not even the children. "They were a pretty sullen bunch," recalls one officer. The bridge noted with satisfaction that nobody made any menacing gestures or by other overt means indicated hostility. (Perhaps this will not surprise anybody who while sitting in a small boat has watched a heavily gunned warship pass by.)

The fishing people did not look friendly, but neither did they have a military air about them. Officers examined them closely through the ship's telescope finding no evidence of military equipment nor even a disproportionate number of young men. As for large concentrations of fishing craft, none exceeded three hundred in number, nor even approached three hundred, although many smaller groups were counted. It all looked like routine fishing.

What did that prove? Not much, really. A lone and conspicuous American warship was not a very effective vehicle for making the search. To men of the *Maddox* it seemed most unlikely that any infiltrators were going to sail out of their way, 8 or 10 miles from shore, in the full glare of sunlight, to take a closer look at the foreign warship—perhaps brandishing aloft their light weapons. Ironically, should any infiltrators have been so audacious, the *Maddox* had no authority to bother them. The ship had instructions not to disturb small craft in any way, such as by steaming too close; and, despite North Vietnamese assertions to the contrary, the destroyer followed those instructions.

In this connection, it should be noted that during the entire Gulf patrol, including the week *Turner Joy* was along, the destroyermen found no infiltrators, no military supplies, and no huge concentrations of small craft. This should have surprised nobody at higher command. Below Tiger Island six hundred South Vietnamese junks manned by 4000 South Vietnamese sailors were not finding much evidence of infiltration, either, even though they had authority to stop any boat and search it. As for seeking large concentrations of small craft, it occurred to officers of the *Maddox* that an airplane could do the job far more swiftly and effectively. A big concentration—like an invasion fleet—would have orders to disperse by the time the old short hull floated into view, saving fuel at 8 knots.

Yet, at the 1968 hearing, Secretary McNamara told senators that the *Maddox*'s primary task in the Gulf was to look for infiltrators. Furthermore, the Secretary implied that the search was highly successsful. Two or three months afterward, he recalled, the U. S. Navy started its big anti-infiltration patrol off South Vietnam: the Market Time operation in support of the South Vietnamese search by junk. What prompted Market Time, said McNamara, was information gathered by De Soto patrols, including the August patrol. Senators were not in a position to challenge this statement. They did not know that the August patrol failed to find a single infiltrator or his equipment.

As for the other De Soto ships, in March observation was limited by unfavorable weather, and in September while the *Edwards* or *Morton* may perhaps have discerned the glint of a gun barrel or a boatful of suspiciously young-looking men, the patrol was cut short in time, and nothing has been said specifically about its finding any evidence of maritime infiltration. The U. S. Government's detailed document on infiltration is *Aggression from the North*, the State Department pamphlet published in 1965 in order to justify the bombing of North Vietnam. It mentions no supply vessel captured before 1965. As for personnel infiltrating by sea, the pamphlet gives but few examples— none of which were discovered after April 1963 when four spies are said to have beached their small boat in a storm.

Although to date it is not known who suggested and planned *Maddox*'s patrol, certainly the facts and circumstances argue persuasively that the essential purpose was not to look for infiltrators. The attempt was unrealistic—even if it assumes that infiltrators sail in daylight. And the scheduled patrol track, for the most part, did not go where the infiltrators were supposed to be. They were thought to embark chiefly from Dong Hoi and points south.[2] Yet the *Maddox* lingered only 1½ days, at most, between Dong Hoi and the Demilitarized Zone. The ship was scheduled to spend most of her time farther north. As a final point, Secretary McNamara, in his midnight press conference of August 5, 1964, denied that *Maddox*'s patrol had anything to do with the movement of junks (or with "any operations" in the Gulf area).

Whatever may have been its primary task, *Maddox*'s patrol was planned and carried out in such a way as to suggest that it had something to do with North Vietnamese *defenses*. Nearly all of the destroyer's checkpoints—Tiger Island, Mui Ron, etc.—have been identified (especially during the 1965 bombing campaign) as military facilities or as being very close to such facilities. The *Maddox* was to loiter near radar stations, gun emplacements, communication facilities, and naval bases.

[2] *Aggression from the North* mentions Dong Hoi as a specific point of embarkation; and a map in the pamphlet shows an arrow proceeding from Dong Hoi to four points along the South Vietnamese coast. Moreover, when the U. S. Navy started its Sea Dragon patrol in October 1965, to interdict waterborne traffic along the North Vietnamese coast, the initial patrol zone extended only up to latitude 17:30, two miles above Dong Hoi.

On Saturday afternoon *Maddox* went back to Mui Ron and, from there, headed farther into the Gulf for Checkpoint Charlie, another 70 miles up the coast. En route the ship passed by the towering monolith of Hon Mat, jutting out of the water about 11 miles from the mainland. (When in later years the battleship *New Jersey* bombarded North Vietnam, her 16-inch shells knocked a big piece off Hon Mat, tumbling guns and radar into the sea.) Between this island and the mainland lay Hon Ngu, the gunboat target where, unknown to men of the *Maddox,* secondary explosions rocked the beach.

So far as the destroyermen could tell, the first two days of patrol went by without incident. "We were fat, dumb, and happy," the commodore said later. The initial tension wore off, and, except for the hot weather, it began to look as though the ship would enjoy a pleasant 10-day cruise. Most of the American sailors had little extra work to do. Off duty, they lounged at the taffrail, privileged to compare notes on a part of the world that was strange and new to them—a part that in later years would become very familiar to those who remained in the service.

The ship's regular routine was carried out, as Captain Ogier's announcement said that it would be. There were additions to it, however, among them the silent GQ. GQ stands for General Quarters, meaning battle stations. The ordinary GQ drill is full of commotion with a loud gong ringing and everybody dashing hither and yon. The silent GQ, men of the *Maddox* learned, required the crew to take battle stations with a minimum of fuss, quietly and inconspicuously. The gong was replaced by a simple announcement over the intercom. Passing the word to one another, the men walked, not ran, to their stations. As much as possible, they took interior routes rather than disturb the placid appearance of the outer decks. The stated purpose of the silent GQ was to avoid alarming the fisherfolk and to maintain a casual, routine ("no sweat") appearance. Speculatively, if the COMVAN were to come up with a warning of North Vietnamese attack, the silent GQ would not tip the American hand. Officers assumed that the ship was under Communist observation at all times. Not only observers ashore but observers in small craft nearby could have been sending reports.

The boys in the black box seemed pleased with their work. They were picking up "good stuff." Perhaps they were listening to local chatter about the *Maddox* and the night raiders. Communications technicians heard that the Gulf patrol was scheduled for this time because a high level of radio activity was expected.

Like the COMVAN, CIC was working "port and starboard watches"—four hours on and four hours off, each man putting in 12 hours per day. There was plenty of tension in CIC where the new elint chores were difficult and frustrating. Local radar was detected and fingerprints were taken, but where were the Communist transmitters? Plotting of radar transmitter locations was not very successful. As noted earlier, the *Maddox*'s old direction finder was deaf to certain frequencies. Furthermore, CIC did not control the ship's course, and to get a reasonably accurate fix three bearings were needed over an arc of 60 degrees. Captain Ogier showed little interest in the problem. Commodore Herrick often visited CIC, but that didn't help the situation either.

I have no information on how the radarscope photography turned out. As to its purpose, some destroyermen agree that the pictures must have been intended for use as navigational aids; and, in support of this theory, I have found two books among the vast literature available on radar, containing instructions on how to photograph the radarscope and use the resulting pictures to help find one's way in the dark along a strange or unmarked coast. Photographs are superimposed on the scope so as to match the radar picture. (A map cannot be used in this way because the angle of view is different.) By such means a gunboat could find its target at night. Whether the radarscope photographs taken by *Maddox* ever provided this kind of assistance, I do not know. But the radarscope photography provides an example of how the ship could have aided future 34-A operations without even knowing it.

It appears that the Foreign Relations Committee were never informed about the radarscope photography. After the 1968 hearing, the Pentagon gave the committee a list of "all men aboard *Maddox* in July and August 1964, who were not part of the regular crew," but the supposedly complete list did not include the radarscope photographer. It also omitted the optical photographer, though the list included names and ranks for all of the COMVAN personnel.[3]

[3] U. S. Congress, Senate, Committee on Foreign Relations; *The Gulf of Tonkin, The 1964 Incidents, Part II;* 90th Congress, 2nd Session (Washington: Government Printing Office, 1968), page 7.

The conviction spread among *Maddox*'s officers that if anything important were happening aboard ship it must be happening in the black box. The other operations looked like busywork. Said one officer, whose description of Friday's and Saturday's activities was typical: "Well, we orbited here and there while the boys in the box were doing whatever they were doing." Enhancing the box's prestige was a rumor that the ship's radio shack had given it a "red line" (special circuit) to Admiral Johnson's flagship, the *Oklahoma City*. One of the Marines stated the even wilder rumor that the box was in communication with a similar unit hidden somewhere in North Vietnam. The Marines, the destroyermen could see, were not just guards. They did some kind of work inside the box.

The COMVAN lieutenant, Gerrell D. Moore, was a soft-spoken Texan who sported a blue baseball cap. Apparently always busy, he sometimes took meals in the clubby atmosphere of the box, sending out for sandwiches and coffee. He occupied a social position comparable in its remoteness to that of the commodore. In his own way, each was bossing the ship, but by Navy custom neither was permitted to get involved with matters of routine—that is, with the ship's discipline and internal workings. The commodore always disappeared at mealtimes. Following tradition, he took meals in his cabin, thus avoiding the give-and-take of the wardroom, where it was the captain's job to tend the balance of power.

Officers of the *Maddox*, by their own judgment, included the usual assortment of outstanding officers, good officers, and those who might have done better elsewhere. The older ones were making a career of the Navy; most of the younger ones were not. One of the more respected of the younger officers was a career man and "mustang" (former enlisted sailor), Ensign Richard B. Corsette. Corsette, an ex-submariner, and known as a "cool head" seemed to know a lot about electronics. Because of the new elint burden, CIC tried to recruit Corsette, but Captain Ogier wanted to keep him in gunfire control. Corsette's battle station was the Main Director, a turret-like box of electronic equipment above the bridge. With its two windows and radar dish antenna, the Main Director looked like a square-faced surgeon wearing his head mirror. Here was the ship's highest manned point, and also the best binoculars. Officers sat there during the day to watch the shore and look at fishing boats. Lieutenant Buehler, an amateur artist, used the binoculars to sketch defensive installations ashore, supplementing the work of the telescopic photographer. Commander Jackson kept a special chart with North Vietnamese defenses marked on it.

Working with Corsette in the Main Director were two enlisted men: a visual gunpointer and a radarman. Naval guns today are aimed by radar and by computer, but there still is room for human skill and human error. The fire control system has its own, specialized radar, which uses the dish antenna on top of the Director. When the automatic equipment fails to put shells on target, it is the job of the fire control officers and their enlisted assistants to notice this and "spot" corrections into the system.

At the rear of *Maddox*'s superstructure stood the ship's After Director, a smaller box overlooking the after 5-inch guns and the two pairs of 3-inch guns. The after fire control officer was the *Maddox*'s resident intellectual, Lieutenant (jg) Keith Bane, a non-career officer, who, after he left the Navy, graduated first in his class at Northwestern Law School.

Keith Bane and Dick Corsette worked for the weapons officer or "gun boss," Lieutenant Raymond P. Connell. "Pat" Connell did not have the formal training that a gun boss was supposed to have. He had learned his job by experience, but the results of his work were considered good. To the amusement of the crew, there was some personality clash between Connell—the "big, tough Mick"—and Captain Ogier—the "sarcastic Frenchman." Each brought out the abrasive qualities in the other. Unlike some of the men, Connell stood up well under criticism.

As military hardware becomes more and more complicated, the armed services find it increasingly difficult to train men adequately and keep them from being lured away by higher-paying civilian jobs. Part of the problem is sheer paperwork, which tends to stifle anybody's enthusiasm for life on the bounding main. (In 1969 the U. S. Navy required the submission of 1.4 million reports, many of them duplicating each other in substance.)

Usually a destroyer's principal business is sonar, but in this department the *Maddox* was not rich in talent. The anti-submarine officer was an ensign who caught a lot of flak for his youthful indiscretions. As for enlisted sonarmen, most of them were green, too. The Defense Department told me several times that the ship had only one rated sonarman, David E. Mallow, sonarman 3rd class.

Through unofficial sources I learned of two more: Patrick N. Park, sonarman 2nd class, and David F. Charba, sonarman 2nd class. The ship did not boast any 1st class sonarman nor any chief sonarman. (Lieutenant White could have met at Long Beach the *Turner Joy*'s chief sonarman.) In addition to the three rated soundmen already mentioned, *Maddox* had several enlisted "strikers" learning the trade from Park and Charba. Charba worked the anti-submarine targeting gear; Park handled the search equipment—known to sonarmen as the "stack." Spelling Park on the stack were David Mallow and some of the strikers.

On the Tonkin Gulf patrol, the ship's lack of "in depth" sonar talent did not seem critical. Nobody expected to find a submarine lurking in the shallow water along the North Vietnamese coast.

North of Hon Mat, the destroyer steamed by Brandon Bay, a wide indentation where the Tonkin Gulf reaches its westernmost limit. Here the coastline curves gently from a northwesterly to a northeasterly direction. The northern boundary of the bay is Cape Falaise, which, pointing seaward, showed *Maddox* the way to Checkpoint Charlie, an imaginary spot 9 miles from shore. The destroyer found Charlie late in the afternoon. The ship eased back some distance, resumed her northward advance, and by sunset was north of Charlie, heading for the island of Hon Me. In darkness the destroyer touched a point 4 miles south of the recently raided island. Without knowing it, the American sailors were probing a sore spot. But there was no trouble yet. The ship quietly turned about and proceeded slowly back to the south.

Hanoi has alleged that the *Maddox* chased fishing boats and, during the night, trained searchlights on them. Men of the ship whom I interviewed unanimously and indignantly denied these charges. Nearly all of the time, they recalled, the destroyer stood well outboard of fishing craft. As for chasing anybody, there was no fuel to waste, and no useful purpose to be served. With respect to searchlights, American warships no longer carry the big ones that used to finger targets at night. They now depend on radar for seeing in the dark. For what illumination might be needed, they retain only their signaling lamps: when the shutter is opened, the "blinker" becomes a small searchlight. On the other hand, it must be kept in mind that fishing craft can be found anywhere in the Gulf, and that fishing stakes, usually with a boat nearby, rise out of the water as far as 25 and 30 miles from shore. The passage of any fair-sized vessel, especially at night, could hardly fail to annoy a few fishermen.

As diagrammed by the North Vietnamese, *Maddox*'s zigzag course might look as though the ship made "runs" at the coast in order to intimidate people ashore, and some American critics of the patrol have made this allegation. If a sped of 5 to 10 knots can be called a "run," the critics might be right. But it probably would be more accurate to say that the ship *sauntered* in and out of the coastal area, hoping in this way to stimulate activity ashore. Presumably defensive facilities would then make extra use of their radio and radar, if only to track the ship and report her movements.

At the 1968 hearing, Secretary McNamara made a peculiar confession. He said that *Maddox* carried some kind of equipment which she turned on to "stimulate" North Vietnamese radar. Senator Morse and other critics understandably made much of this activity as being "aggressive." Former Captain Herrick, however, denied publicly that the *Maddox* carried such equipment; and other ex-*Maddox* sailors with whom I have talked said they never heard of it. A non-*Maddox* officer of considerable rank hinted to me that the ship flicked her own radar on and off in order to stimulate North Vietnamese curiosity. But an ex-*Maddox* officer who was concerned with radar operations advised me that this was preposterous. It would have damaged the equipment, he claimed. It seems possible, therefore, that Secretary McNamara, though flanked by General Wheeler and a Navy captain, misinterpreted the record of *Maddox*'s elint activity. (I do not mean to imply that radar stimulation equipment does not exist. One of the earliest radar countermeasures was a machine for projecting false images. This sort of gadget might well provoke men ashore to switch on every kind of radar they had.)

Steaming southward at a reduced night speed of approximately 5 knots, the *Maddox* again passed Brandon Bay; and, about the middle of the night, the ship was approaching the tall form of Hon Mat when the men on watch experienced their first excitement of the patrol. From what ought to be reliable sources—except for the lapse of time and memory—I have received somewhat conflicting accounts of what happened. There is confusion about a light. Either the destroyer was closing in on Hon Mat when the navigational light there was extinguished or, according to another account, the ship was being *followed* by a light—apparently borne by some kind of surface craft. To add to the excitement, the *Maddox*'s radar indicated small craft massing ahead, as if to surround the destroyer.

What could the small craft do, if anything? *Maddox* officers had heard of a suicide tactic that the Vietnamese reportedly had used on the French. It consisted of a small boat loaded with explosives and piloted by a Vietnamese prepared to be blown up along with the enemy ship. If a kamikaze boat did manage to pull alongside and explode, the *Maddox,* broken in half, might disappear without even tapping out an SOS. Although I was unable to trace the origin of the suicide boat information, a North Vietnamese source confirms that fishing craft were prepared to "engage in combat any time." On June 6, 1964, prior to *Maddox*'s patrol, Hanoi's army newspaper *Quan Doi Nhan Dan* added, ". . . if they [fishing craft] see 'strange' boats, they would make secret signs and surround these strange boats." The article was concerned with the apprehension of spies and commandos who infiltrated in small craft—smaller, anyway, than a destroyer. But it seems clear the North Vietnamese were doing what they could to protect their shores.

Captain Ogier went to the bridge, found out what was happening, and rang Commodore Herrick on the telephone. Herrick was in bed. Without getting up, he authorized an evasive turn to sea. This maneuver eluded not only the massing junks but also apparently the light, if one were following the destroyer. If the small craft were hiding a human torpedo, or perhaps a conventional torpedo boat, they did not press the attack. The crisis was over. One of its effects was to rekindle some apprehension concerning the patrol, though many of the crew, including officers, never heard anything about the Hon Mat incident.

Another effect of the incident had to do with Captain Ogier's motto of Proved Readiness. When he turned to sea, the captain was surprised to learn from the engine room that only one of the ship's four boilers had steam in it. This saved fuel, but in an emergency the power plant could not supply more than 17 knots. At Ogier's suggestion, therefore, the ship's engineer, Lieutenant Stephen B. Tool, started heating an extra boiler. An hour or two later the ship was capable of making 27 knots if need be. Two boilers remained cold—firing them up would have added only 7 knots to the ship's potential speed, because, at 27 knots, the conventional ship's hull begins to encounter tremendous water resistance.[4]

Following the Hon Mat incident, the *Maddox*'s next few hours passed without cause for alarm. Most of the crew continued to sleep peacefully as the ship glided through a smooth black sea. The weather continued hot and humid. Like Commander Jackson, many of the crew lay topside in the open air.

It was about 4 A.M. when Commodore Herrick quietly lit off a rocket to higher command.[5] The ship had intelligence, he reported by radio, indicating the possibility of hostile action from North Vietnam in the vicinity of Point Charlie. Four A.M. in the Tonkin Gulf would have been 5 A.M. in Taiwan, 6 A.M. in Okinawa, and 5 P.M. (Saturday afternoon) in Washington, D.C. What was the reaction to the commodore's message? I've never heard that he received a reply.

Despite the predicted danger, *Maddox* continued her patrol, perhaps a little farther from shore. It was just before dawn when the calm of the South Sea night was shattered by a call to General Quarters. The intercom crackled, and the voice of Captain Ogier could be heard. One astonished sailor later wrote down the words: "All hands proceed to General Quarters via internal routes." Not everybody heard the announcement. One officer remembers being awakened by a runner. Another officer slept through the whole emergency, and, hearing of the incident four years later, could scarcely believe it. Yet there was, in fact, a predawn GQ. The cause of it was a sonar contact.

Amazingly, whoever was on the stack reported the submerged presence of a submarine. For some time the destroyer maneuvered busily around the underwater contact. At last the ping was judged to be false. Reasons of depth seem to have entered into the decision.

---

[4] This helps to explain why, historically, conventional warship speeds climbed to 30-odd knots and stopped there. At that speed water begins to feel like concrete; indeed, a man falling overboard is liable to break half the bones in his body. Speeds substantially greater than 30 knots are achieved by brute force, as with nuclear powered engines, by hydrofoil supports that completely or partially lift the hull out of the water, or by means of an air cushion.

[5] A few of the isolated times in this narrative could be an hour off. They come from a variety of official and unofficial records, some of which do not always indicate what zone they are based on. Official records are almost as bad in this respect as the unofficial records.

Lieutenant Connell called down to the sonar gang: "Do you guys know how deep the water is here?" Wherever the ship was by this time, the water seems to have been too shallow to accommodate a pigboat; the sonarmen shamefacedly gave up their claim. Near Point Charlie the bottom would have been 72 feet; farther from shore the maximum would have been 200 feet. In any case, the soundmen decided that their ping came from a whale or some other natural object.

Was the sonar contact a false one? The ship decided that it was, and Sonarman Park, now a civilian, believes that it resulted from the excitement left over from the Hon Mat incident. Sonarmen are trained to be extremely cautious, calling out everything that they hear. In time of war, far more "submarines" are discovered and "sunk" than actually exist. "Better be safe than sorry" could be the sonarman's motto.

But not everybody agrees that *Maddox*'s ping was a false one. A few weeks after she left the Gulf, one of the crew heard from an apparently reliable source that a submarine, made in the U.S.A., had crept into the Gulf to act as lifeguard for the destroyer. According to this story, if the ship had been blown apart by a suicide boat, the submarine would have been there to pick up survivors. (Several days later a submarine entered the Gulf to lifeguard for aircraft. From what I have heard, this was a different boat.) It is typical of the patrol that years later men who were on it still wonder whether a friendly submersible was following them. I looked up the name of the alleged Sunday morning lifeguard and found it listed as an "electronic research vessel." The same description covered the elint activities of *Pueblo* and *Liberty*.

At the time of the predawn GQ, further mystery was added by the COMVAN. Lieutenant Moore stood on the bridge with a piece of yellow paper in his hand, talking in a low voice to the commodore and captain. Maybe he was talking about the earlier warning; maybe he had a new one. In any event, men in CIC noticed that whenever the lieutenant strode forward with a piece of paper in his hand, things began to happen. Jokingly, they talked of voodoo rituals in the mad box. The crew recently had seen a moving picture about an African witch doctor who worked his magic with a ball of human hair. A few humorists now began referring to the COMVAN lieutenant as the "hair ball man."

Commodore Herrick was taking the COMVAN more seriously than that. About an hour after sunrise he lit off another rocket to higher command. This one said that the earlier intelligence was accurate and that, in the commodore's opinion, the patrol should be canceled. Part of the text: CONSIDER CONTINUANCE OF PATROL PRESENTS UNACCEPTABLE RISK. More than two hours passed. Then, at about 9 A.M., a message came in from Admiral Johnson, Commander of the Seventh Fleet, who ordered *Maddox* to continue her patrol. The original plan, said he, could be altered as necessary, but "when considered prudent, resume itinerary." The De Soto chief, Admiral MacPherson, does not seem to have entered into this discussion. Commodore Herrick thought the prudent thing would be to get out of the Tonkin Gulf but, after hearing from Seventh Fleet, the commodore set course for his next checkpoint. That was Point Delta, an imaginary spot about 27 miles up the coast from Hon Me, in a north-northeasterly direction. Delta stood 11 miles off the mainland, about even with Loc Chao, a river mouth that harbored North Vietnamese naval craft.

The Seventh Fleet commander not only ordered Commodore Herrick to continue his patrol but gave permission to *change the itinerary as necessary*. What happened to the attention that, according to Secretary McNamara, CINCPACFLT and MACV were giving to the precise movements of the *Maddox?* Actually it was not CINCPACFLT but Admiral Johnson who was supposed to coordinate the De Soto patrol with MACV, according to a 1970 statement by Admiral Moorer, the former CINCPACFLT.[6] Moorer at that time was seeking confirmation by the Senate as Chairman of the Joint Chiefs. Moorer admitted to the Committee on Armed Services that he had detailed knowledge of the Hon Me and Hon Ngu raids, which, he said, were not connected with the *Maddox*'s patrol.

Perhaps it was Admiral Johnson who contributed a new safety precaution. The *Ticonderoga* received orders to arm a jet plane and keep it in Condition One—on a hot catapult—ready to help Sindbad at any time. The carrier had only two catapults: one was out of order; the other was needed for regular operations. *Maddox* never

---

[6] U. S. Congress, Senate, Committee on Armed Services; *Nomination of Admiral Thomas H. Moorer;* Hearing, 91st Congress, 2nd Session, June 4–5, 1970 (Washington: Government Printing Office, 1970), page 31.

found this out, but the carrier made alternative arrangements. Today, Sunday, the second day of August, the destroyer would patrol about 150 or 160 miles north of Yankee Station. The carrier's fastest jet, the high-winged F-8 Crusader, was thought capable of reaching the destroyer in about 15 minutes.

Exactly what kind of warning the COMVAN supplied remains very highly classified. The intelligence does not seem to have indicated what kind of attack might develop or at what time. As if covering all bets, the destroyer activated her air search radar for the first time since entering the Gulf. In the ready racks there remained a mixture of shell types and fuzes. The ship was prepared to deal with attack by air or by sea, by night or by day—except that two boilers remained cold.

The air search radar, SPS-40, was a fancy piece of new equipment that the ship had instructions not to use, unless really needed, anywhere that the Communists might be able to collect its fingerprint. Until Sunday not having to deal with the air search radar had been a lucky break for the overworked men of CIC. SPS-40 was known to be powerful but temperamental; it would go out of whack at the slightest excuse. When the new radar was installed back at Long Beach, an officer from another ship, who was familiar with it, predicted, "SPS-40 will be the biggest headache of your naval career."

Sunday brightened into one of the Gulf's typical summer days. A thin haze hung over the sky, and a slight breeze rippled the water. The Tonkin Gulf is like a big lake. On a clear day, land is visible from almost anywhere; in the absence of a storm, the water is calm.

Very few destroyermen, including the officers, knew about the COMVAN's warnings or about the messages exchanged with Admiral Johnson. In later years, former crew members were surprised to hear of the tense situation that had threatened them. They recalled that the captain had set "holiday routine" as if nothing unusual were expected. Most of the crew was permitted to take the day off. On the bulletin board, the Plan of the Day scheduled Protestant services in the morning, Catholic Rosary in the afternoon, and a bingo game for the evening. Orders of the Day chided the crew for leaving empty coffee cups in the pilot house and engineering spaces; meals, it was said, had been delayed for lack of coffee cups. Another note reminded the crew to keep out of any place marked

Restricted Area and, except in line of duty, to stay away from Officers' Country.

An ordinary Sunday seemed to be in progress. Off-duty sailors relaxed wherever some shade might be found. Enlisted men wore, as usual, their blue dungarees, white T-shirts, and white hats. Officers and chief petty officers dressed in tropical khaki. Long trousers were required for everybody. Short sleeves were permitted. Any Vietnamese watching the ship would have seen no evidence of alertness. Nearly everybody in sight was taking it easy, including a few gunners atop Mount 52, the taller 5-inch mount of the two forward. Not visible, of course, were the men of the COMVAN and CIC, where full staffs were on the job.

The Plan of the Day anticipated reaching Point Delta at 10 A.M. (12 noon ship's time), but, actually, the ship was there and turning south as early as 9:45 A.M. *Maddox* reached the checkpoint off Loc Chao earlier than scheduled, despite the time lost in the submarine alert and in waiting for instructions from higher command. Something must have been omitted from the original plan, perhaps a lengthy inspection of Hon Me.

Coming south from Delta, men of the *Maddox* were looking at Hon Me's northern side, a smooth, green dome rising 824 feet. A man standing on the summit would be able to see 33 miles to the sea horizon (and the view would have been most interesting that Sunday afternoon). The destroyer continued southward, keeping at least 4 miles from Hon Me but within the presumed 12-mile limit. From the east the island looked very different. Behind the big dome a series of wooded peaks stepped down toward the water. A few rocks then led the way, like tiny children, toward the small, motherly promontory of Hon Vat. To landward the grandfatherly mountain of Nui Tu Vi dominated the familiar scene.

The photographer's mate snapped pictures of Hon Me and the few man-made structures visible on its seaward side. From the far side smoke curled up into the air. The destroyermen supposed that the smoke came from cooking fires. But a week later, when they read news reports of an alleged gunboat raid, they wondered whether the shelling had not started a blaze which still smoldered when *Maddox* arrived. Hon Me was not the kind of place where one could call a fire engine.

The ship did not circle Hon Me. Since only 7 miles of water separated the island from the mainland, *Maddox*'s navigational guidelines did not permit passing in between. Maps indicated an anchorage on the landward side of the island, a cove sheltered by the grouping of Hon Me, Hon Vat, and a few nameless promontories. Given the *Maddox*'s 8-mile and 4-mile guidelines, the destroyermen's best view of the anchorage would have been from a point 7 miles to the south-southeast. On Saturday the *Maddox* had approached Hon Me from the south, but in darkness, and on Sunday the ship loitered chiefly to the northeast. Nothing on the record indicates that the American sailors took a good look at the anchorage on either Saturday or Sunday; nor do the results of my interviews suggest otherwise.

Southwest of Hon Me and Hon Vat several rocky promontories proceed like steppingstones toward the mainland. The ones farthest south, a little grouping 2½ miles distant, are known collectively as Hon Nieu, and various accounts of the Tonkin Gulf incidents (notably that of Senator Morse) have mistaken them for the raided island of Hon Ngu (sometimes spelled Hon Nieu). Hon Me and its neighbors are part of Thanh Hoa province; Hanoi said that the raided Hon Ngu was in Nghe An province, which includes Vinh and its offshore sentries of Hon Ngu and Hon Mat. Nghe An extends northward from just below Vinh almost up to Hon Me. It is a relatively poor, sparsely populated area known as the birthplace of revolutionaries. From Nghe An came Ho Chi Minh and, before him, the resistance leader Phan Boi Chau.

Turning back north toward Point Delta, men of the *Maddox* found northeast of Hon Me a Sunday morning congregation of fishing craft. Officers counted about seventy-five boats. As usual, the people aboard were fishing. No weapons could be seen.

Delta was supposed to be one of the ship's most important checkpoints. *Maddox* planned to spend at least a day in this area, mostly orbiting between Hon Me and Loc Chao. The ship steamed fairly close to Loc Chao, hoping to see some of the naval craft based there. These patrol craft protected the provincial capital, the town of Thanh Hoa (population: about 16,000), some 10 (statute) miles up the Ma River. From the south bank of Loc Chao rises the high ground of Cape Chao, from which a pagoda looks out over the estuary. On the Gulf side of the cape nestles the fishing village of Sam Son. Radio Hanoi has asserted that the *Maddox* at times could be seen from Sam Son beach. If so, the ship must have been steaming not more than 8 or 10 miles from shore. (Sam Son beach offers another point of historical interest: after the French phase of the war in Vietnam, survivors of the Dien Bien Phu garrison were picked up there and taken south.)

At some time on Sunday morning, officers of the *Maddox* took note of a small tanker that came down from the north, probably from Loc Chao, and disappeared behind Hon Me.

Late in the morning, about 11 A.M., *Maddox* was near Delta, proceeding north, when radarmen discovered three "skunks" (unidentified surface objects) coming out of Loc Chao. The skunks turned southward but did not head for the destroyer. They followed the contour of Cape Chao, departing only a mile or so from land. Since the three blips were making a speed of 20 knots, they could not be fishing boats; most likely, they would be naval vessels. The *Maddox*'s officer of the deck, Lieutenant Bane, reported the news to the captain. Soon the ship's senior officers were assembling on the bridge. Within 20 minutes the boats were in visual range. They still followed the shoreline and still moved at a brisk pace, as if bound on important business down south. The three tiny images kicked up a noticeable amount of white water, clearly visible against the dark headlands. Somebody said they were torpedo boats.

According to Naval Intelligence, North Vietnam had Soviet-designed P-4 and P-6 torpedo boats, each type equipped with two torpedo tubes and two pairs of 25-millimeter automatic cannon. *Jane's Fighting Ships,* whose information on North Vietnamese equipment was remarkably similar to the U. S. Navy's, stated that the P-4s had aluminum hulls made in Russia while the P-6s had wooden ones made in China. The two types were very similar in appearance, each displacing 50 tons, though the 85½-foot P-4 exceeded the P-6 in length by 3½ feet. *Maddox* personnel do not seem to have identified the particular kind of torpedo boat that came out of Loc Chao. Eyewitnesses recall that the North Vietnamese craft passed the destroyer "within 2 miles," "at about 5 miles," and "at least 10 miles" away. The Official Chronology released on August 3, 1964, told of *Maddox* being 30 miles from the coast when she encountered three torpedo boats coming south. However, witnesses agree that the fast boats kept close to shore and that they could be seen with the naked eye. *Maddox,* therefore, could not have been

30 miles from land; she must have been within the presumed 12-mile limit.

If the torpedo boats passed within 5 miles of *Maddox,* their skippers might have cursed their lack of orders to attack. With binoculars they could have seen that men of the *Maddox* continued to take their Sunday ease.

As the torpedo boats went by, a few gunners were still relaxing atop Mount 52. They bestirred themselves to take a look at the potential enemy. Gunner's Mate Robert E. Swift indulged in a bit of speculation. He remarked on how easy it would be for the torpedo boat men to pull into a cove, have a party on rice wine, "and then come out and attack us, just like that!" Swift snapped his fingers.

The destroyer maintained a steady course to the north, apparently minding her business, though, as the torpedo craft dropped below the horizon, CIC's radarmen kept an eye on them. The disappearing boats had no way to watch *Maddox.* As predicted by Naval Intelligence, they carried no radar masts—or, at least, none were observed by the destroyermen.

The neighborhood wasn't quiet for long. Soon it looked as though the Sunday parade had begun. Two more patrol craft came buzzing out of Loc Chao, following the same course as the earlier three, although not moving quite so fast. They appeared to be some kind of gunboat. Witnesses say they were slightly bigger than the torpedo craft. North Vietnam was known to have Swatow gunboats of 67-ton displacement (17 tons more than the torpedo boats), whose 83½-foot length, however, did not vary much from that of the torpedo craft. Naval Intelligence reported radar on the Swatows—perhaps the gunboats were identified as such by their radar masts.

Compared to South Vietnam, North Vietnam did not have much of a navy; in fact, the Communist fleet of patrol vessels officially belonged to the Vietnam People's Army. *Jane's* listed 2200 North Vietnamese sailors, including 200 officers and 2000 enlisted men. Their equipment: four P-6 boats, twelve P-4s, thirty Swatows, and three or four Russian 120-ton S.O.I. submarine chasers. *Jane's* reported the P-4 capable of 42 knots and the P-6 capable of 45. *Jane's* and Naval Intelligence agreed that the Swatows, designed in Russia and built in China, carried 37-millimeter guns. *Jane's* said nothing about the Swatow's speed, which officers of the *Maddox* believed to be 25 knots.

As the American sailors watched from the port side of their ship, the two North Vietnamese patrol craft continued purposefully to the south, dropping below the horizon. The destroyer then turned southward, too, tracking the Communists by radar. By one account, the ship at this time also moved farther to sea. As Gunner Swift had speculated, all five of the patrol craft slipped into a cove—the one behind Hon Me, where the fuel ship had gone earlier. Each torpedo boat carried from twelve to fifteen men. The Swatow complement was seventeen. Counting the fuel ship crew, probably eighty or more North Vietnamese sailors now were gathered at Hon Me, for purposes unknown.

It probably was about 12:30 P.M. when the presumed Swatows merged on the radar with the greater bulk of Hon Me. No more patrol craft came out of Loc Chao. Resuming her solitary course, the *Maddox* lazily started a new figure eight at Point Delta. Most of the destroyermen, seeing that the show was over, went back to their holiday routine. Nothing disturbed the tranquillity of the engineering spaces, except for the admonition to return coffee cups. One boiler was on line; one was standing by; two remained cold. It seems that the officers in command considered attack possible, maybe even probable, but by no means certain. Nor does it seem to have been known what kind of attack, by air or by sea, might develop.

At 2 P.M. (4 P.M. ship's time), the watch changed on schedule. Lieutenant Bane and the junior officer of the deck, Ensign Noel M. Allen, another gunnery officer, left the bridge and retired to the wardroom for coffee. They had been relieved by the new OD, Lieutenant Connell, and junior OD, Ensign C. Ward Bond, an engineering officer. After a quick coffee, Bane went up to the fo'c'sle to conduct a Catholic Rosary. So far as the North Vietnamese could tell, however closely they might watch, the *Maddox*'s patrol was, indeed, routine.

But the new team on the bridge had barely taken the conn when things began to happen. On the radar, CIC found a skunk creeping out of Hon Me. Connell and Bond watched it on the bridge's "repeater" scope. The blip was coming northeast, in the general direction of *Maddox*, but heading for the concentration of fishing craft.

The exact position of the destroyer at this time, says the Defense Department, cannot be told to the American people, though the ship was cruising within plain view of Hon Me and Communist naval craft knew where to find her. The map published by Hanoi puts the destroyer about 7 miles off the coast midway between Hon Me and Loc Chao. The vague Official Diagram from the Pentagon suggests a greater distance than that, but admits that the destroyer approached Hon Me as closely as 10.2 miles. In either case, the ship trespassed on what the Communists considered to be their territorial water, and she did so following a recent night attack by unmarked naval craft.

The skunk continued to move toward the part of the radarscope that was dappled by fishing boats. *Maddox* turned away to the northeast, conserving distance. The destroyer's radarmen leaned closer as the skunk began threading its way through the other green blips.

According to former Radarman James A. Stankevitz, "We figured that they were using those other boats as cover. Those other ones we knew were junks."

The skunk from Hon Me traveled at 5 knots on a definable course while the fishing craft were going nowhere in particular. What sort of boat had come out of the anchorage? Radar could not tell. At a considerable distance, perhaps 12 miles, the shapeless blob of light could be a gunboat. It could be two gunboats close together. It could be three torpedo boats close together. It could even be a destroyer. Gradually, however, the blob creeping northward split like protoplasm into three distinct contacts; and these, emerging from the crowded part of the screen, assumed a V formation pointed straight at the *Maddox*.

Chapter VII

Firefighter

For two mid-career officers, Commodore John Herrick and Captain Herbert Ogier, the moment was one of awesome responsibility. Their country was not at war, but it looked as though their ship was getting into one. Since World War II, with the decline of the British Empire, the U. S. Navy, incomparably more powerful than any other, had ruled the waves without challenge. Was the *Maddox*'s radar now showing the start of a new war? Today it is difficult to re-create the apprehensive mood of the 1950s and early 1960s, the general fear of upsetting the nuclear balance of terror. True, the same fear remains, but much dulled by the experience of continuous and open warfare. (Indeed, recently there have appeared in public print serious discussion of whether nuclear weapons might be needed in Vietnam—an idea unmentionable a few years ago.)

North Vietnam seemed an unlikely challenger for naval supremacy, even within the Tonkin Gulf. But local hostility was evident, according to the COMVAN; and one could read the same message in the faces of fishermen. The officers of the *Maddox* must be prepared to protect their ship.

First of all, were these radar blips actually planning an attack? The answer to that would have to be made clear.

Second, were these blips gunboats or torpedo boats? If gunboats, the Americans could let them have the first shot. While the Swatows' 37-millimeter cannon tried to perforate the destroyer's hull, *Maddox*'s 3-inch and 5-inch guns would make short work of them. The gunboats, at a reported 25-knot speed, were not even as fast as the bigger man-of-war.

If, however, the three skunks were torpedo boats—a likely possibility since three such craft were observed only a short time before—then the game would have a different set of rules. The destroyer's advantage over torpedo boats was not firepower but range. At a certain distance, *Maddox* would have the reach and could not be seriously challenged. At close range, the torpedo boats would have enough firepower to knock out a battleship, a fact which explains why many countries, especially the weak naval powers, buy torpedo boats. Even the biggest warship has to treat them with respect. Theoretically, one of these "mosquito boats" can pull alongside an aircraft carrier, order the ship to get moving, and sink her if she disobeys. The *Maddox,* therefore, could not permit herself to be ringed by hostile torpedo craft at close range. The problem was how to prevent it. If the Americans fired first, they could be accused of making an attack.

Commodore Herrick and Captain Ogier reached a decision. They would leave the patrol area and steam directly east toward the middle of the Gulf.

They reasoned that whether the radar contacts followed the destroyer would serve as a test of North Vietnamese intentions. Further, by keeping a minimum distance, the Americans would preserve their advantage of long-range firepower. And since the destroyer did not wish to get pinned against the North Vietnamese coast, the plan would allow her sea room for maneuvering. Finally, *Maddox* would be able to keep any exchange of fire away from the 12-mile zone, thus making certain that no shells fell within that area.

Perhaps other advantages occurred to Herrick and Ogier. Turning away would give the ship time to build up the speed needed to dodge torpedoes, if any were fired. Also, if a battle should start far from shore, additional patrol craft could not quickly reinforce the first three. Gaining time in which to obtain air cover does not seem to have been discussed on the bridge; nor did the ship immediately ask for it.

The disadvantages of turning east were not tactical but political and psychological. Running away from the coast would imply guilt and fear. As for fear, the North Vietnamese would be rash to count on this. In naval tactics, retreat often is used to gain some advantage, such as drawing the attacker into a larger force. It is not dignified, but it is done; and it often works. The destroyermen knew that they could not outrun torpedo boats, which would present the only serious threat.

As for implying guilt, a more cogent criticism can be leveled against the decision. If the U. S. Navy wished to demonstrate its right to patrol within 12 miles of the North Vietnamese coast, turning seaward like a startled rumrunner would not do that. International law cannot be established in secret. To the contrary, flight and subterfuge tend to be associated with the guilty party. Yet Commodore Herrick took pains to camouflage where the ship had been, and so did top officials in Washington.

It probably was about 2:15 P.M. when the *Maddox* turned due east. The ship speeded up a little and watched to see what the patrol craft would do. The V also speeded up and continued to bear on *Maddox*. Not long after clearing the fishing craft, the blips accelerated to 33 knots. Now they were looking like torpedo boats: Swatows were not supposed to be that fast. *Maddox*'s engineers, too, began to pour on the oil; they soon fired the old short hull up to a speed of 20 knots. More and more water separated the ship from Communist territory.

Thus began the chase to sea announced a few days later by Radio Hanoi. Most of the pursuit took place while the Communists were not even on the horizon. The chase itself did not constitute an attack, although it provided some evidence of hostile intent.

As the destroyer began to gather speed, a cooling breeze swept her open spaces. The crew wondered what was happening. The sea was getting bumpy, too, as if a storm were brewing. Yet the sky remained cloudless. A few men walked to the rail, and saw white water flying up from the prow.

At about 2:25 P.M. Lieutenant Bane had just finished the Rosary service when, for the second time that day, the voice of the captain came over the intercom. This time the occasion was even more unbelievable. The skipper said that high-speed radar contacts were pursuing the ship, that the ship was in international water, and that, if necessary, the ship would open fire in self-defense.

Hearing that North Vietnamese craft were closing from the starboard quarter, sailors ran to the starboard side of the ship and looked back. The sea was blank. At 2:30 P.M. a crowd was still scanning the water when another voice commanded the loudspeaker. This time it was the rough, salty timbre of Bosun's Mate Paul L. Bond.

"General Quarters," rasped Bond. "General Quarters. This is not a drill."

Not a drill! Most of the crew had never heard that before. Some had served in the Navy for as long as ten years without seeing a shot fired in anger. Former Ensign John M. Leeman recalls: "When they say just 'General Quarters, General Quarters, man your battle stations'—and they don't say it's a drill—it's a very eerie feeling . . . all of a sudden you run instead of walk real fast. You really run, you run like hell because you really know that something's going to happen." Wherever possible, men grabbed their helmets and flak jackets. Gunners stuffed trouser legs into their socks to prevent flash burns. The ship's barber, Felix Nerio, ran to his gun mount bare-chested. Except for omitting the gong, this GQ was not the silent type. For most of the men it suddenly turned hot again as they dashed into compartments and slammed the metal doors behind them. Hatches were dogged shut so that if a torpedo struck, watertight compartments would confine the flooding to a limited area. This also cut down the circulation of air; and the temperature in engineering spaces climbed to 140 degrees.

One of those who missed the cooling head wind was Commodore Herrick. As an unmodernized destroyer, the *Maddox* had a small bridge, very crowded at GQ, and the commodore elected to stick with CIC. There he could supervise the electronic nerve center and communicate more easily with higher command. Herrick probably expected advice of some kind from Admiral MacPherson or Admiral Johnson. Whether he did or not, none came. The commodore's operations officer, Lieutenant Frederick M. Frick, got in touch with the *Ticonderoga*.

At GQ the bridge team changes. The ship's operations officer, Bill Buehler, became officer of the deck. Connell, the former officer of the deck, remained on the bridge as gun boss. If there were any shooting, Ogier and Connell planned to direct gunfire centrally. Ensign Bond, who had been junior officer of the deck, sprinted off to his repair party below decks. His place was taken by the communications officer, Lieutenant (jg) John Bayley. The new junior officer of the deck started helping enlisted men stow loose objects. These would become "missile hazards" in the event of a torpedo strike or the jolt of 5-inch gunfire. Sailors began tricing up the windows, but the head wind was getting stiff, and it was decided to let the panes hang loose.

Gunfire would shatter tightly closed windows, but free swinging panes had survived many a practice exercise. Grabbing a telephone, Lieutenant Buehler began to get data on the skunks—range and bearings —from CIC. On the other end of the line was Lieutenant Evans, now CIC officer.

Engineer Tool reported that the superheaters were lit off. With these going and two boilers on line, the *Maddox* could make 27 knots.

The destroyermen were falling into procedures long familiar to them. The GQ began to seem like another drill.

Captain Ogier stood on the starboard wing, looking back at the still-empty horizon. A few moments passed. Then he turned to the men nearby, and said he thought the radar contacts were "hostile." There was something about Ogier's voice that sounded convincing. The men on the bridge really began to feel that they were going into battle.

Ten minutes after the GQ was called, the *Maddox* transmitted a flash message—uncoded, top priority—to Admiral Johnson, Admiral MacPherson, and the *Ticonderoga:*

AM BEING APPROACHED BY HIGH SPEED CRAFT WITH APPARENT INTENTION OF TORPEDO ATTACK. INTEND OPEN FIRE IF NECESSARY.

A few minutes later, at 2:45 P.M., the destroyer was making 27 knots, and she turned southeast, the direction of Yankee Station. The turn provided a new test of North Vietnamese intentions. Passing the test, the three skunks also curved to the southeast. Strangely, however, they did not try to cut in front of the destroyer; instead, they kept bearing on the *Maddox* herself. This tactic, if continued, was bound to result in a "stern chase." It was not the fastest way to overtake the destroyer; nor could it result in a good position for launching torpedoes. But there seemed little doubt that the fast boats meant to catch up. Radarmen now estimated their speed at 46 knots.

As *Maddox* bore to the southeast, Lieutenant Connell reported that his 5-inch guns had locked onto the distant skunks. Men on the bridge were now looking slantwise into four black muzzles. Since the Communist boats were to the rear, the forward mounts had to swivel back as far as they would go. In gunnery practice, the ship avoided this awkward angle to prevent noise, smoke, and bits of cork from fouling the bridge.

At 2:47 P.M. the skunks were still in a V formation, fast overhauling the *Maddox,* which would not have time to get her two cold boilers on line. Commodore Herrick finally called for air support. The *Ticonderoga* already had planes armed and aloft.

The Communist boats were still gathering speed. *Maddox*'s astonished radarmen now reckoned their pace at a dazzling 50 knots. Whether P-4s or P-6s, these boats were much faster than Naval Intelligence thought they were.

It was 2:50 P.M. when CIC reported another fascinating development. Radar showed the boats crisscrossing each other's path. Were they having fun, playing porpoise? *Maddox*'s bridge didn't think so. Officers regarded the "three-boat weave" as intended to break their fire control solution. An unsteady blip usually represents weather phenomena, and radar-directed guns are not supposed to fire at such illusions. *Maddox*'s guns were not fooled. Automatically, the 5-inchers maintained their aim.

Visually the boats came into sight about 3 P.M. The first that could be seen of them was their bowspray, shining white in the afternoon sun. The boats now were in column, zigzagging. The three-boat weave had stopped as unexpectedly as it had begun. Perhaps it was only a trick of the radar. Zigzagging, too, was a battle tactic, as ancient as warfare.

More puzzling to men with high-powered optics were the lollipop masts characteristic of radar. North Vietnamese torpedo boats didn't have any radar. That point had been confirmed just hours ago. Was the destroyer being pursued by gunboats? If so, the enemy could be lobbing 37-millimeter shells within minutes. But the Swatow speed, according to Naval Intelligence, was only 25 knots. Therefore, the pursuing boats could only be torpedo boats—*with radar*. This conclusion turned out to be correct, even though Naval Intelligence was wrong about the speed of a Swatow.

The pursuit was no longer a stern chase. The North Vietnamese now were 7 miles west and aiming for a point ahead of the destroyer, as if they planned to cut her off or charge in from the bow. The pursuers looked more aggressive every minute, but the question remained: Was this an attack? The North Vietnamese still had not fired. If wise, they would *not* fire until they could get into the best position—say, two boats straddling the bow and one on the starboard quarter. Six torpedoes lancing in from three directions would be hard to evade; and *Maddox*'s guns would have to split their fire three ways.

It would be foolish to let the enemy set this up. Yet the Americans did not want to shoot first.

Bill Buehler estimated that the boats might launch torpedoes from as far as 3000 yards, though, of course, they would prefer to get closer. Ogier asked Pat Connell how far he thought the boats could be allowed to come in. Connell wanted to start shooting no later than 8000 yards. In making these estimates, the officers were handicapped by a lack of any experience with torpedo boats, which the U. S. Navy no longer had, and by not having shot at small, fast targets, which the Navy did not provide. In gunnery exercises, American ships fired at airborne targets, representing airplanes, and at large slow surface targets (representing what?). (The experts seem to have felt that hitting an airplane would be easier than a small, fast surface target. But even if true, this would not prove that inexperienced gunners could hit them.) Now, for lack of experience, nobody aboard the *Maddox* knew how effective the ship's guns would be. The men, however, were itching to fire, and the general attitude was one of confidence. As matters turned out, Buehler and Connell made good guesses, and Ogier felt that he had waited until the "last minute."

What worried the *Maddox*'s crew was whether the captain would open fire at all. As the men understood it, the ship was in international water. Why were they running away?

Herrick and Ogier wanted to make a final test of North Vietnamese intentions. To do this, they decided to fire three warning shots at a distance of 10,000 yards. If the Communists kept coming, the ship would begin rapid fire, for effect, at 8000 yards.

The North Vietnamese boats were still pulling up on the starboard quarter, at once closing and passing the American ship. Their profiles came into view. To the naked eye, the torpedo boats looked like "little sticks on the water." Men with binoculars saw their bows thrust upward, throwing a wide spray; astern, each boat sprouted a tall, white "rooster tail." At full speed, the torpedo craft made a pretty sight, and a deadly one. These were aluminum P-4s equipped with a forward "step hydrofoil." The P-4 carries two 18-inch torpedoes, each loaded with several hundred pounds of explosive. In contrast, the typical 5-inch shell packs only a few pounds of powder. As an engine of destruction, the torpedo has another advantage: nearly the entire force of its immense explosion shapes toward the target. This is because water won't compress, but ships do. A single torpedo striking below the waterline can tear a hole more than 10 yards wide. Torpedo men say, "Shells are good for letting the air in, but torpedoes let the water in." Knowing this, engineers and others working in the bowels of the ship tend to get keyed up in combat.

For lack of time, 27 knots were the best that Lieutenant Tool could provide. It was no tremendous battle speed, but it was enough to give the rudder plenty of bite. In daytime, an alerted destroyer has an excellent chance of evading the old-fashioned, straight-running torpedo, which the North Vietnamese were thought to have.

The witnesses disagree considerably on the details of the battle action, including the positions of *Maddox* and the torpedo boats at the time the warning shots were fired. One officer sketched for me the leading boat exactly abeam of *Maddox* with the other two trailing some distance behind. Another insists that the first boat was abeam while the other two angled in from the starboard quarter. An officer who kept watch by radar says that all three boats were on the starboard quarter and still weaving. Most often one hears that the boats were in column, off the starboard quarter, and zigzagging. This recollection is supported by the *Maddox*'s deck log, which says that the boats were due west.[1] Since *Maddox* was heading southeast, due west would have been to the right and to the rear. (Abeam would have been southwest.)

The critical moment came about 3:08 P.M. The torpedo boats were only 10,000 yards away; they were crossing the magic circle. Captain Ogier checked with the commodore, saying something like: "I'm going to open fire now."

By one report, the commodore replied, "Well, go ahead!"

Ogier passed the word. Within seconds, the 5-inch guns blasted away in salvo. The firing range: 9800 yards. As the three mounts roared their mighty greeting to the North Vietnamese, the destroyer was about 30 miles from land.

Reverberations from the big guns cracked and shattered the bridge windows. Everybody there went temporarily deaf, and a few "missile

---

[1] The log gave a bearing of "270 degrees." If a "true" bearing, this would mean directly west. There is also such a thing as "relative" bearing, in which case 270 degrees would be off the port beam. That fits nobody's recollection. Furthermore, the Navy requires that relative bearing be indicated as such. The deck log must have been using true bearing, which amounts to a compass reading.

hazards" came unstowed. But these were minor problems. Would the North Vietnamese turn back? Tension mounted as the destroyer-men waited to see what would happen.

For an endless 30 seconds, the *Maddox*'s shells arched through the fetid air of the Gulf. Then, silently, black puffs of smoke and columns of white water bracketed the distant torpedo boats. Finally, the reports of bursting shells were heard. Nobody on the bridge seemed to notice that there were four explosions instead of three. One of the gun mount captains had told his men merely to "load" instead of to "load one barrel."

The "warning shots" were not aimed over anybody's bow. They were pointed right at the boats. "We didn't want to waste too much time spotting our shots," Lieutenant Connell told Tom Stewart of the Associated Press. Not believing his ears, Stewart asked whether the shells were aimed to hit.

"It was shoot to kill," affirmed the ex-gun boss.

Three years after the battle, Connell's statement gave a jolt to nearly all of the ex-*Maddox* men who heard of it, including the former captain. Those not directly involved with the shooting thought that the "warning shots" were aimed to miss. (Yet the log said nothing about a warning; it used the term "open fire." So did a message that *Maddox* sent to higher command.)

Men of the *Maddox* could not tell whether the four 5-inch shells did any damage to the torpedo boats. Most observers say that this would have been very unlikely. One officer who was on the bridge admits, "It's possible." Nobody could see very well since the boats were still a long way off. The deck log reports 9800 yards. That would have been 4.83 nautical or 5.56 statute miles.

Whatever the physical effect of the warning shots, their psychologi-cal impact was certain. The recipients had no reason to regard them as friendly. If the torpedo boat skippers were American, they would have been required by regulations to shoot back.

Of the dozen or so men at the rear 5-inch mount, only two or three could see out. One was the gunpointer, Felix Nerio. A shipmate asked, "Are they turning back?"

"No," said Nerio. "It sure looks real."

The leading boat continued to pull ahead while the after two now swerved in toward the *Maddox*'s starboard quarter. Captain Ogier later said that he was glad the North Vietnamese did not turn back. He explained:

"Of course, you know, if they had just turned and run away after we'd started firing at them, then we could have been in trouble. Because they could have said, 'Here we were in international waters, too, and you went and fired at us.' But they came on and fired torpedoes at us, which was good."

With two boats headed directly at them, the destroyermen saw no point in waiting for the enemy to cross the 8000-yard line. Turning to Connell, the captain said, "They're all yours."

The range probably was about 9000 yards when the old destroyer shook again with the roar of battle. The time, according to the log, was 3:11 P.M. All six 5-inch guns blasted away. So did the one pair of 3-inchers that would bear to starboard.

The first broadside looked as though it were all that would be needed. Black, oily smoke obscured one of the incoming boats as a shell exploded right in front of it.

"We must've got *that* son-of-a-bitch!" said one of the enlisted men.

But the North Vietnamese kept on through it all, not even slowing their pace. Since the two boats on the starboard quarter presented the more immediate threat, most of the fire was directed toward them. *Maddox*'s guns laid down a murderous-looking blanket of fire and smoke. Only one pair of 3-inchers would bear to starboard; but being faster than the hand-loaded 5-inchers, they seemed more effective—at least for scaring the enemy if not for hurting him.

There were several near-hits. A shellburst would seem to lift one end of a boat into the air, or knock a chunk off it. The destroyermen could hear the *WHANG, WHANG* of shrapnel tearing into metal hulls. Yet the spunky North Vietnamese kept coming.

One of the COMVAN Marines who watched the battle begin, says of the gunners: "They weren't doin' too good, so far as hittin' goes." Lieutenant Buehler thought the shooting was good. "I wouldn't have wanted to be out there," he told the AP.

For a moment the Communists might have thought the ship was striking her colors. Shortly after the rapid fire began, the executive officer, Commander Jackson, ordered the signalmen to put up the ship's biggest American flag. The "steaming ensign" came down on one halyard as the "holiday ensign" went up on another. This is an old battle custom, though Jackson explains that he wanted a big, clean flag in the air so that there could be no doubt of the ship's nationality. The torpedo boat men, who were flagless, ought to have been impressed by the ceremony.

As if in response to the bright, new flag, the charging pair began to fire machine guns. Men of the *Maddox* saw little splashes of water between them and the enemy boats, which were still out of bullet range. By mistake the *Maddox* sent a report of 37-millimeter fire; somebody had the P-4 armament confused with that of Swatow craft. But neither did the torpedo boats carry the 25-millimeter guns they were supposed to have. They were firing slugs from heavy machine guns, the Communist equivalent of .50 or .60 caliber.

Down in CIC, Commodore Herrick watched the battle by radar. On the scope he could see the shells exploding and boats coming. "One thought kept going over and over in my mind," he said. "That was, 'It can't be happening . . . It can't be happening.'" At some point, the incredulous commodore stepped out to get a live view. Reaching the bridge, he saw that a real battle was indeed going on. Nearly the whole of *Maddox*'s fire was still being directed toward the after two boats, and Herrick advised Ogier to pay more attention to the one forward. Because of the din, nobody heard the commodore say a word. Herrick retired to CIC, whence he transmitted the same advice by telephone.

Not only windows but eardrums were being split by 5-inch shells slanting past the bridge. For weeks afterward those present had a tendency to shout at one another; one man says that he couldn't hear his watch tick for a year. Still, the gunfire was "real music" to the men whose lives now depended on it.

The Americans were busy fighting their equipment as well as the enemy. A lot of the radar-fuzed "proximity" shells were exploding too soon, detonated by the radar reflection of the water. Other premature bursts, disconcertingly close to the ship, were caused by a malfunctioning fuze-setter. The fuze-setter was damaged by concussion; so was an electrical cable that started a fire in the mess decks.

Most serious, all of the 5-inch guns were getting low on ammunition. The ready racks held only forty-four shells apiece, and nobody was down in the magazines passing more up. Abaft, Chief Gunner's Mate Petrovitz noticed the ammunition shortage and ordered some idle men down into the magazine. Some of these hands came from the portside 3-inch mount which was unable to bear on the enemy; others came from the standby repair party. The bridge learned of the ammunition shortage when somebody up forward asked for permission to open watertight compartments. Why? To get some shells: the forward gunners were reduced to firing illumination rounds. (With their fuzes on "safe," the inert star shells at least might put some holes in the enemy, like old-fashioned cannon balls.) The gunners received permission to break open the magazine; as they did so, some of the forward guns fell silent. After what seemed a century, they all started shooting again.

Machine guns chattering, the after P-4s continued to bore in. When they got up to 4000 yards (witnesses estimate from 3000 to 5000), the boat farthest to the rear whipped around and sped astern, still throwing slugs. The reason for this maneuver soon became apparent. Two thin, white wakes were streaking for a point ahead of the destroyer. The Communist skipper had made a "launch turn" so that his 50-knot boat would not overtake its somewhat slower (perhaps 45 knot) torpedoes. The Red aim looked good.

"Torpedoes in the water! Brace yourself!" ordered the intercom. If a man is standing flatfooted when a torpedo explosion lifts the deck, the shock can break both of his legs. Those who had the opportunity pressed part of their weight against firm objects or lay flat on the deck.

The steel fish were running shallow. Once or twice they came breaking through a wave, then nosed back into the water. Each trailed a stream of bubbles. Naval Intelligence had been right about steam-driven, straight-running torpedoes.

For a solid minute Captain Ogier did nothing but watch. There was still plenty of time in which to dodge. Besides, the remaining boat on the quarter was surely getting ready to launch its torpedoes, and a turn to port would mask the destroyer's forward guns—they couldn't swivel back any farther. When it looked as though time was running out, somebody asked the captain, "Are you going to turn now?"

"Not just yet," said Ogier.

Then he ordered a turn to port.

Gripping the brass wheel was Gordon J. Cadmus, one of the best sailors aboard. Cadmus turned the rudder, the ship swerved, and Ogier told the helmsman to steady up. The bow had come over about 10 degrees. The ship now paralleled the torpedo tracks. That was standard doctrine: parallel the fish. Just as the book prescribed, the white wakes went by without doing any harm. The wakes had "plenty of zip" in them. Witnesses say they missed the ship by 50 or 100 yards.

The intercom didn't mention the good news to the men below, who still were bracing themselves. But their spirits were lifted by another report, that of aircraft on the way. Two of the COMVAN detachment had been sent below to get lifebelts. Now they were braced in a corridor, their feet planted against one bulkhead, their backs pressed against the other. One said he thought the planes would save the ship. The other figured that *Maddox* could take care of herself.

After the boat farthest to the rear turned back, its partner stayed on course, apparently planning to launch a spread of torpedoes from closer range. Instead, as *Maddox* swerved to port, this boat turned back under a hail of 3-inch shells—apparently without launching a single fish. Maybe the torpedomen were killed or their equipment damaged. It seems to have been this boat's machine gun, however, that holed the pedestal of the After Director, where Lieutenant Bane was sitting. Hot fragments of the slug ricocheted into the 3-inch ammunition handling room below the Director; their fumes at first were taken for another electrical fire. Bane knew nothing of this episode until after the battle was over.

The leading boat now had to make its torpedo run all alone. The *Maddox*'s turn prevented the Communist skipper from getting the ideal bow shot, which would have given his torpedoes a relative speed of about 60 knots, adding part of their velocity to that of the destroyer. The last and most worrisome of the enemy boats had to charge in closer to the beam, which still gave it a better position than the two others had achieved. Their torpedo velocity had been largely cancelled by the forward motion of the *Maddox*. The destroyer's bridge now was relieved of some noise and confusion as the ship's forward guns swung forward. Through some misunderstanding, the guns went too far. They quickly swiveled back again.

Enough of radar and computers. The forward gunners, eyeballing it, "walked" a line of shells into the last boat. One round made a direct hit on the port side, knocking loose a torpedo; the torpedo fell into the water but apparently failed to run. At least one *Maddox* veteran asserts that another torpedo fell off the boat's starboard side. In any event, the most intrepid of the P-4 skippers managed to fire nothing but his machine guns. He was reduced to chasing his friends, pouring out a rather ineffective screen of light gray smoke.

Meanwhile, the two boats astern were still being pummeled by the *Maddox*'s after guns. One of them caught fire, and its partner pulled alongside to render assistance. These boats, too, generated a thin screen of gray smoke. A darker vapor rose from the fire.

All of the torpedo craft now had given up their foolhardy though amazingly determined and aggressive attack. The *Maddox* was in a position to sink or capture them.

Did the ship have the authority to pursue and destroy? Officers on board did not doubt it. The Navy's attitude was made clear, for example, by Regulation 0705 concerning "Action with the Enemy." It states that the commanding officer shall "during action engage the enemy to the best of his ability. He shall not, without permission, break off action to assist a disabled ship or to take possession of a captured one." The meaning of this was clear: once in a fight, win it. Herrick and Ogier, both graduates of the Naval Academy, had been absorbing this philosophy during their entire adult lives. Furthermore, they knew the classified "rules of engagement," which authorized any ship in the Western Pacific to fire back if attacked and to pursue the attacker even into his territorial water. The commodore ordered the *Maddox* to chase the fleeing torpedo boats. The time was 3:24 P.M.

But the *Maddox*'s guns were not destined to finish the job.

Shortly after the ship came about, the officer of the deck, whose task it was to "watch the road," spotted a torpedo in the water. Buehler immediately ordered a sharp turn to the right, then one to the left, fishtailing around the deadly object. The torpedo could have been one of those that the ship had dodged seven or eight minutes before. Its fuel nearly spent, the buoyant cylinder might have been overtaken by the destroyer, which, coming about, almost ran into it. For *Maddox* it would have been the supreme irony to win the battle and then sink. With his artist's eye, Buehler noticed that the torpedo was painted yellow and moving just below the surface of the water. Nobody else saw it.

The fishtailing incident did not waste much time. *Maddox* resumed course, chasing her enemies to the northwest, but again the pursuit was foiled. Planes from the *Ticonderoga* were about to arrive—41 minutes after they had been called. The commodore decided to clear the area, not firing his guns while the aircraft dove on target. If the jets were to make any attack it would have to be while their fuel lasted. Since they didn't have much fuel, they would have to attack right away. (The decision was also sound from the bureaucratic standpoint. Admiral Robert B. Moore aboard the *Ticonderoga* would have to share responsibility for firing on the North Vietnamese, even though, strictly speaking, it was primarily the responsibility of Commodore Herrick as the "onscene commander.")

When help from the carrier flashed into sight, the destroyermen relaxed, thinking that this was "the end"—the end of their work and the end of the torpedo boats. The time: 3:28 P.M. Where had the jets been since 2:47 P.M.?

When Sindbad called for help, Jehovah had a dozen planes in the air. They were engaged in target practice, shooting at the plume of water raised by a towed spar. Most of the planes were loaded chiefly with practice ammunition. Only four were prepared for combat. These were F-8E jet Crusaders, the *Ticonderoga*'s only supersonic type of plane. The Crusader was an interceptor, meaning that it was designed for air-to-air combat. Its speed, however, would make it useful for assisting *Maddox,* should the need arise, which is why the four Crusaders were carrying live ammunition. With a code name of Firefighter, the four had been launched on a contingency basis approximately 10 minutes before the *Maddox* went to quarters. The Firefighter group, prepared for air-to-air as well as air-to-surface combat, carried a "mixed bag" of ammunition: Sidewinder air-to-air missiles, Zuni air-to-surface missiles, and 20-millimeter shells and slugs. Since only four planes were made ready, it would appear that Admiral Moore did not take the *Maddox*'s predicament too seriously. While *Maddox* built up speed, heading for the middle of the Gulf, the Firefighter pilots consumed part of their ammunition in target practice.

One would imagine that as Sindbad signaled for help the four jets immediately banked northward and sped to the rescue. To the contrary, the jets continued to loiter above the carrier, their pilots engaged in mock dogfights and watching their friends shoot at the towed spar. So far as the *Ticonderoga* was concerned the fire hadn't started yet. As one of the officers explained it: "The *Maddox* had a few blips on her radar. So what? We didn't think anybody would attack an American man-of-war."

The jet pilots were eager to go. With their fuel diminishing, they worried about getting replaced by a fresh launch. At last the air controller gave the word. "Firefighter," he snapped, "go to the aid of Sindbad!" The timing seems to have coincided with *Maddox*'s open fire.

The air controller provided directional bearings and gave the departing pilots a new communication channel. Firefighter was told not to shoot at the North Vietnamese unless they shot at the *Maddox*. As the jets winged north, the carrier began recovering the planes left in the sky. Not knowing what escalation might be in store, Jehovah apparently wanted to have a powerful force fueled and armed as soon as possible.

The Crusaders traveled north at 600 knots, a speed just below that of sound. The destroyer was 160 miles away—a 16-minute flight as a jet-propelled crow would fly (one knot representing one nautical mile per hour). *Maddox,* however, did not have the new electronic homing device that would guide the planes in a straight line. The Firefighter group began its journey on the basis of old-fashioned dead reckoning. The destroyer hoped to find the planes by radar and bring them in that way, but SPS-40 became a casualty of the "warning shots." The 5-inch salvo, besides wreaking havoc on the bridge and starting a fire in the mess decks, knocked open SPS-40's little black boxes. Automatically, the doors tripped the circuit breakers that prevent careless repairmen from getting electrocuted, and the great electromagnetic umbrella collapsed. SPS-40 would sit this battle out.

Dead reckoning lost several minutes by the time the Crusaders made contact with the ship by UHF voice radio. Now their direction-finding gear had something to hang onto. Daley Evans, the CIC officer, was on air control. The pilots asked him for a long count: "10 . . . 9 . . . 8 . . . 7 . . ." With their navigation squared away, the flyers next wanted a blow-by-blow description of the battle, which Evans provided. Hearing of the Communist fire, the airmen assumed that they would be permitted to join the fray. An eternity passed. Then a little cloud of smoke darkened the horizon; and the attack radar showed surface blips. It was about 23 minutes after leaving Yankee Station when the jets went screaming over *Maddox* after the enemy.

The airmen found three boats plowing to the northwest while the destroyer steamed southeast. Two of the boats were abreast of each other; one trailed behind. The original V formation had become inverted. Without any debate concerning their right to do so, the pilots went in for the kill. The senior pilot and his wingman would each take one of the leading pair while the other two planes dove on the straggler. This would apportion evenly the Zuni rockets, which the pilots intended to use first. The command pilot and his wingman each carried four Zunis. The others had only two apiece since they were burdened with the heat-seeking Sidewinders. The Zuni is not a guided missile, and a twisting, turning torpedo boat is one of the most difficult things to hit from the air. But the impact of the fragmentation warhead of this air-to-surface rocket, 9.2 feet in length and weighing 107 pounds, is tremendous.

A long way from home, the torpedo boat men must have been just as pessimistic about the impending air-to-surface battle as men of the *Maddox* were optimistic. Instead of the radar, the P-4s now needed their old 25-millimeter cannon. The machine guns were not so powerful. They also lacked tracer bullets.

Two pairs of rockets bracketed the trailing boat, causing sheets of water to fly up fore and aft. Like the destroyermen before them, the pilots thought that the first salvo would do the job. Yet the boat kept moving. The airmen then started strafing runs from different directions, firing the 20-millimeter ammunition: armor-piercing, tracers, ball-type, incendiary, and high explosive. It sounds like a lot, but each plane had ammunition for only a minute or two of firing.

The command pilot and his wingman let go of their Zunis, too, without sinking anything. Pulling out of his dive, the wingman called out, "I'm hit!" His plane shuddered alarmingly. Men of the *Maddox* saw a piece fly off the wing, and Commander Jackson ordered rescue stations. The aircraft, however, got its nose up again and began clawing successfully for altitude. After it leveled off, the command pilot maneuvered in close and diagnosed the trouble as a broken "droop" —eager to do his best with the unguided Zuni missiles, the wingman dove too low and, pulling up sharply, tore a control surface on his wing. The command pilot told him to stay where he was and went back to the battle.

The other two Crusaders continued their strafing runs with one making a perfect dive which looked as though it had riddled its victim with a hundred holes. Within a few minutes, these two aircraft had used up all of their ammunition. Their target stopped moving, and one pilot saw bodies sprawled inside. Low on fuel, the two Crusaders headed back for Yankee Station, refueling from tankers on the way.

Two Crusaders remained behind briefly, the one orbiting above while the other exhausted his ammunition. Before leaving the area, they reported to *Maddox* one boat dead in the water and burning. Then they set a course for Da Nang. The damaged Crusader, vibrating as it was, could not risk landing on the carrier.[2]

There was no immediate replacement for Firefighter.

Alone once more, Commodore Herrick thought over the situation and felt reluctant to pursue the North Vietnamese any longer. The torpedo boats already had been fired upon, repulsed, and then chased —first by *Maddox,* then by aircraft. The commodore wondered "how far they [higher command] would want us to push this thing." Conveniently for Herrick's peace of mind, a message arrived with some instructions. Admiral Johnson, Seventh Fleet Commander, ordered the ship not to pursue the torpedo boats. *Maddox* was to retire from the area, defending herself as necessary. This ended all debate. The destroyer proceeded south at best speed.

The enemy was seen last by radar. All three blips were moving slowly, close together. The original V now was inverted. *Maddox* officers thought it likely that two boats were towing the third.

The North Vietnamese had fought valiantly. But if they meant to sink the American ship, their tactics were second-best. The torpedo craft, in effect, had been neatly mousetrapped.

---

[2] The hard luck pilot, Lieutenant Commander Richard Hastings, made it to Da Nang safely. In the spring of 1966 he died of injuries received in an accident aboard the *Ticonderoga* while acting as landing signals officer.

Chapter VIII

What Happened?

After the *Maddox* "incident" of August 2, some of California's retired Navy salts, according to the news media, snorted that the destroyer's skipper ought to have given his men more gunnery practice.
The criticism was inspired partly by the false impression that aircraft, coming along in the nick of time, saved the ship, and partly
by uncertainty as to whether any of the North Vietnamese boats
had been sunk. Men of the *Maddox* heard of such remarks and resented them. Most of the destroyermen knew that the boats had been
driven off before the planes arrived (some of the men in closed compartments were unaware of it), and most believed that at least one
of the Communist craft had been sunk. To explain the survival of
the other two, they referred to the shortness of pursuit and to the extraordinary toughness of the aluminum craft. During World War
II, the U. S. Navy built its famous PT boats of plywood because
aluminum was needed for aircraft; yet often they would survive gunfire unless hit in the fuel tanks.

The Navy did not admit publicly that its gunnery was less than
perfect, but secretly both the top brass and men of the *Maddox*
were not entirely satisfied. The ship's former enlisted gunners recall
that when *Maddox* earned her E the mounts fired independently.
Some officers criticize the radar-fuzed shells that exploded prematurely, saying that they were designed for antiaircraft use. (Fired
high in the sky, the projectile will not be detonated by "water return" [radar reflection from the water] but by the nearness of a solid
object.) In Sunday's battle, simpler types of fuzes gave better results. As for the shortage of ammunition at the 5-inch mounts, it is

said that the peacetime complement of personnel did not provide enough hands.

A few months before the *Maddox* started her patrol, the professional journal *U. S. Naval Institute Proceedings* carried an article that deplored the Navy's current attitude toward gunnery. The author was Commander John O. Stull (USNR, Retired), who formerly commanded the Fleet Gunnery School at San Diego. Guns, said Stull, remained the principal armament aboard Navy ships but they were being treated like "museum pieces." The newer specialties of missiles and electronics, he observed, provided better opportunities for advancement, so that interest in gunnery already had diminished to a dangerous degree. Even a ship's weapons officer, wrote Stull, often lacked the formal training that he was supposed to have. Vaguely, Stull remarked that the missile age wasn't really here yet. He refrained from going into the awful details: the Navy's antiaircraft missiles didn't work, and American warships carried no surface-to-surface tactical missiles at all.

Following the Tonkin Gulf experience, the Navy made one change in its gunnery training. The lack of a small, fast surface target was remedied by the purchase of the 17-foot Firefish, a radio-controlled boat, smaller than the P-4 torpedo boat and also slower, making only 30 knots. Destroyer skippers eagerly began shooting at their new toy, and were surprised to find out how hard it was to hit.

An important factor in the *Maddox*'s defense was the decision to fight a retiring action. This not only made torpedoes easier to dodge but gave the gunners more time in which to shoot. The inglorious though effective tactic might not have been considered necessary if the *Maddox* had carried the fast-firing weapons of an earlier era. During World War II, *Sumner* ships bristled with eleven 20-millimeter guns, twelve 40-millimeter guns, and a variety of machine guns. The slowest of these, the Bofors 40-millimeter, could pump 120 shells per minute over a horizontal distance of 5200 yards. The fast-firing armament was intended primarily for antiaircraft use, but the shells exploded on contact, and, directed to the water's surface they would pulverize any small craft that came near. American PT men used to say that they feared the enemy's light guns more than the heavy ones—small wonder, when a single minute of fire could produce thousands of shells and a hail of bullets. In 1964 *Maddox*'s rate of fire was not so fast. During 16 minutes of all-out effort, the ship expended a total of 283 projectiles. Where a "quad" of 40-millimeter guns used to stand, there was now an empty space called the "officers' sunbathing deck."

Before World War II, the U. S. Navy was slow to adopt the Swedish 40-millimeter and Swiss 20-millimeter guns. American experts (or somebody in authority) preferred to buy the domestic .50-caliber machine gun. When the Navy realized its error, it began installing automatic cannon in every available empty space, and these guns continued to clutter American warships until the end of the Korean War. When they disappeared, word spread that the old guns weren't effective against jet planes, though the Navy's official history of the Korean War mentions no attack on surface ships by enemy jets.[1]

In discarding the automatic cannon, the Navy ignored the threat of coastal patrol craft; and, strangely, even the experience of the *Maddox* brought no change but the Firefish. In 1967 the USS *Liberty*, with no success, fought Israeli torpedo boats with .50-caliber machine guns. That example was lost on the Pentagon, but apparently, it was not lost on the North Koreans or on Captain Bucher of the *Pueblo*. Bucher tried and failed to obtain automatic cannon for his ill-fated ship; he ended up with the same .50-caliber guns that proved suicidal to men of the *Liberty*. Months after the *Pueblo*'s ignominious surrender, the press reported that the Defense Department again was rejecting suggestions for putting heavier guns on the "spy ships." But after the *Pueblo* men came home, gaunt and tortured, the public outcry was stilled by photographs of high-ranking officers patting 20-millimeter cannon aboard a sister ship of the *Pueblo*. It may seem ungrateful to point this out, but the 20-millimeter gun might not have been the best choice. When I discussed automatic cannon with veterans of the *Maddox*, there was general agreement that the 40-millimeter gun would be very useful against torpedo boats ("just great" was a typical evaluation), but nobody had a good word for the 20-millimeter size.

The *Maddox* was not specifically prepared to deal with torpedo boats—the one type of enemy, if any, that she was liable to run into. But as for armament, the old short hull was better equipped for the job than many a bigger and more modern warship would have been

[1] James A. Field, Jr., *United States Naval Operations: Korea* (Government Printing Office, 1962).

including the cruiser-sized vessel. The missile cruiser *Albany,* for example, mounts only two 5-inch guns, one to port and one to starboard. A three-boat attack from one side would confound the 17,500-ton behemoth. This applies equally to the *Albany*'s sister ships, the *Chicago* and *Columbus.* Another two-gunner is the nuclear-powered cruiser *Long Beach,* a super-sophisticated vessel which cost the taxpayer $332.8 million. It is said that these ships would have had no guns at all if it had not been for President Kennedy's suggestion after watching a missile demonstration fail. Admiral Johnson's *Oklahoma City,* though presenting a bulky target, might have survived the August 2 battle by skillful firing of her three 6-inch and two 5-inch guns.

For the U. S. Navy the missile age had not truly arrived; but for the Russians it had. The *Maddox* seems to have been lucky that Moscow had not given Hanoi any of its guided-missile boats. In 1967 the Egyptians used two of them to sink an Israeli destroyer from beyond the latter's gun range. Following World War II, American PT men recommended such craft as the logical successor to the torpedo boat, a night weapon that seemed outmoded by the development of radar. Submariners, too, wanted anti-ship missiles. By 1964 the Defense Department had spent billions developing missiles, but one would have looked in vain for something that a ship could fire at another ship. Today, from 180 miles' distance, a Russian submarine could launch a guided missile at an American aircraft carrier. It is only a matter of time until other nations achieve the same capability, and so it must be hoped that the ECM people have done a better job than the missile people.

In 1964 North Vietnam was still patrolling its coast with torpedo boats, and later this kind of weapon was good enough to overwhelm the *Liberty* and the *Pueblo.* But these two were auxiliary vessels rather than true warships. The *Maddox* was a genuine, comparatively well-gunned man-of-war. Against a warship the torpedo boat traditionally was a weapon of the night, designed to achieve success through surprise. Yet three of them seemed to challenge the *Maddox* in broad daylight, as if willing to risk shellfire all the way from the horizon to close quarters. Were they in fact trying to sink the destroyer? Was that their original intention?

At the 1968 hearing, Secretary McNamara asserted that even the North Vietnamese admitted the attack. He went so far as to say, "I know of no claim that the attack of *Maddox* on August 2 did not occur." One would suppose that if Hanoi had made such a claim McNamara would have heard of it. One would suppose that the Foreign Relations Committee would have heard of it, too. Strangely, however, neither McNamara nor the committee took note of Hanoi's official position on the matter. That position was defined on August 20, 1964, when North Vietnam's Foreign Minister, Xuan Thuy, sent a message to the United Nations in response to the complaint submitted by Ambassador Stevenson. Xuan Thuy charged that the *Maddox* "opened fire in North Vietnam's territorial waters on patrol boats of the DRV, which were thus compelled to take action in self-defense."

The belief that Hanoi admitted the attack on the *Maddox* probably came from the August 5, 1964, statement by Colonel Ha Van Lau of the Vietnam People's Army, who headed Hanoi's liaison to the International Control Commission. In the portion of his statement dealing with the first incident, the colonel charged:

"Continuing their feverish plan to provoke and sabotage the North, on 30 July the U.S. imperialists and their henchmen dispatched warships to encroach upon North Vietnam's territorial waters and shell Hon Me and Hon Ngu islands, which are part of DRV [Democratic Republic of Vietnam] territory. On the night of 31 July–1 August, the U.S. imperialists again sent a destroyer to encroach upon North Vietnam's territorial waters in Quang Binh province. This warship had been cruising for two days, 1 and 2 August, between Hon Mat Island, Nghe An province, and Hon Me Island, Thanh Hoa province, to intimidate fishing boats of our people, openly infringing upon our territorial waters. On the afternoon of 2 August it encountered our patrol boats between Hon Me and Loc Truong (6½ miles north of Loc Chao) in our territorial waters. In the face of the provocations by the sea rovers, our patrol ships took action to defend our territorial waters and fishermen and chased the enemy ship out of our territorial waters. Afterward, our patrol ships returned to their base.

"This is what happened on the afternoon of 2 August. The U.S. imperialists are making a hue and cry about what they call an unprovoked attack by three torpedo boats of North Vietnam. They have made such a clamor to cover their own acts of provocation and sabotage, their violation of territorial waters and airspace, and their encroachment of the sovereignty and territory of the DRV."

The press at first dismissed this statement as the fuzzy account that it was. They certainly did not label it an admission of attack. Within a day or two, however, American officials in Saigon persuaded reporters that the statement did in fact amount to a confession. Perhaps it did. But the reader will recall that the patrol boats chased *Maddox* away from the coast long before the shooting started. Had that been known in 1964, American reporters probably would not so easily have accepted the official interpretation.

Prior to the firing of "warning shots," few men aboard the *Maddox* really believed that the North Vietnamese were making an attack. Captain Ogier was one who did, and he persuaded the men around him. But most of the destroyermen were puzzled. Said one of the officers who were topside: "For a long time it seemed like they [the torpedo boats] were just following us." After the warning shells exploded, the Communist boats charged directly at the destroyer, and everybody could see that they meant to attack. Captain Ogier's prediction came true. But could it have been the self-fulfilling kind?

Until four 5-inch shells bracketed the North Vietnamese craft, the principal items of evidence for attack were the COMVAN warning and the high-speed approach.

Both Commodore Herrick and Captain Ogier have described the high-speed approach as an "attack." Herrick told the Associated Press:

"The torpedoes are on the boat. The boat is on the way toward you on an intercept run. This is like pointing a gun as far as I'm concerned. The torpedo is sitting there and he's pointing it where it will hit you if he lets it go. That's an attack."

When the *Maddox* opened fire, the boats were not pointing at the ship. They were several miles away, nowhere near a torpedo launching position. That is why Herrick did not order *Maddox* to shoot *at* the boats but to fire "warning shots." He assumed that "warning shots" would be aimed to miss. Lieutenant Connell, however, did not want to waste any time getting his aim sharpened. He explained later: "They [the North Vietnamese craft] were coming in on us at a nice, high speed. I don't care how friendly they are when they come in at that high speed." Presumably, whether a fast-approaching boat was North Vietnamese, South Vietnamese, or Scotch-Irish, Pat Connell would have felt justified in shooting at it.

In itself, the torpedo boats' high speed does not prove anything. If the North Vietnamese had wished to approach the American ship for any purpose, peaceful or otherwise, they would have had to do so at high speed since the *Maddox* herself was moving at a brisk pace. Each side built up speed in response to the other. Furthermore, contrary to the general belief—even within the Navy—a torpedo boat does not usually make an attack with its throttle wide open, dashing at the intended victim in broad daylight (unless the victim is almost helpless, like the *Liberty*). Against a warship, the regular tactic is to sneak up in the dark, saving one's speed for the getaway. My search through a hundred years of torpedo boat literature produced only one instance prior to 1964 of a premeditated daylight charge on a warship. During World War I, an Italian skipper, Luigi Rizzo, in a specially equipped two-man boat, charged a whole fleet of Austrian warships moored in Trieste harbor. The attack failed, and Rizzo left Trieste the way he came in, lucky to survive the shells and bullets foaming the water on all sides.[2]

But one may ask if a torpedo boat *does* charge a warship at high speed, is that not a certain indication of hostile intent? The answer is that while high-speed approach is a reckless one, given the ancient human distrust of a rapidly approaching stranger, it does not necessarily indicate an attack. As an example, at the time of the Suez crisis of 1956, three Egyptian torpedo boats made high-speed passes at an American destroyer; the destroyer ignored them; and, eventually, the Egyptians went away.

In time of peace, it is impossible to tell from the mere approach of a torpedo boat, fast or slow, whether it is going to attack; and the same uncertainty, of course, applies to other vehicles of war. What is the skipper of a Russian ship to do when he is "buzzed" by an American airplane—open fire? The Soviet government complains that such incidents have occurred more than a thousand times, but the Soviet ships have not opened fire. Nor, in the reverse situation, have American skippers fired at Russian planes. And nobody shoots on those occasions when American and Russian destroyers dash at each other on a collision course, playing "chicken." The destroyers end up scraping hulls instead. Even more disquieting are the eerie tales of underwater collisions. They have been known to occur when, for

[2] James D. Sanderson, *Giants in War* (Princeton, N.J.: D. Van Nostrand, Inc., 1962), pages 179–80.

example, an American submarine is ordered to "wipe off" a Russian submarine trailing an American Polaris vessel.

Only a couple of days prior to her battle of Sunday, August 2, *Maddox* herself was buzzed by fast boats. It will be recalled that on Friday three unidentified craft, looking like torpedo boats, came rushing down from the north while the destroyer was tied to the *Ashtabula*. On that occasion the *Maddox* did not open fire. The ship did not even go to GQ, although she might have if the commodore had not been able to identify the strange craft promptly.

On Sunday other factors were more important than the high-speed approach. The *Maddox* was no longer in "friendly water." She was loitering in unfriendly water, and from the North Vietnamese point of view the destroyer's presence was both provocative and illegal. Furthermore, the COMVAN warned of hostility ashore. For such reasons the commodore and the captain were inclined to anticipate attack when fast-moving radar contacts began to close in.

In these circumstances, Commodore Herrick and Captain Ogier could not be blamed for taking steps to protect their ship. They were responsible for three hundred American lives. Some kind of action was needed. But what? In support of what he did, Ogier later referred to Navy regulation 0611, which states in part:

"To the extent which the situation demands, the senior officer present shall be prepared for action, and shall guard against surprise attack. With the means at his disposal, he shall put into effect such measures as are necessary to minimize the possibility of the undetected approach of hostile air, surface, or subsurface forces, and shall take all action possible to destroy such hostile forces prior to their reaching attack positions."

But how can one be *sure* that approaching forces are hostile; and, if one is sure, how can it be *proved?*

The U. S. Navy had been patrolling Communist coastlines for many years, but Herrick and Ogier had no experience with torpedo boats, no instructions on how to deal with their approach (slow speed or high speed), and no practice in firing at this kind of target. With respect to the Tonkin Gulf patrol, the advice of higher command had been, "Don't sweat the North Vietnamese" and, when that proved insufficient, "Be careful." On the spur of the moment, Herrick and Ogier were forced to improvise. Drawing on their Academy backgrounds and combined four decades of naval experience, they chose a retiring tactic, which proved tactically effective. They also chose to fire "warning shots."

What is a "warning shot"? At the 1968 hearing, Senator Fulbright asked whether there was such a thing in naval tactics. Neither Secretary McNamara nor General Wheeler could make a definite reply, although they were flanked by a naval adviser, Captain Henry B. Sweitzer. General Wheeler, to his regret, observed that "as a precautionary measure, he [the commander of the *Maddox*] might very well have fired warning shots rather than directly at them." Fulbright, having read the AP interview with Lieutenant Connell, then sprang his trap: the ship *did* fire directly at them, he said. Even Secretary McNamara lost some of his steely composure. Excitedly, he asked over and over again for the name of the gunnery officer so that he could check the report.

General Wheeler, not unlike many a red-blooded moviegoer, had it fixed in his mind that to put a shot over the bow was a regular naval practice. Captain Sweitzer apparently felt the same way; and, after some research, the Defense Department advised me that warning shots were "an old custom, like a policeman firing his pistol into the air."

Actually, warning shots are more of an *old problem* than an old custom; and sometimes, as we have seen, they are not at all like the shots that a policeman fires into the air. The truly old custom of opening communication was to hail by voice and, if necessary, send a small boat. For example, on June 22, 1807, when the English frigate HMS *Leopard* wished to communicate with the American frigate USS *Chesapeake*, the English vessel hailed the American and then sent a messenger in a boat. (It happened that *Leopard* later attacked the *Chesapeake*, but the hailing procedure still demonstrates what was normal.) That the warning shot even in the days of wood and sail was more of a problem than a custom is borne out by an incident involving the HMS *Beagle*, a 10-gun brig surveying the South American coast. The incident was recorded by not only the *Beagle*'s captain, Robert Fitzroy, but by the ship's official naturalist, Charles Darwin. On August 2, 1832, off Buenos Aires, an Argentine ship fired a blank shot at the approaching *Beagle*. The *Beagle* did not stop, and the

Argentine, trying to enforce a medical inspection, next put a live shot over the English sail. Such "uncivilized" behavior enraged Captain Fitzroy, who never did heave to and who later dispatched an English frigate to deal with the "misconduct" of the Argentine.

In the twentieth century naval vessels still occasionally fire warning shots, and the recipients still are enraged by them. Senator Warren G. Magnuson, Democrat of Washington, has complained of how Latin American warships (supplied by the United States) fire over the bows of American tuna boats. The Latin aim is not good, it is said, and such reckless behavior is liable to cause a serious incident. Nor does the State Department approve of warning shots when employed by foreigners. About two weeks before the *Maddox*'s encounter of August 2, 1964, the State Department protested the action of a Russian patrol vessel, which allegedly put three shots over the bow of an American grain ship. The Russians denied the charge. Their skipper, said the Communists, fired only "signal rockets," doing so after other signals had been ignored. One could hardly imagine Washington's state of mind if the Russians fired over the bow of an American naval vessel.

The fact that warning shots are known to cause misunderstanding and make trouble could explain why the U. S. Navy has established no procedure for firing them. I asked four Navy officers, including a weapons officer, how to fire warning shots, and I received the following four answers: fire long, fire short, fire to one side, and fire blanks (suggested by the gun boss). Nobody recommended aiming live shells directly at the vessel to be warned. In any case, the situation has become increasingly precarious since that day in 1832 when an Argentine cannon ball plopped into the water, infuriating Captain Robert Fitzroy.

Since 1832 much progress has been made in the technology of communications; nevertheless, no senator pointed out to Secretary McNamara that *Maddox* possessed other means of communicating with the North Vietnamese than by shooting at them. The ship could have signaled by flag or flashing light, using the International Code first established in 1857. American destroyers found these techniques adequate in 1962 when they intercepted ships carrying Russian missiles to Cuba. In this case, the destroyers reportedly were supervised by Attorney General Robert F. Kennedy, who knew that the President did not want to embarrass the Russians more than necessary.[3] The destroyers, therefore, made use of visual signals. By both flag and flashing light, the intercepting destroyers showed the two-letter combination Oscar November: "Heave to; stop at once." They did not use the stronger Oscar Lima combination: "Heave to or I will open fire on you," which was how the North Koreans addressed the *Pueblo* in 1968. The Kennedy brothers, both ex-Navy men, judged it wise to speak softly while carrying history's biggest stick.

Two-letter signals such as Oscar November are considered urgent and they require an immediate reply. Even more urgent are some one-letter signals that the *Maddox* could have used. The ship could have hoisted a red-and-white checkered flag, the Uniform signal, which means, "You are standing into danger." That is the message the warning shots were meant to convey. Alternatively, *Maddox* could have flown the Xray (*sic*) flag, a blue cross on a white field: "Stop carrying out your intentions and watch for my signals." The international rules permit the Uniform signal to be transmitted also by flashing light (though not the Xray signal). In clear weather, the blinker standard on Navy ships can be seen all the way to the horizon, even in daylight.

Commodore Herrick and Captain Ogier never discussed the possibility of making a visual signal. A half-dozen signalmen, standing near the bridge with nothing to do, did not discuss the possibility either. Asked why, one of them explained to me: "There was nobody to signal." A signal, these men believed, was something that one sent to a friend, not to a Communist. Their attitude becomes more understandable if one looks at the training manuals available at the time.[4] Neither the basic nor the advanced signaling manual gave any

[3] Informed sources say that the Chief of Naval Operations, Admiral George W. Anderson, thenceforth complained often and bitterly about "civilian interference" in naval matters. For a chilling account of how Secretary McNamara tried and failed to find out what the Navy's blockading procedure would be, see Elie Abel, *The Missile Crisis* (Philadelphia: J. B. Lippincott, 1966). According to Abel, Admiral Anderson refused to explain in detail how the interception would be handled. Instead, the admiral waved a book of regulations in McNamara's face saying, "It's all in there." Because of this quarrel and disagreement over the TFX fighter-bomber (which Anderson, to his credit, opposed), Admiral Anderson was not reappointed CNO in 1963.

[4] *Signalman 3 & 2*, published in 1961; *Signalman 1 & C*, published in 1963.

example of communicating with a Communist ship. The basic manual did include a chapter on international signaling, but, with respect to foreign navies, it mentioned only those of countries allied with the United States.

Historically, naval men have been slow and unimaginative with respect to signaling. The visibility of a flashing light was well known; yet the sun-illuminated blinker (heliograph) was not invented until after the electric telegraph. Why? Because there was no Morse code with which to convey a message. Though one usually associates it with the image of a bell-bottomed sailor waving flags up and down, the semaphore, too, originated on land—a series of wigwag stations erected from hilltop to hilltop speeded up Napoleon's communications.

Coded flags, such as the one for "You are standing into danger," perhaps were a naval invention, but it was not until the eighteenth century that an English officer, Captain Richard Kempenfelt, developed a practical and comprehensive system. Designing the signals was easy; getting them accepted was not. Two admirals rejected Kempenfelt's proposal; it finally was accepted in 1780 by another pioneer in signaling, Admiral Howe of the Channel Fleet.

The argument might be advanced that if the *Maddox* had tried signaling she would have lost valuable time and consequently, perhaps, the battle as well. There are three points to be made in reply. First, the ship was supposed to be gathering intelligence, and to shoot at the local people unnecessarily would confuse the situation that the *Maddox* was sent to observe. Second, if the COMVAN intercepted a message ordering an attack, the normal security procedure would be to conceal this intelligence capability by pretending ignorance of the enemy's intention. Third, the *Maddox* had plenty of time in which to signal. The ship could have started flashing her blinker at 14,000 yards, the distance of the horizon. Had the Communist craft continued to close, warning shots (preferably blank) could have been fired at 10,000 yards, if not sooner. From every standpoint, therefore, visual signaling would have been preferable.

Following the action of August 2, 1964, the Navy ought to have taken notice of its deficiency in signaling, but the facts were covered up, and three years later thirty-four American seamen died as the USS *Liberty* and Israeli forces failed to communicate with each other. As the attacker, Israel bore the responsibility of making a correct identification. But both sides were slow to signal, and when they got around to it, neither side knew the correct international procedure. As a further complication, when the Israeli torpedo boats showed up, the *Liberty*'s blinker was intermittently obscured by smoke resulting from an earlier air attack.

One of the Israeli sailors wrote a newspaper article about the attack, in which he said that the torpedo boats tried to engage the *Liberty*'s attention by firing over her bow. The American skipper did not recognize these or any other shells as a friendly signal.

Seven months after the *Liberty* was torpedoed, the case of the *Pueblo* involved another muddle in the lost art of signaling. Before her capture, the elint ship reported to higher command that she had hoisted flags protesting, "I am in international waters." A year later this report was contradicted by the ship's signalman, Wendell Leach, when he testified in the Court of Inquiry. Leach was going to make such a signal, as ordered by the captain, but he couldn't find the flags. "There was another signal that I sent," he told the startled Admirals of the Court. He did not remember what that signal was. Captain Bucher disagreed. He was sure that the proper signal had been raised, although earlier he had testified that the *Pueblo*'s signals seemed to confuse the Communists, thus buying some time for the ship to edge away.

The predicament of the *Pueblo*'s signalman becomes understandable if one takes a look at the International Code book. There is no simple way of saying, "I am in international waters." I leafed through the book for twenty minutes without being able to put the whole sentence together. I then telephoned one of the Navy's chief signalmen. Offhand, he didn't know how to say it, either. We guessed that a dozen flags would be needed. Whatever Signalman Leach told the North Koreans appears destined to remain a mystery for all time.

As for the *Maddox,* while the ship did not signal, she indicated in other ways that she was preparing for battle. The American warship was building up speed in response to the North Vietnamese approach, and she leveled eight gun barrels in their direction. Yet the Communists kept coming, and they, too, failed to signal. If their intention was peaceful, they ought to have said so.

Up to the time of open fire, the *Maddox*'s best evidence of attack might have been the COMVAN warning or warnings. At the 1968 hearing, Secretary McNamara told the senators: "North Vietnamese reports of their plans had previously been obtained from an intelligence source." How clear were these reports—the texts of which remain very highly classified? Did an intercepted message actually order an attack on the destroyer? Some of the enlisted men with the box bragged later: "We knew we were going to be attacked." One of the men that I talked to recalled that the intelligence became available at "10 A.M.," and that at noontime the situation was tense enough to keep him from leaving the box for lunch. Nevertheless, if the *Maddox* really expected to fight for her life, the ship's defensive preparations were curiously incomplete. So were the *Ticonderoga*'s. Nobody persuaded Admiral Moore that Sindbad was in real danger. Furthermore, after the battle was over, briefings in Washington did not portray the advance intelligence as having been particularly firm. Senator Morse and Senator Lausche, although they differed on other points, agreed that the destroyer had some kind of warning but no certain indication of attack. The Pentagon concluded that the "attack" was an isolated incident, possibly resulting from a "miscalculation" or the "impulsive act of a local commander." Anonymous officials said that *Maddox*'s "warning shots" might have "confused" the Communists.

Could the "impulsive" local commander have been the Communist who got "confused" by the "warning shots"? What then of his orders to attack, which seemed so cut-and-dried when Secretary McNamara testified in 1968? If in 1964 there was no doubt concerning North Vietnamese orders to attack, a lot of things ought to have been said and done differently. Beforehand, the Navy should have made better preparations for dealing with the attack. Afterward, the Defense Department should have been certain that the attack was premeditated.

Though the intelligence firmed up in 1968, allegedly indicating attack, it softened again two years later when Admiral Moorer talked to the Senate Armed Services Committee, before his confirmation as Chairman of the Joint Chiefs. A hard-core dove, Democrat Stephen M. Young of Ohio, wanted to know a few things about the Tonkin Gulf, including why *Maddox*'s patrol was not canceled after Commodore Herrick reported that he faced an "unacceptable risk." Moorer said that the information forwarded by Herrick was "ambiguous."[5] He

---

[5] Senate Armed Services Committee, *Nomination of Admiral Thomas H. Moorer,* page 32.

added ". . . that there was no reason to conclude that the North Vietnamese would attack a U.S. ship on patrol on the high seas which obviously was neither hostile nor interfering with international navigation." The former CINCPACFLT still thought that the attack was the "impulsive act of a local commander," whom he termed "irresponsible."[6] (Moorer, by the way, in a written statement insisted that "the *Maddox* did not open fire until she was under a torpedo attack by the North Vietnamese PT boats . . ." Records and testimony, said the admiral, make that "abundantly clear.")

If premeditated, as McNamara had implied in 1968, the torpedo boats' daylight charge on the *Maddox* was not only unusual—possibly unique—in naval history, it was also unnecessary.[7] Surely planners of the attack could have waited a few hours for darkness to fall. The destroyer obviously meant to stay in the area for a while. Furthermore, why had the North Vietnamese employed only three boats? They had sixteen torpedo craft in all; and, as close as Hon Me, two gunboats were sitting idle. Possibly another three torpedo boats were also anchored at the cove—officers of the *Maddox* were not sure that the three in the attack were the same as the three observed a few hours before. Nobody had noticed radar masts on the original trio.[8] It was bad planning indeed if the North Vietnamese made their attack with two to five boats hanging back at Hon Me. It also seemed as though the attackers were not properly armed. Only three torpedoes were observed for certain, out of a possible six; and the enemy lacked tracer bullets for his machine guns.

Of course, poor tactics do not prove innocence any more than a

[6] *Ibid.*, pages 21 and 33.

[7] There is a precedent for an unpremeditated daylight charge—on three warships, two of them cruisers. Early in the Korean War, one American and two British vessels surprised at dawn four North Korean torpedo boats and two gunboats. The Communist craft during the night had been escorting ammunition trawlers. "As the cruisers put on speed to intercept the enemy, the torpedo boats, with more bravery than discretion, turned to attack . . . The final score of the engagement was three torpedo boats and both gunboats destroyed, and two prisoners taken . . ." See James A. Field, Jr., page 61.

[8] This information comes from interviews. In support of it, I could cite the remarks of Admiral William P. Mack, Navy Chief of Information, at his press conference of August 4, 1964. In reference to the torpedo boats sighted earlier in the day, Admiral Mack said, "Whether they were the same PTs that attacked here [pointing at a map] or not is not known." This quotation comes from the press conference transcript; I did not see it in any newspaper.

high-speed approach proves guilt. The North Vietnamese have never demonstrated any gift for naval tactics. In later years, American ships operated in the Tonkin Gulf almost at will. The Communists have never managed to sink one, not even with a mine.

One could imagine a number of things the three torpedo boats planned to do. They might have intended observation, harassment, perhaps a warning to cruise farther from shore—backed up by force if necessary. Their commander might have declared his intention to reconnoiter, but, secretly hoped to draw fire that would justify an attack. Many possibilities come to mind. Assuming, however, that an attack was ordered, the three boats might have succeeded if in some manner they could have moved in close—say, by successfully using the fishing junks as cover. Only a few hours earlier, when five patrol craft went by, the *Maddox* had appeared somnolent. The ship, far from going to GQ, continued to take her ease. She probably looked an easy target.

Whether the North Vietnamese really planned an attack that Sunday afternoon was not seriously discussed at the 1968 hearing. Everybody assumed that Hanoi had confessed. Besides, it was the "second attack" that precipitated the Tonkin Gulf resolution, and that was the senators' major complaint. Nevertheless, the hearing produced a new piece of evidence for the "first attack." The Defense Secretary disclosed that:

". . . U.S. forces in the 3½ years which have elapsed since the August 1964 incidents have captured several North Vietnamese naval personnel. These personnel were extensively interrogated. One of these, captured in July 1966, stated he had taken part in the August 2, 1964, attack on the *Maddox,* and his account of that attack coincided with our own observations."

Senator Morse, who never questioned the reality of the Sunday attack, later revealed that this prisoner was the torpedo boat squadron's executive officer, and that he had written up the August 2 action report.

Evidence like the above would seem to be conclusive except for two things. First, very little of the Navy's record of interrogation has been made public, and, as will be seen later, Secretary McNamara had a way of quoting very loosely what prisoners had to say about the Tonkin Gulf. Second, McNamara said that the prisoner's testimony "coincided with our own observations." What observations?

Nearly all of the Defense Department's observations have turned out to be inaccurate: torpedo craft were not first encountered 30 miles from land; the North Vietnamese did not shoot first (whether one counts *Maddox*'s "warning shots" or not; no boat was left dead in the water; the *Maddox* was not on a routine patrol; and the attack, if real, was not unprovoked. What did the prisoner have to say about those observations? The Defense Secretary originally thought that the battle resulted from a misunderstanding, or from the impulsive act of a local commander, and in 1970 Admiral Moorer still thought so. Did the prisoner agree with that? To McNamara it was the "second attack" that proved aggressive designs. From one part of the Navy's interrogation that became public, we learn that the prisoner did not agree with that. He denied vigorously that there had been any August 4 attack.

As for Hanoi's view of the August 2 battle, authorities there never protested loudly about it. The Colonel Ha and Xuan Thuy statements have already been mentioned. On other occasions, Radio Hanoi has claimed a great victory while talking ambiguously about how the shooting started. North Vietnamese actions have been ambiguous, too. On Friday, August 7, President Ho awarded decorations to *two* naval units for their work of the previous Sunday.[9] What happened to the third boat? Did it vanish with all hands? Or did its commander overstep his instructions? During the following week, August 12, a North Vietnamese domestic broadcast reported details of the battle in boastful and rather lighthearted terms. In my opinion, the available text of the account, which comes through the CIA's monitoring system, implies that the torpedo boats intended to drive the destroyer away from land and expected a fight in the process. An excerpt follows:

"Because the U. S. Navy destroyer has the strength of long-range firepower, we had to move in close to it. Lively, mobile, witty, and courageous, we were determined to fulfill our duty to protect the

[9] According to Radio Hanoi, President Ho gave two decorations of the 2nd Class and eight of the 3rd Class to ten anti-aircraft units and naval units for destroying "eight" American planes on August 5 and driving a destroyer from territorial water on August 2. Thus it appears that two naval units received the two decorations of the 2nd Class. Supporting that inference is an August 13 broadcast by Radio Peking which, referring to the Hanoi press, announced that 2nd Class awards were presented to naval forces.

tranquil waters of our fatherland. Raising high this determination, the small boats of our combatants increased their speed, gliding over the water as though in flight, and waved signal banners and wished one another success. At 1500 hours the U.S. destroyer, which was identified as the *Maddox* . . ." (here a portion of the broadcast reportedly was indistinct). "It was zigzagging north of Hon Me island near the mouth of the Day River [15 miles north of Loc Chao]. Immediately, boat group X, going full speed, sped over the waves toward the destroyer. Upon seeing our boats, the enemy destroyer immediately attacked. Like thunder, its guns fired one after another, causing high columns of water to spout around our boats. But our boats kept silent and continued to speed swiftly against the enemy ship . . ."

The radio went on to say that *Maddox,* bewildered, fled territorial water at top speed, calling for help. *Five* jets came, said Hanoi. One allegedly burst into flames; another fled in a trail of black smoke. "When the third jet aircraft was hit," exulted the radio, "the two others were panic-stricken, fired innumerable bullets into the sea . . . and finally flew away." The Vietnamese language broadcast mentioned no damage to the torpedo boats.

It was not until August 20 that Foreign Minister Xuan Thuy announced that the torpedo boats were "compelled to take action in self-defense." The Foreign Minister neglected to mention what kind of mission the torpedo boats were supposed to carry out.

Perhaps Xuan Thuy's statement of August 20 was a self-serving afterthought. The torpedo boats might have been ordered to drive *Maddox* from territorial water, using force if necessary. The decision to pursue the ship so far into the Gulf could have been the impulse of a local commander, who—intentionally or not—baited the ship into firing first. If, on the other hand, the Communist high command planned to sink the *Maddox,* wherever she might be found, the North Vietnamese undertook an enterprise of great consequence in a casual and slipshod manner—unlike their Viet Cong comrades in the South who have conducted so many hit-and-run raids with careful planning and spectacular success.

For the American people the most significant aspect of the August 2 incident has been the way the Johnson administration reported it. Under the circumstances, there should have been nothing very surprising about a clash between American and North Vietnamese naval craft; a virtual state of war existed in the Tonkin Gulf. Yet Washington's version of the battle made it completely incomprehensible, as if Asian Communists were suddenly liable to go mad, like dogs in the noonday sun.

For what reason were the elements of provocation concealed? It was no secret to the North Vietnamese that the *Maddox* ventured closer to land than 12 miles. The American people had a right to that information and would probably not have complained about it. Most Americans believed, though incorrectly, that the 12-mile limit was an outrageous Communist whim. Very likely the public would have applauded the Navy's effort to uphold the "traditional" 3-mile limit. Nor were the gunboat raids secret to the North Vietnamese. Why should the fact of such "South Vietnamese" operations be kept from the American people? Far from being embarrassed about the gunboats, Premier Khanh and other South Vietnamese officials were eager to brag about them. American officials wanted Khanh and his friends to keep quiet.

As for the U. S. Navy's public relations, they were not helped by the Johnson administration's account of the August 2 battle. If a more accurate version had been released, the Navy still would have gotten credit for doing a good job. A lone destroyer, after all, defended herself adequately from what seemed to be a surprise attack by three torpedo boats. After she won the surface engagement, four planes carried out a swift, on-the-spot retaliation (or "positive reply"). The public would have derived satisfaction from these facts, and there would have been less critical concern as to whether any of the Communist boats had been sunk. It could have been said that *Maddox* was "patrolling" in the Gulf. There was no need to say that the ship was on a "routine patrol," which she was not. True, the Navy might have come in for a little criticism on the timing of the patrol—the *Maddox* ought not to have entered the Gulf shortly after gunboat raids. In the future, the admirals would have had to step more carefully, and that could have saved a lot of trouble. Some extra caution would have prevented the tragedies of the *Liberty* and the *Pueblo,* both of which patrolled, unprotected, within combat zones. Finally, in one of the professional naval journals, some retired officer might have pointed out that warning shots were getting to be outmoded as a means of communication—especially since the inert cannon ball had been replaced by explosive shells—and maybe the time had come to take a look at the International Code.

For reasons best known to itself, the Johnson administration did not respect the people's right to know. Nor did it respect the Congress's right to know. In secret briefings, members of the Congress were given a cover story very similar to the one dispensed in public. The secret information was more detailed, but not much more accurate. I have found no evidence of a Navy man being present at the August 6 hearings. The House Foreign Affairs Committee never published a transcript of its meeting, but the Senate Foreign Relations Committee did; and according to the text of the senators' hearing, the naval action was explained by Secretary McNamara (an ex-Army man), General Wheeler (an Army man), and even by Secretary Rusk (an ex-Army man) whose primary task was to explain the requested Congressional resolution. The absence of Admiral McDonald, the Chief of Naval Operations, might have been related to his reputation for "unvarnished honesty."[10] Many are the anecdotes illustrating McDonald's penchant for uttering the blunt truth.[11] In any event, the Congress accepted as adequate non-naval sources of information, and in so doing did not respect sufficiently its own right to know, particularly if one considers the perplexing nature of the Tonkin Gulf incidents.

Nothing could shake senatorial complacency, not even a warning from Senator Morse, who asserted that the administration's story was very questionable. The Oregonian's opposition to the Tonkin Gulf resolution was not based simply on his knowledge of constitutional law and his dislike of the administration's policy in Vietnam. A friend in the Pentagon had told him that things in the Tonkin Gulf were not what they seemed. Late one night a man "still in uniform" telephoned the senator. The *Maddox,* he said, had not been where the administration said she was, and her mission was not what the

---

[10] Captain John N. Horrocks, Jr., "The Art, Science, and Innocence Involved in Becoming Chief of Naval Operations," *U. S. Naval Institute Proceedings* (January 1970).

[11] Concerning the start of the *Pueblo*-type elint operation, Admiral McDonald has been quoted as saying: "I remember feeling, 'Well, okay, let's get two or three of these damn spitkits, then wait and see how they're paying out before we go for the whole program.'" Trevor Armbrister, *A Matter of Accountability* (New York: Coward-McCann, Inc., 1970), page 84.

administration claimed it to have been. "Get the logs," urged the man on the telephone. For Morse the warning was sufficient. At Thursday's hearing, he asked that *"Maddox*'s log" (no doubt thinking of the deck log) be made available. Secretary McNamara refused, though the log was not even classified. A heated quarrel ensued. "That meeting was no tea party," Morse told me. The argument Morse referred to did not appear in the published transcript, which further angered the senator.

As a maverick, anti-war senator, Wayne Morse could not expect any favors from the Defense Department, nor even a routine respect for his rights. But another senator, a loyal conservative who demanded the facts, didn't get them, either. This was Frank J. Lausche, Ohio Democrat, who strongly supported the Tonkin Gulf resolution against Morse's attacks on it. At the August 6 hearing, Lausche told McNamara and Wheeler: "I want to get clear in the record and in my own mind exactly what happened on the 2nd." Lausche got the same cover story that Morse did.

The Johnson administration did a skillful job of carrying water on both shoulders. It opposed speculation while, at the same time, it portrayed the Tonkin Gulf as a great Oriental mystery. To this day, the U. S. Government has suggested no motive for the North Vietnamese attack.

After Sunday's battle, men of the *Maddox* wondered why the North Vietnamese were "hopping mad" at them. Years later the destroyermen recalled their bewilderment, saying things like:

"It was an amazing attack. Very aggressive and determined . . . We couldn't understand it. We hadn't been doing anything that serious."

After the patrol was over, light began to dawn. The destroyermen read in a news magazine about the alleged gunboat raids. Then they understood better the situation around Hon Me. "A lot of people," said one ex-*Maddox* officer, "began to wonder if somebody wasn't behind it all—maybe the CIA."

During the Tonkin Gulf controversy of the winter of 1967–68, senators made much of the gunboat raids without, however, uncovering information on exactly who had been responsible for them—other than the fact that CINCPACFLT and MACV were to make sure that the gunboats and the destroyer did not "interfere" with each other. The Foreign Relations Committee heard from an anonymous informant, who seemed knowledgeable about the Pentagon, that the CIA was involved. I do not know to what extent the committee investigated CIA responsibility. It could be significant that Senator Fulbright at last managed to become a member of the select group of lawmakers who are supposed to supervise the cloak-and-dagger agency. This was one of Fulbright's long-sought goals, since the CIA has much to do with the making of foreign policy. (Later, the senator complained that the supervisors didn't meet very often.)

Another gap in the public record has to do with alleged provocations, other than the gunboat raids, which somehow never figured in the Tonkin Gulf controversy so far as the American people were concerned. If one reads the transcript of Radio Hanoi, it appears that the index of provocation took a record-breaking jump during the months just before the *Maddox*'s patrol and even *during* the patrol.

By Radio Hanoi's calendar, provocations were few during the first several months of 1964. In early March four South Vietnamese frogmen were caught trying to land at Quang Khe; there was nothing very unusual about this. At the end of March Hanoi protested two American destroyers violating territorial water along the coast of Nghe An province. This must have been the De Soto patrol that was hampered by rainy weather. (Though Radio Hanoi complained about two ships, it gave the number of only one—DD 885, which would have been the *John R. Craig,* a "long hull" commissioned in 1945.) In April six South Vietnamese were caught parachuting into the mountains of Nghe An province. It was in late May that alleged provocations started to become more varied and more frequent. The expanded anti-infiltration patrol conducted by motorized South Vietnamese junks led to clashes with North Vietnamese small craft, which allegedly were chased into Communist water. Then on June 30 the North Vietnamese claimed capture of another South Vietnamese commando team.

Alleged provocations increased considerably in July. On the 8th South Vietnamese aircraft are alleged to have raided the town of Linh Phung on the North Vietnamese side of the Demilitarized Zone; on the 13th South Vietnamese aircraft hit Tan Binh across the DMZ, and an air-directed artillery barrage followed.[12] On the 25th South Vietnamese boats reportedly seized eleven North Vietnamese fishermen. On the night of July 30–31 "U.S.-South Vietnamese" gunboats fired on the islands of Hon Me and Hon Ngu. On the 31st the destroyer *Maddox* entered the Gulf, sauntering slowly up the North Vietnamese coast.

On Saturday, August 1, *Maddox* was patrolling "fat, dumb, and happy" along the Gulf side of Nghe An province when, according to Radio Hanoi, *American* aircraft strafed two targets the far side of the province, along the border with Laos. These aircraft, said Hanoi, flew from the direction of Laos and were T-28 fighter-bombers (a type of propeller plane used by the CIA). They allegedly attacked Nam Can border post and the village of Noong De. Allegedly American planes again hit Nam Can on Sunday, while men of the *Maddox,* oblivious, were enjoying their holiday routine. Loitering within plain view of bases and fortifications, the American destroyer offered a tempting target for revenge.

On Sunday Radio Hanoi protested the alleged Saturday raid, but this news was pretty well swamped by *Maddox*'s astonishing fight with torpedo boats. Some American papers mentioned the Communist report briefly, along with a denial from the State Department, which said that reports of gunboat raids and air raids were "without foundation." The State Department had "no knowledge of any such attacks being made by anyone." Whether or not the State Department had knowledge of gunboat raids, the Defense Department later admitted that they were real. What would have happened if the Foreign Relations Committee had investigated the alleged air attacks?

The State Department did not have to deny the alleged air attack of Sunday August 2, because apparently nobody asked about it. I have never found any report of this attack in the American press. Hanoi did not complain about it until August 5, and subsequent editions of American newspapers were to be jammed with details of the

[12] It might be worth noting that in 1962 American "air commandos" began flying planes with South Vietnamese markings on them. These were part of the daredevil Special Operations Force which in 1970 tried to rescue American prisoners in North Vietnam. See Donald Robinson, "America's Air Guerrillas —Will They Stop Future Vietnams?", *Parade* magazine (January 31, 1971).

carrier-based air raids, the President's television speech, Tuesday night's torpedo assault, and so forth. Still, the alleged air raids of August 1 and August 2 *ought* to have been big news. They were the first that Hanoi blamed specifically on the United States rather than on "U.S.-South Vietnamese" forces.

Left out of the calendar of alleged provocations are some other events that disturbed Hanoi. Among them were the Navy's air operations in Laos, President Johnson's rejection of negotiations, Saigon's "To the North!" threats, and President Johnson's announcement of more "advisers" going to South Vietnam. Hanoi accused Washington of escalating the war in South Vietnam and Laos, of preparing a bombing campaign against North Vietnam, and of planning to invade North Vietnam and Cambodia.

In short, the North Vietnamese were angry enough to harass or sink the *Maddox*. It must have been galling, indeed, to suffer daily attacks while an American warship lazily drew figure eights within sight of land, apparently assisting in plans for future assaults and observing the results of previous ones.

But one wonders what the North Vietnamese hoped to achieve by bothering the *Maddox*. Certainly an attack would be followed by increased American naval activity, including, perhaps, severe retaliation. By playing their cards carefully, the North Vietnamese might score some propaganda points. But their propaganda was too little and too late. Is it possible that the North Vietnamese, with their fleet of patrol craft, hoped to bar the U. S. Navy from the Tonkin Gulf? If so, they gave up very easily. For years afterward, despite heavy bombing from carriers in the Gulf, they did little to bother the U. S. Navy.

As of May 1964, the U. S. Navy found cause to be provoked, too. On the second day of the month, just before violent clashes began accelerating north of the DMZ, the Viet Cong attacked an American ship. The guerrillas planted a bomb near the bottom of the USNS *Card,* an aircraft transport vessel; ignominiously, the former "baby flattop" (small aircraft carrier) sank in the Saigon River. Seven men were injured; nobody died. The *Card* was floating again in a few days. To the American people, the thought of jungle guerrillas sinking an "aircraft carrier" was more humorous than significant. The Navy could not have been pleased, for example, when *Time* magazine exhorted its readers to "Remember the *Card!*" To the Navy the incident had serious implications: before long American warships stopped calling at the South Vietnamese capital. The last such visitor was the cruiser *Oklahoma City,* bringing Admiral Johnson to confer with Ambassador Taylor.

Unnamed American officials declared that the sinking of the *Card* was instigated by North Vietnam; at the time, Hanoi was complaining about a build-up of American air power in South Vietnam. Speculatively, the Pacific Fleet had now acquired its own motive for a show of force along the North Vietnamese coast. As a further speculation, somebody in North Vietnam, if only a torpedo boat commander, might have wondered whether he could clear the Tonkin Gulf as effectively as the Viet Cong were clearing Saigon harbor.

Chapter IX

An "Uneventful" Day

As Firefighter winged north to help Sindbad, Jehovah began recycling his planes, landing the target-shooters in the air and getting a large force fueled and armed. Some of these planes, at least, were launched northward after the *Maddox*'s battle was over. What were they supposed to do? I do not know. In any case, they were called back. As one possibility, perhaps somebody hoped to get approval for a retaliatory strike. For a month the carrier had been practicing strike exercises on a contingency basis.

An hour or two passed between the time Firefighter left the *Maddox* and the time a few more planes showed up. Two men who were with the box remember that the GQ had just been secured when, to everybody's surprise, a couple of propeller planes were "right on top of the ship," undetected by radar. The crew ran back to battle stations. Then the intruders were recognized as friendly, and the ship relaxed once more.

As Winston Churchill remarked, there is nothing more exhilarating than to be shot at without result, and men of the *Maddox* would have agreed with him. The encounter with torpedo boats lifted the destroyermen to a high state of morale. They had taken part in an old fashioned ship-to-ship battle; they had won it; and they had come through without a scratch. It was like a boyhood dream. A number of sailors declared that they would enjoy having that kind of workout every week.

The ship's only personnel casualties were several cases of heat exhaustion down in the engineering spaces. As for damage to the destroyer, *Maddox*'s own gunfire did more harm than the enemy. A broken electrical cable had to be repaired. SPS-40, the Humpty Dumpty of radar, got put back together again. A few cracked and broken windowpanes remained as the ship's major battle loss.

North Vietnamese fire accomplished nothing more serious than to leave a ½-inch hole in the pedestal of the After Director (which, after the patrol was over, became a popular backdrop for memorial photographs). Below the Director, on the deck of the 3-inch ammunition handling compartment, gunners found the smoking fragments of an armor-piercing slug. The gunners wanted to keep the fragments as souvenirs but had to turn them in, and senior officers decided that the three pieces of metal would be retained, one each, by the commodore, captain, and executive officer. News of the battle relic continued up the chain of command, and somebody, so men of the *Maddox* heard, conceived the idea of giving it to the President. The reassembled slug, encased in plastic, ended up at the Pentagon; in later years it served as Exhibit A in lectures to suspicious senators. The reality of one battle could be proved. I have been told, however, that the bullet is a military secret and cannot be shown to the general public.[1] If so, the Navy had better start looking for a couple of other secret slugs. They were found abaft the COMVAN and escaped official cognizance.

The North Vietnamese were poor shots, firing too high or too low. Their lack of tracer bullets helps to explain this. Officially released information said that the boats closed to 5000 yards, which would have been 2000 yards or more within the maximum range of a heavy machine gun. Former *Maddox* officers assert that, according to fire-control data, at least one boat came within 1700 yards of the destroyer—a bit less than one land mile. That was the forward boat stunned by a 5-inch shell.

The experience of battle not only exhilarated the crew but drew the men together into a friendlier, closer-knit group. After the noise died away, Chief Quartermaster McRae looked around the bridge and sensed that something had changed. Realizing what it was, the hoarse-voiced chief declared, "Well, you're all men-of-warsmen now!" Until that afternoon only a few old-timers like McRae had

[1] Surfacing the bullet would help to determine its caliber, which has been reported as 12.7-millimeter and 14.5 millimeter.

seen combat. Now all were united in the ancient brotherhood of warriors.

Captain Ogier underwent a complete change of status, becoming a popular hero for having given the order to open fire. The men vowed that "Herbie" was "all right." Anybody who said, "Yes, but . . ." got stared down.

Word of the COMVAN's warning spread throughout the ship, though it shouldn't have. The "mad box" turned into the "ol' box." No ship should be without one.

The younger officers were as happy as the enlisted men. One of them wrote home to his wife:

"The scene in the wardroom that night was straight from a World War II movie. Critique and rehash . . . each man had an observation. No one ate much dinner—there was excitement and the smell of victory. We were all 'VFW' . . ."

The American people naturally supposed that the destroyer *Maddox,* new symbol for freedom of the sea, would continue her patrol, challenging all comers. Men of the ship, however, knowing how rickety she was, felt equally certain that she would be replaced. They assumed that the Navy would send some of its newer ships into the Gulf, with an umbrella of air power. But while *Maddox* sailors were contemplating the delights of shore leave, an astonishing decision thudded down from higher command: *Maddox* would continue her patrol. The news *"struck a bit of realism into the victory celebration,"* said the letter writer.

Men of the *Maddox* were partly right. The ship was to have air support and she would be accompanied by a newer vessel, the *Turner Joy,* DD 951. As a member of *Maddox*'s squadron, the *Turner Joy* had left Long Beach, California, on the same day, Friday, March 13. Since arriving in WestPac, the two ships had not seen much of each other, but men of the *Maddox* recalled that all of *Turner Joy*'s guns were automatic. That was encouraging. Of course, the battle-weary veterans would have preferred to loaf around Keelung, telling war stories over a cold beer; but, at least, it looked as though the North Vietnamese would think twice before starting any new trouble.

As in the days of her youth, *Maddox* would become a flagship. Commodore Herrick, staying aboard, would command both the *Maddox* and the *Turner Joy.* But Herrick no longer would look to Admiral MacPherson for instructions. Operational command was being assumed by Admiral Moore on the *Ticonderoga*. Moore himself asked for the change. Sunday's battle demonstrated that he was close enough to keep in touch—closer, anyway, than Admiral MacPherson; besides, Moore would have to provide the air support. The change in command seems to have been very informal: the two destroyers were known as "Task Group 72.1"[2] using Admiral MacPherson's numerical prefix of "72" rather than Admiral Moore's prefix of "77." Men of the *Maddox* recall no announced change in the command structure. As they saw it, the faceless Admiral MacPherson simply dropped out of the picture, and there was Jehovah in all his airborne glory.

The light-haired "Whitey" Moore was a bluff, plain-spoken Southerner, a former pilot, and a graduate of the Naval Academy—in sum, a typical Admiral of the U. S. Navy. Recently he had commanded a task force in the Indian Ocean. Before that he was in Iceland as commander of the anti-submarine Barrier Force patrolling the Atlantic. The President of Iceland pinned on the admiral an impressive-sounding decoration: the Grand Knight's Cross with Star of the Icelandic Order of the Falcon. Moore won this recognition for his work in improving relations between American servicemen and the people of Iceland.

The *Turner Joy*, as mentioned earlier, was named for the late Admiral C. Turner Joy. During the Korean War, Admiral Joy commanded Far Eastern naval forces at the time of the brilliantly successful Inchon landing. Inchon, however, was General Douglas MacArthur's great gamble, and to him went the fame, no matter who did the work. Admiral Joy became better known for a less glamorous task—heading the UN delegation to the Panmunjom peace talks. For a year Joy suffered insults as the Communists fortified their line across the peninsula. After he left, the talks dragged on for another year before the Korean truce materialized. Thus it is difficult to resist speculating that the selection of DD 951 to accompany *Maddox* represented somebody's desire to remind the world of Communist haggling at Panmunjom. Newspapers did mention the ship's indirect connection with the Korean talks; and, it will be recalled, the John-

---

[2] Actually "Task Group 72.1.2." The number usually is shortened to 72.1, sometimes even in official documents.

son administration was rejecting proposals for a Vietnam peace conference.

As men of the *Turner Joy* understood the situation, however,
joining *Maddox* was the result of a series of emergencies which continued to deprive them of an overdue shore leave. It all began with a
trip to the Philippines. The *Turner Joy* moored at Subic Bay on July
21 for liberty and repairs, anticipating a stay of at least three days.
Part of the crew went ashore. Late that night, the crew heard, Admiral Moore, up at Yankee Station, demanded a destroyer posthaste
to replace the USS *Brush*. The *Brush,* an old *Sumner* ship like the
Maddox, was having trouble with her propulsion plant. Of all the
destroyers at Subic, *Turner Joy,* being the latest arrival, was best able
to get under way in a hurry. She had some steam, and she was moored
in the outermost position. The squadron engineer had all this figured
out by 2:30 A.M. (local time in the Philippines). By 6:30 A.M. the
Turner Joy had recovered her shoreborne revelers, and the ship was
ready to go.

"We left Subic so fast," says the former captain, "we had to leave
laundry, pump parts, and valves on the beach." The skipper was
Commander Robert C. Barnhart, a forty-three-year-old Naval Academy graduate from Johnstown, Pennsylvania. Recently Barnhart had
attended the National War College at Washington, D.C. The
assignment marked him as an up-and-coming officer.

On the morning that *Turner Joy* rushed out of Subic Bay, the
Maddox departed Yokosuka. The Seventh Fleet flagship, *Oklahoma
City,* was moored in the Saigon River.

Captain Barnhart's ship was a happy one and a hard-working one.
The skipper knew how to tend morale, and he had a sense of humor.
Being fairly new, the ship herself instilled pride and confidence.
Former crew members say she was the "steamin'est" destroyer in
the Western Pacific. Though needing repairs herself, *Turner Joy*
dashed north to replace the *Brush* and, within a week, she was standing in for two more stricken vessels. One was the *Edson,* which had
two cases of hepatitis aboard and possibly a fouled water supply.
Another was the "Sammy" *Moore,* an old short hull on which, as a
lieutenant (jg), Commodore Herrick had once served as engineering
officer. Like *Brush,* the *Moore* had propulsion problems. At the far
end of this chain of misery and circumstance, the *Turner Joy* found
herself on a lone patrol at Watchdog Station, close to Hainan.

What was Watchdog? The *Turner Joy* men understood that they were on radar picket duty, keeping a lookout for jet aircraft based on the big Chinese island (about half the size of West Virginia). The destroyermen heard that the Red Chinese, having instigated the war in Vietnam, themselves might decide to jump in at any minute. If they did, a logical first move would be to attack American ships at Yankee Station. Hence a radar picket was needed. The best place for that would be about 15 miles southwest of Hainan, just outside Red China's 12-mile limit.

Dutifully, the *Turner Joy* cruised back and forth, but she felt rather useless since her radar wasn't finding any airplanes. The men joked that the Chinese had "jets but no gas." Nor did the ship's code name, Ballroom, inspire any sense of urgency.

When the *Maddox* pulled up to Tiger Island, the *Turner Joy* already was standing off Hainan, about 100 miles to the northeast. Whether at that time the *Turner Joy* was in the Tonkin Gulf is a matter of opinion. If one were to draw the Gulf's boundary straight eastward from Tiger Island, she was well inside, being as far north as Mui Doc; if one drew the line from Tiger Island northeastward to Hainan, she was tethered at the entrance like a real watchdog.

In my opinion, this account of how Captain Barnhart's ship got to Watchdog and what she did there makes a coherent and plausible story. The information comes from unofficial sources and probably is true as far as it goes. There is, however, one complication: Admiral Moore, now retired, told me that the *Turner Joy* at the time of the Sunday battle was *not under his command*. Like Tom Stewart interviewing Lieutenant Connell about the "warning shots," I couldn't believe my ears. I thought we must be talking about different days. But, no, this was August 2, the day of the first battle. "They were up there," said the admiral. He referred to the *Maddox* and *Turner Joy*, which, he thought, were working together.

At the crucial hearing of August 6, 1964, senators did not ask where *Turner Joy* fitted into the picture. They do not even seem to have known about the De Soto patrol and Admiral MacPherson. General Wheeler told them that on August 2 the *Maddox* opened fire upon receiving instructions from the "task force commander—who was on the *Ticonderoga*." Every other piece of information I have collected indicates that the ship opened fire on her own authority with no instructions from anywhere, and that she was *not* part of the carrier's task force. Apparently the *Turner Joy* wasn't, either. Were both destroyers nominally under Admiral MacPherson? Radio Hanoi complained of a two-destroyer visit in March. Two destroyers patrolled the Gulf in September. How about the August patrol? Were men of the *Turner Joy* on a De Soto assignment without even knowing it? Unclear, in any event, is where Captain Barnhart fitted into the chain of command and why the *Maddox* was cruising alone.

On Sunday, August 2, the *Turner Joy* was at Watchdog Station enjoying holiday routine. The men believed that they soon would be replaced by the *Moore,* and there was talk of a forthcoming liberty in Hong Kong. One officer lay on his bunk, reading a magazine, when a shipmate poked his head through the hatch:

"You aren't going to believe this," said the newcomer.

"Believe what?"

"It's the *Maddox*. They're up in the Gulf, and they have high speed contacts on the radar. The captain says he might have to open fire."

"*W-h-a-t?*"

The conversation ended as the two scrambled for the bridge. Eavesdropping there, one could get a play-by-play account. *Turner Joy* was tuned in to *Maddox*'s radio transmissions. Possibly she was relaying the *Maddox*'s messages to higher command, as the *Moore* would do at Watchdog later in the week.

Most of the crew was slow to find out what was happening. The intercom grated, "Now hear this . . ." and informed everybody that the ship had a new assignment, another emergency. With that, *Turner Joy* spun about and started north, not bothering to wait for "Sammy" *Moore.* At first the intercom said nothing about *Maddox*'s battle with torpedo boats. Curses scalded the deck as men of the *Turner Joy* anticipated another postponement of their long-awaited liberty. After a while, news of the battle reached the crew. This was no everyday emergency. It sounded like war.

The *Turner Joy* revved up to 70,000 horsepower. This was more steam than the *Maddox* could generate, but because of the newer ship's greater weight and bulk, her speed was no better, if as good. Below *Turner Joy*'s hull, a big sonar dome (transducer) dragged the sea. Eventually, however, the two ships began to close the gap between them at a combined speed of more than 65 knots. By sunset, as the water glistened like pink pearl, the destroyers caught sight of each other. Men of the *Turner Joy* expected the *Maddox* to slow down. Instead, the flagship "went right on by." Obediently, the *Turner Joy* faced about, fell into column, and made haste southward.

Maddox's signalmen at last had somebody to signal. On behalf of Commodore Herrick, they blinked out this spirited greeting:

"Welcome to the club. Hope your gunnery is sharp. Those boys are hopping mad up there. Anything can happen and probably will. Require Condition 3 watch with liberal sprinkling of GQs. Full battle dress with flak jackets. More dope as we go along. Will head north after UNREP [underway replenishment of fuel, etc.]."

Men of the *Turner Joy* groaned as they read "liberal sprinkling of GQs." Running to battle stations and breaking out the necessary equipment involves extra work and loss of sleep. Both ships were to get progressively tired and strained as the patrol wore on.

As the Task Group proceeded southward, the two members engaged in a long discussion by blinker. This method of transmission was more secure than voice radio and much faster than the encryption-decryption process. Commodore Herrick believed that the Task Group stood a very good chance of getting into further combat. To the message quoted above, he added:

"It is apparent that DRV [Democratic Republic of Vietnam] has thrown down the gauntlet and now considers itself at war with the United States. It is felt that they will attack U.S. forces on sight with no regard for cost. U.S. ships in Gulf of Tonkin can no longer assume that they will be considered neutrals exercising the right of free transit. They will be treated as belligerents from first detection and must consider themselves as such . . . Consider situation not unlike war patrol and demanding of maximum alertness and readiness."

In short, Commodore Herrick now saw himself at war. He and the North Vietnamese would shoot on sight. This was a very different view from that expressed in Washington by Secretary McNamara, who seems to have thought that peace reigned in the Tonkin Gulf. In a Monday briefing for lawmakers, McNamara described Sunday's encounter as an "isolated incident" and predicted no more trouble.

Somewhere there was a serious breakdown in communication. It is unfortunate that distance prevented a face-to-face meeting of the commodore and the Secretary. But even when Herrick was stationed near Washington, D.C., at Portsmouth, Virginia, McNamara made no effort to meet him. Before the 1968 hearing, the Defense Secretary preferred to write his statement with the help of the "best lawyers" in the Pentagon.

Distance did not prevent a meeting between Commodore Herrick and Captain Barnhart, but they did not have a face-to-face talk, either, at least until after the patrol was finished. The two ships steamed within waving distance of each other and either man might have taken the high line to visit the other. Instead, *Maddox* and *Turner Joy* communicated by radio and by flashing light.

The stated purpose of the patrol now was changing. Until Sunday afternoon the primary purpose—as senior officers understood it—was to collect intelligence. Now the primary purpose—as understood by everybody of the two ships—became one of showing the flag. As Admiral Sharp told newsmen in Honolulu:

"Here was a United States Navy ship attacked on the high seas. You can't accept any interference with our use of international waters. You must go back to the same place and say, 'Here's two of us this time, if you want to try anything.' "

The De Soto information-gathering duties continued as a secondary responsibility, and the *Maddox* discussed with the *Turner Joy* certain tasks to be shared, such as taking fixes on the shore-based radar. The two ships also discussed gunnery, *Maddox* advising that proximity-fuzed shells were not effective. *Maddox* decided to improve her ammunition-passing capability by assigning gun repairmen to the magazines—if there were no shells to fire, a smooth-working gun would not be needed.

No longer alone in enemy territory, men of the *Maddox* took a new look at the *Turner Joy,* the Navy's latest type of DD. If one appreciates the esthetic qualities of warships, as sailors do, the *Turner Joy* offers a smooth, uncluttered beauty. Gunhousings are not squared-off but rounded, with a single barrel protruding from each. The two stacks rake backward so that the ship seems to lunge forward. Ahead of each stack stands a tripodal mast, aggressively perpendicular as if disdaining a strong head wind. One would hesitate to call the *Turner Joy* a "tin can." She belongs to the sleek, aluminum superstructured, air-conditioned generation of destroyer. The *Turner Joy* was completed in 1959 as one of the *Forrest Sherman* class. She displaces 4200 tons, nearly a third more than the *Maddox.* Her 418-foot length adds 41½ feet to that of the old short hull.

Late Sunday night found the *Maddox* and *Turner Joy* at Yankee

Station, where the *Maddox* began to refuel and rearm. Some distance away cruised the *Ticonderoga,* an old fighting companion of the *Maddox.* During World War II they suffered two of the first *kamikaze* attacks, limping off together for repairs.

While the *Maddox* was getting her oil transfusion, again from the *Ashtabula,* a suspicious radar contact appeared. Captain Ogier ordered preparations for an "emergency breakaway." But, before the GQ alarm was sounded, the skunk vanished.

By first light of Monday, August 3, the two destroyers were steaming back into the Gulf. The ships maintained a high degree of alertness—Condition "One Easy"—with a certain number of battle stations manned constantly. *Turner Joy*'s CIC established "port and starboard" watches. Four hours on, four hours off, the *Turner Joy*'s radarmen squinted at every speck on the scope, finding out what *Maddox*'s CIC had been going through.

In one respect the patrol became less provocative. At the 1968 hearing, Secretary McNamara advised senators that the Task Group did not approach the mainland as closely as the *Maddox* had done before. The 8-mile guideline was replaced by an 11-mile guideline. Commodore Herrick, always cautious, added to that distance a 5-mile cushion so that he now gave the mainland a very wide berth, 16 miles. McNamara said nothing to the senators about a new guideline for islands. The Official Diagram shows that the Task Group patrolled up to 9.2 miles of Hon Me. In 1970 Admiral Moorer told of a 7-mile approach to Hon Me and Hon Ngu. In short, the new navigational guidelines were less provocative, but nevertheless still provocative.

Monday's patrol was "uneventful," according to Secretary McNamara's testimony of August 6, 1964. Compared to Sunday's fireworks, this description was correct; but *less* eventful would have been more accurate.

The Task Group made what preparations it could to deal with a Communist attack, should one come about. At 9 A.M. Monday the *Maddox*'s physician, Dr. Sam Halpern, started a series of first-aid classes for off-duty personnel. Another precaution was somewhat chilling—the doctor gave syrettes of morphine to several officers and explained their use. If necessary, the drug would be used to ease the pain of wounded men. (Somebody started the rumor that in the event of imminent capture certain men were to be "done away with," but I have found no evidence to substantiate this. Certainly nothing of the sort happened aboard the *Pueblo*.) On both *Maddox* and *Turner Joy* a number of officers strapped pistols to their waists. The sidearms were supposed to help repel boarders, if any. In battle they also can be used to keep discipline.

One incident testified to man's abiding faith in fast-firing armament. Two of the COMVAN Marines sought permisssion to set up a machine gun. Permission was granted, and from somewhere the Marines dragged out a .30-caliber gun. Part of a railing was cut away to let the barrel swing freely.

Commodore Herrick retained his quiet, even-tempered manner, but, having judged North Vietnam to be hostile, he might have been concerned about a number of tactical problems.

For one thing, the *Turner Joy*'s presence was less reassuring than had been expected. The ship was having troubles with her equipment, including a gun that was not in operating condition. The gun was the lone 5-incher that stood forward. The other two faced to the rear.

Then, too, the air cover didn't cover. During the day it was intermittent, chiefly because of the low endurance of the jet planes. The prop-driven Skyraiders were more satisfactory. At night—when one would most expect a torpedo boat attack—the carrier provided a "15-minute reaction time," whatever that meant. Events later in the patrol caused me to suspect that it meant no combat air patrol at all, and I verified this suspicion by studying flight logs from the *Ticonderoga*. I found further confirmation in the following statement by Admiral Sharp in his book *Report on the War in Vietnam:* "In accordance with a Presidential directive, the Tonkin Gulf patrol was reinforced by a second destroyer, the *C. Turner Joy,* and *during daylight hours* [italics mine] by a combat air patrol from the *Ticonderoga . . .*" Admiral Sharp, the reader will notice, attributed the CAP schedule to President Johnson. The President, however, said nothing publicly about a daytime-only air patrol.

By order of CINCPACFLT, the destroyers at night were to steam in the center of the Gulf, where surprise attack would not be so easy for the North Vietnamese; but whether the Task Group could be sure of detecting hostile craft was problematical. Commodore Herrick advised the *Turner Joy:* "DRV PTs have advantage, especially at night, of being able to hide in junk concentrations all across the

Gulf of Tonkin. This would allow attack from short range with little or no early warning."

If attacked at night, how could the destroyers dodge torpedoes? They would have to rely on sonar for warning, and the prospect of this looked slim. On Sunday the *Maddox*'s sonarmen, despite their ability to find a submarine, heard no torpedoes at all, even though two went chugging by at close range. Whether the fault lay with equipment, personnel, or the high level of noise, Sunday's sonar performance was far from encouraging. Nevertheless, because of gunnery troubles on Sunday, 2nd Class Sonarman Patrick N. Park transferred back to his previous job in the Main Director. Now the old "E" team was together again, but Park's transfer left Sonarman 3rd Class David Mallow as the *Maddox*'s only rated soundman available to listen for torpedoes.

What if the Nasty gunboats continued their nocturnal forays into the Gulf? Lashing out in a fury, the Communists might try to avenge themselves on the destroyers. Available for a combined assault, the North Vietnamese had at least thirteen, maybe fifteen, serviceable torpedo boats and some thirty gunboats. Also, one could not rule out the possibility of help from the Red Chinese, who had plenty of patrol craft and, reportedly, jet airplanes based on Hainan.

The amateur observer might think, as did Commodore Herrick, that the Task Group was in a precarious situation. But the former CINCPACFLT, Admiral Moorer, has disagreed, asserting that even a mass attack on the ships would have presented only a slight danger. In 1970 Admiral Moorer, as prospective Chairman of the Joint Chiefs, advised senators: "A mass attack on one of these ships could well have resulted in major damage to the ships (*sic*). With two ships, the risk became minimal." In background Admiral Moorer is a Naval Academy graduate of 1933 and a bemedalled aviator. He wears a Silver Star, Distinguished Flying Cross, and Purple Heart. The Alabama-born flyer has a reputation not only for bravery but for an exceptionally keen mind. In 1964, at the age of fifty-two, he was the Navy's youngest four-star admiral. By the Navy's standards, however, Moorer never qualified to command destroyers.

In evaluating the risk Admiral Moorer had the help of a large staff plus the headquarters of CINCPAC. Admiral Sharp was a surface sailor who had commanded both destroyers and cruisers. Nonetheless, even a "black shoe" can be fallible in these matters. In 1968

Admiral Sharp—still CINCPAC—judged the mission of the USS *Pueblo* to be one of "minimal risk" even though the virtually defenseless elint ship was going to visit a hot spot alive with Communist torpedo boats. Sharp, a native of Montana, graduated from the Naval Academy in 1927. In 1964 he was fifty-eight years old. Among his decorations are two Silver Stars and two Bronze Stars.

One former *Maddox* officer recalls that the messages from Admiral Moorer were the most aggressive that he saw during the patrol. After Sunday's battle, CINCPACFLT told subordinates that it was necessary to "assert right of freedom of the seas and resume Gulf of Tonkin patrol soonest." Moorer planned to continue the original navigational guidelines, but somebody overruled him. The 8-mile guideline turned into an 11-mile guideline which, in effect, became a 16-mile guideline. That no doubt helped Secretary McNamara to feel safe in predicting no more trouble. Perhaps McNamara did not know about the separate guideline for islands.

Admiral Moorer gave new instructions for the itinerary. On Monday and Tuesday the ships were to cruise between Charlie and Delta, in the general vicinity of where the trouble started. From Wednesday through Friday, they were to proceed farther into the Gulf and then return southward. During hours of darkness, the ships were to move away from the coast, toward the middle of the Gulf.

On Monday night the ships were to stay away from a certain zone along the southern part of the North Vietnamese coast. Commodore Herrick must have suspected that some kind of 34-A activity was scheduled for that area.

In the 1968 hearing Secretary McNamara gave a vague though technical-sounding description of the location of the prohibited zone. He said it was "an area set by a line between 17 degrees and about 17 degrees, 50 minutes north and a line running north-south into which the patrol was not to penetrate." In effect, McNamara did not say where the boundary lines were. As for the east-west line, McNamara placed it somewhere between the Demilitarized Zone (latitude 17:00) and a point 50 miles north of it (latitude 17:50—one minute of latitude equals one nautical mile). Later in his testimony, McNamara indicated that the east-west line was in fact 40 miles north of the DMZ, at latitude 17:40.

If Commodore Herrick suspected that gunboats were coming into the Gulf to visit the prohibited zone, he was partly right. They were

1. The destroyer *Maddox* on March 21, 1964, the day she left Pearl Harbor, Hawaii, for the Far East. *U. S. Navy photo.*

2. *Turner Joy*, the other half of Captain Herrick's Task Group 72.1. *United Press International photo.*

3. North Vietnamese P-4 torpedo boat approaches the *Maddox* at high speed on the afternoon of Sunday, August 2, 1964. *U. S. Navy photo.*

4. Another photograph taken from aboard the *Maddox* shows a torpedo boat with an apparent shellburst in its wake. Note radar antenna on the boat. *United Press International photo.*

5. Commander John J. Herrick (left) and Captain Herbert L. Ogier (right) in battle dress aboard the *Maddox. U.S. Navy photo.*

6. Lieutenant Keith Bane, a fire control officer aboard the *Maddox,* points to a bullet hole, the sole damage caused by Communist fire on August 2, 1964. A machine gun slug punctured the pedestal of the After Director, in which Bane was sitting, and fell into the 3-inch shell handling compartment below. *United Press International photo.*

7. Close-up of the bullet hole. The Defense Department has not permitted public inspection of the slug. *U. S. Navy photo.*

coming into the Gulf, but in order to shell targets just *north* of the prohibited zone, that is, on Herrick's side of the line.

In his statement of Wednesday, August 5, Colonel Ha Van Lau catalogued a number of grievances without saying anything about gunboat raids on Monday, August 3. In his statement of Thursday, August 6, however, the colonel told of two raids that had taken place on Monday night:

"At 11 P.M. on 3 August they [earlier defined as "U.S. imperialists"] again sent four small ships escorted by two big ones to encroach upon DRV territorial waters and use 40-millimeter cannons and 12.7-millimeter heavy machine guns to shell and fire on Ron and Deo Ngang areas, Quang Binh province."

Deo Ngang is a pass on Mui Doc. Through this parting of the hills runs North Vietnam's most important road, Route 1. Just south of the cape, the road cuts through the town of Ron, and continues south over a bridge crossing the Ron River. The northern boundary of the prohibited zone, latitude 17:40 lay two miles south of the Ron River bridge and almost 17 miles south of Deo Ngang.

The geography of the raided area might suggest that the gunboats were trying to interdict infiltration at a bottleneck or two along the north-south highway. Hanoi, sparing with the facts, as usual, added no details to the August 6 complaint; and the U. S. Government did not confirm the raids until the hearing of February 20, 1968. Secretary McNamara then acknowledged the reality of the second gunboat operation as well as that of the first: ". . . on the night of the 3rd of August certain patrol boats of the South Vietnamese bombarded Ron River in North Vietnam and Vinh Sonh radar in North Vietnam."

Vinh Sonh is a village near the sandy tip of Mui Doc, from which one or two trails lead to Deo Ngang, a short distance away. The radar station in that area ought to have been sighted by the *Maddox* on Saturday morning—and vice versa.

To have "bombarded Ron River," as McNamara put it, would surely have been a waste of ammunition. Senator Morse reported that the targets included "radar sites and a security post." Evidently, the gunboats shelled radar on Mui Doc and a security post near Ron, perhaps also the Ron River bridge.

Were Ron and Vinh Sonh "points associated with infiltration" as McNamara described 34-A objectives? Knocking out a bridge might temporarily inconvenience infiltrators, but McNamara said nothing

about a bridge. Whether the gunboats hit one is a matter of speculation. As for the radar station and a security post, what did they have
to do with infiltration? Speculation on this point is more fruitful if one
recalls that the infiltration was going *both ways,* from south to north
as well as from north to south. According to Radio Hanoi, the June
20 group of Southern infiltrators was caught somewhere along the
coast of Quang Binh province, which includes Ron. Perhaps, as the
gunboat men understood their mission, Monday night's shelling
would prepare the way for safer landings in the future and also
punish the North Vietnamese guard post which captured the last
team. However, in connection with the bombing campaign, the
Defense Department in 1965 identified Vinh Sonh radar as an "early
warning" facility; the radar facilities there might have been designed
for air search. In any case, Vinh Sonh radar obviously was a defensive military facility.

At least a few American officials had advance knowledge of the
August 3 raids. Among them were Admiral Moorer, Admiral Johnson, and, at the headquarters of General Westmoreland, the mysterious MACV liaison man. As for the North Vietnamese, they
presumably had no prior knowledge of the raids, even though they
gave chase to one of the attacking boats for an hour.

Among those in ignorance, both before the raids and afterward,
were the U. S. Congress, which voted for the Tonkin Gulf resolution,
and the American people, who were to contribute their blood and
treasure to the expanding war. Also among the ignorant, by his own
account, was the Secretary of Defense, Robert S. McNamara. In
his prepared statement of February 20, 1968, McNamara told the
Foreign Relations Committee:

"I learned subsequent to my testimony of August 6, 1964, that
another South Vietnamese bombardment took place on the night of
August 3–4."

It was on August 6 that McNamara, Rusk, and Wheeler explained
to key lawmakers what happened in the Tonkin Gulf and why a
congressional resolution was needed in order to discourage further
Communist aggression. These meetings took place three days after
the latest gunboat raids and several hours after Colonel Ha Van Lau's
public report of them. It was surely the responsibility of the Defense
Secretary to make certain that no gunboat raids occurred while the
President's flag-showing patrol continued. Experienced Washington

observers regarded McNamara as the only Secretary of Defense who ever achieved a substantial measure of control over the military services. Is it possible that he did not know what was going on?

While the American people, their elected representatives, and, apparently, the Secretary of Defense were groping in the dark, so was Commodore Herrick, both literally and figuratively. Herrick was one of those who did not hear through official channels about the projected raids.

Exactly what the Task Group did on that "uneventful" Monday night is the subject of conflicting reports. Some officers recall that the ships "night-steamed" in the center of the Gulf. The term refers to letting most of the crew sleep while the ship steams very slowly in a square. The rectangular course enables the ship to maintain a certain position; it also keeps the bridge officers alert by requiring them to plot turns and give orders to the helmsman.

On the face of it, the idea of steaming on a predictable course seems dangerous. The ships would seem to be sitting ducks for torpedo attack. Any surface blip could be either a fishing junk or a patrol boat. A herd of such blips could mean anything. Nevertheless, the overwhelming weight of testimony shows that the Task Group did plan to steam in a 24-mile square. Other information, equally impressive, indicates that the plan was not carried out. Indeed, the Official Diagram of the patrol track shows the course proceeding in a southeasterly direction; it then turns straight north; finally, it doubles back toward the North Vietnamese mainland.

The Official Diagram supports the recollection of an officer who told me that the night-steaming plan was changed in order to avoid operations of North Vietnamese patrol craft. (It was this report that prompted me to ask for a diagram that would include Monday night's course.) According to this same officer, the patrol craft were picked up by radar early in the evening. The skunks were not heading directly toward the Task Group, but their presence was enough to stimulate a change of plan. Instead of steaming in a square, the two destroyers adopted a defensive zigzag (not shown in the diagram), which lasted until shortly after midnight. (To foil torpedo attack by submarines, every warship carries a set of pre-planned zigzag courses which, if adhered to with precision, will enable the ship to maintain the over-all direction which she wants.)

When Colonel Ha said that the gunboats were escorted by two

larger vessels, he seemed to imply that *Maddox* and *Turner Joy* accompanied them. They did not. Nor did their guns help the boat that was chased for an hour. Did the Task Group, however, become involved in some way with the gunboat operations, perhaps inadvertently?

At the 1968 hearing, Secretary McNamara said that the ships were "at least 70 nautical miles to the northeast" when the raids took place; and the Official Diagram indicates a southernmost approach of 70 miles from Mui Doc. The diagram is not very accurate; but, in any event at some point toward the middle of the Gulf, perhaps 70 miles from Mui Doc, the Task Group stopped zigzagging and turned straight north. Whatever the reason for the turn, it was not because the destroyers ran afoul of the prohibited zone, which began farther south. They may, however, have wanted to keep well clear of it. Or they may have turned to keep well clear of the gunboats, which at that time could have been in the middle of the Gulf.

What did the North Vietnamese make of this situation? At a minimum, they knew that both the destroyers and the gunboats were out there, somewhere in the dark. The Communists naturally would assume that the destroyers were helping the gunboats—a reasonably prudent commander would have to make that assumption.

But, in point of fact, was there any kind of assistance that the Task Group *could* have given to the gunboat operations, assuming that Commodore Herrick knew little or nothing about 34-A plans? There was. Advance scouting comes to mind. Two days before the attacks, the destroyers could have reported details of the Vinh Sonh radar and its defenses. On Monday night the destroyers could have served as lookouts. The Task Group's radar swept a large part of the Gulf, spotting North Vietnamese patrol craft when they departed from a base along the coast. Routinely, this information probably found its way to higher command, whence it could have been forwarded to MACV. Most important could have been the assistance rendered by radio intelligence. The COMVAN might have got wind of defensive plans or the dispatch of intercepting patrol craft.

In order to provide help of this sort, the destroyermen would not "need to know" anything at all about 34-A plans. They had only to make regular reports to higher command, where the information could be processed and forwarded to MACV.

I have found no evidence that Commodore Herrick thought he was aiding the gunboat operation. Herrick, however, believed that Hanoi thought so. Sensing that his patrol was provocative and dangerous, the commodore was not satisfied with the part-time air cover. Sometime on August 3, he transmitted this forceful message:

"(a) Evaluation of info from various sources indicated DRV considers patrol directly involved with 34-A ops. DRV considers U.S. ships present as enemies because of these ops and have already indicated their readiness to treat us in that category.

"(b) DRV very sensitive about Hon Me, believe this is PT operating base, and the cove there presently contains numerous patrol and PT craft which have been repositioned from northerly bases.

"(c) Defense against PTs very difficult when in close proximity to Hon Me in that they can hide behind it until the opportune moment and start their run leaving very little time for tracking and spotting and allowing no international water working space for aircraft.

"(d) Under these conditions 15 minutes reaction time for obtaining air cover is unacceptable. Cover must be overhead and controlled by DDs [destroyers] at all times."

The commodore's message provides an example of how the Task Group's reconnaissance was reported to higher command and hence could have helped 34-A planners. Surely MACV would not order further gunboat raids on Hon Me while "numerous patrol and PT craft" were stationed there.

Herrick might well have been convinced that the torpedo boats at Hon Me were poised to attack *him* rather than the gunboats. In the first place, it would be virtually impossible to hit a fast, shallow-draft gunboat with a torpedo; and in the second, the torpedo is too expensive a weapon for that kind of target. On the other hand, the torpedo boats were very fast, and, equipped with radar and machine guns, they could have been used against Nasty craft.

The Seventh Fleet commander, Admiral Johnson, had not agreed to canceling the patrol on Sunday morning, but sometime during Monday's "uneventful" hours he changed his mind. Obviously, the Tonkin Gulf was getting too crowded for all of the activities scheduled there.

At the 1968 hearing, Secretary McNamara disclosed that the Seventh Fleet commander "reported his intention to terminate the patrol on the evening of August 4 in order to move it away from the area and avoid any possibility of conflict with 34-A." Specifically,

Admiral Johnson feared that the destroyers and 34-A gunboats would *shoot at each other*. Navigating in the dark by radar, either type of vessel was liable to regard any fast-moving skunk as the enemy. But the Seventh Fleet commander was overruled by his superior, Admiral Moorer. McNamara would not admit that conditions in the Tonkin Gulf were becoming too explosive for demonstrating the American position on freedom of the sea. Commodore Herrick, he contended, had no information on which to base his report that Hanoi associated the Task Group with 34-A boats. Herrick, said McNamara, knew nothing of 34-A but the term itself. Therefore, the Task Group could not have helped the gunboats, and, for that reason, Hanoi could not possibly have regarded the two operations as related in any way. As proof of this, the Secretary brought up the testimony of a North Vietnamese naval prisoner. The prisoner, said McNamara, ". . . told his interrogators that it was clear in his mind that the De Soto patrol was separate from 34-A operations."

As for the commodore's report that Hanoi associated his destroyers with the gunboats, this represented "sheer speculation, unfounded speculation," said the Defense Secretary. "Herrick himself," declared McNamara, "now says that he can recall no basis for coming to that conclusion."

"Well," observed Senator Fulbright, "you are not saying that this cable (Herrick's) was not sent."

"I simply stand on what I said, Mr. Chairman. Of course it was sent."

"You are not saying that it was not sent."

"But I am saying that it is a complete distortion of the fact to leave the record indicating that the commander of the *Maddox* had any basis whatsoever for believing that North Vietnam confused 34-A and De Soto. He did not have the basis."

Herrick's revised opinion was obtained by somebody in McNamara's office, not by the Secretary himself. To the end, the Defense Secretary was to rely on indirect reports gathered by his staff, although he professed to base everything he said on cold, hard fact. It was, according to McNamara, experienced naval officers with first-hand knowledge of events who indulged in speculation.

When Admiral Moorer decided to continue the patrol, he said that the Seventh Fleet commander's plan "Does not in my view adequately demonstrate the U.S. resolve to assert our legitimate rights in these international waters." Presumably the President would have been far from pleased with cancellation of the patrol. He already was dissatisfied with the Navy for not having annihilated three torpedo boats on Sunday, and he already had announced to the world that two destroyers would cruise in the Gulf. If only because of the President's attitude, the Task Group had to stay there, showing the flag. If the destroyers were attacked, the Navy would have to take drastic action in reply. This would be true in normal times. The election campaign made it doubly imperative.

Politicians themselves, the members of the Foreign Relations Committee no doubt could understand why, in view of Sunday's battle and the President's subsequent statement, the Task Group had to remain in the Gulf. But why did the gunboat raids have to continue? When asserting historic rights, would it not be better to do so with clean hands? Why confuse the issue with mysterious marauders and 40-millimeter shells? Unfortunately, no senator asked these questions.

Secretary McNamara talked as if great care had been taken to insulate the destroyer Task Group in every way from 34-A operations, but this concern does not seem to have been fully shared in 1964 by Admiral Sharp and Admiral Moorer. On the night of August 4, they wanted the destroyers not only to demonstrate a point of international law but to help the raiding gunboats at the same time. In order to "accommodate MACV," Admiral Moorer directed the Task Group to spend Tuesday night farther north, above latitude 19:10. The new boundary was 4 miles north of Cape Falaise and 12 miles south of Hon Me.

The purpose of the northward move, Admiral Moorer's directive stated, was to "demonstrate our determination to continue these operations," "possibly draw" North Vietnamese gunboats away from the area of 34-A operations, and "eliminate" the destroyers' "interference" with 34-A operations. Evidently there had been some interference if it was now necessary to eliminate it. And evidently Admiral Moorer thought the destroyers might be able to help the gunboats by drawing North Vietnamese patrol craft away from the area scheduled for attack. Why would North Vietnamese patrol craft follow the destroyers? To attack them? Or because on the previous night the

Task Group had led the way to the area of 34-A operations? Admiral Moorer's telegram was quoted by senators at the 1968 hearing.[3] At the 1970 hearing, Admiral Moorer attributed to CINCPAC the plan to help 34-A. Trying to draw Communist craft away from the gunboats' target area was recommended to the Joint Chiefs by Admiral Sharp, said the former CINCPACFLT. (This conflicted with McNamara's assertion that the Joint Chiefs never considered such a plan.) Under the circumstances, it seems wise to assume that both Sharp and Moorer were involved with the decoy recommendation; both have been linked to it, and both were at Pearl Harbor. Admiral Moorer denied that the decoy plan actually was carried out. Neither he nor anybody else has said that the Joint Chiefs rejected the plan.

At the 1968 hearing, Senator Morse declared that the destroyers were being used as decoys, and this, he said, amounted to an act of war. In those circumstances, Morse argued, the North Vietnamese had a right to attack the destroyers. The ex-law professor challenged McNamara: "You are not arguing, are you, that the North Vietnamese had no right to attack them on the high seas?"

The Defense Secretary never answered that question. He retorted that the purpose of the northward move, above latitude 19:10, was "to further separate the *Maddox* from 34-A operations in order to assure that there was less reason for anybody, including the North Vietnamese, to associate the two." McNamara cited the testimony of his prisoner, and he ignored what Hanoi said officially on the subject. McNamara flatly denied that the destroyers were intended to decoy North Vietnamese patrol craft. He explained:

"Senator Morse, had we been using them as a decoy, we would not have so substantially increased the restricted area. This move to north of 19 degrees 10 minutes was a move of about, I would say, 90 miles, moving the northerly boundary of the restricted areas farther and farther away from the 34-A operations."

(Here, when it suited his purpose, McNamara revealed the location of Monday night's boundary—which, if 90 miles south of 19:10,

[3] The message said in part:
"The above patrol will clearly demonstrate our determination to continue these operations.
"B. Possibly draw NVN [North Vietnamese] PGMS [Patrol Gunboats, Motor] northward away from the area of 34A OPS [operations].
"C. Eliminate DeSoto patrol interference with 34A OPS."

would have been latitude 17:40. Senators failed to notice that neither 17:50 nor 17:40 would have been adequate.)

In the Defense Secretary's view, the admirals in Hawaii were guilty of poor judgment (not to mention an act of war) if they thought that moving the destroyers so far north would enable them to act as decoys. As usual, McNamara put his naval judgment above the Navy's. Who was right?

The new prohibited zone extended 75 miles north of Vinh Sonh, one of Monday night's targets, but it fell 12 miles short of Hon Me, one of Friday night's targets. As for Tuesday night's targets, where were they to be? McNamara did not say. The Foreign Relations Committee seems not to have asked, and since the raids were canceled, Radio Hanoi could not reveal their location.

Why were the raids canceled? This is not known, either. But one fact has been well publicized: the Task Group on Tuesday evening reported itself under continuous attack by Communist torpedo craft. The attack, if real, proves that as a decoy the Task Group was *too* effective.

Chapter X

The Hubs of Hell

After their midnight change of course, the destroyers stopped zigzagging and steamed north for several hours, mostly in a straight line
(course 000 from 12:10 A.M. until 4:03 A.M., with frequent changes
thereafter). By dawn, 5:46 A.M., the Task Group was well above
the latitude of Hon Me and still midway between North Vietnam and
Hainan. The destroyers were parting a low, white mist when the
men on watch caught sight of an island, whose long summit floated
above the mist like a green wafer on ice cream. This was Bach Long
Vi (White-Tailed Dragon), a solitary piece of North Vietnamese
territory in the middle of the Gulf. Historically, the island has provided a home for fishermen and, no doubt, for the pirates who used
to infest the South China Sea. Europeans called it Nightingale Island,
but the local term is more descriptive of the island's fighting potential. The long ridge provides an excellent, centrally located platform
for radar and guns. Like Tiger Island, another promontory convenient for Gulf-watching, Bach Long Vi became an early target for
the 1965 bombing campaign.

According to the U. S. Official Diagram, the destroyers turned
westward about 20 miles south of Bach Long Vi (not shown), and,
as they approached the coast, angled a bit farther north before retiring
southward toward Hon Me. Unofficially, I have heard that the Task
Group not only inspected the lonely isle in the middle of the Gulf, but
proceeded far enough northward along the coast to examine the island
approaches to Haiphong. The Task Group lingered in that area for
a while in order to count traffic in and out of the port; then it mean-
dered back south toward Hon Me.

After sunrise, aircraft from the *Ticonderoga* resumed their Combat Air Patrol duty, shuttling back and forth two at a time. The planes scouted far and wide for Communist naval craft but found none. The morning passed without any sign of hostility.

The destroyers spent most of Tuesday's daylight hours patrolling the now-familiar areas of Point Delta and Point Charlie. They again sliced through the 12-mile limit as drawn from islands. They again steered 16 miles clear of the mainland. One ominous development was a change in the weather. A gathering overcast began to darken the surface of the Gulf. If a storm were brewing, the reduced visibility could assist torpedo attack at night.

The unaccustomed shade did not make the destroyermen more comfortable. The air hung moist and heavy like a wet towel. Steel helmets, long-sleeved shirts, and flak jackets became increasingly irksome. Men of the *Turner Joy* tried quenching their thirst with large quantities of "bug juice," a soft drink available from the mess. Like the ship's air conditioning, however, the ice-making apparatus was overtaxed, and the sugary liquid barely cooled one's tongue.

The *Maddox* was a floating oven. Buttoned up compartments reduced ventilation and caused more cases of heat exhaustion. Dr. Halpern gave one of the snipes an intravenous injection to bring him around. Fortunately, the prostrate seaman resumed breathing before any brain damage could occur. So far as the old short hull was concerned, not a great deal of progress in tropical living conditions had been made since 1898 when Commodore George Dewey defeated the Spanish squadron at Manila Bay. The only American who died there keeled over from heat exhaustion.

Commodore Herrick's men were facing a sustained emergency, waiting for the other side to make its move. Day in, day out, there were extra watches to stand and more work to do. The Condition "One Easy" readiness for battle cut into sleeping time. Many of the *Maddox*'s key personnel had enjoyed little or no rest since Saturday night—and even that had been disturbed by the Hon Mat incident and the submarine alert.

By Tuesday the destroyermen were growing tired, but, at least, they were not bored. *Turner Joy* men knew that they were along to ride shotgun; and from what the commodore had told them, they fully expected a chance to pull the trigger. Aboard *Maddox,* the command ship, there were more shades of opinion. Some expected a fight; others did not. But a larger number of officers wore pistols on Tuesday than on Monday; and even a few bayonets made their appearance. When *Maddox*'s officers went to lunch, they found the wardroom equipped as a casualty station. Intravenous rigs festooned the compartment. Looking over one's shoulder were surgical lamps; and lying nearby were a set of shiny instruments which had nothing to do with eating. Dr. Halpern was prepared for the worst. On the bulkhead he posted first-aid instructions to be consulted if, as the result of enemy action, the doctor should be unavailable.

The pessimists, believing that "next time" the North Vietnamese would organize a more intelligent attack, discussed what to do if the ship sank. The favorite plan: commandeer a junk at pistol point and sail south. The optimists contended that North Vietnam would not be so foolish as to try anything again: a second attack would invite retaliation. Some thought it was a mistake not to bomb North Vietnam after Sunday's attack. Everybody agreed on the need to be alert.

Among the *Maddox*'s pessimists were those who were concerned not only about the hostility of the North Vietnamese but about the puzzling attitude of their *own side*. Why was there no air cover at night? As the commodore had reminded CINCPACFLT, the torpedo boats could use hide-and-pounce tactics, lying in wait behind rocks or mingling with fishing craft. At night, aircraft could check out suspicious-looking radar contacts by dropping flares on them. However, despite the commodore's demand for constant cover, the "President's directive" remained the same: Combat Air Patrol only during the hours of sunlight. After dark, the *Ticonderoga*'s planes folded their wings and went to sleep. Equally puzzling was the directive to stay north of 19:10. The prohibited zone now reached 90 miles farther into the Gulf; and from what I have heard unofficially, it stretched eastward all the way to Hainan. The destroyers now were boxed into the upper part of the Gulf. At the 1968 hearing, Secretary McNamara would make it sound as if the Task Group were better off the farther it went north, allegedly putting more water between it and the scheduled location of gunboat raids. At the time, the destroyermen felt more secure the farther south they went, putting less water between them and the source of air cover.

Few of the destroyermen, if any, knew about Admiral Moorer's plan to "draw" North Vietnamese craft away from gunboat raids. Those who did suspect the motive behind the 19:10 line felt more like pigeons than decoys. The *Maddox* already had been shot at; did higher command now want a sunken destroyer? Perhaps it made no difference how careful the ships were; the odds against them were continually being raised. At the 1970 hearing, Senator Young asked Admiral Moorer whether he had hoped the North Vietnamese would "challenge the U.S. presence." Moorer replied that he had not.

If the *Maddox* were on a pigeon assignment—a not uncommon naval tactic—it would not have been the first time. During the Korean War the ship was known to meander along the North Korean coast, drawing shellfire in order to divert attention from landings. The ship claimed a record for getting shot at: 720 rounds of major caliber fire. Not all of them missed.

Down at Yankee Station there was little sympathy for Commodore Herrick, whose request to cancel the patrol had met with contempt. "If he can't take care of himself up there, with all of his guns, it's too bad," was the general attitude. Some added: "Maybe he's in a tough spot, but that's what the Navy is for." The carrier men were not at all sensitive to the danger of expanding the war in Southeast Asia. To the contrary, they were tired of Washington's pusillanimous attitude. So far the paperwork at Yankee Station weighed more than the ammunition that pilots were allowed to fire at Communist guerrillas.

As for the view from higher command, it could not have failed to take into account that the destroyer's presence in the Gulf would severely test the North Vietnamese willingness to fight. At some point, the Communists would have to resist. Sunday's experience seemed to testify that that point had been reached. If, however, the North Vietnamese were to attack the Task Group with everything they had, the most the U. S. Navy could lose would be two destroyers. Massive air power, readily available on the *Ticonderoga* and *Constellation,* could then take over and teach the Communists a lesson. No matter what the North Vietnamese tried to do, higher command could take comfort from the prospect of a happy ending. Medals would be awarded. Speeches would be made. Everybody, including the Communists, would be aware of the convenience and mobility of carrier-based air power.

The Defense Department's "Chronology of Second Attack" starts out with a few words bringing the reader up-to-date:

"After the first attack on the USS *Maddox,* on Sunday, the *Maddox* joined with its sister destroyer, the USS *Turner Joy,* in the Gulf of Tonkin and resumed its patrol in international waters, as directed by President Johnson. The patrol was uneventful during most of the daylight hours of Tuesday, August 4."

Nevertheless, there were a few small events. One was the receipt of news from home. The destroyermen heard that President Johnson had "doubled" the patrol in the Gulf, and the President's choice of words inspired a round of sarcastic jokes. Adding one ship to the patrol did not amount to an overwhelming show of force, such as one might find at Yankee Station or some liberty port.

Another event had to do with *Maddox*'s sonar. The ship reported that something was wrong with it. Perhaps the report told of Sunday's failure to hear any torpedoes; it might have noted, too, a defect in the gyro apparatus that oriented the sonar with the direction of the ship.

There was also a momentary flurry of excitement. At 2:30 P.M. the ships were near Point Delta, maintaining their battle-ready alertness, when radarmen discovered a faster-than-sail contact about 15 miles to the west, near shore. The skunk evidently was a naval vessel which was painting the Task Group with radar of its own. But within minutes the Communist radar was identified as the "skinhead" type associated with Swatow gunboats. The Swatow could have been scouting for radarless torpedo craft. In any event, no attack developed. The Task Group reported the contact as a "suspected Red Shadow." The North Vietnamese, of course, had every right to patrol their own coastline, and indeed, were staying within territorial water. (After Sunday's battle the U. S. Government drafted a warning of "grave consequences" should there be any further "unprovoked" action against U.S. forces, but the warning could not have reached Hanoi by Tuesday, according to newspaper accounts of Wednesday, August 5. At present the State Department, which I have queried several times, does not seem to know whether the official text *ever* reached Hanoi or how it was transmitted.)

The Official Chronology continues:

"Late afternoon, August 4, the *Maddox* reported radar contact with unidentified surface vessels who were paralleling its track and the track of the *Turner Joy*."

In the recollections of destroyermen I have found no basis for that report. Several *Maddox* sailors, including radarmen and the officer of the deck, told me that they knew of no significant skunks until nightfall. Nevertheless, the Official Chronology reads on as if the paralleling contacts were observed until their actions threatened "imminent attack" at 7:40 P.M., the approximate time of darkness. I would have given up my investigation of this point much sooner except for the recollection of a non-destroyerman, Commander George Edmondson, who remembered an alert that took place aboard the *Ticonderoga* about 5 P.M. Edmondson commanded the carrier's only squadron of prop-driven Skyraiders. He and the other squadron leaders were called to the Ready Room, where they heard about radar contacts to the northwest of the destroyers. The situation was not considered dangerous enough for anybody to take off. In half an hour the alert was over, and the squadron commanders went to dinner. A few pilots, including Edmondson, were designated as CAP should another emergency arise.

Assuming that the now-retired Commander Edmondson's recollection is accurate, the alert was a brief one. No menacing contacts were observed continuously from late afternoon until 7:40 P.M.

Exaggeration crept into the official accounts of what happened. So did error, which sometimes is even more disturbing. A major source of confusion has been the Defense Department's astonishing carelessness in dealing with time zones. The reader will recall that in 1964 the Pentagon gave two different times for the night attack: 10:30 P.M. and 9:30 P.M. The difference represented a discrepancy in converting time, an error that was still being committed 3½ years later. At the 1968 hearing, McNamara and Wheeler presented a chronology which sounded as if the attack started at about 9:30 P.M. When I raised a query, Pentagon officials restudied the chronology several times and finally decided that it was an hour off. To convert what McNamara called "Tonkin Gulf time" to Eastern Daylight time required the subtraction of 11 hours, not the officially recommended 12 hours. In conversation "Golf time," the phonetic term for the "G" time zone that properly applies to Indochina and the Tonkin Gulf, often is confused with "Gulf time," the habitual term for whatever time Navy ships are using in that area. "Gulf time" tends to be the same as South Vietnamese time, an artificial zone that runs an hour faster than Golf time. What Secretary McNamara called "Tonkin Gulf time" was, indeed, the same as South Vietnamese time. This book uses Golf time as much as possible when narrating events in the

Tonkin Gulf. It happens to fit the Official Chronology of Second Attack if one remembers to subtract 11 hours in order to arrive at Eastern Daylight time.[1]

The official Tonkin Gulf chronologies are so confused that it took me more than a year to establish the correct time of anything (and I'm still uneasy!). Fortunately, one of the *Maddox*'s officers kept copies of the ship's Plan of the Day, and they provided a clue. The Plan did not specify what zone was being used but two copies out of three gave the time of sunrise; and from the astronomically correct time of sunrise it became possible to reckon the zone being used —or, more accurately, the *zones* being used. In the Plan of the Day it appears that between Sunday and Tuesday the *Maddox* turned her clocks back two hours. Here, again, is the Mystery of the Clocks. Nobody from the *Maddox* seems to remember any readjustment of clocks or why it was done. One might guess that Commodore Herrick decided to get in step with Admiral Moore rather than continue on Japan time with Admiral MacPherson. But the two-hour shift put *Maddox* on Golf time, and the *Ticonderoga* was keeping South Vietnamese time. The shift did put *Maddox* in step with North Vietnam, which uses Golf time.

The sun, our basic timekeeper, settled behind the mountains of North Vietnam at about 6:30 P.M. (Golf time) Tuesday, August 4. As its light faded from the still-overcast sky, the destroyers turned toward the middle of the Gulf, again planning to steam in a square. The area designated for that purpose lay midway between North Vietnam and Hainan. The base of the square rested just above the 19:10 line established by Admiral Moorer; the sides reached 24 miles to the north. Correctly, the Official Diagram indicates that the Task Group turned seaward just north of Hon Me. The course, however, did not slant in a southeasterly direction but proceeded due east.

When two warships steam in company, they customarily improve radar efficiency by dividing the range. One ship concentrates on "far search," the other on "near search." In this case, *Maddox* took the

---

[1] Running eastward, the three adjacent zones are Golf, Hotel, and India. North Vietnam uses Golf time, which technically is called "zone time" for that area. South Vietnam and Taiwan use Hotel time, which is the correct zone time for Taiwan. Japan uses India time, the correct zone time for Japan. "India," of course, refers to the letter "I." Eastern Daylight time corresponds to Quebec time; Eastern Standard corresponds to Rome time.

extreme range while the *Turner Joy* watched close in. The *Maddox*'s radarmen, having been in the Gulf longer, were becoming accustomed to the exceptional performance peculiar to the area. On the high sea, "normal range" extended 20 or 25 miles for picking out ships. In the Tonkin Gulf the radar did much better. On Sunday, August 2, for example, the *Maddox*'s radarmen spied the *Turner Joy* at a distance of 98 miles. The reason lies with weather conditions peculiar to warm, coastal areas, especially a tropical, nearly landlocked body of water like the Tonkin Gulf. Heated air from the land flows over the cooler water, forming an upper layer of thin atmosphere that acts like a radar lens. The hot, thin air bends the radar waves downward so that they reach over the physical horizon instead of shooting out into space. This phenomenon, called "super-refraction," is similar in principle to a desert mirage. Next, the super-refracted waves tend to bounce off the water, then bend down again from the sky, and proceed in that way, alternately reflecting and refracting, farther and farther from the transmitting antenna. This is called "severe super-refraction" or "ducting." The waves act as though ducted through a channel of mirrors. When the ducted waves encounter an obstruction, such as a ship or an island, they come surging back again, bearing the imprint of where they have been. Ducting has been known to return the images of objects more than a thousand miles away. An upper layer of hot air is the usual cause for super-refraction. A sharp decrease in humidity can have the same effect (waves bend toward the denser medium).

Ducting can be an invaluable aid to radarmen. But the interpretation of such far-fetched images is a tricky affair. That blip drifting over the scope: Is it an island 40 miles away, a boat 20 miles away, or the top of a mountain 200 miles away? Could it be a distant thunderstorm? The radarman must learn to recognize what is happening to his scope and to distinguish one kind of blip from another. He also must learn to cope with the inquisitive bystander who, spotting a few whales, asks why that "enemy concentration" hasn't been reported. On the other hand, the non-radarman faces a vexing problem when the technician points to a featureless green blob and declares that it is a fast-approaching torpedo boat.

At sunset of August 4, the *Maddox*'s radar was ducting in its normal Tonkin Gulf fashion. Radarmen say the reception was "great." The bridge navigated on Bach Long Vi 90 miles to the northeast.

Standing there as officer of the deck was Lieutenant James D. Copeland, assistant engineer; sharing the 4–8 watch with him was Ensign John M. Leeman, the junior officer of the deck.

Copeland, when I talked to him, had left the Navy and was studying architecture. He recalled that at twilight the *Maddox* was pushing eastward at 20 knots. There was a stiff head wind; spray flew over the bow; and the water felt choppy. The water actually was choppy, Copeland recollected—it was not just the speed. For some reason not known to him, then or later, all four boilers were hot.

By 7:30 P.M. it was getting fairly dark, and there were no signs of trouble, so far as the bridge or Combat Information Center could tell. At about this time, however, Lieutenant Copeland began studying some fast radar contacts far away. Various persons have reported them at distances of anywhere from 20 to 36 miles. The skunks, at any rate, were beyond the physical horizon. Copeland at first thought the contacts were clouds, but they demanded further scrutiny because they more or less surrounded the Task Group. One of them, at least, paralleled the destroyers' path. Still, the picture was not sufficiently threatening to justify calling the captain—not until a northerly contact, coming closer, split into three parts, in the same way Sunday's blip had done as it closed the range.

The split persuaded Copeland that he was looking not at a cloud but at naval craft. "A cloud," he told me, "will disappear as it breaks up." Copeland does not remember how the closing came about. Either the contact was on a course intercepting the Task Group or, as another officer recalls, the destroyers now had turned northward along one side of the proposed night-steaming square. The picture on the scope at this time later became known as the "original ambush."

CIC confirmed the OD's observation of three firm contacts closing from the north, and so did the *Turner Joy.* Apparently the CAP had already left for the day. In any event, no visual sightings confirmed the radar information.

Captain Barnhart told me that in his opinion the North Vietnamese were able to lay this trap because, having watched the Task Group on the previous night, they knew about the night steaming square. As noted earlier, the destroyers did not steam in a square on Monday night; moreover, the southern boundary had been moved up 90 miles. However, a night attack would make more sense than a day attack, and the North Vietnamese must have noticed that the CAP disappeared at sunset.

To the destroyermen, the split contact looked like three patrol craft. More could be lurking in the as yet unsplit contacts elsewhere on the scope. By telephone Lieutenant Copeland made a report to Captain Ogier. As he did so, the prospective officer of the deck and junior OD, Lieutenant Bane and Ensign Noel M. Allen, climbed up the bridge. The time now must have been 7:45 P.M. or 7:50 P.M.—the Navy requires the relief men to get on station early. Since the OD was busy and could not brief them, Bane and Allen stepped over to the radarscope; Copeland still remembers seeing their faces illuminated by the green glow, disembodied in the dark. Only a few traces of sunset now lingered in the sky. Lieutenant Bane counted three firm skunks. So did Ensign Allen. The new men apparently did not count the "unsplit" contacts. Copeland and Leeman did count them. At the 1968 hearing Secretary McNamara told of five contacts in all.

Captain Ogier made his decision. He told the officer of the deck to ring General Quarters. Copeland's GQ would be a "real" one, using the gong. After Sunday's battle there no longer seemed to be any point in playing the "sneaky Pete" game. Besides, the silent GQ had failed to alert everybody. At least one officer on Sunday reached his post 15 minutes late. Now, on both destroyers, there was no mistaking the loud *BONG, BONG, BONG*. Hundreds of feet pounded the metal decks. Bulkheads reverberated with the clang of hatches and the clatter of emergency equipment.

Bane and Allen left the bridge for their battle stations. Allen ran to CIC where he again found three solid skunks on the radar. They reminded him of Sunday's contacts. "Once you see them," says Allen, "you don't forget them." Lieutenant Bane did not run straight to the After Director. He took an interior route to pick up a morphine syrette in his stateroom, and the trip through lighted areas of the ship ruined his night vision. Topside, everything went black.

Lieutenant Copeland remained on the bridge for a while, helping the GQ tenants to get organized. As an engineering officer, Copeland's battle station was damage control, and the situation did not look as though there would be any damage for a while. Before leaving the bridge, the former OD took another look at the radarscope and saw that a southwesterly contact, too, had split into three parts. I have found nobody to confirm this observation.

Senior officers decided to use Sunday's tactic: open the range and watch whether the blips would follow. The immediate threat came from the split contacts approaching in echelon from the northwest. The reciprocal course would plow through Admiral Moorer's 19:10 barrier, but that could not be helped. *Maddox* leaned her prow to the left and, looping around, started another run to the southeast. Without comment, Captain Barnhart ordered his ship to do the same— nearly all of the *Turner Joy*'s usable weapons faced to the rear in any case. Soon both ships looked like huge motorboats, churning the water at 30 knots. The commodore did not immediately request air support. Perhaps having been turned down once, he did not want to be refused again.

Says the Official Chronology:

"7:40 P.M., August 4. The *Maddox* reported that from actions being taken by the unidentified vessels, an attack by them appeared imminent. The *Maddox* was heading southeast near the center of the Gulf in international waters approximately 65 miles from nearest land."

The term "unidentified vessels" refers to the previous entry concerning "late afternoon" radar contacts. According to my information, the ships turned southeast not at 7:40 P.M. but closer to 8 P.M. The chronology was correct in saying that the Task Group was far from land.

Apparently not only radar but intelligence of some kind warned of an attack in the making. At the 1968 hearing, Senator Fulbright put into the record this message transmitted by Commodore Herrick:

"RCD info indicating attack by PGM/P-4 imminent. My position 19-10.7 N 107-003 proceeding southeast at best speed."

The time of the message has not been made public, but the information on speed and position indicates a time between the ringing of GQ and the crossing of the 19:10 line, that is, approximately 8 P.M. According to Secretary McNamara, the first intelligence of attack reached Washington at the equivalent of 8:20 P.M.

Men of the *Maddox* waited for the shooting to start. One of the ship's former officers:

"My men were on station in record time, as was the whole ship. The captain did not come up with any information as to what was happening so we sat there wondering. Little bits of information began coming over the phones . . . Somebody on the phone asked what was going on. Main Control said he didn't know. Finally, Main Control announced: 'All stations, this is Main Control. The bridge talker thinks it's PTs . . . lots of them.' I told my guys to lie down in the passageway in case any machine gun fire was encountered."

The "bridge talker" wears a telephone apparatus and relays messages. He is a man "in the know."

In another part of the ship, sailors heard that torpedo boats had boxed in the two destroyers.

Captain Ogier probably was saying nothing because he knew nothing. After he turned to the southeast, the radar contacts did not follow. They stayed in the same area or, as one man remembered it, they "converged" on the area that the destroyers had left. The attackers, if real, evidently were unable to see what they were doing. Were the skunks mere illusions? Or had the Task Group by its quick maneuver escaped a trap? After the 7:40 P.M. entry, the Official Chronology said no more about these contacts.

By 8:15 P.M. the *Maddox*'s radarmen were beginning to relax. Their scopes were clean. The Task Group, however, continued on to the southeast, still anticipating attack. The night was young.

Ten minutes later the radar showed one or two new skunks, this time coming from the direction of Hainan. The commodore now, at 8:25 P.M., asked for air support. The new menace suggested the possibility of Red Chinese activity. So did the subsequent discovery of radar contacts in the air. The Official Chronology continues:

"8:36 P.M., August 4. The *Maddox* established new radar contact with two unidentified surface vessels and three unidentified aircraft. At this time, U.S. fighter aircraft were launched from the USS *Ticonderoga* to rendezvous with the *Maddox* and the *Turner Joy* to provide protection against possible attack from the unidentified vessels and aircraft, in accordance with the President's previously issued directives."

According to this, despite Commodore Herrick's earlier report of "imminent" attack, the first CAP launch did not take place until after he reported three unidentified aircraft. Did the President's "previously issued directives" specify CAP only when the enemy also had CAP?

It struck me as incredible that the *Ticonderoga* would not launch any aircraft until 8:36 P.M. The Defense Department allowed me to examine the carrier's master flight logs, and they told a different story, though one almost as strange:

8:03 P.M.	Skyraider
8:07 P.M.	Skyraider
8:43 P.M.	Crusader
8:46 P.M.	Crusader
8:46 P.M.	Skyhawk
8:48 P.M.	Skyhawk

Two Skyraiders left the carrier not long after the Task Group rang GQ. They were flown by Commander Edmondson and Lieutenant (jg) Jere (pronounced "Jerry") Barton. The airmen were in the wardroom, drinking their after dinner coffee, when called to action.[2] The planes were gassed up and ready to go.

The two "Spads," as carrier men called the prop-driven Skyraiders, sprang into the air within minutes, but to reach the Task Group they would need approximately 1½ hours. The carrier, south of Hainan, was quite a distance from the destroyers in the Gulf. For that matter, even jet planes could not have fulfilled the 15-minute reaction promise —unless the plan called for getting planes *into the air* within 15 minutes.

Whether he knew of the Spad launch or not, Commodore Herrick requested CAP at 8:25 P.M. Eighteen minutes later jet aircraft began whooshing into the sky.

The first two jets were F-8 Crusaders, the supersonic interceptor type of plane that had made up the Firefighter group on Sunday. The Crusaders were fast enough to reach the destroyers well ahead of the Spads launched half an hour before. Shortly after take-off, however, one of the F-8s developed a mechanical difficulty and turned back. The other F-8, piloted by a squadron commander, streaked on ahead.

The last two jets were subsonic "attack" aircraft. These were A-4 Skyhawks, relatively slow but well armed for air-to-surface fighting. Flying the delta-winged A-4s were Commander Wesley McDonald, leader of a Skyhawk squadron, and his wingman, Lieutenant Thomas Gehman.

The *Ticonderoga*'s launching pattern represented a typically American, competitive situation. Every type of squadron was getting a piece

---

[2] Thus it seems possible that the alert Commander Edmondson remembered took place not around 5 P.M. but around 7 P.M.

of the action, and the slowest planes were launched first. Speculating on the preference for Spads, one recognizes that they did offer certain advantages: the most endurance, the most ordnance, and the only flares. The Spads carried no radar.

As Jehovah began to stir himself, Sindbad was getting very busy. In CIC radarmen studied carefully the new pair of skunks to the east. They approached in a formation straddling the Task Group: one to the northeast, one to the southeast. Their speed: from 10 to 20 knots. The blips were somewhat irregular in shape as if caused by weather, and at first *Maddox*'s CIC did not know whether to take them seriously. Commodore Herrick reminded the men that on Sunday one irregularly shaped, moderately paced skunk had given birth to three torpedo boats. As the discussion continued, more straws came flying in the wind. SPS-40, the erratic air search radar, found three bogeys in the sky. CIC now had a use for its aircraft plotting board, the vertical plastic slab. Everyone speculated on a Chinese attack. Next, the radar monitor (ECM) crackled with waves sweeping in from a northerly direction. Here, it seemed, was final confirmation of real enemies closing in.

Within minutes, however, everything vanished. The surface contacts faded away. The ECM went dumb. Fortunately for the lone Crusader, the three bogeys disappeared. Men who observed these phenomena still disagree on whether any of them were real. The air contacts, somebody at the Pentagon later told the press, probably were flocks of birds. As for the ECM, one might expect the detection of radar waves to be certain evidence of a man-made object somewhere, but ECM equipment, essentially a radio receiver, is subject to atmospheric interference. If genuine, the radar waves could have been coming from Bach Long Vi.

Says the Official Chronology:

"9:08 P.M., August 4. The *Maddox* reported that the unidentified aircraft had disappeared from its radar screen and that the surface vessels were remaining at a distance. The U.S. aircraft from the *Ticonderoga* arrived and commenced defensive patrol over the *Maddox* and the *Turner Joy*."

The "U.S. aircraft" arriving at 9:08 P.M. might have been the lone F-8 launched at 8:46 P.M. A 22-minute flight would have been fast, but perhaps not impossible. The trouble with this report is that

I have found almost no destroyerman to back it up. All but one of those interviewed on this point either did not remember when aircraft arrived or, more often, insisted that *no* aircraft showed up until later —after the shooting started.

Radarmen picked up more skunks at 9:11 P.M. Fourteen miles to the northeast, three blips were making 40 knots on a course intercepting the destroyers' still southeasterly path. Before vanishing, their closest approach was 11 miles. The destroyers did not shoot at them. Nor did the "U.S. aircraft" reportedly on station find any big, 40-knot wakes.

"You'd have beautiful pips for a while, and then they'd disappear," says Radarman James A. Stankevitz. He and Herbert O. Hazelwood, both now civilians, were the *Maddox*'s most experienced radarmen. Sometime after dark, they remember, the radar stopped ducting. Indeed, the range shortened to *less* than normal.

As the destroyers continued southward, they ran into the beginning of a line squall edging into the Gulf from the open sea. Perhaps a layer of cold air was causing sub-refraction, which is the opposite of super-refraction. If an upper layer of hot, thin air will bend radar waves downward, thus extending the range of a surface search radar, then an upper layer of cold, dense air will bend the waves upward, *decreasing* the range. Sub-refraction, while more common along polar coastlines, can take place in tropical areas, just as super-refraction sometimes will occur in the frigid latitudes.

On this night the U. S. Navy was in for some weird electronic effects. Yet no storm roiled the surface of the Gulf. Published accounts of the night action have tended to exaggerate the weather, as if the destroyers were pitching and tossing in a heavy thunderstorm. In fact, the Task Group plowed through waves only a foot or two high. It was the airmen who fought wind and rain. Storms bedeviled their route between the middle of the Gulf and Yankee Station.

In the destroyers' location, the weather presented more subtle problems. Aboard *Maddox,* Chief McRae called it an "electrified night." Radarman Stankevitz looked outside and declared it "darker than the hubs of hell." Layers of cloud stacked up to a tremendous height, completely blotting out the stars (a thin moon would not rise until after 2 A.M.). The *Turner Joy* steamed only 1000 yards behind the *Maddox,* but the two destroyers, blacked-out, could not see each other except by radar. With their eyes, topside sailors could make out nothing but the occasional flash of lightning and the phosphorescence of their own wake. From her highest manned point, the Main Director, Lieutenant (jg) John J. Barry estimated the *Turner Joy*'s luminous trail of water to be visible for only 100 yards.

The Official Chronology says nothing about the radar contacts of 9:11 P.M. It resumes the story at 9:30 P.M. when new contacts appeared ahead of the destroyers and to the left:

"9:30 P.M., August 4. Additional vessels were observed on the *Maddox* radar, and these vessels began to close rapidly on the destroyer patrol at speeds in excess of 40 knots. The attacking craft continued to close rapidly from the west and south and the *Maddox* reported that their intentions were evaluated as hostile."

Evidently this was the 9:30 P.M. attack that Secretary McNamara described to reporters. As *Maddox*'s radarmen recall it, the skunks again shuffled off or disappeared. Perhaps *Turner Joy* radarmen kept them on the scope. In any event, men of both ships had the impression that they were surrounded by a "swarm" of hostile torpedo craft that kept dancing in and out of range. The Official Chronology's next entry came 22 minutes later:

"9:52 P.M., August 4. The destroyers reported that they were under continuous torpedo attack and were engaged in defensive counterfire."

At some unspecified time between 9:30 P.M. and 9:52 P.M., all hell broke loose. A "continuous torpedo attack" is no everyday affair. The Official Chronology does not mention at what time the first torpedo was heard, at what time the destroyers opened fire, or whether aircraft joined the fray. It implies that the North Vietnamese shot first and that the Americans defended themselves. Senator Frank J. Lausche, Ohio Democrat, tried to clarify this point at the secret hearing of August 6, 1964. Lausche already had been told that the Communists shot first on Sunday. He asked of Tuesday's battle:

"The shots again were initiated by the North Vietnamese?"

"Yes," replied Secretary McNamara.

"That is correct," said General Wheeler.

As one of the staunchest hawks in Washington, Senator Lausche had bitterly opposed holding another hearing in 1968, but information disclosed at that time did not justify the confidence he had placed in the Pentagon a few years earlier. In his prepared statement, Secretary McNamara now said that the Task Group opened fire *"when it was evident from their maneuvers"* [italics mine] that they (the North Vietnamese) were *pressing in for attack positions* [italics mine]." An unofficial authority, the *Turner Joy*'s "cruise book" (a memorial volume similar to a school yearbook) put it this way:

"Turner Joy's guns were ready long before the contacts reached torpedo launching range and commenced firing when there could be no doubt of the contacts' intentions."

These written sources make it appear that Tuesday's open fire was like Sunday's—minus the "warning shots."

In describing the action to me, several men recalled that the destroyers opened fire before hearing any torpedoes. A few disagreed, saying that the first torpedo was detected by sonar before the guns fired. One of the best informed officers of the *Turner Joy* admitted that the first torpedo was *heard* after the open fire but insisted, nonetheless, that the North Vietnamese still could have shot first. According to this officer, which side shot first depends on an unknown fact: how long the torpedo was in the water. "You could study this to your dying day," he said, "and you wouldn't know who shot first. It was that close."

The destroyermen, in any case, did not plan to let the other side shoot first. They intended to open fire as soon as a torpedo boat came close enough to hit. The run to the southeast, as on Sunday, was meant to keep a safe distance while separating peaceful craft from hostile pursuers. What about reconnaissance by air? It seems that, so far as decision-makers knew at the time, no aircraft were present, not even the "U.S. aircraft" that, according to the Official Chronology, arrived on station at 9:08 P.M.

To backtrack again, the critical events unfolded as follows.

By 9 P.M. Commodore Herrick was under great pressure and distinctly disturbed by the way things were going. Believing himself about to be overwhelmed, Herrick had broken through the 19:10 barrier established by CINCPACFLT. The destroyers ought to have come under attack, but so far not a shot had been fired. Instead, impish radar contacts played on the scope outside of gun range. Everything was being reported to higher command, including the Pentagon and, no doubt, the White House. Not only Herrick but the whole Navy was on the spot. A message asked the commodore: "Have you engaged yet?" No, he had not, even though a whole posse of torpedo boats had been observed. Somewhere between the Tonkin Gulf and the Pentagon, a disgusted admiral pounded his fist. "Why doesn't the son-of-a-bitch *shoot* at them?" he wanted to know.

At last the long-awaited attack presented itself. As Lieutenant Barry of the *Turner Joy* observed it, sometime after 9 P.M., perhaps about 9:15, a single skunk appeared ahead of the Task Group and off to one side. The destroyers were still in column, steaming southeast. Barry watched the contact "drift" aft, then start closing from that direction. Aboard *Maddox* it seems to have been the same contact that flashed into the scope at 9:34 P.M.—from absolutely nowhere, so far as CIC could tell. The skunk was astern and closing. Radarmen measured its speed at 38 knots. From the northeast, an apparent torpedo boat was overtaking the destroyers at a relative speed of about 6 knots. Hard and clear, this was *Maddox*'s best contact of the night; the after-fire control radar had it, too. Watching the scope there was Lee E. Burton, a radarman of three years' experience.

Astern the *Turner Joy* was a thousand yards closer to the enemy, and Captain Barnhart did not need permission to open fire. It already had been decided that any fast-moving skunk within a certain distance would be treated as hostile. Why would a 38-knot boat be chasing the destroyers if not to attack them with torpedoes? At 9:35 P.M. the skunk was 10,000 yards off *Turner Joy*'s port quarter, and the ship's after guns opened up. With an ear-splitting roar, the 5-inch rifles abaft began spitting shells as fast as the automatic mechanism could move them.

As on Sunday, the enemy was not easily discouraged. He kept coming. At 9:39 P.M. four minutes after the *Turner Joy*, *Maddox*'s after guns opened fire.[3] According to a man who was topside, "Both 3-inch mounts started firing and so did Mount 53. I remember the 5-inch gunners hadn't changed over to flashless ammunition the way they should have, and Mount 53 lit up the whole sky. There was some comment from the bridge about that . . . No, the ship wasn't dodging torpedoes yet."

By other accounts, the 3-inchers did not fire at this time and the 5-inch guns lobbed only star shells. Either way, the sky lit up, and Lieutenant Bane again lost his night vision.

For several minutes the lone torpedo boat charged the two de-

[3] At the 1968 hearing, Secretary McNamara asserted that the *Maddox* and *Turner Joy* opened fire "at about 9:39 P.M." Logs indicate that the *Turner Joy* started shooting at 9:35 P.M. and the *Maddox* at 9:39 P.M.

stroyers, through shellfire and shrapnel. Finally, down to 6000 yards range, the boat pulled away, turning to port, still under heavy fire. Some describe the blip's entire course as a shallow curve; others remember a fish hook, with the shank on a line for the destroyers and the hook pointing back to the northeast. Destroyermen took the curving motion for a launch turn.

On each ship approximately twenty men were topside, straining their eyes into the darkness for a glimpse of the enemy or—God forbid—a torpedo wake. On a night like this, by the time an incoming wake could be seen, its explosion would not be far off. Sonar had better provide warning, if warning should be needed. Down in the bowels of the *Maddox*, Sonarman David Mallow crouched over his instruments, six feet below the waterline. Mallow waited for the characteristic *Zzzzzt!* of the tiny, fast propellers of a torpedo. The inexperienced 3rd class soundman's performance now could mean life or death for himself and the whole crew. Would he fail to give warning—as the sonar watch did on Sunday afternoon?

By *Maddox*'s logs, everything important happened at 9:39 P.M., each event within seconds of the other. The guns opened fire, David Mallow sang out, and the ship swerved to avoid torpedo attack. Witnesses differ on whether Mallow reported a "torpedo in the water," a "hydrophone effect," or a "noise spoke" (another term for an acoustical effect). Whatever it may have been, the noise was on the port quarter—*the direction of the launch turn radar contact*. Evidently a spread of torpedoes was on the way. Captain Ogier ordered a hard right rudder. *Maddox* heeled over, dodging the track of the presumed missiles.

Turner Joy's sonarmen heard nothing. Their ship steamed right through *Maddox*'s turning point before Captain Barnhart, warned by radio, ordered a starboard swerve of his own.

As the *Turner Joy* swung around, Lieutenant Barry and Seaman Larry O. Litton, both in the Main Director, saw a thin, straight wake run up the port side. The apparent torpedo sped harmlessly by. The same wake, according to Secretary McNamara, was observed by two more *Turner Joy* men: the port lookout, Edwin R. Sentel, and a visual spotter in the After Director, Seaman Rodger Bergland.

Following David Mallow's first alarm, the night became chaos. The soundman called out another "noise spoke" or whatever, and the *Maddox* leaned over again. Losing their balance, crewmen grabbed anything handy. In CIC the big Dead Reckoning Tracer table served the purpose. Men knelt beside it, flexing their knees and turning their faces away from the glass and plastic dials and scopes lest they shatter if a torpedo struck home. Commodore Herrick, who again made CIC his battle station, gripped both sides of the hatch and leaned out into the passageway, keeping his weight off the deck.

Below decks, one of the men lying flat changed his position. He noticed that several filing cabinets would start sliding his way in the event of a concussion.

After the second torpedo was evaded, David Mallow called out another, and another, and another. The destroyer veered crazily.

"The captain really swung her around," says one of the men who were on the bridge. "I didn't think the old *Maddox* would turn like that."

The torpedo assault continued, incredibly, for about two hours. Between hard-over turns, Radarman Leonard G. Smith tried to sketch the whole action on the DRT scroll. The paper filled up so rapidly that it had to be turned three times. Smith later joined the Army and found himself with the infantry in Vietnam, but he never forgot the details of the harrowing night at sea. From Vietnam, he wrote in a letter:

"We had a speaker in CIC from Sonar. The Sonarmen passed bearings over the speaker which I plotted in order for the ship to turn and evade the torpedoes. I had several bad dreams after that, and I would keep hearing those bearings coming over that speaker. It would sound something like this: 'Torpedo in the water bearing 280 . . . getting louder, getting louder, getting louder, getting very loud, getting very loud, decreasing range. Three hundred yards, bearing 280 . . . 270 bearing . . . 280 . . . 280 to 200 . . . 280 to 150 . . . 280 to 275.' Everyone waited for the bridge to make a turn to evade the torpedo. My palms would sweat . . . It was hot outside and even hotter inside because of everybody crammed into CIC. No one had had time for a shower in about 48 hours, and everyone was sweating under the tension."

Radarman Smith, who stayed on the job throughout history's worst cross fire of torpedoes, or apparent torpedoes, takes great pride in having been present. "CIC was like one precision made watch," he said, "and every spring and wheel making two little hands go round."

While Smith jumped up and down to mark torpedo tracks on the DRT, Gunner Norman Leavitt was closed up inside the rearmost gun mount bracing himself. Leavitt couldn't figure out when to relax. "They would tell us 'torpedo in the water,' he recalls, "and they would never tell us where the torpedo went."

With Leavitt was Felix Nerio, who recollects, "They passed the word every couple of minutes to brace yourself, torpedoes coming, and I kept grabbing the gun. I grabbed it so hard the stone flew out of my ring finally and flew across by Leavitt." The ring, crushed out of shape, later had to be cut from Nerio's hand.

The Official Diagram shows the destroyers steaming on a fairly direct course, aiming for Yankee Station. At the 1964 press conference, Secretary McNamara described it as the normal course of the patrol, which, every time it was mentioned in the news, was proceeding routinely to the southeast. Actually, the two ships quit the southeasterly course when the battle started. They maneuvered independently for a couple of hours within a big oval between Hainan and Mui Ron. No doubt shellbursts and gun flashes could be seen from the high ground behind Mui Ron.

The rapid-firing *Turner Joy* was quite a spectacle. Looking out of *Maddox*'s rear mount, Gunner Robert Swift greatly admired the *Turner Joy*'s weapons. "They were so fast," says Swift, "that a continuous yellow blaze hung off the barrel."

Maddox's gunners had plenty of time to brace themselves and watch the battle. After the first minute or two, they were not moving any shells. Noticing the dead silence from the weapons department, Commodore Herrick asked the reason for it. The answer came back: No targets on the fire control radar. Yet the water was full of torpedoes, and the *Turner Joy* was claiming hits on enemy boats. "Well, shoot at something!" barked the commodore, losing his temper for the only time that week. Hearing of this order, Lieutenant Connell didn't know what to do. Reportedly he went to confer with the skipper, who advised him to fire some star shells. Perhaps that would flush the enemy.

The illumination rounds soared high into the night, ejecting flares suspended by little parachutes. But where was the light? Looking upward, the destroyermen could make out only a few lumes, gradually getting brighter. The flares were caught in the overcast. Eventually they came burning through, lighting the water on all sides, but after a brief moment of glory they sputtered out and fell invisibly into the sea. The short-lived incandescence silhouetted no enemy boats. The *Maddox,* however, was bathed in a white glare, and the men topside lost what was left of their night vision.

Turner Joy avoided the flare mistake by not having any flares. There was some kind of bug in the Navy's 5-inch .54 caliber star shell that made it dangerous. But Captain Barnhart's After Director was finding plenty of targets, and the gunners there were busily engaged. The Mark 56 radar and computer were operated by two enlisted men from Texas: Melvin Royce Bow and Marshall L. Hakala. The Texans had a compartment to themselves while, above, the After Fire Control Officer, Lieutenant (jg) Wayne Whitmore, sat in an open tub with the visual spotter, Rodger Bergland. Bow and Hakala did the critical work of aiming and firing the guns. Whitmore had no scope of his own, but he had implicit confidence in the Mark 56 radar. "We used to track gulls with it," he told me. One of the ship's officers went to see how Bow and Hakala were getting along. They were too busy to talk, and the officer went away.

The *Turner Joy*'s forward 5-inch gun fired once or twice, blinding the bridge, then reverted to its inoperative state. Except for a few moments when both were "down" with mechanical difficulties, the after 5-inch guns worked beautifully. The two pumped an enormous number of shells, as did the fast 3-inchers. No figures have ever been mentioned.

Radarmen of both ships agree that near search became extremely difficult because of "knuckles" in the water. When a ship turns, it leaves a welling in the wake called a "knuckle." Two ships swerving around can make a welter of knuckles, which on the radar look like solid objects.

It was a rare kind of engagement. The *Maddox,* dark and silent, made a poor target for torpedo attack; yet she continually twisted and swerved to escape sudden death. The old short hull fired only about sixty rounds during the lengthy battle. The *Turner Joy,* glowing with gunfire, made a spectacular target, but her zigzagging was a routine defensive measure. She never heard any torpedoes, not even the one or two spotted visually.

The *Turner Joy*'s Chief Sonarman Joseph E. Schaperjahn could not believe that a real battle was in progress. If twenty-three-year-old David Mallow knew what he was doing, the chief, a veteran of

World War II, was sitting through one of the biggest torpedo assaults of all time without hearing a thing. On a few occasions, the younger sonarmen on Schaperjahn's staff thought they had a suspicious noise. Schaperjahn would then check his radarscope and tell the younger men to forget it—they were picking up the *Maddox*'s screwbeat. Usually, Schaperjahn could see the flagship on his scope; otherwise, he would ask the bridge where she was.

As in *Turner Joy*'s CIC, the sonar compartment's radar showed surface blips bright and clear. Schaperjahn did not believe in them, either. "At first I did," recalls the chief, now retired. "But when a single shell would make four of them disappear, I began to wonder."

Like any technician, Schaperjahn had to put his faith in his training and his equipment. He did not believe that any torpedoes were in the water, and he kept saying so.

According to Secretary McNamara, North Vietnamese radio messages told of a battle in progress. Two Communist boats were reported "lost," an airplane was shot down, and a destroyer "wounded." In fact, no airplane was shot down and no destroyer "wounded." But there were such reports on the air, and *Turner Joy* claimed the sinking of two or three torpedo boats. She also reported the sinking of one torpedo boat by another torpedo boat, so horrendous was the cross fire.

Before the shooting started, it was hoped back at Yankee Station that aircraft would confirm or deny the presence of attacking torpedo craft. The story now switches to the pilots' point of view.

Tom Gehman was just finishing a stint as landing signal officer when, unknown to him, the emergency arose up north. Gehman walked into the Ready Room, eased into a chair, and heard the intercom demand two A-4 (Skyhawk) pilots. On an impulse, the lieutenant went over to his squadron leader, Commander Wesley McDonald, and said, "I'd like to go." McDonald intended to fly the other A-4 himself, and he was glad to get a volunteer. "I had no idea of what was happening," Gehman told this writer, "but Wes [McDonald] filled me in as we got ready."

By 8:48 P.M. the two Skyhawks were in the air, and, according to McDonald's recollection three years later, the trip north took 30 or 40 minutes. That would indicate a 9:28 P.M. arrival at latest—seven minutes before the *Turner Joy* opened fire. But, having reached the area, it then took some time to locate the destroyers visually. The Skyhawks flew dark except for McDonald's winglight, which Gehman kept his eyes on. McDonald alone searched for the destroyers. After a while, the Skyhawk commander spotted a luminescent wake. There was *Maddox,* steaming at the bottom of the inkwell. McDonald doesn't remember seeing the ship fire her guns, nor does he recall whether *Turner Joy* had begun shooting yet. Gehman doesn't remember whether the destroyers were firing, though he recalls that "Things were going hot and heavy when we got there." In any case, the Skyhawk pilots, like the F-8 presumably on station already, were soon looking for torpedo boats. But the jets' narrow-angle attack radar proved to be not so good for sweeping the Gulf (though the F-8 radar had performed well on Sunday); and the pilots wanted precise ranges and bearings from the destroyers in order to find surface targets on that dark night.

As flagship, the *Maddox* took primary responsibility for the air control. On the job as air controller was a chief petty officer nicknamed "Shaky," a man of nervous temperament who, lacking formal training in air control, had picked up what he knew from experience. (Lieutenant Evans, trained in air control, was in his regular job as CIC officer.) Shaky talked the planes in as Evans had done on Sunday, but what happened next is not at all clear. Hoping to get his side of the story, I managed to find the *Maddox*'s former air controller, now retired. He did not wish to be interviewed, but he did say that he could not recall whether the planes reached the scene before or after the shooting started. Also retired from the Navy was the *Turner Joy*'s former air controller, Chief Robert Johnson. Former Chief Johnson is one of the many ex-destroyermen who believe that *no* aircraft reached the scene until after the shooting started. "That's why," says Johnson, "we didn't direct any planes to look at the launch turn contact."

In any case, no pilot saw a torpedo boat making a launch turn; and after the battle definitely was under way, the pilots, according to their recollection, still could not find out where to look. They unanimously describe the air control as "chaotic," "confused," and "garbled." Evidently the *Maddox*'s radar could not hold a target long enough for Shaky to prepare the necessary directions. The *Maddox* did have plenty of information on torpedoes, thanks to Sonarman Mallow, and Shaky excitedly called out their bearings. If the enemy boats were real, there ought to have been plenty of high-speed wakes in the immediate vicinity. But the pilots saw none.

Maddox's CIC officers observed that the air control was not effective; and, knowing that the *Turner Joy* claimed excellent radar targets, they decided to give the aircraft to the other ship. The *Turner Joy* refused. Her air controller, Chief Johnson, was having trouble with his radio transmitter. He could hear the airmen talk, but most of the time he was unable to get through to them. His transmitter, Johnson told me, wouldn't carry more than 10 miles. Since the *Turner Joy* was firing at targets less than 10 miles away, one might expect the range to be sufficient. However, the *Turner Joy* repeatedly refused to take over the air control, and most pilots agree that it was difficult to establish radio contact with that ship. Her continuous firing and zigzagging made everyone's job difficult. Radioman Gary Stephens told the AP: "I had to watch one of my transmitters close because it had a tendency to switch off, and I had to hit the reset button. Whenever we'd fire, it would shake the ship pretty bad and had a tendency to knock us off the air."

The Skyhawks circled around, waiting for an opportunity to attack the enemy. Gehman said later: "We were too high. We were at 5000 or 7000 feet, just below the overcast. It was a good altitude for rocket runs, but not for searching."

At last McDonald located a high-speed wake and reported it to one of the destroyers—he could not be sure which. Despite the difficulty with its transmitter, sometimes the *Turner Joy* would come through.

"That must be a torpedo boat," said one of the air controllers.

"Just to be sure," said McDonald, "the wake is on bearing 120."

The air controller thought this over. Then he yelled, "Don't shoot! We're on 120!"

On another occasion, the *Turner Joy* came through "calm and clear," as McDonald recalls. The ship sounded much better organized than the *Maddox*. Chief Johnson said, "We're shooting at a target over at . . ." and gave directions. "Can you give us a hand?" asked the chief. McDonald and Gehman saw a stream of "red hot balls" moving in the direction indicated. The two Skyhawks followed the trail of shells and saw them impacting about 3000 yards astern of the destroyer. No torpedo boats were visible, but the jets nevertheless unloaded half of their rockets in the same place, hoping the enemy was there. It did not seem as though a better target would be found. Each Skyhawk loosed a pod of nineteen rockets, achieving a buckshot effect. These were not the big Zunis carried by the F-8s but clustered missiles only 2.75 inches in diameter.

Lumbering along at a mere 160 knots, the two Skyraiders that took to the air first probably reached the destroyers' area shortly after the Skyhawks. Commander Edmondson remembers talking by radio to Commander McDonald on the way up. Edmondson says that the ships were not in column when he found them and that they were under torpedo attack, although Edmondson did not hear anything about gunfire when he arrived. By the time *Maddox* opened fire, she must have had about five planes to take care of, either on station or just about to get there. Among the pilots were three of the *Ticonderoga*'s five squadron leaders. To the layman it may seem wasteful to put all of that talent and equipment under the control of a chief petty officer with no formal training in his job, but that is how the Navy did it.

From the *Maddox* Commander Edmondson heard of a "threat area" just a couple of thousand yards to the northeast. Immediately the two Spads darted over there and began their search routine. Edmondson and Barton had practiced night search many times. Barton now orbited in the "attack position" while Edmondson flew over the designated area, dropping flares. Offensive doctrine called for a Communist skipper to be caught in the bright lights, and for Jere Barton to clobber him. But where to put the flares, says Edmondson, was "largely a matter of guesswork" owing to imprecise air control. Besides that, the ceiling was only 3500 feet (lower than Gehman reported), and some of the flares were defective. In Edmondson's first run, only two out of four flares lit off; they burned only a short time before hitting the water. Very little light resulted, and no boats were found. The Spads took turns laying flares and waiting in the attack position.

It was Commander Edmondson's idea to suggest by radio that the carrier send up a radar plane. The pilots were used to being directed by the twin-engine "Willie Fudd" (WF-2), a propeller craft with full-time radarmen. *Ticonderoga* had three Fudds. Unfortunately, only one left the deck that night, and instead of searching the Gulf it orbited between the destroyers and the carrier to relay messages for the CAP. Ironically, Edmondson never learned whether *his* messages got through. His radio, like that of the *Turner Joy*'s air controller, was malfunctioning. (Strangely, Edmondson claims to have been able to communicate better with the *Turner Joy* than with the *Maddox,* though other pilots had the opposite experience.)

While the lone Fudd relayed messages for the CAP, the destroyers had their own middlemen. Two ships, the *Moore* and Herrick's *Berkeley,* helped the Task Group. They were known, respectively, as Watchdog and Bulldog. The Bulldog position seems to have been near Tiger Island. I never found out why *Berkeley* happened to be in the area.

By radio Commander Edmondson was able to reach Commander McDonald, who warned him that the jets were "coming down through" the clouds for a search closer to the water. Knowing the jets were low on fuel and would have to leave soon, Edmondson marked the northeastern threat area for them with his last flares; the two Spads, not wishing to "get into the middle of the jets' program," then departed for a new threat area to the west. Like the Spads, the Skyhawks found nothing in the northeast; they, too, complained of poor illumination.

The Spads' new domain lay just a few miles from the *Maddox.* Edmondson and Barton resumed their flare-dropping routine, this time with the commander in the attack position. Now the ceiling dropped even lower, down to about 1000 feet. Barton laid his flares as best he could. Edmondson swooped through, and called out, "Jere, I'm being shot at!" The commander saw what looked like "fireflies" or tracers in the air. He thought they might be reflections of ordnance fired by the jets, but, no, the "fireflies" were arching up from the sea and falling down again. They looked like anti-aircraft tracers. Jere Barton didn't see the tracers at all; he could have been facing in the wrong direction. The enemy fire or whatever didn't last long, and Edmondson failed to locate their source. The commander made another pass, saw more "fireflies," and again failed to locate a target. The two planes milled around for some time but saw nothing of interest. Neither Spad fired a shot.

Like Commander McDonald, Commander Edmondson could have fired blindly into what seemed to be the enemy's general location. Edmondson explained to me that he didn't know exactly where the destroyers were, hence feared the effect of ricochets. At about this time the propeller pilots were close enough to the Task Group to see an F-8 firing into the wake of what Edmondson thought was the *Maddox*. The Spad men were startled by how close to the destroyer the F-8 would dive and strafe.

Turner Joy men tell of an apparent attack on them by a jet plane. From the bridge, Captain Barnhart saw rockets or tracers leave the plane. Yelling for everybody to hit the deck, Barnhart grabbed the man next to him and pulled him down. Fortunately, nothing hit the destroyer. Possibly the jet was diving on a knuckle in the wake.

Both ships thought torpedo boats were "bore-sighting" on the wake, a tactic by which the enemy follows a destroyer's big luminous wake and fires torpedoes when she turns, presenting a broad target. The radar showed contacts astern. Air attack, however, failed to wipe them out. The ships next tried depth charges, which occasionally since World War I have been tossed at surface craft astern. The Task Group's first cans were set very shallow. They failed to discourage the enemy, but "they rattled us pretty good," says one destroyerman. Another recalls getting splashed with water though his position was well about the fantail. After dropping a few more cans, set to explode at greater depth, the destroyers abandoned that tactic and, in utter disgust, reached back in history for the oldest of naval weapons. They turned to ram. The "bore-sighting" theory lost some plausibility when the ships found themselves cutting through nothing solid— just water and air.

The Official Chronology has this to say:

"10:15 P.M., August 4. The destroyers reported that they had avoided torpedoes and had sunk one of the attacking craft.

"10:42 P.M., August 4. The destroyers reported that they had evaded additional torpedoes and had sunk another of the attacking craft. Other protective aircraft arrived overhead, but weather and darkness were hampering operations."

The "destroyers" were not evading additional torpedoes. Only the *Maddox* was.

The "other protective aircraft" could have referred to the earlier arrivals of McDonald, Edmondson, and their wingmen. The term also could have referred to a pair of F-8s that flew as CAP but, for some reason, were not listed in the master flight logs. One of the F-8 pilots later flew with the Navy's acrobatic team, the Blue Angels.

When I talked to him, he remembered only that it was a "very dark night."

The Task Group reported sinking two enemy boats. The estimate was based on radar contacts disappearing as shells burst upon them, on visual observation of secondary explosions, and on visual observation of burning targets. Although *Maddox*'s radar was outclassed by *Turner Joy*'s in its ability to find targets, Commodore Herrick vouches for the disappearance of radar contacts as shells poured onto them. He saw this happen on two occasions. From the *Turner Joy*, Lieutenant Barry saw secondary explosions; and Rodger Bergland, using high-powered optics in the After Director, twice discovered boats burning in the water. Bergland, however, could not tell whether the fiery wrecks were fishing junks or torpedo boats.

The airmen, unable to find good targets, were really baffled. As they risked their lives darting around "on the deck," the pilots gritted their teeth, fuming at the weather, darkness, and air control. Commander Jackson, who had been an air show parachutist in his 'teens, marveled at how the F-8s and Skyraiders performed amazing stunts in their eagerness to find the enemy. "One of the F-8s," he says, "came down at a tremendous speed, just a hundred feet above the water. He was either insane or one of the best pilots I ever saw." Whenever the executive officer saw planes coming his way, he flicked on the *Maddox*'s running lights or Grimes light—a rotating beacon similar to that on police cars. Jackson thought he saw Crusader searching with photoflash bombs; but an F-8 pilot told me that the F-8s were not equipped with these. More probably the jet was expending ordnance. Fortunately, the pilots didn't shoot any destroyers, snag a wave, or run into each other.

On at least one occasion, a destroyer fired at a radar contact that turned out to be an airplane. No damage was done.

Low on fuel, the original F-8 returned to the carrier, its pilot telling Admiral Moore that he could not find any torpedo boats. The Skyhawks turned back at about the same time, approximately 10:30 P.M.; McDonald and Gehman remember struggling back to the carrier "through hairy thunderstorms." By the time the slower Skyhawks returned, the *Ticonderoga* had run out of sea room; she was closing the Paracel Islands south of Hainan. The Skyhawks plugged into tankers and waited for a chance to come down, which they did at midnight. Admiral Moore collected another negative report. So far not a single returning pilot had seen anything.

Meanwhile, to replace the original jets, the *Ticonderoga* began launching aircraft again shortly after 10 P.M. A lone Spad took off at 10:07. Two Skyhawks followed at 10:21; another Spad took to the air at 10:25. These were the last planes to be launched by the carrier before midnight. Perhaps more should have been; but, except for the radar plane, the pilots themselves did not want any more. On that dark night, with a low ceiling and imprecise air control, the search involved a high risk of collision. (The number of CAP planes, nevertheless, greatly increased when the *Constellation* pulled into launching distance.)

There was a lull in the battle that started perhaps at 10:30 P.M. and lasted until about 10:50 P.M. The Official Chronology resumes:

"10:52 P.M., August 4. The *Maddox* reported that the destroyers were again under attack."

The second wave of CAP ought to have been arriving at about this time, joining Edmondson and Barton, who were still hard at work.

According to one report, it was sometime after 11 P.M., maybe around midnight, when the *Maddox* trained all six of her 5-inch guns on the *Turner Joy* and almost blew her "clear out of the water." The quotation is from Patrick N. Park, the sonarman who, because of Sunday's trouble with gunnery, had transferred back to his old job in the Main Director. Park says that he was ordered to fire at a good, hard radar contact only 1500 yards abeam. Park was about to fire when, looking closely at the radarscope, the presentation there—a pencil-thick line and two smaller, dancing ones—reminded him of a nearby destroyer seen broadside. Where's the *Turner Joy?* Park wanted to know. Curses blasted the headphones. The ship was in danger, but the man with the firing key refused to obey orders. Ensign Corsette now had the authority to draw his pistol and force Park to do his job. Instead, the bridge asked the *Turner Joy* to show her lights. There she was—right in the cross hairs of the Main Director.

Ensign Corsette, now Lieutenant Corsette, flatly denies the whole *Turner Joy* incident, labeling it a post-action "sea story." Corsette adds that the Main Director did not have control of all six guns that night but only of the two mounts forward. Both Park, now a fast-food store manager in La Mirada, California, and Corsette, still in the Navy, are convincing. I asked Park why the 3-inch guns didn't take the radar contact under fire. Park didn't know. He supposed that they must have been busy with another target.[4]

Before the *Turner Joy* incident, Patrick Park remembers the bridge kept pressure on the gunners to find some targets and shoot at them; about ten minutes afterward, the pressure let up. If it happened, the near-destruction of the *Turner Joy* ought to have been a very sobering experience. If it did not happen, those in command would in any event have grown skeptical of the battle, because David Mallow was finding too many torpedoes. One of the men below decks counted seventeen and gave up. A man in the COMVAN kept track of twenty-seven. In all, the *Maddox* made eighty-four hard-rudder turns, though perhaps not all of them were caused by sonar alarms. In its action report, the Task Group settled on twenty-two enemy missiles.

The absurdity of the situation gradually became apparent. A few of the men in CIC, including the commodore, began to joke about the torpedoes. Even the *Turner Joy* wasn't finding enough attackers to account for them. A few years later Captain Ogier recalled: "Evaluating everything that was going on, I was becoming less and less convinced that somebody was out there." Someone (various persons take the credit) pointed out that a new torpedo seemed to follow every hard-rudder turn; perhaps the ship herself somehow was generating the noise. Commodore Herrick reported later: ". . . he (Ogier) was able to verify this by producing similar hydrophone effects by making full rudder turns. We were amazed that there would be such similarity to actual torpedo noises." The officers decided that the "torpedo noise" actually was the beat of the ship's own propellers reflected from the hard-over rudder. By an unofficial report, the *Maddox* heard her last torpedo at 11:36 P.M. The Rudder Reflection Theory, however, did not account for Mallow's first torpedo, discovered when the ship was steaming in a straight line. Most of the *Maddox*'s crew, both officer and enlisted, kept their belief in a North Vietnamese attack.

---

[4] Park's story was first reported by Joseph Goulden in *Truth Is the First Casualty*. Goulden timed the incident "around midnight." Park, when I talked to him, thought it could have happened as early as 11:30 P.M.; he was not at all sure about the time. There was a third man in the Director, 2nd Class Radarman Timothy G. Deyarmie, now employed by IBM in El Paso, Texas. Deyarmie, Park told me, supported his refusal to fire. When I found Deyarmie, early in 1970, he "vaguely" remembered something like the *Turner Joy* incident, but said he could recall "nothing specific."

The Official Chronology:

"Midnight. The patrol reported that, even though torpedoes had been fired at them, they had suffered no hits nor casualties and that the defensive aircraft from the *Ticonderoga* were illuminating the area and attacking the enemy surface craft."

The original Spads were still on the job, still searching threat areas. Toward midnight, the *Turner Joy* gave them a vector to the southeast (155 degrees). Heading in that direction, Edmondson and Barton flew over the two destroyers, which they could see were back in column zigzagging to the southeast. The Task Group now was leaving the big oval between Hainan and Mui Ron, where most of the action took place. Shortly after passing over the destroyers, Commander Edmondson spotted a thin, crooked line of foam which he took to be a high-speed wake—smaller than that of the destroyers. "Jere, I think I've got one," said the commander. The phosphorescent streak lay to the right, at 1:30 o'clock, on a line to the southwest. The Spads were only 400 feet above the water; "I couldn't have seen that wake from a thousand feet," Edmondson told me. The commander wanted to roll his plane over to starboard at once, but Jere Barton was there at 5 o'clock. The Spads, therefore, banked to port and circled back, now only 200 feet over the surface of the Gulf. It was too late. The apparent wake had dissolved; nothing could be seen.

If a boat were there, the skipper's best tactic upon hearing the planes would have been to stop his engines and lie perfectly still. Then no breaking water would have marked his presence. "In that case, we would never have seen him," says Edmondson.

The two Spads searched the area for eight or ten minutes. As they did so, Edmondson radioed the Task Group, asking whether the destroyers' radar had a surface blip in his area. Word came back that planes from the *Constellation* now were on station and that the destroyers seemed to be out of danger. Edmondson and Barton were released from duty.

The Spad pilots headed home through heavy weather, and by the time they found the carrier she again was closing the Paracels. The returning airmen didn't get to bed until after 3 A.M. Before turning in, Commander Edmondson made a report to the admiral's staff. Then, after a couple of hours of sleep, Edmondson was awakened to learn that the ship was planning a strike on North Vietnam. "Fine, if anything comes up, let me know," said the groggy flyer, and went back to sleep. Edmondson doubted that the raid would actually come off.

As the original Spads went home ten or so jets from the *Constellation* started looking for the enemy. The supercarrier, having dodged perilous shoals at flank speed, was still east of Hainan, but within launching distance of the destroyers. At the height of the air search, between midnight and 1 A.M., *Maddox*'s CIC counted approximately twenty-five planes in the air. One group the destroyermen didn't even know about until they announced their departure.

The men from the *Constellation* brought a Willie Fudd along. This reduced their dependence on the Task Group for air control, but the airmen still found nothing that looked like a North Vietnamese boat. Evidently the best opportunity was lost when the Task Group advised Edmondson it was out of danger.

The Official Chronology says nothing about the *Constellation*. It continues:

"12:32 A.M., August 5. The patrol reported that at least two enemy craft had been sunk and that low ceilings continued to hamper the aircraft operations."

"12:54 A.M., August 5. The *Turner Joy* reported that during the engagement, in addition to the torpedo attack, she was fired upon by automatic weapons while being illuminated by searchlights."

The *Turner Joy* fought until shortly after midnight, perhaps half an hour longer than *Maddox* stayed with the battle. The Official Chronology carries the action even farther:

"1:30 A.M., August 5. The destroyers reported that the attacking craft had apparently broken off the engagement."

Aircraft continued to shuttle overhead from the *Constellation*. The supercarrier's pilots had not made a night take-off for about three weeks, and that can be long enough to make a man rusty. But the *Constellation*'s big umbrella opened and closed without incident.

The Chronology ends:

"The *Maddox* and *Turner Joy* were directed to resume their patrol in the Gulf of Tonkin at daylight on the 5th of August."

The ships did not immediately resume their patrol. On the order of CINCPACFLT, they began searching the battle area for debris. Higher command wanted some physical evidence of the swirling, nighttime engagement—some wreckage, lifebelted survivors, anything tangible.

Chapter XI

The Evaluation

In Washington, D.C., it was 10:35 Tuesday morning when, over on the dark side of the globe, *Turner Joy* began flinging shells at elusive blips on the radar. Officials at the Pentagon, State Department, and White House were disposed to accept reports of torpedoes and shellfire as evidence of a battle in progress, as confirmation of a predicted attack. Nobody "in the know" wanted to let the Communists get away with this—a vile ambush at night on the high seas. The National Security Council met at noon, and to the dozen-or-so men present, President Johnson declared his intention of striking back at the North Vietnamese mainland. As he spoke, Johnson could not have known that the destroyer *Maddox* was dodging her last torpedo, and that senior officers of the ship were having second thoughts as to what was going on. Approximately an hour later, at 1:27 P.M., the President and his closest aides were engrossed in the selection of air raid targets when a message from Commodore Herrick dropped like a bombshell into the Pentagon:

REVIEW OF ACTION MAKES MANY RECORDED CONTACTS AND TORPEDOES FIRED APPEAR DOUBTFUL. FREAK WEATHER EFFECTS AND OVEREAGER SONARMAN MAY HAVE ACCOUNTED FOR MANY REPORTS. NO ACTUAL VISUAL SIGHTINGS BY MADDOX. SUGGEST COMPLETE EVALUATION BEFORE ANY FURTHER ACTION.

The commodore was confiding his doubts. He feared that some kind of action would be taken on the basis of his earlier reports. Perhaps already there was talk of retaliation on the high command circuit.

The ordinary citizen might expect his leaders to sigh with relief upon hearing that Communist forces might not have attacked the

U. S. Navy after all. The President and his aides might indulge in a few jokes, order an investigation, and, shaking their heads, move on to more pressing business. Instead, consternation reigned. A few hours before, the lowly Commodore Herrick had been on the spot, wondering whether he ought to open fire. Now the whole chain of command quivered with the same uncertainty, all the way up to the Commander-in-Chief. The Defense Department already had reported a North Vietnamese attack. The President already had taken personal responsibility for a momentous decision—the biggest so far of his career. If there had been no attack, if no retaliation could be justified, there would be hell to pay. The whole story was bound to leak out, right in the middle of an election campaign. The Democrats were calling Senator Goldwater "trigger happy." Goldwater would throw the charge back at them, and make it stick. Then, after the best moment for retaliation had gone by, it probably would be decided that the North Vietnamese had made an attack after all. The Republicans would add bungling and utter foolishness to their list of charges—along with a certain softness on communism.

Of course, the President could stand on the fact that the naval commander on the scene was doubtful, and let the controversy rage, if rage it must. The Navy could bomb North Vietnam any time, if need be.

In point of fact, the plan for a quick retaliation was carried out, after some hand-wringing at the Pentagon.

At the 1968 hearing, Senator Fulbright brought up the commodore's message and asked why it was not followed by "some reasonable investigation or delay." Secretary McNamara replied:

"What do you think we would do when we got it? Well, obviously we were concerned, and we immediately began to examine it, and I have here a whole series of steps we took at that point as to what was done. I personally called Admiral Sharp and brought this to his attention, and said we obviously do not want to carry out retaliatory action unless we are 'damned sure what happened.' Those were the exact words."

(Apparently Admiral Sharp in Hawaii already knew about the decision to retaliate.)

"Did you see the cable?" Fulbright asked McNamara.

"I am not sure whether I saw the cable or whether it was brought to my attention in an oral report," replied the Defense Secretary.

The investigation had gotten off to a limp start. McNamara did not necessarily read Commodore Herrick's message. As the Secretary went on to explain, perhaps he relied on an oral report from the Air Force officer, Lieutenant General David A. Burchinal, who was Director of the Joint Staff.

A few days after the raids on North Vietnam, reporters had heard that top officials in Washington spent a leisurely Tuesday afternoon discussing targets. Maybe they did. Or maybe some of them did. But the way McNamara told the story four years later, he and the Joint Chiefs wrestled all afternoon with the question of whether the raids could be justified. The debate lasted 4½ hours. Did that period of time represent the "complete evaluation" recommended by Commodore Herrick? McNamara insisted to the senators that it did.

Following is a chronology of the evaluation on Tuesday, August 5, compiled from the transcript of the 1968 hearing, later revelations by Senator Morse, and other sources (times are Eastern Daylight unless otherwise specified):

1:27 P.M.—Herrick's message arrives in Washington. The commodore added these words (exact time uncertain):

JOY ALSO REPORTS NO ACTUAL VISUAL SIGHTINGS OR WAKE. HAVE NO RECAPS OF AIRCRAFT SIGHTINGS BUT SEEM TO BE FEW . . . ENTIRE ACTION LEAVES MANY DOUBTS EXCEPT APPARENT ATTEMPT TO AMBUSH AT BEGINNING.

Secretary McNamara telephoned Admiral Sharp and told him to make "damned sure" of what happened or, as McNamara said later in the 1968 hearing, to "be damned sure that no retaliatory action was taken until any doubts as to what went on were eliminated, at least to the point of retaliation."

Except for not being in the Tonkin Gulf, Admiral Sharp was eminently qualified to supervise an investigation. He not only was an experienced surface sailor but had commanded the Navy's sonar school in San Diego, California.

2:45 P.M.—Commodore Herrick reported visual sightings to CINCPACFLT and certified that the "original ambush" was genuine. McNamara told senators:

"Details of the action present a confusing picture, but he had made positive visual sightings of cockpit lights or similar lights passing near the *Maddox,* and the *Turner Joy* reported two torpedoes passed near her."

Herrick personally had seen no lights at all. As for the "original ambush," that took place two hours before the shooting started.

3 P.M.—Secretary McNamara met with the Deputy Secretary of Defense, Cyrus Vance, and the Joint Chiefs of Staff, except for General Wheeler who was on a trip to New York. McNamara did not yet have Herrick's message of 2:45 P.M. Presumably it was being held up in Hawaii with the hope that something more positive would come in. Shortly after 3 P.M., McNamara met with the President. At that time, McNamara told senators, the air strike was "tentatively authorized subject to the final information on the details of the incident earlier in the afternoon." By "the incident" McNamara seems to have meant Herrick's warning of 1:27 P.M.

During the afternoon, Secretary McNamara talked with the President five times, often with Secretary Rusk on the same telephone line. Between those conversations, McNamara evaluated reports from the Gulf with the help of the Joint Chiefs and other advisers. The Pentagon men frequently referred to several Communist radio messages intercepted by some elint facility or facilities. (I have found no specific indication that the intercepts came from *Maddox*'s COMVAN.) One message seemed to order an attack on the destroyers. Others told of two boats lost and of airplanes shot down.

4:40 P.M.—Admiral Sharp finally telephoned Secretary McNamara and told him about Commodore Herrick's message of 2:45 P.M. Apparently nothing better had come in. Sharp was impatient to get on with the air raids. *Time* magazine[1] reported that the admiral spent a lot of time watching clocks and that he made "about 100 calls to Washington." By 4:40 P.M. Sharp had reason to be impatient. In two hours the sun would start rising over North Vietnam. But Commodore Herrick had not yet confirmed an attack, and the Defense Secretary wanted more information. Despite Sharp's call, McNamara still would not agree to an air strike.

5:11 P.M.—Admiral Moorer, whatever the wisdom of his previous decisions, now took a sensible step. He ordered a search for debris. In 40 minutes, twilight would glimmer on the surface of the Gulf. However, at about the time CINCPACFLT transmitted this order, the White House was inviting congressional leaders to an urgent meeting scheduled for 6:45 P.M.

[1] August 14, 1964.

5:23 P.M.—Sharp again telephoned the Pentagon "stating that he was convinced that the attack had occurred and that all were satisfied that it had," McNamara told the senators. The Defense Secretary's testimony, however, does not indicate that Admiral Sharp knew any more at 5:23 P.M. than he did at 2:45 P.M. As for "all" being "satisfied," Commodore Herrick still had not confirmed anything beyond the "original ambush."

6 P.M.—The National Security Council began gathering at the White House, expecting to hear more about the President's plan to bomb North Vietnam. At "about 6 o'clock," McNamara told the senators, President Johnson gave his "final authorization" for the air raids.

6:07 P.M.—The Secretary of Defense, though authorized to order the bombing of North Vietnam, still had not made up his mind concerning the reality of the North Vietnamese attack. Admiral Sharp was on the telephone, and McNamara apparently tried to avoid talking to him. He told the senators:

"I spoke to the Director of the Joint Staff [General Burchinal] and asked him to make certain that the Commander-in-Chief, Pacific, was willing to state that the attack had taken place, and therefore that he was free to release the Executive order because earlier in the afternoon I had told him that under no circumstances would retaliatory action take place until we were, to use my words, 'damned sure that the attack had taken place.' "

Secretary McNamara wanted General Burchinal to give Admiral Sharp the go-ahead *if* Admiral Sharp "was willing to state that the attack had taken place." This would put Sharp in the position of being *the* man in the Defense establishment who had reaffirmed the attack. Commodore Herrick still had not done so. Neither had Admiral Johnson, Admiral Moorer, Admiral Moore, nor Admiral Guest.

McNamara's bureaucratic gambit was an old one, and Admiral Sharp did not fall for it. He managed to get the Secretary on the telephone. At the 1968 hearing, McNamara remembered the conversation this way:

"We discussed it, and he [Admiral Sharp] stated that he was fully assured that the attack took place. I stated that I was then convinced that it had, and I released the Executive order on the strike."

The Defense Secretary's protracted indecision must have been a trial to CINCPAC and to the President. What if Admiral Sharp had not convinced McNamara at the last minute? What would the Defense Secretary have done? Would he have given congressional leaders a lukewarm briefing, quoting CINCPAC on the critical points? Or would he have quit his job and gone home, leaving the government in chaos? McNamara really had little choice. He took the pledge.

As McNamara made his decision, the Tonkin Gulf lay still and gray in the faint light of dawn. The search for debris was getting underway.

6:10 P.M.—It is difficult to imagine that within the space of three minutes McNamara settled his differences with Admiral Sharp, hung up the telephone, and flashed the green light to the Pentagon's newsroom. Nevertheless, at 6:10 P.M. the news staff logged in the announcement of a second attack, and the Pentagon's PR battalions were ready to tell the world. (The New York *Times* later said that the announcement was made at 5 P.M.[2] Copies of the press release are unusual for having no date stamped on them.)

6:30 P.M.—Admiral Sharp passed along the air strike order, probably to CINCPACFLT. (It is my opinion that Sharp and McNamara finished their conversation between 6:20 and 6:30. I have no explanation for premature action by the news staff except to note that the air strike was fated to go ahead with or without a "complete evaluation.")

6:37 P.M.—The upper rim of the sun began to shine over North Vietnam.

6:45 P.M.—The President and his top aides from State, CIA, and Defense started briefing congressional leaders. No mention was made of the fact that the officer commanding the destroyers did not seem to know for certain whether he had been attacked.

7:06 P.M.—Admiral Moorer "cabled the *Maddox* and *Turner Joy* to report immediate confirmation of the earlier attack on them." The quote is from Senator Gore at the 1968 hearing. McNamara explained to Gore: "This was simply a response to the earlier inquiry of Sharp who got the information by other channels before that time."

What "information" did Sharp get? McNamara did not say. Herrick still doubted that there had been a real battle. He had not cabled any confirmation to Admiral Sharp. Also doubtful was Captain

[2] Edwin L. Dale, Jr., "Tonkin Gulf Decision: 12 Tense Hours Led to Swift U. S. Move," New York *Times*, August 9, 1964.

Ogier. Of the three senior officers in the Gulf, at this time only Captain Barnhart believed that there had been any attack.

Perhaps the following message, quoted by Senator Morse, was the one that CINCPACFLT sent to Herrick at 7:06 P.M.:

"1. Can you confirm absolutely that you were attacked?

"2. Can you confirm sinking of PT boats?

"3. Desire reply directly supporting evidence."

Was there some kind of hint in part 3? If so, Commodore Herrick paid no heed. Senator Morse quoted Herrick's reply:

"*Maddox* scored no known hits and never positively identified a boat as such. Furthermore, weather was overcast with limited visibility . . . air support not successful in locating targets. There were no stars or moon resulting in almost total darkness throughout action . . . No known damage or personal (*sic*) casualties to either ship. *Turner Joy* claims sinking one craft and damaging another."

Commodore Herrick still did not confirm the reality of the attack. He only discussed the situation and relayed claims from the *Turner Joy*.

CINCPACFLT, according to Senator Morse, tried again:

"A. Can you confirm that you were attacked by PT or Swatow?"

Admiral Moorer was willing to settle for an attack by gunboats carrying only 37-millimeter weapons. But Herrick refused to give him even that satisfaction. According to Senator Morse, the commodore made no reply.

The *Turner Joy*, however, came up with a bill of particulars. Captain Barnhart reported that he could confirm the attack on the basis of sighting one torpedo, a target seen burning when hit, black smoke seen by many, and target silhouette sighted by "some topside personnel." But, said Captain Barnhart, sinkings were "only highly probable" because target tracked on radar; "shell bursts observed on radar all over contact"; hits reported visually; targets disappeared.

At some point, the *Turner Joy* reported two negative factors. Senator Fulbright put into the record of the 1968 hearing this message text:

"Estimate two PT's attack originally. However, must admit two factors defer (*sic*). No ECM. However, tactics seem to be bore-sight on wake thus accounting for lack of radar signals. No sonar indications of torpedo noises even that which passed down side. Self noise was very high."

This must have been surprising news. The *Turner Joy* detected no enemy radar during the night. Nor did she hear any torpedoes.

8:15 P.M.—President Johnson concluded his meeting with congressional leaders. He had told them about the attack. He had given them a pep talk on the need to stand firm in Southeast Asia. He now obtained from the most influential Republican and the Democratic legislators their personal assurances of support for the Tonkin Gulf resolution (which, unknown to them, had been germinating since spring).

8:22 P.M.—The White House Press Secretary, George Reedy, announced that the President would make a statement on national television later that night.

9 P.M.—Admiral Johnson, the Seventh Fleet Commander, asked *Turner Joy* urgently to amplify her reports. Senator Morse quoted this portion of the telegram:

WHO WERE WITNESSES, WHAT IS WITNESS RELIABILITY? MOST IMPORTANT THAT PRESENT EVIDENCE SUBSTANTIATING TYPE AND NUMBER OF ATTACKING FORCES BE GATHERED AND DISSEMINATED.

9:30 P.M.—Admiral Johnson ordered the *Turner Joy* to "locate debris to substantiate."

11:35 P.M.—Five hours after sunrise in the Tonkin Gulf, no debris had been found. Neither destroyers nor aircraft located a stick of wood, a lifebelted survivor, or even a slick of oil. The destroyers, having given up, already were resuming their coastal patrol. President Johnson went on television, anyway. He announced air action "now in execution."

Commodore Herrick was not told about the order to bomb North Vietnam. What would he have said? It seems that higher command did not want to find out.

At the 1968 hearing, senators did not have all of the foregoing information, but what they got convinced Senator Gore that he had been "misled" and that the administration (of his own party) had acted "hastily" and "unwisely." Secretary McNamara disagreed. The evaluation was complete, he asserted. McNamara even went so far as to say that Commodore Herrick "did not doubt there was any attack."

After top officials had made up their minds about the August 4 action, the process of agreement continued at lower levels. On Friday, August 7, General Burchinal completed his examination of message traffic and reported to the Defense Secretary: "The actuality of the attack is confirmed." McNamara relayed this information to the senators as further proof of the attack; he did not say which message had convinced the Air Force general. Another week passed before the Seventh Fleet commander made up his mind. On August 14 Admiral Johnson finished his review of the Task Group's "combined chronology and track charts," and, according to Secretary McNamara, confirmed the attack. Admiral Moorer concurred.

The reader might find it interesting to speculate on when, for the purpose of ordering an air raid, the evaluation came to an end. Obviously, Admiral Johnson and Admiral Moorer were living in a dream world when, after congressional leaders gathered at the White House, they desperately sought confirmation of the attack. By then the attack was a *political fact,* with all of the President's prestige behind it. Even as early as 6:07 P.M., the pressure was too great for Secretary McNamara to resist.

It seems to me very possible that President Johnson made up his mind by shortly after 3 P.M. when, said McNamara, the air strike was "tentatively authorized." In any case, from the President's point of view, it would not have been convenient to postpone the decision beyond 5 P.M. If by that time congressional leaders were not being invited to the White House, they would scatter to their homes in the suburbs and to a variety of social engagements. It might prove impossible to round them up. And if the sixteen key lawmakers were not consulted, so to speak, they would not be so eager to support the President's action. They certainly would not feel obligated to steamroller a resolution through both Houses of Congress. The meeting perhaps could have been postponed until late at night, but by then the prime television time would have passed. As for meeting on Thursday morning, North Vietnam would be dark again; the raids then would have to wait for Thursday evening, Washington time.

In short, after 5 P.M. Wednesday, any delay would seem to demand a 24-hour postponement. Secrecy probably would be lost, and Hanoi, which still had said nothing about Sunday's battle, might seize the initiative, accusing the United States of aggression. The world would not know which side to believe, and the Tonkin Gulf would become a damaging issue in the American election campaign.

President Johnson did not lose the initiative. He stayed on the course that had been charted so quickly after Commodore Herrick's first reports. One can only speculate on whether the President and Admiral Sharp talked directly to each other, puzzling about what to do with the recalcitrant McNamara, a problem that got ironed out just in time. In any event, President Johnson, as the man with the facts, encountered no difficulty in selling his version of the crisis to congressional leaders, obtaining their pledged and fervent support for the Tonkin Gulf resolution. Within hours, Johnson sold the same package to the American people. Ironically, it was Secretary McNamara, the apparently reluctant member of the team, who ended up chief spokesman and apologist for the President's course of action.

Chapter XII

Play Ball!

After their wraithlike, exhausting night battle, the *Maddox* and *Turner Joy* hoped to stay at the edge of the Gulf for a while to rest, refuel, and rearm before undertaking any new assignments. Wednesday morning had not even dawned, however, when Commodore Herrick received CINCPACFLT's order to go and look for evidence of the battle. Herrick did not tell his men that there was any doubt as to whether a real battle had taken place. Most of the bone-tired sailors of both ships believed that they had just fought off a whole posse of torpedo boats. *Turner Joy*'s radarmen had counted twenty or thirty enemy craft.

Dawn was leaden, overcast sky. Destroyermen, as usual, recall seeing few aircraft. The *Ticonderoga,* however, launched about a dozen planes that might have helped the search (from the log, one usually cannot tell what the planes did); the *Constellation* definitely contributed Phantoms and Skyhawks. The destroyers charted the most likely area for debris and covered it methodically. Nobody found anything. There were no North Vietnamese survivors, no flotsam or jetsam, no life preservers—nothing at all. Not even a spot of oil stained the surface of the Gulf, where hundreds of shells—maybe thousands—had rained just hours before. The destroyers did not search for long. By midmorning they resumed their coastal patrol. *Constellation* aircraft provided CAP and continued to look for signs of battle. Perhaps the most intensive search, however, was conducted by a pair of Spad pilots who left the *Ticonderoga* before dawn and did not return until 10 A.M.

The negative results of the search disappointed gunners of the

Turner Joy, who fully expected to find a few North Vietnamese sailors clinging to bits of charred wreckage. Nonetheless, the gunners later painted two "kills" on their mounts. A photograph in the ship's cruise book shows Melvin Bow smiling as he finished the job. Bow painted the silhouettes in red, using a broad brush and a template. The outline of the template did not resemble the P-4 torpedo craft observed by *Maddox* sailors on Sunday; nor did it look like the P-6 boat as pictured in later years by *Jane's Fighting Ships* (1968–69 edition). The silhouette did, however, bear a strong resemblance to a picture printed in the August 5, 1964, New York *Times.* The *Times* obtained this photograph from the Defense Department, which said that it showed a torpedo boat of the type used by North Vietnam. Probably the photograph came from Naval Intelligence.

The *Maddox*'s gunners discussed painting a "kill" or two on their mounts, but the ship's officers would not permit it. There was no proof that any boat had been sunk, either on Sunday or on Tuesday. It was quite possible, officers recalled from Sunday's experience, to hit a boat and make it burn. It also was possible for the same boat, having many watertight compartments, to stay afloat.

If the *Turner Joy* did destroy or badly damage any patrol craft, there ought to have been something floating on the water. The example of the famous PT-109 bears witness. After a Japanese destroyer rammed Lieutenant John F. Kennedy's boat, breaking it in half, the young skipper and several members of his crew clung for eleven hours to the bow section. Then they abandoned the still-floating wreckage to swim ashore.

The blank surface of the Gulf did not surprise Bosun's Mate Eusebio B. Estrada aboard the *Maddox.* "Those Chinese can clean up anything," was his comment. Some destroyermen already were writing letters about the incredible night battle, wondering if they ever would get an opportunity to put these thoughts into the mail. It seemed that the destroyers would stay in the Gulf until they themselves became debris.

The Task Group now enjoyed plenty of air cover. Visible or not, planes constantly buzzed overhead, searching for wreckage and keeping a lookout for attackers. Many shuttled from the *Constellation,* still far from the Gulf.

Commanding the *Constellation*'s Task Force was Rear Admiral William S. Guest, a Naval Academy graduate of 1935. As a carrier pilot, Guest achieved distinction during World War II. His decorations included a Navy Cross and four other awards for bravery and achievement. The Admiral's office provides upon request an impressive four-page single-spaced biography, which, curiously, says nothing whatever about the Tonkin Gulf. It touches lightly on 1964 with a half-sentence that mentions a transfer to southern Europe. (In 1966 Admiral Guest commanded naval forces which searched for the hydrogen bomb lost by the Air Force off the coast of Spain. After that ticklish assignment, a Distinguished Service Medal was added to the admiral's long list of decorations.) As a rear admiral, Guest was three years junior to Admiral Moore. By 1964 Guest had moved ahead of Moore in one respect: his carrier was bigger and newer. However, as the senior officer at Yankee Station, Admiral Moore became the onscene commander, taking responsibility for both carrier forces.

Early Wednesday morning, a message from higher command warned the carriers and Task Group 72.1 to watch out for a possible air attack from the northwest (though the North Vietnamese at this time had no combat aircraft). But SPS-40, the *Maddox*'s temperamental air search radar, found nothing coming from the direction of North Vietnam.

It was lunchtime when SPS-40 picked up some contacts in the opposite direction, the southeast. At first the bogeys looked like replacements for the CAP, but before long the vertical plotting board showed too many marks for that. Yet these planes were real. By radio, *Maddox* got in touch with the approaching airmen and, to CIC's relief, identified them as American. Nothing was learned of their mission. Next, three formations, two of jets and one of propeller craft, soared overhead. As the airmen began dropping to lower altitudes, the destroyermen realized what was about to happen: a raid on North Vietnam! A fresh excitement gripped the tired surface sailors. As usual, they were in the thick of things . . . as usual, without knowing it.

During the night the carriers heard that Washington might order a strike on North Vietnam, but the event didn't seem likely. It was too much to hope for. During the Korean War American airmen were not permitted to bomb the enemy's source of supply in Manchuria. Nor did American aircraft help the desperate Cuban exiles struggling at the Bay of Pigs. In 1962 even the strategic missile sites in Cuba did not unleash a surprise attack by air; President Kennedy chose a naval blockade instead. In addition, there now existed some doubt as to whether the North Vietnamese had made an attack the night before. Certainly the airmen could not prove anything. Yet they did not regard the question of an attack critical. Since the North Vietnamese attacked on Sunday, reasoned the airmen, why worry about whether they did it a *second* time. Let's let 'em have it! was the attitude at Yankee Station.

At breakfast the airmen were disconsolate. So far as they knew, the strike had not been approved and was growing more doubtful by the minute. The carrier men had not heard about Secretary McNamara giving his approval shortly after 5 A.M.; nor did they know that the impatient Admiral Sharp supposedly flashed the final word at 5:30 A.M.

Even without the green light, planning for the strike went ahead on a contingency basis. Washington made inquiries about the smallest details without realizing that the biggest question had yet to be settled. Washington wanted to know what types of planes would fly, what weapons they would have, how much the bombs and rockets would weigh, and so forth. Targets were designated and redesignated; prohibited zones were drawn. Civilian casualties were to be avoided. Communist patrol boats could be chased here but not there. The carriers were having a preview of the later bombing campaign when President Johnson would boast, "They can't bomb an outhouse without my permission!"

The carriers' latest teleprinter equipment, speedy though it was, could not keep up with the demands of human curiosity. Messages concerning the air raids plus queries to the sleepless Commodore Herrick, jammed the radio circuits so badly that a high priority item could take four or five hours to get through. It was unfortunate that nobody had thought to send a communications ship to Yankee Station.

From all I have been able to gather, the go-ahead for the air strike bogged down for approximately five hours somewhere between CINCPAC and Yankee Station. Apparently, the clogged circuits were responsible for much of the delay. But men who were close to the operation say that one critical hour was lost because of an "ambiguous message," originating in Washington, which confused the time zones. In view of the confusion normally rampant among official times, this seems not improbable. Very possibly someone confused "Golf time" with someone else's notion of "Gulf time."

In any case, when the President stepped into the Fish Room to make his telecast, the *Ticonderoga* was just finding out that an air strike had been approved. The first wave of aircraft reached their targets 1½ hours afterward.[1]

When a Republican congressman from Texas, Ed Foreman, learned of the discrepancy in timing, he complained angrily on the House floor: "Why, this is better notice to the enemy than they could get with an alert radar system!" Foreman's objection struck the only sour note in the House's brief consideration of the Tonkin Gulf and the resolution to be voted on. Within hours the Defense Department had an explanation ready. Arthur Sylvester, Assistant Secretary of Defense for Public Affairs, took note of some "confusion in news reports." In the name of Secretary McNamara, who did not make himself available for questioning, Sylvester released a statement giving five reasons why it was an excellent idea for the President to have gone on the air when he did. But McNamara based his whole argument on a false premise—that attacking aircraft had been on the way to their targets for one hour when the President began to speak. Therefore, said McNamara, the attacking aircraft already were in North Vietnamese radar; it was important for the President to tell the American people what was happening; it was important to tell the world that this was a limited strike; and so forth. After the Tonkin Gulf affair the Defense Secretary installed his own communications facility, rivaling that of the Joint Chiefs.

In 1964 Ed Foreman and a few other disgruntled congressmen wondered whether the President's television address had warned the enemy, but that question may be academic. According to columnist Jack Anderson, the Tonkin Gulf incidents provided the first important use of the "hot line" between Washington and Moscow. If so the Russians did not need a hasty report from their ambassador watching his television set; President Johnson gave them the word directly by high-speed teleprinter. Presumably Moscow would pass

[1] Errors of timing are not new in modern naval operations. In 1941 a zone discrepancy delayed the Atlantic rendezvous of President Roosevelt and Prime Minister Winston S. Churchill, whose navies were using different times. Japan's initial plan for the Pearl Harbor attack involved a miscalculation of time. That was corrected soon enough, but, evidently for other reasons, the naval bombardment of Malaya began 2 hours and 15 minutes before the air attack on Pearl Harbor.

the word immediately to Hanoi, although this is sheer speculation.

While listing five reasons for timing the raids the way he did, Secretary McNamara repeated his earlier claim that the attack was a huge success. The North Vietnamese, he said, "did not have time to move their forces; our attacking aircraft found the torpedo boats at their docks; the attack was highly successful." At the August 6 hearing, McNamara and Wheeler agreed with the senators that complete surprise had been achieved; the Communist boats, said McNamara, were found "lying dead in the water." There was satisfied agreement that the raids had gone off like Pearl Harbor. Actually, that was not quite correct.

The code name of the air operation was Pierce Arrow, an appellation which to the younger generation might suggest a swift, accurate blow while reminding the older generation of a stately, old-fashioned limousine. The operation was meant to be a swift, accurate blow, and it can be said for Washington strategists that they succeeded in advertising it that way—as a triumph of the Pentagon's expensive "command and control system." In fact, what destruction was accomplished owed everything to the skill and determination of men on the scene; it owed nothing to a flow of computerized genius from the nation's capital.

As for the nature of the targets, President Johnson announced air action "against gunboats and certain supporting facilities which have been used in these hostile operations" (two North Vietnamese attacks). Whatever the President meant by that, the major target of the day was a concentration of oil tanks near the town of Vinh. These tanks, a dozen or so, held 10 percent of North Vietnam's petroleum supply, imported from the Soviet Union. The tanks reportedly were thrown in "to show we meant business." (Personally, I suspect that somebody hankered to improve on the Pearl Harbor raid. American naval experts long had criticized the Japanese attack for neglecting oil tanks, the destruction of which might have crippled the Pacific Fleet more than the loss of its battleships.) The town of Vinh (the word means "gulf") was a port for general cargo, utilizing the Ca River to the sea. The oil tanks were far enough from Vinh to avoid the risk of extensive civilian casualties. They stood across the river at the village of Ben Thuy. The *Ticonderoga* assigned sixteen aircraft to the Ben Thuy mission. Of that number, four Spads would do the actual bombing, and twelve jets would insure the Spads' success by strafing anti-aircraft emplacements. On their way back to the carrier, the jets were to seek patrol craft as targets of opportunity. Some boats were said to be at the mouth of the Ca River not far from Hon Ngu. Six other *Ticonderoga* jets would hit a naval base at Quang Khe, whose white, sandy beaches *Maddox* passed early in her patrol. As for the *Constellation,* she would devote her efforts entirely to naval targets. Her planes would attack patrol craft at Loc Chao, the estuary north of Hon Me, and patrol craft at Hon Gay (not an island), a port at the northern end of the Gulf. From Hon Gay the North Vietnamese exported anthracite coal mined nearby.

Such was the plan. It envisaged a succession of bombs and rockets going off along the North Vietnamese coast while President Johnson addressed the astonished American people. However, the strikes came off late and in stages. So much for the Defense Department's elaborate, costly and much-vaunted "command and control system."

At some point, Admiral Moore must have found cause to regard the air strikes as a live possibility. At 9:33 A.M. he began launching four Skyraiders which, if they ever got the tip-off word—"Play Ball!" —were to bomb the oil tanks at Ben Thuy. Until then the four Spads were to buzz around the carrier. Their leader was the Skyraider Squadron's executive officer, Commander Lee McAdams, his wingman: Lieutenant (jg) Paul Carter. The other two pilots were the squadron operations officer, Lieutenant Commander Lawrence Brumbach and his wingman, Lieutenant (jg) Richard Moore.[2] Among the younger Spad flyers, Carter and Moore were particularly good dive bombers. Each of the sturdy, single-engined Spads carried a thousand pound bomb and a dozen 250-pound bombs (ordnance equivalent to the payload of a four-engined World War II Flying Fortress).

While in orbit, the propeller pilots hardly dreamed that they would get the opportunity to test their skill in combat. Commander Brumbach recalls that he "was sure that this was just another drill.

---

[2] The reader will notice that some pilots are mentioned by name while others are not. Because of the possibility of capture, the Defense Department asks that publicity for pilots be kept to the minimum. I do not give the names of any pilots still on flying status with the Navy unless the name has been published before in the same context.

I had just gotten a degree in international relations, and I knew that the United States did not respond in this way." Besides the weather was terrible—heavy clouds and a low ceiling. The weather could be different on target, but the flyers had no information on that. Sitting on the *Ticonderoga*'s flight deck were reconnaissance jets, also waiting for the word. For a month the different types of squadrons had been practicing coordinated strike exercises.

The four Spad men had been in the air for about one hour when, to their amazement, the strike order actually came through. The mission was a real "go." And right away! Off went the startled Spads, disappearing into the overcast. There was no time for reconnaissance. As men of the *Ticonderoga* understood the situation, they had only one hour in which to prepare and launch armed jets. Frantically, the carrier men began to reload the on-deck planes and rebrief the pilots.

The bomb-laden Spads droned along at about 160 knots. If launched on time, the supporting jets would catch up before the propeller planes were on target. The Spads flew in a straight line, one pair ahead and one pair behind.

The carrier men knew nothing about the President's telecast, nor about the hot line. They naturally hoped to achieve total surprise. Commander McAdams and his men did not surprise the U. S. Air Force, which sent a jet from Da Nang to look them over. Presumably Air Force radar had picked them out. The Spads, however, were not expected to alarm the North Vietnamese. They were shielded by heavy clouds from visual observation. As for Communist radar, supposedly there would not be enough time for passing the word to defensive positions. The early warning stations were thought to be ineffective for lack of communications—perhaps the 34-A raids were to have destroyed their radio facilities.

In a record 45 minutes the men of the *Ticonderoga* began flinging armed jets into the sky. The four Spads were still droning northward when a half-dozen Crusaders neared Quang Khe.

The slope-winged F-8s flew northwest in the sparkling sunlight and clear air of 33,000 feet, well above the feathery mass of cloud below. Near the mainland, they dipped into the weather, now a gray fog, and, still descending, their radar began painting the coast at 20 miles. How far down would the weather go? In luck, the Crusaders broke through at 15,000 feet. With Quang Khe in clear view, they penetrated the Communist airspace. Visibility was fine. The time: 12:15 P.M.—1 hour and 40 minutes after the President began his speech.

To the Crusaders' surprise, they were being shot at. Below the airmen could see little puffs of black smoke. The flak seemed to come from patrol boats. Fortunately, the shells were not climbing as high as the jets, which still flew at 10,000 feet.

The jets were not ready to engage yet. They were to cross the coastline from the southeast, fly past Quang Khe, and circle back to hit the boats. In that way, anyone disabled by flak would have a chance of parachuting into the Gulf, where he might be rescued. The jets flew as directed, circled back, and dove into the speckled air below. The pilots saw little boats scurrying this way and that. These were Swatow craft with 37-millimeter guns. "They were firing like hell," says one of the flyers. "There was no surprise." Another pilot describes his experience:

"The boats were moving when I first saw them. But they were in the area where they were briefed to be. They were between a peninsula and the mainland. We made a couple of runs firing Zunis. We had eight rockets apiece. You can't see your own rockets hit because you have to pull out. You aren't even supposed to look back. I did look back, though, and once I saw my rockets straddling a boat. The boat must have been hurt, but I can't say for sure that I sank anything. We made more runs with the 20-millimeter stuff, diving from 2500 feet. I believe we got about five boats. Some of them went onto the beach to keep from sinking."

One flyer reports that two boats ran aground. He estimates that five or six were destroyed or damaged. The Defense Department released no specific count for Quang Khe.

Meanwhile, the original four Spads, which had been in the air close to three hours, were approaching the coast farther north. The weather, instead of improving, was getting worse. The Spad men plunged into a mist so thick that they couldn't even see each other. To prevent collision they stepped down to lower altitudes, each plane putting a vertical separation of 500 feet between it and the one following. As they did so, the supporting jets were making a rendezvous in the clear air above. Next, the Skyhawks and Crusaders dropped almost to water level and, like silver arrows, sped toward the mainland. They were to sneak under the defensive radar, if any, while the Spads plowed their way through the overcast.

At this, the last minute, no one could tell whether the Ben Thuy raid would come off. The orders were clear: no halfway measures. If the weather on target were not favorable, not a single bomb was to be dropped. The Spad men, up in the soup, would decide. They had the bombs.

As the four dive bombers bored into Communist airspace, the heavy mist fell away completely, revealing a blue sky and fluffy, white clouds. Beyond a green and white shoreline, Vinh and Ben Thuy lay exposed on the ground. Suddenly it was a beautiful day.

The jets still did not have the word. Skimming the surface of the Gulf, their commander, Wesley McDonald, asked by radio: "Can you see the target?"

"Sure," said McAdams. "Let's play ball!"

That was what the jet pilots wanted to hear. They dashed ahead, zoomed over the beach, and started hedge-hopping across the countryside. Abruptly, a bus stopped on Route 1, and its passengers, like so many marbles, poured out, seeking depressions in the earth. Everybody in sight took alarm. Everybody knew what to do. A farmer threw down his hoe and dove into an irrigation ditch.

Wryly, one of the pilots sums it up: "Nobody came out to wave at the American good guys."

The jets now pulled up to rocket-launching altitude, without attracting any fire, and swooped down again, seeking targets. Intelligence couldn't be sure of all the triple-A positions, but the pilots had instructions on several. Some of the guns were poking out of earthen revetments. Others were in a courtyard that looked like a school yard. Working independently, the Skyhawks and Crusaders showered the known emplacements with rocket missiles—the big Zuni and the smaller 2.75-inch size. One of the Skyhawk pilots, not finding his target, loosed a podful at the oil tanks, setting one ablaze. For a moment, his wingman feared that the dive bombers were on the job too soon. On the next run, both of these planes fired their remaining pods at the triple-A. The flak suppression was over in a couple of minutes. As the jets pulled away, their pilots saw a few black puffs in the air.

Now the Skyraiders came in for the kill. Arriving exactly on time, the Spad men watched the flak suppression from 13,000 feet. Thanks to the Skyhawk pilot who had fired at the oil tank they had a smoke marker, just as in target practice. McAdams and Carter rolled into their diving runs, hindered by very little flak, and put their bombs on a line for the target. The Spads pulled away at 2500 feet, keeping clear of any possible small arms fire. Now it was their turn to hedge-hop. The lightened pair accelerated back toward the Gulf. Behind them, black smoke and orange fire boiled up from the ground.

Brumbach and Moore, still at 13,000 feet, saw that the Communist gunners, who knew the range, were beginning to make trouble. Skillfully, the Spad men detoured to the left, sinking down to 8000 feet to evade flak. Already smoke from the oil tanks had reached this level. The Spads started their dive, angling toward the base of the black pillar. As he let go of his bombs, Brumbach saw a few tanks still intact. Seconds later, Moore pitched his cargo into the burning mess, and, pulling away, wobbled his wings. This signaled an F-8 photo plane that from somewhere whipped in to take pictures. Heading back to the Gulf, the last two Spad men looked back over their shoulders, gratified to see the tank farm blazing. As targets for bombing, oil tanks rate among the most satisfying.

The jets, having used up their rockets at Ben Thuy, retained 20-millimeter ammunition for patrol craft. As on Sunday two Crusaders proceeded to Da Nang because a pilot thought his plane had been hit. Four Crusaders followed the Ca River toward Hon Ngu and reportedly discovered a half-dozen patrol boats near the hamlet of Phuc Loi. The score: four boats "moderately damaged" and two "lightly damaged." Flying southward, the Skyhawks inspected about 75 miles of coastline before finding any targets of opportunity. Leading the way were Commander McDonald and Lieutenant Gehman, who had searched the Gulf so fruitlessly the night before. This time they had better luck. After whizzing by Mui Ron and Mui Doc, they spotted near the town of Ron an official-looking boat with a red flag on it. The two immediately dove in for the attack. Gehman had sprayed the hapless craft with three-quarters of his 20-millimeter ammunition when his guns jammed. McDonald remembers the battle this way:

"The boat was laying in close to shore. As I dove in, I thought I saw a couple of men jump overboard. The boat had guns on it, but they didn't fire—I guess because the gunners went over the side. That skipper was one of the best seamen I ever saw. He'd dodge, and then he'd turn around and come right at me. I fired all of my 20-millimeter ammunition. That boat had plenty of holes in it, but it wouldn't sink. Finally, I thought about trying to hit it with my empty fuel tanks, but, in utter disgust, I decided to call it a day. Somebody said later that he saw a boat on the beach in that area."

While McDonald and Gehman were dive-bombing one lone boat, other Skyhawks sped on toward Quang Khe. There they caught about five boats a mile or so downstream from where the F-8s were still working. A shore battery opened up on the new arrivals. Commander Henry Urban pounced on one of the boats and hit it pretty hard. The target spun completely around and caught fire. The other jets made hits but failed to stop a boat. One of the Skyhawks had guns that jammed.

The *Ticonderoga*'s first wave did not achieve total surprise, but it was the most successful strike of the day, and everybody got back safely. At Quang Khe the North Vietnamese were ready to repel attack. At Ben Thuy the defenders were not ready, even though the planes arrived about ten minutes later. One pilot explained the difference by saying that the North Vietnamese *army* was responsible for defending the oil tanks; the navy, he said, was more likely to be alert because of the attack it had made the night before. One also might recall that President Johnson talked about hitting gunboats and their supporting facilities. He didn't say anything about oil tanks.

It was going to be a bad day for the *Constellation*. During the morning the supercarrier shuttled planes to and from the Gulf, providing CAP for the destroyers and searching for debris—both of which seemed important at the time. Simultaneously, the *Constellation* suffered through Washington's method of planning an air strike. The junior carrier had her targets changed four or five times; in the end, she was left with the most northerly places to go, even though she was farther from the Gulf. Roundtrips of more than 600 miles would be required. For the light bombers of an aircraft carrier, the distances would be extraordinary; in-flight refueling would be needed to get the jets back. The target changes required a great deal of extra briefing, extra planning, and a tremendous flow of message traffic. The glut of encrypted messages not only slowed communications with Washington but blacked out completely the *Ticonderoga* only a hundred miles or so to the west. *Constellation* officers tried to contact the senior carrier by radiotelephone, in veiled terms (not a recommended security procedure), in order to find out when or if the strikes would come off. They were told only to "wait." Neither carrier sent an officer to visit the other: staying aboard one's own ship seems to be a firm naval tradition. In any event, the prospect of a strike did not seem very likely. So far nobody even had a weather report on the targets.

Men of the *Constellation* learned of the strike order in the most shocking way possible: by the receipt of a "launch message" from the other carrier. At this time, evidently, the *Ticonderoga* already had reloaded the on-deck jets and put them into the air. Now it was the *Constellation*'s turn to scramble.

Equally stunned were officers of the *Ticonderoga,* who had imagined that the distant supercarrier was all set. Admiral Moore's staff was "mad as hell," one observer recalls. But there were more surprises to come. As *Ticonderoga* pilots neared their targets, wondering how the weather would be, Washington demanded repeatedly to know the *results* of the operation. The Pentagon could not seem to understand why reports were lacking.

At last in the air, the *Constellation*'s raiders started their long dogleg around Hainan, passed some returning CAP pilots, and turned right into the Gulf, where they soon saw the column of smoke at Ben Thuy. The Russian oil was topping out at 12,000 feet. It was 2:45 P.M., four hours after the President's speech ended, when the party of raiders destined for Loc Chao found at sea a half-dozen patrol craft, apparently making a dash for the estuary. Spads and Skyhawks blanketed the fleeing boats with unguided 2.75-inch rockets. Gamely, the North Vietnamese fought back with machine guns. They must have been driving torpedo boats, perhaps from Hon Me. One of the Skyraiders, piloted by Lieutenant Richard C. Sather, crashed into the sea. Sather did not bail out. Another Spad took a hit but made it safely back to the carrier. Watching the battle from above was Lieutenant James C. Scanlon, a radar observer in one of three Phantom jets acting as CAP in case Communist aircraft showed up. Scanlon recalls that the Spads made a very aggressive attack, moving close in and delivering the most accurate fire.

After exhausting their ammunition, the Loc Chao party turned back, one fewer than when it had started out. The supercarrier made a conservative claim: two of the six boats "seriously damaged."

At about the same time, the Hon Gay raiders were passing over the islands that fringe the Gulf's northern shore. Skyhawks arrived first, plummeted in for the attack, and found themselves enveloped by smoke and shrapnel. Guns were positioned on hilltops overlooking the harbor. The raiders made no attempt to knock out the guns; correctly, officers of the *Constellation* interpreted Washington's orders as not permitting flak suppression. The Hon Gay aircraft were to touch nothing on the mainland or tied to it. Had they done so, there probably would have been charges of bombing the coal mines.

The Skyhawks found no patrol craft where they were supposed to be, and in the midst of heavy fire this called for a change of plan. A quick look-around discovered five boats behind a rocky islet. These—dead in the water—could have been the ones Secretary McNamara talked about. The enemy craft, however, immediately scampered for the sea—which was a mistake. Had they dashed for the mainland piers, they would have been immune from attack; but the Communist skippers had no way of knowing the airmen's orders. The Skyhawks chased their covey, surprised by how fast the enemy's 37-millimeter guns could shoot. Missiles, bullets, and shells thickened the air. As at Loc Chao, one of the attacking aircraft plunged into the water. This was the Skyhawk of Lieutenant Everett Alvarez. His companions saw no parachute, though they heard the automatic beeper on one. The Skyhawks, low on fuel, could do nothing but go home, along with the Phantoms acting as CAP. As the jets departed, four Spads, fending for themselves, buzzed in and took their turn pouring fire onto the stricken patrol craft. All of the Spads got away safely. When last seen, the surface craft were smoking. The Defense Department said that all five were destroyed.

As the *Constellation* planes belatedly carried out their assignment, the *Maddox* and the *Turner Joy* cruised in the middle of the Gulf, south of Bach Long Vi, wondering whether their services would be needed. Hearing of downed aircraft, the Task Group started a dash for Loc Chao and another for Hon Gay, but in each case the destroyermen learned that nothing could be done. Lieutenant Sather was dead. Lieutenant Alvarez, if alive, must have been captured.

The *Ticonderoga,* having made the first strike, had time left over in which to make another. A few oil tanks were reported still standing at Ben Thuy. The original four Spads, returning to the carrier, knew nothing of the restrike plan, and they were surprised to find themselves diverted to Da Nang for landing. By voice radio the carrier could not explain that the decks were busy arming another flight.

At Da Nang the Spad men shook hands and slapped each other on the back. Air Force mechanics refueled the Navy planes—not an unusual task—without even asking where they had been. Nor did the jubilant flyers volunteer any information. Before leaving the carrier, all of the *Ticonderoga* pilots had been ordered to say nothing in the event that they landed at the Air Force base. This is how tight security was locally in the absence of information on the President's telecast. The mechanics at Da Nang carefully removed from one of the Spads a 1000-pound bomb that failed to "pickle" and rolled it away on a cart.

From the *Ticonderoga,* ten Skyhawks and four Crusaders revisited the Ben Thuy area at 3:45 P.M., encountering much heavier flak than did the first wave. Here was another indication that the first wave had taken Ben Thuy by surprise. A Skyhawk pilot remembers the defensive fire:

"We were flying low, and we could see the ground pretty well. I thought I saw some explosions down there. Somebody said, 'No, you dope, those are guns firing—muzzle flashes.' They had 57-millimeter and 85-millimeter guns. I know that now, having seen the various types since then. The guns were arranged in the classic circular patterns. I saw some black puffs creeping up on the man ahead of me. I warned him, and he Rogered. Then somebody yelled at me, and it was my turn to move. After we carried out our mission and left the mainland, we even saw a lot of crap falling into the water—shrapnel, I mean."

This time four Skyhawks plastered gun emplacements around Ben Thuy, and another four attacked the remaining tanks, two or three of them in the northeastern corner of the area. The mission of the other six jets, including four Crusaders, was to look for patrol boats. Flyers told me about a gunboat discovered south of Mui Ron. A Skyhawk pilot loosed a pod of rockets and, in the words of one observer, "knocked the tail off." Other jets strafed the same unfortunate craft, which still did not sink but managed to beach itself. Again, all of the *Ticonderoga* planes made it home safely.

Even after the restrike on Ben Thuy, two tanks reportedly were left standing. Photographs showed their tops bashed in and holes in the sides, sprouting fluid; but, as if by a miracle, they did not burn.

The indestructible pair, Navy Intelligence heard later, contained water. Even those tanks, however, disappeared in the bombing campaign of 1965–68. "Anything that looked like a tank," says a veteran pilot, "got worked over pretty good."

How successful was the strike of August 5? Certainly the attack on Ben Thuy was an unqualified success; and the pilots who took part in it are very proud of it. "Had we practiced that raid," says one, "we probably would have screwed it up. But, with no preparation, everything went perfectly."

Attacking patrol boats was another story. As flyers learned during World War II, the fast-moving boat with its rapid-fire guns not only is difficult to hit but makes a fairly good anti-aircraft weapon.[3]

The Pentagon reported that the August 5 raiders sighted thirty North Vietnamese boats and "destroyed or damaged" twenty-five of them. Secretary McNamara claimed the "bulk" of the North Vietnamese fleet had been "eliminated from operational use."[4] Incipient hawks pointed at the score with pride, and incipient doves viewed it with alarm—regarding the extent of retaliation as excessive since neither American destroyer had been damaged. In any case the Pentagon's score probably was somewhat exaggerated. Some of the destroyermen, who were decidedly hawkish, doubted that the North Vietnamese fleet had been hit so hard as Washington claimed. They wondered how pilots could tell a burning boat from one that was just making smoke. I asked two pilots that question. One looked puzzled and said that he hadn't heard of any smoke-generating capability on the boats. Commander Urban stated firmly that he saw flames coming from a boat that he hit.

Of the two carriers, *Constellation* found less to shoot at, and she suffered the only casualties. The supercarrier traded two planes lost for five boats destroyed and two seriously damaged. Some former *Constellation* men say that the delay in launching made the difference; others believe that the timing did not really matter. The two-seater Phantoms coolly observing the scene might have tended to make the

[3] In World War II a reported thirty Japanese planes swooped down on two American PTs, and four planes crashed while the PTs got away. On another occasion, twenty-two American planes strafed two American PTs by mistake. This time the two boats sank while only one plane was downed. Commander Edward I. Farley, *PT Patrol* (New York: Exposition Press, 1957), pages 55–58, 63–64.

[4] CBS-TV interview of August 5, 1964.

Constellation's claims relatively conservative. In any case, it was the *Ticonderoga* that got credited with a brilliant score: eighteen of the twenty-five boats "destroyed or damaged."

The Pentagon announced later that aircraft destroyed or severely damaged seven anti-aircraft installations in the Vinh area, and newsmen exulted that the raids had been "even more successful" than first reported. Actually, as mentioned earlier, Washington intended to prohibit flak suppression. Since the *Ticonderoga* did it anyway, another achievement was proclaimed.

At the August 6 hearing, Senator Clifford P. Case, Republican of New Jersey, wondered why the American planes did not have guided missiles to use against surface targets. Secretary McNamara and General Wheeler replied that *they* were satisfied with the results obtained, and Senator Case—a member of Foreign Relations, not Armed Services—refrained from pressing his query. Two of the *Constellation*'s Phantom interceptors are said to have tried firing air-to-air guided missiles at patrol craft. One Phantom launched a heat-seeking Sidewinder at a burning boat; the missile "went ballistic" and strayed—possibly the boat was just making smoke. Another Phantom tried a radar-guided Sparrow missile and claimed a hit, although "water return" (the reflection of radar from water) tends to make radar guidance unreliable for this kind of target.

Senator Case's question ought to have been taken more seriously. In four years of intensive aerial warfare against North Vietnam, the United States lost about 1400 airmen (the exact number is secret) and caused a great deal of unnecessary damage while trying to knock out bridges and other difficult, well-defended targets. One of the bridges on Route 1 never was destroyed, even though craters opened up all around it. Neighboring farmers said that bridge was the safest place in the whole country. Somehow the Pentagon had failed to get beyond the aerial techniques developed in World War II. Nearly all the assigned targets stood less than 50 miles from salt water. Reliable surface-to-surface guided missiles, if available, could have done the job far more quickly and far more cheaply—in both human and material cost.

Hanoi, too, claimed a great victory on August 5. The North Vietnamese reported eight American planes shot down. Three more, they said, were damaged. As proof the Communists showed off Lieutenant Alvarez. The flyer's parachute did not open, but, splashing into the water from a low altitude, he somehow escaped fatal injury. Armed militia in a fishing boat picked him up.

In 1964 Lieutenant Alvarez was twenty-six years old and newly married. Now, seven years later, he is the dean of more than three hundred American prisoners in North Vietnam. (The Defense Department estimates that 378 of the downed airmen should be alive; North Vietnam has revealed the names of 339 prisoners, saying twenty died of wounds and other causes.) For years the North Vietnamese, who regard the American flyers as "war criminals," would not release any kind of list. They finally did so after a publicity campaign generated by the airmen's wives.

Most of the August 5 veterans whom I talked to remarked on how well-drilled in civil defense the North Vietnamese people appeared to be, and some pilots reported seeing elaborate defensive facilities on the ground. The coast was protected not only by guns but by trenches as if the Communists were anticipating invasion. After August 5, North Vietnamese publications boasted of the nation's readiness for defense. They said that the raids came without warning but that everybody responded with rapidity and skill. One periodical told of the skepticism that had been expressed by a member of the International Control Commission, who, seeing a bomb shelter under construction, had assured the local people that the Americans would never harm them. On August 5, said the Communist periodical, the ICC man took cover like everybody else, and emerging from the bomb shelter, wrote his name over the door.

One might well ask why the people of North Vietnam knew more about American plans—or at least made a better guess—than did people of the United States. In this country few people anticipated a bombing campaign against North Vietnam, either before or after August 5. The American attitude is easy to explain: the voters were against bombing, and they thought President Johnson was against it, too. But how did the North Vietnamese know so much?

It could be argued that North Vietnam, as the real aggressor in South Vietnam, planned to step up the war and, for that reason, expected retaliation by air. It never has been proved, however, that North Vietnamese forces played any major role in South Vietnam until mid-1965 when the bombing already had begun and American ground forces were landing in South Vietnam. Did Hanoi, then, plan a big push by the Viet Cong? This has not been proved, either, though some U.S. officials might have believed it. Much simpler it is to look at the record from the North Vietnamese point of view. Radio Hanoi not only predicted bombing but listed many items of evidence for such a plan. Since 1964 other evidence, too, has come to light. Here is a partial summary:

The gunboat raids, first of all, ought to have had some military purpose. If there were no plan to bomb or invade North Vietnam, why blow up the coastal radar? (It would be interesting to know which facilities were capable of air search; in 1965 the Defense Department cited Vinh Sonh as an "early warning" station.) We also noted earlier the alleged South Vietnamese bombing attacks of July, 1964, and the alleged American (CIA?) air attacks of August 1 and August 2. These rumbles of the coming storm might have been fictitious. Washington never admitted them. But it was a matter of public record that the South Vietnamese Premier, General Khanh, was drumming up support for a "To the North!" campaign; and, simultaneously, Air Commander Ky publicly threatened North Vietnam with air attack. Even if the North Vietnamese did not take Khanh and Ky seriously, they must have observed the U. S. Navy's new combat role in Laos, as well as the strike exercises being practiced at the North Vietnamese doorstep—now termed "Yankee Station." Furthermore, the American press reported that air base facilities were being expanded in South Vietnam, and that a large number of Skyraiders and F-100 jet fighters were moving in. The latter activity portended some kind of increased American commitment. Meanwhile, according to Radio Hanoi, reconnaissance planes were flying over North Vietnam. The truth of that is evidenced by the fact that on August 5 Navy planes knew where to look for their targets.

Radio Hanoi flagged some interesting leaks from the Pentagon and Congress. One concerned 50 medium bombers which, said the Communist radio, were in the Philippines training with U-2 photographs of North Vietnamese territory. Similar information recently had appeared in the June 9, 1964, New York *Herald Tribune*. In an article titled "We Point Bombers at North Vietnam," the aviation editor, David Hoffman, reported that a wing of Air Force B-57s was training to destroy targets in North Vietnam. The planes, Hoffman wrote, had been scheduled for return to the United States and distribution among Air National Guard units; but the airmen's dependents went home, instead, and the wing transferred to Clark Air Base near Manila. In that context, Hoffman quoted the Air Force Chief of Staff, General Curtis E. LeMay, as telling congressmen: "We are swatting flies when we should be going after the manure pile." Hoffman added, "The manure pile, in the military's view, can be found and destroyed in North Vietnam."

Radio Hanoi attributed its information about U-2 photographs to a statement by Melvin R. Laird, then a Republican congressman from Wisconsin and a member of the Defense Subcommittee of the Committee on Appropriations. I do not know whether Congressman Laird said anything about U-2 flights, but on May 30, 1964, he caused a momentary stir in the press with a statement that the Johnson administration "plans to prepare to move into North Vietnam." (In 1969 Melvin Laird became President Nixon's Secretary of Defense. He had come a long way since World War II when, as an ensign, Laird served aboard the destroyer *Maddox*.)

Whatever happened to those bombers in the Philippines? On August 4, 1964, Secretary McNamara secretly ordered thirty-six of them to South Vietnam.[5] These were the B-57s that went flying into the country on Friday, August 7—as a part of the military build-up that McNamara did not mention in his two press conferences of August 5. The bombers landed at Bien Hoa, a "secret" base which, said American journalists, harbored U-2 planes.

Clearly, bombing North Vietnam was not just Senator Goldwater's "crazy idea" as many voters thought it was back in 1964. While the American people rejected this plan and scoffed at it, preparations for carrying it out were moving ahead step by step.

Within the Johnson administration there was one man at least who opposed sending the B-57s to South Vietnam: William Bundy, Assistant Secretary of State for the Far East.[6] At Bien Hoa, Bundy argued, the aircraft would present a tempting target for Viet Cong attack. Secretary Rusk then asked Secretary McNamara whether he needed the planes in South Vietnam. McNamara replied that he did

[5] Committee on Foreign Relations, *The Gulf of Tonkin, The 1964 Incidents, Part II,* pages 2–3.

[6] Joseph Kraft, "The Dean Rusk Show," *New York Times Magazine* (March 24, 1968).

(but for what?), and Rusk, as usual, fell into step with the armed forces. He was not known for backing up his subordinates when they opposed a plan sponsored by the Pentagon. Rusk, for that matter, never quite liked thinking of himself as a diplomat. He sometimes reminded his staff that, counting time in uniform and in mufti, he had served longer in the defense establishment than in the State Department.

The North Vietnamese could see with their own eyes the advancing preparations for an American bombing campaign; and they sensed keenly every leak from Washington. It may be that President Johnson did not intend to go through with the bombing plan—that question will be discussed in the final chapter. In any case, Hanoi's prediction proved accurate. Bombs did rain on North Vietnam—in total nearly 50 percent more than U.S. aircraft dropped in all of World War II, including both the Pacific and European theaters. Vinh and the other towns along Route 1 were destroyed; at this writing they remain ghost towns while the former inhabitants remain in the countryside for safety. Air power ruralized North Vietnam as it urbanized South Vietnam—approximately 60 percent of the 17,000,000 South Vietnamese people now are huddled in urban areas, most of them dependent on American spending. In the narrow, southern "panhandle" of North Vietnam even a large part of the rural area was hard-hit. Massive bombing converted the view along Route 1 into a "ghastly moonscape," according to one American visitor, Robert S. Boyd, Chief of the Knight Newspapers' Washington Bureau.[7] The American bombers refrained from destroying North Vietnamese agriculture, which they could have done by blasting holes in dikes and levees; they also left undisturbed the center of Hanoi and the maritime traffic at Haiphong.

William Bundy's prediction, too, proved accurate. Less than three months after the B-57s landed at Bien Hoa, American blood boiled as the Viet Cong attacked the secret base. Early one Sunday morning, carefully aimed mortar shells destroyed five bombers, damaged fifteen, and ruined several smaller aircraft. Five Americans died and seventy-six were injured. The guerrillas made good their escape, af-

[7] Washington *Evening Star* of June 3, 1970. See also Amando E. Doronila's article in the *Star* of April 17, 1970; and Richard S. Gott in the February 28, 1970, *Weekly Guardian*.

ter doing $50,000,000 in damage with only $800 worth of shells—all made in U.S.A. Secretary McNamara called the Bien Hoa disaster a "sneak attack." News media termed it the "worst setback of the war," a "little Pearl Harbor," and "retaliation" for the August 5 raids on North Vietnam. Yet the American airmen, like William Bundy, had known how vulnerable the base was. Snipers, they told newsmen, often shot at them as they landed and took off. The bombers, nonetheless, were parked wingtip to wingtip without revetments —an easy target for mortar attack.

William Bundy's warning remained unheeded. President Johnson ordered the damaged aircraft replaced. The U. S. Air Force, like the U. S. Navy, could not back down in the face of a Communist challenge. In Saigon MACV officers said that American *troops* now were needed *to protect American equipment*. As Secretary Rusk remarked when he approved sending the B-57s to South Vietnam: "In for a penny, in for a pound."

Chapter XIII

Wrapping It Up

In the tense aftermath of the air raids, the American people were inclined to forget about the *Maddox* and *Turner Joy,* but the two destroyers were still cruising in the Tonkin Gulf, still persuaded that they were engaged in a hazardous enterprise. To the west that column of black smoke reminded the surface sailors of North Vietnamese hostility. To the east lay the mysterious island of Hainan. Would the Chinese Communists not back up their puppets in Hanoi? On Wednesday afternoon a Willie Fudd radar plane picketed Hainan. The Fudd found no hostile aircraft, but it discovered a good many Chinese patrol boats buzzing up and down the 12-mile limit, as if to challenge the Americans to violate *their* territorial water.

At some time following the air raids, a large group of Chinese patrol craft appeared to menace the "Sammy" *Moore* at Watchdog Station. The *Ticonderoga* dispatched a few planes in that direction, and the Chinese boats went away. Admiral Moore recalled this incident four years later when the USS *Pueblo,* while desperately calling for air support, was captured by North Korean patrol craft.

It seems to have been Wednesday afternoon when the destroyer Task Group found another hostile-looking radar contact on the surface. A fat skunk was closing the destroyers at high speed. Would the Communists dare another attack, this time in broad daylight? The *Maddox*'s radarmen by this time realized that many of Tuesday night's radar contacts were false; and Captain Ogier had declared to a few officers that he didn't believe in the torpedo attack at all. CIC, therefore, examined the new skunk with great care. It looked perfectly solid and steady. The destroyermen, guns ready, waited for the blip to make visual range. When it did, however, there was nothing at all to be seen. The sea in that direction was completely blank.

"Where's that PT boat?" Captain Ogier taunted CIC.

Mystified, the radarmen could only point to their equipment. The skunk was still there. Indeed, it stayed on course until the green blip was almost touching the *Maddox*. Then, slowly and gracefully, it blossomed into a huge cloud, covering the entire scope. In darkness, the same contact surely would have drawn fire, stimulating a report of North Vietnamese attack.

In later years, this kind of false radar contact became known as the "Tonkin spook." An ex-*Maddox* officer told me that once in 1966 when he was officer of the deck on another ship, a Tonkin spook came barreling right over the bow in daylight and perfectly clear weather. By this time the Navy was so accustomed to the local apparitions that the skipper did not even come to the bridge, though the former *Maddox* officer thought he should have.

One of the *Maddox*'s senior officers told me that the South China Sea has been notorious for weird electronic effects ever since radar began to be used by ships. This he learned after the De Soto patrol was over. Before the patrol, men of the *Maddox* could not have learned much by looking into the current radar manual, *Radarman 3 & 2*. The manual had this to say:

"Radar contacts made on targets that cannot be seen visually are often given the erroneous title of phantom contacts when actually they are caused by clouds, birds, fish, weather conditions, and wakes. All of these will reflect radar pulses to some extent. In general, echoes from these sources can be recognized by the alert operator."

The same manual, published in 1962, informed radarmen that in the South China Sea problems with refraction could be expected during the winter months. No information, said the manual, was available for the other three seasons of the year.

Today, in 1971, Navy men still do not know the cause or causes of the "Tonkin spook." This I have heard from officers having recent experience in the Gulf.

Whether or not it had anything to do with the spook, on Wednesday the *Maddox*'s radar was ducting again. One of the ensigns felt certain that he was tracking a Communist boat at 5 or 10 knots, but, after some argument, older hands dismissed the contact as a far-off island. The apparent motion could have been an illusion generated by the ship's own speed, just as a person in a stationary railway train sometimes thinks that he is moving when he sees another train rumble by.

On Wednesday evening the *Maddox* and *Turner Joy* retired from the Gulf and passed the night at Yankee Station. The destroyermen did not know it, but they were destined not to prowl up north again after dark, not on this patrol. One could speculate that Washington was determined to avoid any additional nighttime incidents. If no more trouble erupted, the Tonkin Gulf resolution would coast through Congress on the impetus of two unquestioned attacks. But if the ships again opened fire in the dark of night, there was no telling what might happen. The President would be pressured to order another air raid—bigger this time. Inevitably the Congress would debate the merits of declaring war, and in the midst of these events Commodore Herrick might decide that he was shooting at ghosts. It seems possible that Washington officials decided to simplify everything by keeping the destroyers away from trouble, at least during hours of darkness.

The Nasty gunboats, too, were held in check. For many nights to come, the waters of the Tonkin Gulf would lap in peace.

On orders from above, the Task Group lingered at Yankee Station not only Wednesday night but all day Thursday, and took this opportunity to replenish fuel and ammunition. Both ships had burned a great deal of oil on Tuesday night, and the *Turner Joy* had expended a large number of shells. The destroyers *Edson* and *Moore* provided ordnance.

At dawn on Friday, August 7, the Task Group headed north, making a gingerly probe. The destroyers looked around the Vinh area, encountering no sign of hostility. At sunset they again retired to the south. By this time Premier Khanh had seized emergency powers in South Vietnam, apparently anticipating invasion from the North. On Friday evening Ho Chi Minh was presenting decorations to antiaircraft units and naval units for their work on August 2 and August 5; as for August 4, no awards were mentioned. Just after midnight, while the *Maddox* and *Turner Joy* cruised peacefully at Yankee Station, the U. S. Senate stamped its seal of approval on the Tonkin Gulf resolution.

As Premier Khanh inspected the Demilitarized Zone on Saturday,

August 8, the destroyer Task Group waited all day at the edge of the Gulf for instructions from Washington. The naval build-up was in full swing. With mounting excitement, Commodore Herrick's men counted friendly silhouettes: two attack carriers, one helicopter carrier, two cruisers, submarines, numerous destroyers, and every kind of auxiliary vessel. It looked like a replay of World War II, and men of the Task Group were impressed.

Predictably, it was the tired and sweaty men of Task Group 72.1 who, on orders from Washington, were again to reconnoiter the enemy's lair. Early Sunday morning they started out. The two ships had not proceeded far when a warning reached them: watch out for air attack. This made at least the fifth attack warning in ten days. *Maddox*'s CIC kept a close watch on SPS-40. Perhaps, remembering Wednesday's experience, the radarmen looked with as much curiosity to the south as to the north. The air search radar painted a few planes over land, but, as usual, the Communist aircraft did not venture in the Task Group's direction. (Perhaps the attack warning was stimulated by North Vietnam's acquisition of the MiG fighters mentioned earlier.)

It was late Sunday afternoon when *Maddox* and *Turner Joy,* departing the Gulf, completed their historic patrol. For men of the *Maddox,* the Gulf cruise lasted a very long eleven days, one more than Captain Ogier had predicted. The destroyermen looked forward to a well-deserved rest in port, but the Navy had other plans. Yankee Station needed more escort vessels, the destroyermen heard, as their little Task Group dissolved into the huge armada parading off Da Nang. Men of the *Turner Joy* were vexed to see another chance for liberty go glimmering; men of the *Maddox* were equally chagrined. As a minor irritant, the destroyermen noted how remaining at sea kept them away from the news media, though it did not keep the flyers of the *Ticonderoga* from being interviewed. A press conference aboard the carrier "made it look as though they did everything," complained the surface sailors.

The *Maddox* began plane guarding for the *Ticonderoga.* Most disgusted with the assignment were the COMVAN men, who no longer had any work to do. Before long, however, the faceless technicians transferred to the carrier and flew to Taiwan. From there they dispersed to their regular duty stations, bearing vivid tales of life in the basic Navy. One was about the conscientious Lieutenant Moore. On

August 2 some off-duty elint men took cover on the weather decks to watch the battle, and after a few moments one of the sightseers poked his head into the COMVAN, asking the lieutenant: "Aren't you going to watch?"

"There's nothing I can do about it," said Moore, and went on writing a report. Later he sent the sightseers below.

Even before the Gulf patrol ended, the Task Group wanted to make a port call, and not for purposes of recreation or publicity but to get a high priority job done—the preparation of an "action report." After Tuesday night's go-around, higher command demanded a quick, complete, written report of what had happened. Obviously, the work would go better ashore where the key men of both ships could get together and work in comfort, free from other duties. But the ships remained at sea even when they had little to do.

Aboard *Maddox* the operations officer, Bill Buehler, and his assistant, Daley Evans, were assigned to write the report, and they set up shop in the wardroom where, to some extent, they could spread out the necessary papers and charts. Swallowing pep pills to keep awake, the two got to work and kept at it for a couple of days until the report was finished. Visiting them once or twice was the *Turner Joy*'s executive officer, Lieutenant Commander Robert B. Hoffman. On the night of the 4th, Hoffman had supervised the other ship's CIC. Many problems cropped up. It appeared to *Maddox* personnel that the *Turner Joy* was claiming too much, and they wanted to tone down the information she submitted. Commander Hoffman reportedly objected to associating any of his ship's visual sightings of torpedoes with the *Maddox*'s sonar bearings, though Hoffman denied that when I talked to him. Discrepancies plagued the two destroyers' deck logs, CIC logs, and Dead Reckoning Tracer scrolls; even aboard the same ship different men tend to record the same events in different ways and at slightly different times. After an important incident, the Navy likes to prepare a "smooth log" as soon as possible, while the participants' memories are fresh.

To supervise completion of the action report, Commodore Herrick began taking meals in the *Maddox*'s wardroom. The Buehler-Evans draft was revised a few times. Then it was forwarded to higher command.

When there are important questions concerning a ship incident, a Court of Inquiry normally convenes. This is an international custom dating back for centuries. In similar manner, the U. S. Navy investigated the cases of the *Liberty* and *Pueblo*. But the adventures of the *Maddox* and *Turner Joy* were not investigated so formally.

After the action report was completed, selected representatives of the Task Group made a visit to the *Ticonderoga*. Hoisted up from the *Maddox* were Commodore Herrick, Lieutenant Buehler, and Lieutenant Evans. From the *Turner Joy* came one officer, Lieutenant Barry, and a few enlisted men, including Bosun's Mate 3rd Class Donald V. Sharkey and Seaman Kenneth E. Garrison. All of the *Turner Joy* representatives were men who claimed some kind of visual sighting on the night of the 4th. Remaining aboard their ships were Captain Ogier, Captain Barnhart, and the two executive officers, Commander Jackson and Commander Hoffman.

Aboard the *Ticonderoga*, the visiting destroyermen were impressed by the spaciousness of an aircraft carrier as they were led through passageways and into a roomy compartment. The group sat down around a table. At the head of it was not Admiral Moore, as the destroyermen half-expected, but a member of his staff, a balding captain. He did not waste any time on courtesy.

"I haven't had any sleep for forty-eight hours!" growled the host. "During my whole career in the Navy, I've seen something like *two* flash messages. Now I've seen seventy-five! I've been called out of bed for all sorts of ridiculous reasons."

This outburst, coming as it did before the enlisted men, shocked the destroyer officers. All of the battle-weary veterans gave up any hope for the red carpet treatment. The carpet they were on was the plainer kind. But the most interesting statement was to follow:

"I suppose you people think," blustered the captain, "that you were pigeons up there. Well, *that's exactly what you were.*"

Did the host speak from certain knowledge of the Task Group's mission? Or was he expressing an opinion? This was not clear. The writer obtained the quotation from one of the men present, who, thinking it over, was not sure whether the captain said "pigeons" or "sitting ducks." I tried to check the quotation with another witness. He would not confirm what the carrier officer had said. He did say enigmatically, "A lot of people thought that."

In any case, the balding staff officer's point seemed to be that the destroyermen ought to have taken this assignment in stride, with more aplomb, and without disturbing his sleep. Most of all, he resented the scores of flash messages that resulted from faulty sonar reports. Regulations require that a warship send a flash message every time a torpedo is detected. If the ship then disappears, higher command will know what happened. I cannot say how many flash messages were transmitted. Perhaps there were not more than twenty-two, which sometimes has been mentioned as the number of torpedoes detected. However, during the night action, the *Ticonderoga*'s CIC was flooded with flash messages owing to the zeal of the Navy's communications station at Subic Bay, which *repeated* each flash to a larger number of addressees—including the *Ticonderoga*. Thus the carrier received every flash at least twice, and officers did not always examine them carefully enough to distinguish the originals from the repeats.

Having been shaken by the captain's tirade, the most unsettling experience since Tuesday night, the destroyermen next were called, one by one, into the presence of Admiral Moore—Jehovah himself. First Commodore Herrick disappeared, remaining with the admiral for a lengthy talk. After that was over, each of the other men, in order of decreasing rank, was called into the admiral's compartment. Before his turn, each man went over in his mind the things he had to say, trying to prepare a creditable statement. But, except for the commodore, nobody stayed long with the admiral. One man described the interrogation as going this way:

"Do you believe you were attacked?"

"Yes, sir."

"Do you believe your captain did the right thing?"

"Yes, sir."

That was it. As for whether the captain had done the right thing, it was not clear which of the three "captains" in the Task Group the admiral was talking about, but in the Navy it is well known that the captain always does the right thing. It seemed that Admiral Moore's job was to collect affirmations of faith.

The battle witnesses learned that they would be making a trip to Subic Bay. Each of them received orders that authorized travel to the Philippines and, if necessary, to Washington, D.C., and New York City. At this time officials in Washington thought some destroyermen might be needed to testify at the United Nations.

For once the blustering carrier captain was favorably impressed.

"I've never seen orders like these," he marveled. "You could go any-where in the world and endorse them yourselves."

The selected destroyermen traveled to Subic Bay aboard a prop-driven transport of the type the Navy calls a "COD" (Carrier On-Board Delivery) plane. Upon landing they were met by the base's commanding officer, an admiral, who whisked them off to sleeping quarters, incommunicado. Early the next morning, which was Mon-day, August 10, the sailors from the Tonkin Gulf enjoyed a land-cooked breakfast; then, still unsteady on *terra firma,* they proceeded to a big meeting room. Also assembling there were several Navy officers from Washington and Hawaii. But the principal figures ap-peared to be two civilians from Washington. (At the 1968 hearing Secretary McNamara was incorrect when he gave senators the im-pression that no investigators traveled to the Far East after the August incidents.) One of the destroyermen described the meeting this way:

"We were very impressed by the civilians. They had come out from Washington in a big jet. One looked very young, about thirty. He was fairly stocky, had black hair. The other man was older. He had gray hair. The younger one was the senior of the two in rank. He was an Assistant Secretary of Defense in charge of United Nations affairs or something like that. He wore a coat and a tie. I'd say he was conservatively dressed. Both of the civilians had been yanked from the States in a hurry. The gray-haired one had been on vacation or something. He was wearing a Madras plaid sportcoat, and he had brown-and-white shoes. He looked like a bookie. We liked him. He was very witty. Both the civilians were very intelligent, but I don't think either of them had any technical Navy background. The older man did understand what we were saying—the sequence of events—pretty well, and he explained things to the younger man. The younger man worried about what he would say to Mr. Stevenson at the United Nations. That was his main concern. No, we didn't get their names. I don't think anybody was introduced except the commodore."

The chief purpose of the civilians' investigation seems to have been the gathering of evidence for Ambassador Stevenson to use, if need be, at the United Nations. Both of the civilians were lawyers by training and, coincidentally, graduates of Cornell. The younger man was Alvin Friedman, thirty-four, dark and husky, who recently had become Deputy Assistant Secretary of Defense for International Security Affairs. Friedman was not a professional civil servant but a political appointee; he had enjoyed quick promotion since joining the Defense Department on the recommendation of Dean Acheson, the former Secretary of State. (Acheson was associated with Friedman's previous employer, a Washington law firm.) Friedman's military experience amounted to two years' active duty as an Air Force officer. During the Korean War he taught international relations at an Officers Candidate School. Traveling with Friedman to Subic was Jack L. Stempler, forty-four (and prematurely gray), a career civil servant who had been with the Defense Department since 1948. During World War II Stempler served four years with the First Marine Division.

For the destroyermen Lieutenant Buehler did nearly all of the talking. He believed firmly in the night battle. He had done most of the report writing, and he knew the whole complicated story by heart—so far as the Task Group's activities were concerned. Now and then Lieutenant Evans, who had drawn diagrams for the report, would help Buehler out. Most of the time, Commodore Herrick sat quietly. Sometimes he exchanged a few words with the officers from higher command.

I have heard that the two civilian lawyers were entirely satisfied that an attack had taken place on the night of August 4. I also have heard that one of them said, "Even if we had the North Vietnamese here, we probably couldn't find out what happened."

But, in either case, the lawyers were far from satisfied with the evidence available. When the meeting broke up, they cornered the junior officers.

"What do you have for us?" the men from Washington asked. "Don't you have any evidence for the attack?"

Lieutenant Buehler began to repeat his monologue on radar, sonar, and eyewitnesses.

"All you're giving us is a bunch of talk," broke in the civilians. "That isn't going to do us any good. Don't you have something real?"

"We have some photographs," said Buehler, apparently in reference to the August 2 battle."

"Oh, that's no good," scoffed the civilians. "They'll just tell us we staged those photographs."

(Ambassador Stevenson had made it clear that he was not going to hold up any pictures. At the time of the Cuban invasion, three years before, Stevenson had shown the UN a photograph that, unknown to him, was staged by the CIA as part of a cover story. To the ambassador's mortification, the cover crumbled almost immediately under the weight of a few questions from newspaper reporters.)

The lawyers asked Buehler: "Don't you have the arm of a Chinaman, or a piece of a boat, or *something* that we can go up there and show them, that nobody can deny?"

The answer was negative.

"Well, why didn't you go back and *get* something?"

"How should *I* know?" was Buehler's rejoinder.

After the meeting the destroyermen sent telegrams to their families in the States, reporting that they were safe and sound. The admiral in charge of the base personally examined the telegrams, crossing out references to Subic Bay. With some exasperation, he explained, "Nobody's supposed to know you're here."

Though pressed for time, the Pentagon lawyers decided to interview some more veterans of the night battle. On Tuesday morning the whole group boarded the civilians' jet and flew to Da Nang, thence hopping by two COD flights to the *Ticonderoga*. Aboard the carrier a brass band greeted the VIPs and their gold-braided escorts. Alvin Friedman rated the honors of a vice admiral. He and his entourage then took lunch with Admiral Moore while the destroyermen were hustled back to their ships. When I interviewed Friedman in 1968, he remembered meeting "several young pilots" who reported seeing wakes. However, because of Tuesday night's very poor visibility, Friedman considered their testimony the "least authoritative." Nobody aboard the carrier expressed any doubt concerning the reality of the night attack. At about 2 P.M. the investigative party took the high line to visit *Turner Joy*.

Captain Barnhart greeted the VIPs and guided them to a comfortable compartment. Commander Hoffman seemed very knowledgeable. He talked about radar and explained the DRT tracings of torpedo tracks and enemy boats. Hoffman's presentation and the ensuing discussion lasted more than two hours. The men from Washington could understand why, on that pitchblack night, the destroyermen had to rely on electronic detection of the enemy. They were puzzled, however, by the Communists ability to get along without electronic help. Without using radar, how did the enemy manage to find the destroyers, then fire torpedoes with such accuracy? *Turner Joy* officers explained that the enemy's tactic was "bore-sighting" on the wake.

The civilians next interviewed several enlisted men who had seen lights, explosions, torpedo wakes, etc. Stempler recalls, "We didn't try to shake their stories, but it was worth something to look them in the eye and find out what they had to say."

Friedman remembers meeting the *"Turner Joy*'s sonarman." This witness told of detecting what Friedman thought a "more reasonable number of torpedoes" than the *Maddox* had reported. Chief Schaperjahn, now retired and living near Richmond, Virginia, says that he never reported any torpedoes to anybody.

The men from Washington discussed with gunners the reliability of firing at night by radar. "These were men who fire guns every day," says Friedman. "They knew what they were doing. I asked them whether they could tell the difference between a boat and orange crate floating in the water. They assured me that they could tell the difference."

Nobody aboard the *Turner Joy* expressed any doubt, and for this there was good reason. Before the visitors arrived, members of the crew had been ordered to see a designated officer if they had any statements to make about the battle. Those who offered information in support of an attack were welcomed, and some of these men were introduced to the investigators. Those who had had any doubts about an attack were not welcomed, and were given no opportunity to meet the two lawyers. Some may find this shocking, seeing in it evidence of a plot; but others, with experience in the armed forces, will perhaps find it no different from the usual method of dealing with outsiders. Any civilian is an outsider, no matter how many bells may be rung or guns fired in his honor. (Secretary McNamara, perhaps, did not fully realize this when making his several fact-finding trips to Saigon, known locally as "Saigon's first snowstorm," "Saigon's second snowstorm," and so forth.)

Convinced that the attack was real, and having collected the best evidence available, the two Washington lawyers departed the *Turner Joy* late in the afternoon and flew back to Washington. Industriously, Friedman wrote his report on the way. Although the two lawyers had traveled halfway around the world to investigate the Tonkin Gulf incidents, one of the most crucial episodes in the nation's history, they did not visit the destroyer *Maddox*. Before starting the trip, they knew that the *Maddox* was "at a loss"; besides, officers from that ship were interrogated at Subic Bay. The *Turner Joy,* Friedman observes, was a "newer ship, more modern, and it seemed to have more information."

Midway in our conversation, Friedman remarked, "I had no negative evidence." But in point of fact, the investigators were not looking very hard for negative evidence. Their primary mission seems to have been collecting information that Ambassador Stevenson would find useful if the North Vietnamese tried to prove that the battle was a fabrication (although, in that case, one might wonder why the State Department did not send out an investigator). Obligingly, the Navy did its best to make available the least confusing, most helpful information. As matters turned out, North Vietnam rejected the UN's invitation, and Ambassador Stevenson did not have to argue the case further.

Following the pattern of Washington lawyers who go in and out of public service, Friedman later left the Defense Department, and, at this writing, practices law in his own firm of Epstein and Friedman. Jack Stempler presently holds the title Assistant to the Secretary of Defense for Legislative Affairs. In Washington he is known as the man who coaches military officers in the art of lobbying on Capitol Hill. Stempler's 1964 trip later proved useful when, as one of the "best lawyers" in the Pentagon, he helped Secretary McNamara prepare for the 1968 hearing.

Information from the *Turner Joy* not only gave the civilian investigators the kind of evidence they needed but even convinced Commodore Herrick that the attack was real. It was Captain Barnhart, the commodore told me, who eliminated his doubts. If, immediately after the battle, Herrick had traveled by high line to the *Turner Joy,* he might have saved Washington many anxious hours. Then, again, he might not have, as we shall see.

Men of the *Maddox* at last got their cold beer and a chance to trade war stories after their ship docked at Subic Bay on Sunday, August 23. For a time, whenever they were on liberty with men of the *Turner Joy,* the reminiscences were enlivened by disagreement. It was not easy to decide which ship had been the hero of August 4 and which the goat. True, the *Turner Joy* had done most of the fighting—if there had been any fighting. But would *Turner Joy* not have been sunk, literally, without the *Maddox*'s timely warning—if a warning had been needed? The argument was endless, and some blows were exchanged.

On August 25, Captain Ogier turned the *Maddox* over to a new skipper and transferred to a planning job aboard the *Constellation*. The apparent suddenness of the change in command sparked a rumor within the Navy that the *Maddox* skipper had been relieved for cause. As mentioned before, however, Ogier's transfer was scheduled before the Tonkin Gulf patrol began.

On the second day of October, *Maddox* and *Turner Joy* were among forty ships that docked at Long Beach, California, completing their WestPac deployment. *Maddox* was the last destroyer to throw out her lines. Perhaps the delay had something to do with the Southern California press standing on the pier, waiting to interview veterans of the Tonkin Gulf. Recently Senator Morse had been in the area, casting doubt on the government's version of what happened. Morse said that the *Maddox* had shot first on August 2, and he accused the Navy of patrolling closer to shore than had been admitted.

Commodore Herrick, who came in aboard the *Picking,* refuted these intimations of wrongdoing. He reassured newsmen: "It cannot be charged that we fired first in the Tonkin Gulf on August 2." Herrick at this time did not know that the warning shots were aimed to kill. As for the rapid fire, he later explained to me that nobody could be sure of when the first torpedoes were *launched* even though two were first *observed* after the commencement of rapid fire. This explanation must rest on the improbable assumption that a torpedo boat discharged its missiles at a range of more than 9000 yards, and then braved murderous shellfire, closing in long after the missiles were gone.

As to how close to shore the *Maddox* patrolled, the commodore at Long Beach gave a figure of 16 miles. Herrick told me that he had in mind the distance of land when Sunday's attackers appeared on the radar.

Perhaps it should be noted that naval officers, like other government personnel, are required by law to protect classified information. In order to preserve a military secret, an officer may be forced to take refuge in a misleading statement. And what is a military secret? Whatever the government *says* is a military secret, even if the same "secret" is obviously in the hands of the enemy.

The Los Angeles *Times* printed the interview with Herrick and other destroyermen back on page 13. Toward the end of the story appeared a quotation from the commodore that surely deserved more prominent treatment. Said Herrick:

"We considered the boats we saw August 2 as North Vietnamese. What were encountered two nights later—whether they were Chinese or North Vietnamese—we're not sure. It happened in the dark of night."

One immediately wonders about the special intelligence. Weren't the intercepted messages in Vietnamese? Or didn't the messages, if in Vietnamese, order an attack? Herrick later explained to me that during the battle there was much speculation as to whether Chinese craft were "supporting" a North Vietnamese attack. In other words, the commodore's statement at Long Beach was based on the theory that boats of two nationalities might have attacked the destroyers.

While the ships were at Subic Bay, the Navy decided to make a film about their historic patrol. The *Turner Joy* steamed out to sea, fired her guns for the camera, and helped with other footage. *Maddox* played a role, too, after disposing of the black box. The destroyermen were eager to see the completed motion picture, but, as it turned out, the Navy prepared only a brief film on the air raids. The surface footage got "shelved," heard the destroyermen. Sagely, the battle skeptics nodded their heads. The *Turner Joy,* however, enjoyed one colorful bit of public recognition. Captain Barnhart flew to New York and appeared on a television program: "To Tell the Truth." It became the skipper's job to camouflage himself between two impostors, then stand up when the "real Captain Barnhart" was demanded. Men of the *Maddox* thought that was quite a gas.

Ambiguity would plague the patrol for years, perhaps forever. President Johnson refused to give the Task Group a citation. But the Secretary of the Navy signed one, authorizing all Task Group personnel to wear the Navy Unit Commendation Ribbon. By telegram the ships already had received the compliments of the Chief of Naval Operations, CINCPAC, and the Commander of the Seventh Fleet. I have found no record of a commendation from CINCPACFLT, except for one that he sent to men of the black box. Admiral Moorer did speak highly of the ships at the 1970 hearing, when he sought confirmation as Chairman of the Joint Chiefs. On that occasion Admiral Moorer attributed the Task Group's survival to the "superb performance of the men and officers of the *Maddox* and *Turner Joy* and the manner in which they conducted themselves during these sea battles." Nonetheless, the decorations for destroyermen were few and modest. There had been talk of promotions and Silver Stars, but Commodore Herrick got nothing beyond the Unit Commendation; and the two skippers, Ogier and Barnhart, received only Bronze Stars. For some unspecified but "extremely meritorious" service, a Navy Commendation Medal went to Lieutenant Frick, the commodore's operations officer. Chief Petrovitz, who kept the ammunition moving on August 2, seems to have received no particular recognition for his service. A few of the carrier pilots earned Silver Stars in the air raids. Posthumously, Lieutenant Sather was awarded the Distinguished Flying Cross.

The careers of both Herrick and Ogier were shelved like the Tonkin Gulf movie. Since 1964 neither officer has enjoyed the command of another ship or promotion in rank. The ex-*Maddox* skipper retired as a commander in 1970. The former commodore, still a captain in rank, remains on active duty in a shore job. A few officers who in 1964 were familiar with the thinking at higher command have hinted to me that, in its judgment, somebody with the Task Group panicked. This judgment apparently did not apply to the *Turner Joy*'s skipper, Commander Barnhart. Barnhart later made captain and obtained the command of a guided missile ship.

Perhaps the worst experience that Ogier and Herrick endured after leaving the Tonkin Gulf was a dinner sponsored by the Navy League, a venerable lobbying organization which calls itself the "right arm of the Navy." Admiral Moore also was at the dinner, and the three Tonkin Gulf veterans were called up to the dais apparently to receive awards. A band struck up a few stirring notes, the room quieted down, and Admiral Moore was handed a scroll of appreciation. The band struck some more stirring notes, the room quieted down, but to everyone's embarrassment the Navy League had run out of scrolls. Nobody knew what to do, including the band. Somehow the awkward tableau finally dissolved.

In the fall of 1967 I found an opportunity to visit the *Maddox*. She had been in the Gulf every year since 1964; now the old short hull was in the Long Beach drydock, all torn up for an overhaul. Even Lieutenant Connell's guns were missing. Where they had stood, big, rusty holes gaped in the deck. The holes were to be filled with reconditioned guns from a depot in Indiana. Still aboard ship were a few of the men who had been on the De Soto patrol. All were gunners—specialists for whom the Navy finds little in the way of shore duty. One of the old hands was Robert Swift, the Tennesseean who envisioned a North Vietnamese drinking party at some secluded cove, to be followed by a wild attack. By 1967 Swift had spent a lot of time in the Tonkin Gulf. Asked for his impressions of the area, the gunner replied with some feeling, "I wish I could forget it."

Admiral Moore, the former Jehovah, retired in 1967. He was still a rear admiral in rank. Privately, Moore doubted the reality of the August 4 attack.

Admiral Sharp continued as CINCPAC until his retirement in August of 1968. In his four years of commanding the Pacific area, Sharp took some measure of responsibility not only for the Tonkin Gulf affair, but for the escalation of the war in Indochina and the *Pueblo* disaster.

General Westmoreland continued in command of MACV until 1968. Following the Communists' Tet offensive against major South Vietnamese cities (one cause of President Johnson's sudden retirement), General Westmoreland got "kicked upstairs" to Army Chief of Staff. In that position he has gathered many of his former MACV colleagues to help run the Army.

When the regular bombing of North Vietnam started in 1965, Admiral Moorer was still in Hawaii as CINCPACFLT. In April of that year, he transferred to the Atlantic Fleet, in time to supervise the Dominican intervention. Two years later Moorer became Chief of Naval Operations, and in 1970 he replaced General Wheeler as Chairman of the Joint Chiefs. Admiral Moorer is the first Navy man to hold the top military job since Admiral Radford, who in 1954 urged President Eisenhower to save the French cause in Indochina. As Chairman-designate of the Joint Chiefs (before his confirmation by Congress), Moorer is said to have played an important role in President Nixon's decision to invade Cambodia.

Chapter XIV

Phantom Battles

To date the most frequently asked question concerning the Tonkin Gulf has been whether a "real battle" took place on the night of August 4. Two American destroyers and numerous aircraft were on the scene. Official reports told of radar contacts, sonar reports of torpedoes, visually sighted torpedo wakes, silhouettes of attacking boats, enemy gunfire, other sightings, and "special intelligence." The attackers, it was said, even trained searchlights on the American ships in order to shoot at them with automatic guns. At least two of the brash boats were sunk. How could anybody doubt such a mass of evidence?

As Pentagon officials have pointed out, it is impossible to believe that a large part of the Seventh Fleet, including gold-braided admirals and bell-bottomed sailors, got together to plan a deliberate hoax. Such a suspicion would be more than "monstrous," to use Secretary McNamara's term. It would be absurd. Nevertheless, the August 4 attack has been doubted, and the skeptics, to my personal knowledge, have included several of the best-informed officers who were involved. Could an entire naval battle be imaginary? Could such a conflict result merely from overwrought nerves, weird electronic conditions, or a combination of the two?

Experienced military men know that soldiers, sailors, and airmen are liable to "see things" and shoot at them, later describing a fictitious enemy. Fear can stimulate such apparitions. Other emotions can have the same effect. In peacetime maneuvers, a simple eagerness to do one's best can generate illusions. In time of war, a strong desire to fight can, through wishful thinking, produce the image of an enemy.

In naval warfare, the small but lethal torpedo boat is a potent stimulus to overreaction. As early as 1891 the British navy learned that gunners are liable to "see" one anywhere. In night exercises of that year, the rules required that defending warships make certain that they were not taken by surprise. Consequently, the gunners were under pressure to discover the "enemy" and shoot at him as soon as possible. In his book *Torpedoes and Torpedo Vessels*,[1] Lieutenant G. E. Armstrong described the results:

"Aligning the sights at the supposed enemy was a matter of quite secondary importance. The chief thing was to blaze away, and blaze away as fast as they could directly the alarm was raised, so as to bring the torpedo boats 'under fire' at the earliest possible moment. On more than one occasion, and notoriously so on the night of the 29th, several of the ships were actually firing right into their friends, and it is more than probable that if the guns had been properly loaded the ships in harbour would have done far more damage to themselves than any of the enemy's torpedo boats could have inflicted on them. Captain Durnford, than whom no better authority could be found, and an exceedingly practical officer as well, gave it as his opinion that as regards a night torpedo boat attack 'the accuracy of the fire of guns has to be considered,' and considering the 'extraordinary way people think they see torpedo boats when none are there,' he thinks that the 'boat has an excellent chance of not being hit.' "

If such mistakes could occur before the invention of long range electronic detection devices, what kind of problem do we face now? Interpreting the blips and squeaks of electronic gadgets is more of an art than a science. As mentioned earlier, sonarmen are trained to err on the "safe" side, reporting everything they hear. Having no time to argue, the man on the bridge has no choice but to take evasive action. If there is reason to expect attack, the skipper will start shooting back.

As for radar, World War II produced a classic case of error that, within the U. S. Navy, became known as the "Battle of the Pips." The great illusion began on the night of July 26, 1943, when a Navy plane reported seven contacts 200 miles south of Attu, one of the Aleutian islands that had been occupied by the Japanese. Admiral Robert C. Giffen charged northward with a Task Force of two or

---

[1] Published in 1896 by George Bell and Sons, London.

three battleships, several cruisers, and four destroyers. For most of Giffen's men, it was their first opportunity to get at the enemy, and they were spoiling for a fight. The night was crisp and clear. Admiral Samuel Eliot Morison relates the incident in his World War II naval history:

"*Mississippi* reported radar contacts 15 miles on the port bow. *Idaho, Wichita,* and *Portland* chimed in that they 'had 'em too.' In every ship the General alarm tolled excited sailors to battle stations as 'Ike' Giffen jockeyed his disposition into battle formation and set course due north. When the strange contacts registered eight miles from the cruisers and 12 miles from the battleships, the Admiral altered course to 340° to clear enemy torpedo water. Battleships and cruisers opened fire at 0013, throwing shells at the places where radar indicated that the enemy lay, while destroyers were detached to deliver torpedo attacks. Radar spotters gave salvo corrections; lookouts reported torpedo wakes, flares, and light; men below decks felt concussions similar to those they had experienced of near-misses; gunners noted star shells apparently thrown up by the foe; there was even a mental breakdown by a neurotic sailor! It seemed odd, though, that no return fire came from the enemy, and that neither *San Francisco* nor a single destroyer had any radar contact whatsoever.

"When the Admiral ordered Cease Firing at 0044 because the radar screens were clear of targets, the battleships had expended 518 rounds of 14-inch shell and the three cruisers 487 rounds of 8-inch. When dawn broke, Giffen circled back to the vicinity of the 'battle' and launched a plane which found nothing—no ship, no debris, no wreckage, not even a dead whale; nothing but the cold, gray surges of the North Pacific. Suspicion had already dawned that the 'targets' had been mere radar phantoms, and suspicion now became certainty. What had shown up on the radar were return echoes from the mountains of Amchitka and other islands 100 to 150 miles distant."[2]

Undoubtedly Admiral Giffen's radar had been super-refracting. With normal radar vision, the highest peak on Amchitka ought not to have been visible for more than 60 miles. Yet there it was, with other peaks, cluttering the scope from distances of 100 to 150 miles. The Task Force opened fire, and this in turn triggered delusions

[2] *History of United States Naval Operations in World War II* (Boston: Little, Brown, and Company, 1951), VII, page 60.

among young, alert human beings who were trusting not to radar but to their everyday bodily senses. The Battle of the Pips lasted only 31 minutes. It became a huge joke, though an expensive one, considering the expenditure of shells and the deterioration of gun barrels.

A smaller but very tragic mix-up occurred more recently in Vietnam. In June of 1968, U. S. Marines and South Vietnamese soldiers reported enemy helicopters operating at night over the Demilitarized Zone. They heard the distinctive sounds of chopper engines, and looking upward they saw lights in the sky. To the Air Force, such reports were a perennial nuisance. They came sporadically from the DMZ and from troops stationed near Cambodia, but the presence of Communist helicopters in or near South Vietnam never had been confirmed. Nonetheless, jet fighters dashed northward from Da Nang. To their surprise, the pilots actually found radar blips that looked like enemy aircraft flying low. The Americans immediately took advantage of this rare opportunity for air-to-air combat; afterward, they reported the "possible destruction" of Communist helicopters. Without knowing it, however, the airmen had tangled with friendly *naval vessels*.

Unfortunately, men on the surface thought they had withstood a North Vietnamese attack from the air. Consequently, another battle took place the following night. The two-day score: one American gunboat sunk, the heavy cruiser *Boston* damaged, and the Australian destroyer *Hobart* "extensively damaged." Air attack killed five of seven men aboard the gunboat. Two Australians died and seven were injured. The Air Force came through unscathed. Evidently the Navy's anti-aircraft missiles accomplished nothing (though in 1968 missiles fired by the *Long Beach* at last knocked down two North Vietnamese MiG 21 fighters). The *Boston* sought help from Yankee Station, but the Navy jets did not arrive in time to deal with the Air Force jets. Down in Saigon, MACV announced that a Swift gunboat, PCF-19, had been sunk by "hostile fire from the beach." Other surface vessels, said MACV, were attacked by helicopters and winged aircraft.

What stopped the nightly duels were suspicions voiced by the two gunboat survivors and the destroyer *Hobart*. The gunboat men insisted that they had been attacked by American jets. The Australians thought they had been hit by Sparrow missiles. These charges stimulated an investigation, and six weeks later MACV admitted the mix-up. The fast-moving jet pilots, it was explained, had difficulty seeing the tiny radar screens installed in their cockpits. Nobody explained how men on the surface, with their slow speed and big screen radar, could mistake the speedy jets for cumbersome helicopters.

It happened to be June 16, 1968, the day between the two night battles of mistaken identity, when General Creighton W. Abrams, Jr., the normally taciturn successor to General Westmoreland, hailed publicly the development of a new secret weapon. It was designed, said Abrams, to "put a stop" to the Viet Cong's rocket and mortar attacks. Hitherto the problem had been timing. The guerrillas would set up their weapons, let fly a well-aimed barrage, and make a fast getaway before the Americans could defend themselves. But all that had changed. The defenders were now able to shoot back at a greatly accelerated speed. Just recently, said Abrams, the new gadget had helped to discourage a Communist rocket assault.

One of the first miracle machines was set up at the base camp of the 9th Division, and seven months' after Abrams's announcement a story on it made the press. The gadget was a radar-eyed computer, designated AN/MPQ-4. Its purpose to spot enemy projectiles in the air and, calculating from their trajectory, give their point of origin to defending artillerymen. A trained technician sat up night after night watching the radarscope. At last, tell-tale streaks of light appeared. Literally hundreds of enemy shells were funneling in. Quickly, the technician passed firing data to nearby howitzers, and they started blasting away even before the enemy shells could hit the ground. In fact, the enemy shells never did hit the ground. All was quiet except for the howitzers; and soon they, too, stopped firing. Something was wrong. At dawn foot soldiers reconnoitered the source of the ghostly barrage. They found no traces of the Viet Cong—just a Vietnamese farmer plucking a lot of dead ducks.

The Army's trouble with the radar-eyed computer would be more amusing if, later on, a big rocket assault had not hit the same base. Furthermore, the AN/MPQ-4 must remind one of the even more automatic targeting system planned by the Army for its nuclear-tipped Anti-Ballistic Missiles (ABMs), which have been scheduled for installation within the continental United States.

Another battle in the Tonkin Gulf almost exactly paralleled the action of August 4, 1964. This was the incident of September 18, 1964, about which Fireman James J. Kress wrote to his family in Dubuque,

Iowa. Again two destroyers were on De Soto patrol. Again they opened fire on high-speed radar contacts and reported themselves under attack. This time, however, the Defense Department reacted with caution. Secretary McNamara issued this brief statement dated September 18:

"Preliminary and fragmentary reports have been received of a nighttime incident in international waters in the Gulf of Tonkin. There has been no damage reported by American vessels and no loss of American personnel. The reports of the incident are being investigated. We will have nothing further to say until our investigation has been completed."

Upon receiving the first report of an attack, the Defense Secretary broke away from a press conference to telephone Admiral Sharp. Next, as on August 4, McNamara gathered his top aides, civilian and military. The group discussed the problem at lunch, then proceeded to the White House. President Johnson, according to what he said later, rejected advice to bomb North Vietnam immediately. The President did not say who gave this advice; it was probably not Mc-Namara, who was so hesitant on August 4. In any case, Johnson decided to wait for the results of daylight reconnaissance, which was fortunate because, as in August, the search turned up nothing. The President decided not to order an air raid.

On September 19 the Defense Secretary issued another statement, again very cautious in wording and tone. McNamara made no accusations and did not use the word "attack." He did not even identify the American ships. Nor did he say anything about a debris search. The statement attributed to Admiral Sharp, CINCPAC, the information that the two destroyers on a routine patrol "were menaced by four unidentified vessels which, because of their dispositions, courses and speed, indicated hostile intent. The destroyers, after changing course to minimize danger to themselves and after the un-identified vessels continued to close, fired warning shots. In spite of these warning rounds the unidentified vessels continued toward the destroyers. The destroyers then properly opened fire and the ap-proaching craft disappeared without closing sufficiently to open fire on the destroyers. The destroyers are continuing their patrols in the international waters in the Gulf of Tonkin and U.S. air and sea forces remain prepared to respond immediately to any attack."

Clearly, on this occasion the Johnson administration did not wish to arouse public opinion or congressional opinion. Instead of exaggerating what was known about the new incident in the Gulf, the Pentagon actually omitted or covered up evidence of an attack. For example, an anonymous official told the press that everything happened not only at night but in a "heavy fog." Actually, according to Senator Morse, who obtained access to the Navy's records in 1968, the battle took place on a moonlit night with good visibility for four miles. In his letter home, Fireman Kress provided some vivid details:

"We picked up seven contacts on the radar screen. The *Edwards* blew two of them out of the water for certain and shot up another one. I don't know if the *Morton* destroyed any or not."

Kress was aboard the *Richard S. Edwards,* DD 950 (not to be confused with the older *Edwards,* DD 619, built in 1942). Both she and the *Morton,* DD 948, were up-to-date *Forrest Sherman* class ships like the *Turner Joy.* In September there were no old short hulls steaming around "at a loss."

As in August there seems to have been bore-sighting on the wake. Kress noted in his letter: "One of those boats like to got us. It was trying to sneak up on our rear and almost succeeded. It came within 2000 yards before we blew it up." Two men on the *Morton,* he added, signed statements saying that they had seen torpedo boats. According to Senator Morse, men of the *Edwards* reported seeing the enemy's tracer bullets and shellbursts.

"That little battle we had," wrote Kress, "sure did build up morale for a while. I think that it was so high that if they would have told us that liberty was cancelled for two months, the morale of the crew wouldn't have dropped too much."

James Kress somehow managed to mail his letter from the Philippines, where the destroyermen, having cut short their patrol, underwent a secret interrogation. Even though the September 18 reports were almost identical to those of August 4—or perhaps *because* they were almost identical—the Navy decided that a formal inquiry was needed. A Board of Inquiry convened at Subic Bay on September 21, the day after the two destroyers arrived there. (The *Pueblo* and *Liberty* were investigated by Courts of Inquiry. In Navy terminology, a Board is similar except that not all of its members are commissioned officers; probably in this case civilian technical advisers were included.) The Board of Inquiry was chaired by Admiral William S. Guest, who was embarked in *Constellation* at the time of the August 4 incident. Guest must have had plenty of time to compare notes with the former skipper of the *Maddox*, Commander Ogier, who before the new fracas had transferred to *Constellation*.

For two days the Board took evidence and cross-examined the destroyermen. Its conclusion: there was "no credible evidence" for an attack. The quotation is from Secretary McNamara's testimony at the 1968 Tonkin Gulf hearing. How the Board reached its decision has not been revealed, but the lack of post-battle debris seems to have been a factor. Secretary McNamara told the senators that no special intelligence confirmed the September attack.

In charge of the September patrol was Commodore Ernest Hollyfield. The commodore admitted to the Board that it was "unfortunate" he had reported the destroyers under attack. As in August, the destroyers opened fire at the approach of high-speed radar contacts. I have heard that, as in August, there were sonar reports of torpedoes. Yet when a skeptical higher command deluged Hollyfield with messages, asking such questions as whether the enemy was shooting back, the commodore was unable to make up his mind. He told the investigators:

"I refused to say we were fired on when I did not know we were, and still do not know. I know that careless or inaccurate reports would provoke more questions as they had in the *Maddox* case."

Whether or not Commodore Hollyfield's reports were more accurate than Commodore Herrick's, both men essentially took the same actions. Both opened fire on high-speed radar contacts; both reported an attack; both, subsequently puzzled, refused to confirm an attack. The two commodores even opened fire in the same general area. Each battle started approximately on a latitude with Vinh, with Hollyfield somewhat farther west. The evidence for both attacks was about the same except that, according to Secretary McNamara, no special intelligence confirmed the September attack.

For years the existence of the Board of Inquiry and its findings were kept secret. After the Board met, the Pentagon told newsmen in Washington that a team of civilian and naval investigators had reduced the number of "hard targets" from four to two.

It appears that the full findings of the Board, whatever they might have been, were kept not only from the public but even from most or all of the destroyermen involved. Upon completing his period of command, the skipper of the *Morton*, Commander John S. McGill, on March 30, 1965, submitted a routine review of the ship's activity to the Chief of Naval Operations. In this report, McGill recalled, "While patrolling the Gulf of Tonkin with the USS *Edwards* . . . *Morton* engaged hostile small craft with gunfire." McGill also noted that his ship won an Armed Forces Expeditionary Medal for her patrol and for her performance in a subsequent training exercise.

Commodore Hollyfield's career was not damaged by his performance in the Tonkin Gulf. He later commanded the guided missile cruiser *Providence* when she was flagship to the Seventh Fleet. In 1970 he died following a long illness.

At the 1968 hearing, Secretary McNamara acknowledged the lack of "credible evidence" for a September attack but continued to believe in the August 4 attack. The uncanny resemblance between the two attacks did not embarrass the Secretary. To the contrary, he drew strength from it. Some of those who didn't believe in the August 4 attack, McNamara asserted, had confused it with the September 18 affair, thinking *that* was the "second" attack. Said the Defense Secretary:

"Many individuals who were not aware of all the facts about all three incidents, that is, August 2 and 4, and September 18, have made the mistaken assumption that descriptions of the September 18 incident were referring to the second Tonkin Gulf incident. Aware of the negative findings on September 18, they have mistakenly assumed that there is serious doubt as to whether the 'second' Tonkin Gulf attack in fact took place."

It is true that in conversation some Defense Department people tended to confuse the "second" incident with the September incident. On the other hand, "many individuals" had never heard of the September board or its findings; and the skeptics included persons who could not possibly have confused events in August with events in September. In short, the simple truth is that naval officers have not been able to agree on whether an attack took place on either August 4 or September 18.

Oddly, when in 1969 I tried to check a minor point concerning the September investigation, the Defense Department reverted to its original story. Seemingly nobody had heard of a Board of Inquiry. Only a "survey team" had studied the matter, it was said, and the team never produced a "written" report, only a "verbal" one. For the content of that, I was referred to a newspaper article published in September of 1964—when hard-nosed investigators reportedly cut down the number of radar contacts from four to two.

At the 1968 hearing, Secretary McNamara told the senators that he doubted the September attack because there was no special intelligence to back it up, but that he would believe in the August 4 attack even without the special intelligence. The Secretary, of course, had plenty of reason to believe in the August 4 attack whether he wanted to or not.

Chapter XV

"Something Was Out There"

A lengthy naval engagement ought to leave some wreckage, oil, and survivors. A blank sea, as noted in the previous chapter, has been taken for convincing evidence of a phantom battle. But the importance of whatever happened on the night of August 4 does not permit dismissing it on the basis of the Navy's rather brief search for debris. It is necessary at this point to examine all of the available evidence for an attack, both official and unofficial.

In the statement that he prepared for the 1968 hearing, Secretary McNamara said in part that the following evidence was available at 6:30 P.M., EDT, when Admiral Sharp allegedly transmitted the air strike order:

"An intelligence report of a highly classified and unimpeachable nature received shortly before the engagement, stating that North Vietnamese naval forces intended to attack the *Maddox* and *Turner Joy.*

"Reports from the ships that their radars indicated they were being shadowed by high speed surface craft.

"Reports from the ships that they were being approached by the high speed vessels and an attack appeared imminent.

"Reports from the ships that they were under attack.

"A report from the ships that searchlight illumination had been utilized by the attacking craft and that gunfire against the patrol had been observed.

"A report that two torpedoes had passed close to the *Turner Joy* and that there had been positive visual sightings of what appeared to be cockpit lights of patrol craft passing near the *Maddox.*

"An intelligence report stating that North Vietnamese naval forces had reported that they were involved in an engagement.

"Reports from the U.S. ships that they had sunk two and possibly three of the attacking craft.

"An intelligence report stating that North Vietnamese naval forces had reported losing two ships in the engagement.

"A report from the onscene Task Group commander that he was certain that the ambush had taken place, although precise details of the engagement were still not known.

"A report from the Commander in Chief, Pacific, that he had no doubt that an attack had occurred."

Here was a very persuasive list. McNamara's statement made an excellent press release, and that is why he came to the hearing with two hundred copies, even though he and the senators had agreed not to release anything except by mutual consent. The Defense Secretary could not hope to win over his critics in the Senate, who had become exceedingly skeptical of any information from the Pentagon. He could hope to reassure the public, and he did.

The list of evidence, however, is not so convincing if one realizes that after the battle two of the three ranking officers in the Gulf did not fully accept it. True, Commodore Herrick certified that the "ambush" had been real. But McNamara did not explain that the "ambush" was what Herrick called the "original ambush"—a radar picture that had faded away long before the shooting started. This chapter will examine the evidence listed above, evidence that became available later, and some evidence that did not come out at the 1968 hearing.

First of all, let us take into account the eyewitness reports. The major problem with this testimony is that all of the original statements are secret. It would be important to know exactly what the witnesses signed and the time put down for each sighting. It also would be important to know whether the witnesses claimed more than we have been told. My approach to the problem of evaluating the eyewitness testimony has been to communicate directly with as many of the witnesses as possible. After some difficulty, I managed to obtain from the Defense Department an address of record for each of the witnesses named at the 1968 hearing. (This would not have been possible had I not appealed directly to Secretary McNamara's successor, Clark Clifford.) Whenever possible, I interviewed the witnesses by telephone or by traveling to their residences. Otherwise, I

sent letters asking for confirmation of what they saw. A large pro-
portion of the addresses were out of date. Some witnesses, still in
the Navy, reportedly were at sea, and none of these men answered
my letters. However, I did manage to get in touch with many of the
listed witnesses. Below, the results of these interviews are categorized
according to the type of sighting:

Torpedo Wakes—From firsthand interviews I can confirm that at
least two of the four *Turner Joy* men listed believe that they saw
torpedo wakes. The two are former Lieutenant (jg) John Barry,
presently employed by IBM in Irwin, Pennsylvania, and ex-Seaman
Rodger Bergland, now a draftsman-designer in Minneapolis, Minnesota. Seaman Larry Litton, though officially still in the Navy, had
disappeared by the time I began to look for him. At present the ex-
seaman is listed as having received an administrative discharge and
is not reachable through the Navy's address of record. Fortunately,
before I began looking for him, Litton had been interviewed by the
Associated Press and by David Wise, who wrote a magazine article
on the Tonkin Gulf incidents.[1] The fourth torpedo wake witness was
the *Turner Joy*'s port lookout, Edwin R. Sentel. Sentel was at sea and
did not respond to my letter.

The record of torpedo wake sightings is rather confused, partly
because no one seems to have reported a torpedo to the bridge at
the time he saw it. After the battle, Commodore Herrick told higher
command that neither ship had made any visual sightings. Then the
Task Group was ordered to gather evidence, and the *Turner Joy* came
up with sightings of two torpedoes. Admiral Sharp examined the reports and agreed that there had been two torpedoes. At the 1968
hearing, however, Secretary McNamara told of four *Turner Joy* men
seeing *one* torpedo. This reduced the number sighted, but it strengthened the evidence for one torpedo, which was all McNamara needed.
The Secretary tacked onto these four sightings David Mallow's first
sonar alarm and, of course, the launch turn radar contact. Now three
kinds of evidence dovetailed beautifully. The Foreign Relations Committee did not know that the witnesses had failed to report their torpedoes immediately, nor that the times of sighting were in doubt.
One must admire Secretary McNamara's skill in handling congres-

---

[1] "Remember the *Maddox!*," *Esquire* (April 1968). The title was ironic, not
hawkish. Wise doubted the August 4 attack.

sional committees, although such legerdemain erodes the trust needed between the executive and legislative branches of government.

Barry and Litton sat together in the *Turner Joy*'s Main Director. Rodger Bergland was in the After Director. All three have confirmed seeing a thin, straight wake pass by from astern. All remember that the ship was turning to starboard and that the wake was on the port side. Astern would have been the direction that David Mallow's torpedo ought to have come from, and also the direction of the launch turn radar contact. So far, so good. Barry remembered that his torpedo went by on an early swerve, perhaps the first. Bergland was not clear on the sequence of events. He remembered only seeing a wake "during an interval in the firing."

The Barry-Litton and the Bergland wakes differ greatly in two respects: length of time in sight and distance from the ship. If valid, the sightings must pertain to two different wakes, as Admiral Sharp and others thought they did. Litton estimated the Barry-Litton wake at 200 to 400 feet away; Barry said it was probably 300—the maximum possible distance, he reasoned, since the *Turner Joy*'s own, relatively immense trail of water could be seen for only 300 feet. The Barry and Litton statements agree fairly well. Rodger Bergland, however, said that his torpedo flashed by at a distance of only 20 or 30 feet. True, distance is not easy to judge at sea, especially at night. But the Barry-Litton torpedo passed at the very limit of visual range, and the Bergland torpedo barely missed the ship. As for time in sight, Barry would not make any kind of estimate; Litton said three or four minutes. Bergland estimated 20 seconds. Again, the wakes sound very different. Nobody, of course, saw a torpedo itself; just a streak of white water.

All three of these witnesses sat and watched an apparent torpedo travel the length of the ship without making any report to the bridge. I asked former Lieutenant Barry why he didn't speak up. Barry explained that the telephone lines were busy with fire-control information. "I didn't want to clutter the circuit," he said. But he did grab Seaman Litton and call his attention to the water. "I didn't even say, 'Look at the torpedo.' I asked him what he saw," Barry told the Associated Press.

Larry Litton did not remember the situation exactly that way when he was interviewed by David Wise. Said Litton: "Mr. Barry saw it and pointed down and yelled, 'Look, there's a torpedo!'" I asked Barry about the discrepancy. He replied that he did not remember exactly what it was that he had said to Litton.

In his conversation with David Wise, Seaman Litton continued, "There definitely was [a torpedo]. I never want to see one that close again. He [Barry] asked me if I saw it, and I said yes, I did. It kinda looked like a porpoise going through the water. But it wasn't no porpoise. We watched it for four or five minutes. It was 200 to 400 feet from the ship, about two or three feet below the water . . . we turned to starboard and it went up our port side."

A hair-raising story, but not so convincing if one thinks about the relative speeds of the torpedo and the ship. With only a 100-yard radius of visibility, an overtaking torpedo could not possibly have been in sight for four or five minutes—nor even for one minute. Passing near the outer limit of visibility, a 45-knot wake could have been seen for only a few seconds; even if it shaved the hull on a parallel course, the wake would be in sight for only 30 seconds or less, depending on how much momentum the destroyer lost in her turn. Perhaps Barry and Litton saw part of *Maddox*'s wake. As the *Turner Joy* turned east, the flagship was coming back north, spreading long V's of white water. Barry and Litton traveled right through *Maddox*'s wake, and probably did so without realizing it.

Sitting in the After Director, Rodger Bergland made his sighting independently. The torpedo zipped by at close range, but Bergland kept quiet about the near-destruction of his ship. I asked him why, and he explained, "I was so surprised that I just gaped at it." (I related this statement to Chief Schaperjahn, and even he thought it had the ring of truth. Schaperjahn recalled the first time he saw Japanese airplanes during World War II. "I just stood there and stared at them," he said.) Bergland was reluctant to estimate the time his wake was in sight. Finally, he smiled and said, "Well, it couldn't have been very long, could it?" He then gave a time of about 20 seconds. Although Bergland's wake came much closer to the ship than did the Barry-Litton wake, Bergland did not seem nearly as positive about his sighting. He refused to even confirm it unless I interviewed him personally in Minneapolis, which I did. Bergland then confirmed his sighting, but said that he thought the radar information was more conclusive.

Not only did Bergland fail to report his torpedo to the bridge; he didn't even mention it to the officer sitting next to him in the After Director. Former Ensign Wayne Whitmore, now a civilian living in Tallahassee, Florida, told me that he did not see Bergland's wake and that he knew nothing about it at the time. As for why he failed to see it, Whitmore explained, "The guns were firing and the bright, orange rings hurt my night vision." Later in our conversation, Whitmore told me about a lull in the battle (presumably the one prior to 10:52 P.M.), during which he thought he might have seen "some kind of wake."

No details have become known of Edwin Sentel's sighting. As the port lookout, Sentel was to keep alert and report immediately everything he saw. From the record of messages on visual sightings, it does not appear that he called out any torpedoes as soon as he saw them.

Besides the four men already mentioned, at least fifteen or twenty others were scanning the surface of the water, looking for torpedoes and for attacking boats. There were deck hands, bosuns, signalmen, torpedomen (anti-submarine), and others. None of these men saw phosphorescent wakes. Nor did the *Turner Joy*'s sonarmen report the sounds of any torpedoes.

But what about the timing—the impressive *coincidence* of radar, sonar, and visual evidence? It is not certain that visual sightings occurred on the *Turner Joy*'s first swerve, but what if they did? Then wouldn't the three kinds of evidence dovetail, reinforcing each other? No, not if one examines the coincidence mathematically. A 45-knot torpedo launched at 9:39 P.M. could not have overtaken the *Turner Joy* in less than eight minutes, which would have been *six minutes after* the ship's 9:41 P.M. turn. (My calculation assumes that a torpedo boat was 6000 yards off *Maddox*'s port quarter at a 45-degree angle; that *Maddox* was 1000 yards ahead of *Turner Joy;* and that both ships were making 30 knots. The 45-degree angle is somewhat arbitrary, but no reasonable change would alter the basic conclusion.) Whatever the eyewitnesses might have seen, it could not have been a torpedo from the "launch turn" viewed by radar. It could have been a torpedo from somewhere else—but where?

Silhouettes of Attacking Boats—Secretary McNamara listed four *Turner Joy* men who claimed to have seen boats in the water. They were Donald V. Sharkey, Bosun's Mate 3rd Class; Kenneth E. Garrison, Seaman; Delner Jones, Gunner's Mate; and Arthur B. Anderson, Fire Control Technician. Apparently none of these men saw torpedo wakes. None of them responded to my letters asking for confirmation of boat sightings. According to Secretary McNamara, the witnesses saw P-4 torpedo boats silhouetted by flares "dropped" by "aircraft and ship." The *Turner Joy* had no flares. *Maddox* and a few of the aircraft did. McNamara said that each man sketched from memory the shape of a P-4 boat even though none had ever seen a picture of a P-4. (The critic might ask *why* these men had never seen the picture of a P-4 boat. Normally a prudent Navy distributes recognition silhouettes to men whose job it is to keep an eye open for the enemy. The *Maddox* had photographed P-4s on Sunday.) But if *Turner Joy* men finally learned the shape of a P-4 during the battle, why didn't Melvin Bow paint one on his gun mount? The available facts suggest that *Turner Joy* men did not know what a P-4 looked like either before the battle or after it.

McNamara told of a boat sighting by one of *Maddox*'s gunners, Jose R. San Augustin, Gunner's Mate 2nd Class. Reportedly, the ship's officers did not take this sighting very seriously, but evidence for an attack was demanded and was supplied.

Enemy Gunfire—Secretary McNamara brought this up again in 1968. I have found nobody from the ships who would vouch for it. The *Turner Joy* did report automatic gunfire, which at the 1964 hearing McNamara inflated to "3-inch" shells. But Captain Barnhart told me that he did not know of any gunfire directed at his ship. Apparently, some person or persons reported tracer bullets or the like, but since no slugs or scars could be found, the claim was dropped, so far as the ship's officers were concerned.

Column of Black Smoke—If there is one fact that is generally agreed upon, it is that the night of August 4 was extremely dark—indeed, completely black. Yet we have a sighting of black smoke. Who saw it? At the 1968 hearing, Secretary McNamara told the Foreign Relations Committee: "The commanding officer and other *Turner Joy* personnel observed a thick column of black smoke from this target" (a radar contact that disappeared after shells burst upon it). Again, we have a sighting from the *Turner Joy*. I have found no witnesses for the smoke other than Captain Barnhart. The captain admitted that it was strange for a column of black smoke to be visible on such a dark night. I asked in which direction the smoke was located. Barnhart said he thought it was to the north, where the ship was aiming her fire, but he could not be sure. The ship was zigzagging so much that it was hard to keep track of direction. As noted before, there was no moonlight or starlight in any direction. To David Wise, Captain Barnhart explained that the smoke was illuminated by "gun flashes in the distance." Wise's article did not mention whose guns might have made these flashes. Barnhart himself said that no North Vietnamese gunfire was visible. If American guns were flashing near the column of smoke, some American other than Captain Barnhart ought to have seen it.

Searchlights—After the Associated Press team interviewed scores of Tonkin Gulf veterans, the writers decided that one item of evidence could not be explained away: a powerful searchlight. Secretary McNamara thought it was good evidence, too. He told senators at the 1968 hearing: "Later, 10:47 P.M., during the attack a searchlight was observed by all signal bridge and maneuvering bridge personnel including the commanding officer of the USS *Turner Joy.* The beam of the searchlight did not touch the ship, but was seen to swing in an arc toward the *Turner Joy* and was immediately extinguished when aircraft from the combat air patrol orbiting above the ships approached the vicinity of the searchlight." McNamara's story implied that North Vietnamese boats were going to fire their small guns at the destroyer, using a searchlight to illuminate the man-of-war, but that the approach of aircraft discouraged the hitherto intrepid gunners. McNamara did not mention any of the alert flyers by name. I have found none who claims to have seen a searchlight.

The principal searchlight witness was Captain Barnhart. He told me that the beam of light did not "swing in an arc." It went straight up into the sky, he said, "like a Hollywood searchlight." What was the purpose of this light? Not to direct fire at the destroyer but to signal the end of the attack, thought the captain. At 10:47 P.M.? The searchlight, said Barnhart, appeared not in the middle of the battle but toward the end. Barnhart estimated that the battle lasted 2½ hours (about one hour less than the Official Chronology). Therefore, Barnhart must have seen his searchlight shortly after midnight. Somehow the *Maddox* and the large number of aircraft overhead, from the *Ticonderoga* and the *Constellation,* failed to see this tall beam of light.

Closer to McNamara's version was that of a man whom he did not mention by name as a searchlight witness, Seaman Larry Litton. Litton told David Wise: "We had a couple of searchlights thrown on us. Once off port side and once off starboard." If Litton claimed that lights touched the ship twice, how about Lieutenant Barry, who sat next to Litton? According to the AP story, "Barry remembers the searchlight, too. He said that the attack seemed to break off at that point." When I asked Barry about the searchlight, he said the AP sentence was a "misquote." Barry told me that he did not see any searchlight.

One searchlight witness listed by the Defense Secretary had retired from the Navy, and I found him at his home in Long Beach, California. This was Senior Chief Quartermaster Walter L. Shishim, a man of brusque manner, who aboard the *Turner Joy* had the reputation of being very strict. Chief Shishim was one of several men with Captain Barnhart on the bridge. He said to me: "Sure I saw a light. A lot of men saw it. But it was a *point* of light, not a *beam*. It was the kind of light you might see on a coastal freighter. Or you might see one like that on a submarine that didn't want to get run down in the dark." Shishim saw his light near the end of the action, as did Captain Barnhart. At that time, the Task Group was near the edge of the Gulf, where some traffic might be expected.

Four of the searchlight witnesses did not answer my queries by mail. They were Richard B. Johnson, Signalman 1st Class; Richard D. Nooks, Quartermaster 3rd Class; Richard M. Bacino, Signalman 2nd Class; and Gary D. Carroll, Signalman 3rd Class.

Very possibly, the "searchlights" were navigational lights and flares. *Maddox* turned on her running light from time to time. So did the aircraft.

Cockpit Lights—Here we have a visual sighting from the *Maddox*. Two of the COMVAN Marines claimed to have seen the "cockpit lights" of a patrol boat pass at high speed up one side of the ship, go out ahead, turn around, and come back down the other side. The Marines, Sergeant Matthew B. Allasre, and Corporal David A. Prouty, did not respond to my inquiries by mail. Allasre was supposed to be in Hawaii. Prouty was still in the Corps, but the Defense Department would not say where he was located. All mail to Prouty, I was told, must be directed to the Marine Corps Headquarters for forwarding. I sent a registered letter but received no reply.

This sighting, like that of San Augustin's boat silhouette, was not taken very seriously aboard *Maddox*. Officers could not understand why no one else would see the lights or hear the boat's engine.

Allasre and Prouty were the two Marines manning the .30 caliber
machine gun, but they did not open fire. When asked why not, they
explained that nobody *told* them to open fire. Nobody *could* have
told them to open fire because, like the torpedo wake witnesses
aboard the *Turner Joy,* the Marines kept their discovery to themselves.

Secondary Explosions—At the 1968 hearing, Secretary McNamara
did not mention any men who saw North Vietnamese craft exploding
and burning in the darkness, but the Associated Press heard about
explosions from former Lieutenant Barry and from Bosun's Mate
Kenneth Garrison, one of the *Turner Joy* enlisted men who accompanied Barry to the meeting at Subic Bay. Garrison claimed to have
seen two spectacular explosions. He also spotted a boat about one
mile away. In conversation with me, Barry confirmed seeing two or
three explosions and a fire. The very first target, he said, blew up.
Off the port quarter, the lieutenant saw a "burst of light." This was
the first of two or three times, said Barry, when a secondary explosion
was accompanied by the disappearance of a radar contact.

Lieutenant Barry was sitting in the Main Director, from where he
should have had a good view of what was going on. However, if a
torpedo or a shell magazine were to explode, this would be a truly
spectacular occurrence. Even a mere fire would be conspicuous on
a dark night. Yet the flyers saw no pyrotechnics of this kind. Neither
did men of the *Maddox.* When there was a "burst of light" on the
port quarter, Rodger Bergland in the *Turner Joy*'s After Director
ought to have been facing in the proper direction. He was the visual
spotter for the guns that were firing. Yet Bergland saw no explosions
at all. Twice during the evening, Bergland thought he saw a boat on
fire but could not tell whether it was a patrol boat or a fishing junk.

The *Turner Joy*'s gun boss, Lieutenant (jg) Charles A. Monia,
saw some "flashes" in the distance. He says they could have been
shellbursts instead of secondary explosions.

The reports of secondary explosions I find most difficult to believe. Many people ought to have seen them, and visible debris should
have resulted. If real, the explosions must have been shellbursts from
the destroyers or rocket bursts from the planes. The reader will recall that Commander McDonald and Lieutenant Gehman fired thirty-
eight rockets into an area where *Turner Joy* shells were falling.

Sightings from the Air—McNamara told the senators that Commander Edmondson and Lieutenant Barton "sighted gun flashes on the surface of the water as well as light antiaircraft bursts at their approximate altitude. On one pass over the destroyer, both pilots positively sighted a 'snakey' high-speed wake 1½ miles ahead of the lead destroyer, USS *Maddox.*" When I talked to the retired Commander Edmondson at his home in Moraga, California, he described his experience in detail. Edmondson did not mention any gun flashes on the surface, so far as the enemy was concerned. He did confirm seeing antiaircraft tracers twice. He also confirmed glimpsing a small, high-speed wake, which, as noted earlier, disappeared when Edmondson and his wingman dove down to get a better look. Edmondson could not speak for what Lieutenant Barton might have seen. Barton, still in the Navy, would not confirm anything. By mail he advised me that the subject was "classified."

Edmondson definitely believes that he saw a wake. Its crookedness, he says, might have been caused by the "sea condition," that is, waves. I asked whether the same line of foam could not have been produced by the breaking of a long wave. He replied, "It definitely was a *streak*. A wave would make *patches* of fluorescence on the water." Secretary McNamara placed the wake only "1½ miles ahead of the lead destroyer, USS *Maddox.*" The Task Group did not see or help look for Edmondson's torpedo boat, which, to escape his observation, must have been lying dead in the water just 3000 yards ahead of the destroyers.

This completes the list of visual sightings. It will be noted that a disproportionate number come from the *Turner Joy.* Secretary McNamara listed fourteen witnesses from that ship. Probably more could have been mentioned. Bosun's Mate Dean Abney, for example, told the Los Angeles *Times* that he saw an enemy boat just 2000 yards away. *Turner Joy,* he said, "opened fire with the 5-incher. I saw a light burst in the sky. I am sure it was a direct hit—that we blasted a boat right out of the water." After Sunday's battle, men of the *Maddox* did not expect so much. They saw no boats blow up, not even with direct hits. They saw a torpedo *fall overboard.* Their experience in daylight combat could explain why men of the *Maddox* reported no secondary explosions.

San Augustin's boat silhouette, if it resembled a P-4, would be the only *Maddox* sighting that matched a *Turner Joy* sighting. No aircraft sighting confirmed any destroyer sighting.

Maddox's officers placed little faith in the visual sightings made by either ship. As Lieutenant Connell put it: ". . . they [the *Turner Joy*] claim everything. We claim nothing." Another of *Maddox*'s more experienced officers said to me: "How you write up that night depends on whether you accept their story or ours. The *Turner Joy* hadn't been in combat before, and they did everything right."

Turner Joy men—even the skeptics—showed a lot of ship spirit. When I remarked to John Barry that the night engagement was very confusing, he replied, "There was no confusion aboard the *Turner Joy*. We had a lot of good radar contacts on all three systems. We knew what we were doing." He described Captain Barnhart and Commander Hoffman as "outstanding officers who would do well in any kind of work." Barry, then a field sales manager for IBM, is an articulate and persuasive young man. Every time I talked to him, I came away feeling that the *Turner Joy* must have been a taut ship.

As the Gulf patrol continued, certain of *Maddox*'s officers became leery of reports from the *Turner Joy*. Somebody there had a very active imagination. In plotting shore-based radar, I am told, the ship came up with a pair of weird fixes. Two sets of radar bearings, probably inaccurate, failed to cross near the shoreline. In one case, the *Turner Joy* decided that a previously plotted transmitter had moved up a mountain side. In the other case, the ship decided that the transmitter was *moving aboard a railroad train* (rails did parallel the shore). For some time I was inclined to disregard these stories as the result of ship-to-ship rivalry. Then a former senior officer of the *Turner Joy* told me something that fit the pattern. We were discussing the extremely hot weather that the destroyermen had to put up with in the Tonkin Gulf, and this officer, quite seriously, recounted that once when the *Turner Joy* slowed down from a fast speed to 10 knots, the temperature on the bridge shot up from 89 to 110 degrees. Doubting that wind could have any appreciable effect on a thermometer, I consulted two Navy quartermasters and a professional meteorologist. All assured me that the story could not be true. (Incidentally, the Navy's shipboard thermometers are enclosed in louvred cabinets.) The *Turner Joy* officer probably based his story on the very common, but mistaken, notion that moving air is cooler than still air—a mistake which derives from the noticeably chilling effect that wind has when evaporating moisture from the skin.

The really important question concerning visual sightings is whether Barry, Bergland, Litton, and Sentel saw any torpedo wakes. Other than Litton's 4-minute estimate of time, the chief weaknesses in this testimony include the failure to report torpedoes immediately, the lack of any discovered sources for these missiles, and the *Turner Joy*'s tendency to be uncritical of visual sightings. On the other hand, if a man says that he saw something, it is very difficult to prove that he didn't. A more definitive judgment must await the release of the original, signed statements. Hopefully, all of the statements, not just a selected few, will be released someday.

Next, let us consider the electronic evidence: sonar, radar, and "special intelligence," that is, the intercepted radio messages.

Sonar—There can be no doubt that David Mallow, Sonarman 3rd Class, made plenty of mistakes. The Foreign Relations Committee uncovered a report of twenty-two torpedoes, and even Secretary McNamara had to admit that the number "probably" was in error. It certainly was. The presence of twenty-two torpedoes would require eleven torpedo boats in the vicinity of the fast-moving *Maddox,* but her radarmen were unable to find them. Looking down from above, airmen were equally mystified. They could make out the fox but not the throng of pursuers galloping after it. *Turner Joy* managed to survive the battle without hearing any torpedoes at all. This is doubly strange because her sonar equipment was much more elaborate,[2] and the men operating it far more experienced. Chief Schaperjahn had nineteen years experience as a soundman and recently had completed an additional eleven months of formal training. Yet this impressive assembly of talent and equipment heard nothing. The *Turner Joy*'s sonarmen also had a radarscope, which David Mallow did not have. Unlike Schaperjahn, Mallow was unable to check easily the position of the other ship to see whether he was picking up the beat of her screws.

Radar—The Task Group's radarmen came to realize that they had

---

[2] A Defense Department spokesman (Richard Fryklund, formerly a reporter for the Washington *Evening Star*), once explained that *Maddox*'s sonar gear was more sensitive to torpedo-like sounds. If so, this is a sad commentary on the *Turner Joy*'s SQS-23 system, the same type of sonar as that installed aboard the super-electronic, nuclear powered cruiser *Long Beach*. Also, if *Maddox*'s sonar were more sensitive to the high whine of torpedo motors, this leaves unexplained what happened to Commodore Hollyfield's sonar in September; both of his ships were of the *Turner Joy* type.

been victimized to some extent by peculiar weather conditions and other problems. Yet even *Maddox*'s radarmen, the most skeptical, retained confidence in the launch turn contact; and all of the scope-watchers interviewed by me insisted that "something was out there." Weighing against this assertion is the fact that pilots found nothing, or almost nothing, visually. Neither did aircraft radar turn up any good targets. To be sure, the airmen's radar was not so elaborate as that of the destroyers. But on August 2 the Firefighter radar managed to see both destroyers and patrol craft, from as far as 50 miles.

If one did grant that "something was out there," it still would not necessarily establish the fact of an attack. The Task Group's increase of speed to 30 knots or more was intended to separate the sheep from the wolves, but this tactic was based on false information. The Swatow gunboat's top speed was not 25 knots, as the destroyermen thought; it was 40 to 43 knots.[3] Repeatedly my interviews turned up the fact that officers of the Task Group were misinformed as to the speed of a Swatow. Indeed, they were still misinformed when I found them. When in 1967 I told a former senior officer of the *Maddox* the presently estimated speed of a Swatow, he would not believe me—until we looked into a recent edition of *Jane's*. By that time the annual reference book was crediting the Swatow with a speed of 40 knots, though it had not given any speed three years before. In sum, shadowing gunboats could have been mistaken for attacking torpedo boats. Strangely, the 40-knot figure was available in Washington in 1964. At his midnight press conference of August 4–5, Secretary McNamara told reporters that the gunboat speed approximated 40 knots. This might help to explain McNamara's reluctance to make up his mind about the reality of an attack.

Also "out there" were a variety of other radar-reflecting objects: scattered thundershowers, fishing junks, schools of fish, and American aircraft. *Maddox*'s fire control radar would seldom lock onto anything. Ensign Corsette thought weather was the problem; Lieutenant Connell decided that some unstable contacts were aircraft zipping in and out of the radar lobe. Lee Burton, the radarman in *Maddox*'s After Director, told me that on one occasion he shot at an airplane without realizing it.

[3] In its 1965–66 edition, *Jane's* began listing 40 knots. At the 1968 Tonkin Gulf hearing, General Wheeler gave a speed of 43 knots.

The aircraft factor could explain a great deal. After combining official and unofficial reports to make a detailed chronology of the night action, I was struck by the repeated coincidence of aircraft activity and radar activity. By the Official Chronology, "U.S. aircraft" swept overhead at 9:08 P.M. My unofficial chronology tells of surface contacts menacing the destroyers at 9:11 P.M. At that time, men of the Task Group do not seem to have known about aircraft being on station. As for the "U.S. aircraft," it (or they) did not find any torpedo boats. Next, at 9:30 P.M., according to the Official Chronology, "attacking craft closed rapidly from the west and south and the *Maddox* reported that their intentions were evaluated as hostile." At the same time, two Spads and two Skyhawks ought to have been approaching from southerly directions. Aboard the *Turner Joy,* Lieutenant Barry saw a radar contact "drift" to the rear. At 9:34 P.M. something astern flashed into *Maddox*'s scope. A firm blip then described a curving motion, and vanished. The maneuver of an airplane, perhaps the original F-8, might account for that.

Most intriguing is a lull in the battle which coincided with the temporary reduction of CAP. The original jets departed by 10:30 P.M., leaving the two Spads, which operated in outlying areas. The *Ticonderoga* launched two Skyhawks at 10:21 P.M., and they must have been approaching the destroyers by 10:52 P.M. when, by the Official Chronology, the Task Group "again" was attacked.

In brief, the battle seems to have ebbed and flowed with the CAP.

As for why the *Turner Joy* had "better" contacts during the battle than the *Maddox, Turner Joy*'s radar could have been tuned differently so that it would hold a blip longer. Both ships were using SPS-10 surface radar, but, as the radarman's manual cautions, the state of radar tuning varies markedly from ship to ship.

At least once the *Maddox* poured 3-inch fire into her wake because of advice from the *Turner Joy*. Attempts at ramming demonstrated that a contact reportedly 2000 yards astern was only a knuckle in the wake. Evidently the *Turner Joy*'s radar could hold the image of a knuckle longer and brighter than could the *Maddox*'s. The *Turner Joy*'s radar might have held airplanes better, too.

In many ways, the situation in the Tonkin Gulf appears to have been made to order for a phantom battle.

Special intelligence—At the 1968 hearing, Secretary McNamara regarded this information as conclusive evidence of attack, although he did not seem to feel that way in 1964. Unfortunately for our analysis, the intercepted message texts are very highly classified, that is, beyond Top Secret. Why? Certainly the North Vietnamese have heard by now that somebody was reading their mail. Besides, so far as I have noticed, it never has been stated authoritatively that the messages were transmitted in code. In fact, it recently has been reported that they were not transmitted in code but in clear text. If true, this could indicate an emergency situation rather than a preplanned attack. The clear text disclosure appeared in a magazine article by John P. Roche, former special consultant to President Johnson.[4] Roche believed in the attack and remarked that he did not know why the intercepted messages were being kept secret. Roche did not say that he himself saw the messages. When in 1968 Senator Morse asked why the messages were being kept secret, it was explained that if the intercepted texts were made public they would compromise the American code in which they were retransmitted back in 1964. Even if valid, this objection does not weigh heavily compared to the question of whether the North Vietnamese planned an attack on the night of August 4. But I doubt that the objection is valid. By 1964 highly classified information—such as communications intelligence—normally was protected by an *unbreakable random encipherment*. In such a case, even if the enemy knows the text of a message transmitted, he cannot recover the key and unlock other messages with it; there is no key to recover.[5] One result of the super-secrecy was to prevent examination of the intercepted messages by William Bader, the Foreign Relations Committee staff member who conducted the investigation of the Tonkin Gulf. At the 1968 hearing, only senators were permitted to see the special intelligence.

Although exact texts of the intercepted messages are not available, McNamara's prepared statement and the transcript of the 1968 hearing provide in paraphrased form much of the information which top officials relied on back in 1964. After clearing the room of Senate staff members, McNamara showed senators four messages that had

[4] "The Jigsaw Puzzle of History," *New York Times Magazine* (January 24, 1971).

[5] For detailed information on this subject, see David Kanh, *The Codebreakers* (London: Weidenfeld and Nicolson, 1967), pages 398–401.

been "flowing back and forth among various stations." The first of them, "from a highly classified and unimpeachable source reported that North Vietnam was making preparations to attack our destroyers with two Swatow boats and with one PT boat if the PT could be made ready in time."

This would have been a curious and foolhardy plan. Two days before, the *Maddox* by herself had fought off three torpedo boats. But now the North Vietnamese were going to attack two destroyers with only two gunboats and one torpedo boat—if the torpedo boat could be made ready in time! According to one of my American informants who saw the special intelligence, the torpedo boat in question had a broken fuel line, and it was one of the three P-4s that had been shot up, if not sunk, in Sunday's battle. McNamara's statement was ambiguous as to whether the North Vietnamese plan of attack depended on getting the torpedo boat ready in time, or whether the two Swatows were to go ahead by themselves if necessary. The gunboats had no weapons suitable for attacking destroyers. As for the lame P-4, it carried only two torpedoes.

(What was meant by getting the torpedo boat ready "in time" actually might have been too fine a point for the Defense Department's linguistic ability. During the *Pueblo* investigation, it came out that this multi-million dollar eavesdropping vessel relied on the linguistic talents of only two American enlisted men, both Marines, who, in the later words of Commander Bucher, were the beneficiaries of a "long-past 16-week course." Since it takes years to produce a good Oriental linguist, the Marines protested their assignment to the *Pueblo,* but to no avail; and the first time Bucher asked one of them to translate something, the available linguist proved unable to read "rice paddy" without fetching a dictionary. Commander Bucher believes that his ship probably would have avoided capture if she truly had been able to understand the North Korean messages that were intercepted.[6])

McNamara's prepared statement: "The same source reported, while the engagement was in progress on August 4, that the attack was underway."

Senator Gore objected to this "flatfooted" statement. Apparently

[6] Commander Lloyd M. Bucher, *Bucher: My Story* (New York: Doubleday, Inc., 1970), pages 170, 175, 387.

the word "attack" did not appear in the intercepted message. Mc-Namara backed away slightly. "I submit," he said, "that any reasonable interpretation of these messages *leads one to the conclusion* [italics mine] that the attack was underway."

A continuing argument between the senator and the Defense Secretary unearthed additional information on the contents of the special intelligence.

McNamara: "Let me put in at this point in the record, if I may, the four messages, starting with the first at (deleted) indicating there were two objectives, enemy attack vessels, located at a point at which the *Maddox* and the *Turner Joy* were located or located within 3000 yards of them; and the second message, which stated that—"

Gore: "Directing them to make ready for military operations."

McNamara: "Make ready for military operations, again referring (deleted) and the third message indicating that the Swatow boats reported an enemy aircraft falling and enemy vessel wounded, and that message coming twelve minutes after our ships reported that they were being attacked.

"The fourth message later reporting that they had shot down two planes and sacrificed two ships, and adding further details of the engagement."

Actually, no planes were shot down, and the search for debris did not confirm the destruction of any patrol boats. The messages do not seem to have reported the launch of any torpedoes; otherwise Mc-Namara would surely have mentioned it.

Of those persons who have seen intercepted messages, few seem to have been convinced by them. Commodore Herrick would not confirm the attack despite the strongest pressure immediately afterward. The former Seventh Fleet Commander, Admiral Johnson, waited for additional information; he now will say only that "something was out there." Among certain Defense Department sources I am not at liberty to name, one officer who had access to intelligence said that he had "reservations" about the attack. Another person summed up the intelligence: "It proved surveillance. It also proved an engagement." He did not think that the intelligence proved an attack.

The Associated Press's review of the Tonkin Gulf said that "classified information" convinced Captain Ogier of the August 4 attack. When I talked to Ogier, he said that he believed in the attack but not because of classified information. The AP sentence, he said, was a "misunderstanding."

More information about special intelligence came out of the 1968 hearing in connection with the very interesting subject of North Vietnamese prisoners and what they had to say about the Tonkin Gulf incidents. In his prepared statement, Secretary McNamara brought up the testimony of a captured North Vietnamese naval officer as providing evidence for an attack on the night of August 4:

"As a final point on this issue, U.S. naval forces in the 3½ years which have elapsed since the August 1964 incidents have captured several North Vietnamese naval personnel. These personnel were extensively interrogated. One of these, captured in July 1966 stated he had taken part in the August 2, 1964, attack on the *Maddox,* and his account of that attack coincided with our own observations. He professed no knowledge of the August 4 attack and said that he believed that PT boats were not involved in that attack. He stated that Swatows could have been used for that attack. His disclaimer of PT participation is contradicted by information received from a later captive. A North Vietnamese naval officer captured in July 1967 provided the name of the commander of a PT squadron. In intelligence reports received immediately after the August 4 attack, this commander and his squadron were identified by name and number as participants."

This was the first time the Foreign Relations Committee had heard of the 1967 prisoner. Complained Fulbright: "They told us about the prisoner in 1966, but Mr. Nitze never indicated that you had a further prisoner in 1967 who testified. I think you should have notified us of that."

"I think so, too, Mr. Chairman," McNamara agreed. "I must say I wish we had. We would have avoided some of the controversy because the testimony of the 1966 prisoner was not nearly as comprehensive or as illuminating on the participation by North Vietnam in the August 4 attack as was the testimony of the prisoner of July 1967 which, I think, came to light only within the past few days."

"I see," said Fulbright.

If one examines closely McNamara's prepared statement, it quotes the 1967 prisoner as having given the name of a torpedo boat squadron commander, but not as having said anything else. Why? He didn't *say* anything else. He did not say that the squadron commander took part in an August 4 attack. He didn't even say that there had been such an attack. He only gave the name of a squadron commander (Le Duy Khoai), and the Navy already had gotten the same name from the officer captured in 1966. In short, the 1967 prisoner contributed nothing new. His testimony was neither "comprehensive" nor "illuminating." The truth, however, was not established by Senator Fulbright until four months after the 1968 hearing. In June the Defense Department finally confessed that the "discrepancy" was caused by "changes in cognizant personnel," through normal duty rotation, from 1964 to 1968.[7] By this time Secretary McNamara had made his own "duty rotation," transferring from the Pentagon to the World Bank.

The central fact about prisoners' testimony is that no prisoner ever has agreed that an attack took place on the night of August 4, 1964. Of nineteen sailors captured in 1966, all "definitely and emphatically" denied that there had been such an attack. Following is a part of the Navy's own report which Senator Fulbright put into the transcript of the 1968 hearing:

"Extensive interrogation of all potentially knowledgeable sources reveals they have no info concerning a NVN [North Vietnamese] attack on U.S. ships on 4 August 1964. They state definitely and emphatically that no PTs could have been involved. They do have knowledge of a U.S. air attack on 5 August in which at least one and possibly three Swatow PGMs [gunboats] were sunk by ACFT [aircraft] in vicinity of the Gianh River [Quang Khe area] . . .

"2. The possibility that Swatows could have committed the 4 Aug attack has also been carefully explored. Here again, however, all sources disclaim any knowledge of such an attack. Based on the experience of interrogations thus far it is very possible that PT boat crews in general might not have heard of this attack since they apparently have little contact with other ship types. On the other hand, source (deleted) obviously has traveled in higher circles and has proved himself exceptionally knowledgeable on almost every naval subject and event of interest. Yet he specifically and strongly denies that any attack took place. When pressed further on this issue, he

[7] Committee on Foreign Relations, *The Gulf of Tonkin, The 1964 Incidents, Part II*, page 13.

states that if such an attack did take place it could only have been committed by Swatows."

The "exceptionally knowledgeable" source was the 1966 officer who although admitting an August 2 attack, denied that there had been any attack on August 4.

Of course, one might question the truthfulness of these prisoners. But interrogation techniques do have some effectiveness, and the 1966 officer, otherwise cooperative, gave his captors a great deal of information that led to the destruction of North Vietnamese facilities. Before his capture, this man was second-in-command of the P-4 squadron whose leader was supposed to have been driving a torpedo boat on the night of August 4. It is scarcely credible that the squadron leader could have taken part in a battle without the knowledge of his executive officer.

Senator Morse added these details about the interrogation of the 1966 prisoner:

"The question of the Gulf of Tonkin attacks did not arise until the interrogation was well under way. When the subject was finally raised, the Navy shifted all reports on the Tonkin incidents into a sensitive communication channel. The information on the attacks was not included in the formal report. However, the Defense Department has provided the committee with that report.

"It should be noted that source of this information is a North Vietnamese officer—a prisoner—who was interrogated for over 100 hours after his capture. He was described by the U. S. Naval officers as cooperative and reliable.

"It is nothing new for a prisoner under those circumstances to be cooperative."

The Defense Department made a special effort to keep secret the testimony of the 1966 prisoner. Had there been any attack of August 4, he ought to have known something about it. For that matter, so should the other eighteen men captured at the same time. Only when "pressed further," did the cooperative and reliable officer say that *if* an attack took place, it could only have been committed by lightly armed gunboats. No wonder the Navy shifted these reports into a "sensitive" channel.

In bringing up the meager testimony of the 1967 prisoner, McNamara shed a new and most disturbing light on the special intelligence, when, to repeat the sentence from the Secretary's prepared statement, he revealed: "In intelligence reports received immediately after the August 4 attack, this commander [Le Duy Khoai] *and his squadron* [italics mine] were identified by name and number as participants." In short, a swarm of torpedo boats appeared not only in the *Turner Joy*'s radar but in the available *intelligence*. In fact, however, there could not have been a whole squadron of torpedo boats maneuvering in the Gulf that night. Aircraft could not find them. Neither could the *Maddox*. Furthermore, special intelligence, according to a later statement by Commodore Herrick, intercepted no messages from torpedo boats.[8] The intercepts apparently came from Swatows and/or other sources. Exactly who was it, then, that claimed a squadron of torpedo boats was chasing the destroyers? Secretary McNamara averred that the special intelligence came from a "highly classified and unimpeachable source." Without question, the source was highly classified; it certainly was not unimpeachable.

McNamara said the intelligence above became available immediately after the attack. Did it arrive in Washington just in time to help convince the Secretary that a real attack had taken place? Where did the information come from? In his magazine article, John P. Roche said that his knowledge of the special intelligence came from a "high Vietnamese official." Is it possible that the "highly classified and unimpeachable source" was located in South Vietnam?

We now have covered the available evidence for and against the August 4 attack. What does it all mean? How does it fit together? If one were to take all of the official information and put it together in chronological order the result would be a wildly improbable story —which perhaps is why Secretary McNamara did not do that at the 1968 hearing.[9] For the convenience of the reader, I shall try to put

[8] Goulden, page 153.

[9] The story did not improve in 1970 when Admiral Moorer testified to the Senate Armed Services Committee. In answer to questions from Senator Young, the admiral provided in writing (thus presumably with the benefit of careful consideration) the following assertions:

"Our best estimate is that three to five North Vietnamese PT boats took part in this attack" (elsewhere in the statement, Moorer specified that these were P-4s, not Swatows) . . . "Personnel aboard *Turner Joy* actually observed 5-inch shell bursts and hits on the attacking North Vietnamese torpedo boats . . . It is possible that the attacking boats were severely damaged only,

in narrative form the essential and more believable elements of the official story. Then I shall discuss Hanoi's case for a fabrication.

An undetermined but not very large number of North Vietnamese patrol craft by some means located the destroyers in the dark, far from land, and launched torpedoes at them, chiefly at the *Maddox,* for some period of time. It is not certain which side fired first, but, in any case, the pursuing torpedo craft planned to make an attack. Special intelligence predicted the attack. Special intelligence reported details of it taking place. Afterward, special intelligence confirmed the attack. Fortunately, neither destroyer was hit by a torpedo, even though the *Turner Joy*'s sonarmen failed to hear any coming. Visually, men of the *Turner Joy* saw one or two missiles pass by. One torpedo the ship was able to dodge because of a timely warning from the *Maddox,* whose old-fashioned sonar performed more effectively. The *Maddox* fired at only one good radar target. The *Turner Joy,* whose radar was performing better, took many targets under fire, destroying at least two of the attacking boats. The *Turner Joy*'s automatic gunfire destroyed the enemy craft so thoroughly that not a trace of them could be found the next day. The torpedo craft were accompanied by Swatow gunboats which either did not fire at the destroyers or, if they did, failed to inflict any damage. Some kind of surface vessel shot twice at an American plane as it dove repeatedly through a flare pattern. Neither the pilot nor his wingman was able to find the source of this fire. The same two airmen, propeller pilots, later discovered a high-speed wake that marked a patrol boat fleeing to the south; unfortunately, the enemy again escaped without being seen clearly. The other airmen, mostly jet pilots, found nothing at all. The night was extremely dark. As an item of negative evidence, it must be admitted that North Vietnamese naval prisoners never have confirmed the attack of August 4, even though one officer admitted the attack of August 2. The Communist motive for any attack, either on the 2nd or on the 4th, remains a matter of speculation. The two attacks, however, fit a larger pattern of systematic Communist aggression.

---

but we believe that two were sunk . . . Search lights and gunfire from the attacking craft were observed by the U.S. crews."

Like Secretary McNamara, the new Chairman of the Joint Chiefs insisted that Commodore Herrick was skeptical only of the details of the attack, not of the fact that one took place.

Although somewhat vague about what happened on August 2, the North Vietnamese consistently have denied the August 4 attack, calling it a "fabrication." The American motives, they alleged, were to cover up American aggression in South Vietnam, and to obtain an excuse to attack North Vietnamese territory. As evidence of pre-arrangement, Hanoi cited the *Turner Joy*'s quick appearance after Sunday's battle, and the *Constellation*'s departure for Hong Kong Tuesday morning. Rushing westward at flank speed, the supercarrier was just able to catch the tail end of the August 4 battle; she did arrive in plenty of time (theoretically) for Wednesday's bombing. The fabrication of the night battle was a clumsy one, said the Communists, as they pointed with scorn to oddities in Washington's story, especially the confusion in official times. The North Vietnamese attributed great significance to an alleged pre-incident meeting of the destroyer *Harry E. Hubbard* (DD 748) with two South Vietnamese vessels. The latter, said Hanoi, were numbered HQ609 and HQ11. (HQ609 is a 243-ton gunboat named the *To Yen*. HQ11, the *Chi Linh,* is a 650-ton ex-minesweeper, now an escort ship. Both vessels formerly belonged to the U. S. Navy.) At a meeting 60 kilometers east of Da Nang, said Hanoi, the South Vietnamese received instructions as to how to fabricate the night attack. Hanoi's version would seem to require bogus attackers on the scene, perhaps launching dummy torpedoes (the Navy's practice torpedoes might do), and the preparation of phony messages as "special intelligence." The plotters ought to have written more convincing messages.

In the light of presently available information, I would suggest that a premeditated North Vietnamese attack on August 4 seems to have been improbable, though not absolutely impossible. The Communists definitely were provoked, as on August 2, if one considers the circumstances as well as the nature of the destroyer patrol. Rather than a premeditated attack, I personally would consider more likely a shadowing operation that went wrong. On the night of August 3, for whatever reason, the destroyers had led the way toward raiding gunboats. Expecting the same thing to happen on Tuesday night, the North Vietnamese might have dispatched hastily a few patrol boats which, drawing fire from the destroyers, scattered amid excited radio chatter. I suggest this as one possibility. Another possibility might be shadowing by the Red Chinese.

Having been warned by Commodore Herrick, top U.S. officials had their doubts about the August 4 attack but gave no hint of them to the people or the Congress. The "second attack" was portrayed as an absolute, spectacular, premeditated certainty. Of course, if the administration were committed to the bombing of North Vietnam, there could be no public soul-searching. It would not look well to bomb a foreign country because of a *possible* attack, nor even because of a *probable* attack. Yet, however one looks at it, taking into account the political realities, the Johnson administration went too far. Officials exaggerated the facts and distorted them. They concealed the elements of provocation. They alleged repeated bolts from the blue to be explained only by the implacable nature of aggressive communism; and they trumped up a great threat to the peace, insinuating that Red China was behind this flagrant challenge on the high seas. With the encouragement of anonymous public servants, the news media speculated on the imminent invasion of South Vietnam, Laos, South Korea, and even Taiwan. Against that lurid backdrop, the Tonkin Gulf resolution, a gesture of support for the Commander-in-Chief, looked the very soul of caution and prudence.

President Johnson's private attitude differed markedly from his public one. On Wednesday, August 5, he reportedly was chatting with a few friends about the recent, exciting events. Chuckling, he waved to a pile of conflicting messages from the Tonkin Gulf and said, "Well, boys, I guess we'll never know what happened, will we?"

Chapter XVI

The Blank Check

One could make a strong case for the *Maddox*'s having served as a pigeon in the Tonkin Gulf, starting with her arrival or sometime thereafter. That is what a "lot of people" (meaning some Navy people) thought; and the circumstantial evidence is plentiful.

First of all, what was the *Maddox*'s mission supposed to be? The ship was not on a "routine patrol" unconnected with operations in the Gulf area, as was said in 1964. Then, as explained four years later, was the destroyer primarily looking for evidence of infiltration? It is true that the Navy, in a bureaucratic way, was concerned about the possibility of maritime infiltration. Market Time patrol went into effect soon after *Maddox* visited the Gulf, even though the De Soto ship did not find a single infiltrator. The Navy wanted the *job* of looking for infiltration, the way the Air Force wanted to find employment for its old B-57s, which otherwise would be transferred to the Air National Guard. Ambitious, high level planning is not often to be deterred by facts or common sense. (Similarly, the observation of sullen fishermen and scared farmers did not impair Washington's faith that the oppressed North Vietnamese people were eagerly awaiting liberation by the American good guys.) If, however, the major purpose of *Maddox*'s patrol was to look for infiltrators, why was the ship to spend most of her time so far north, well beyond the reported bases for infiltration? It seems more likely that the destroyer's primary task was to investigate North Vietnamese defenses. With that general aim, the mission could have been a multiple one, a Christmas tree-like affair with something attached to it for everybody: radio eavesdropping, radar studies, depth soundings, scouting for 34-A, and so forth. Admiral MacPherson might have been collecting suggestions when, as reported by Radio Hanoi at the time, he visited Saigon in June of 1964.

But, whatever the De Soto chief was doing in June, he later demonstrated a curious lack of interest in the Gulf patrol. Admiral MacPherson never laid eyes on Commodore Herrick or the *Maddox*. He never even sent the patrolling destroyer a message, so far as I have been able to determine. Perhaps the reason for this was that higher levels of command took over the planning and supervision. Even by De Soto standards, the *Maddox*'s patrol does not seem to have been routine.

As Admiral MacPherson, for whatever reason, lost touch with the Gulf patrol, it became increasingly provocative and dangerous. The provocations were many and mysterious, often with an air of being deliberate as well. Admiral Moorer and his colleagues must have known in advance that the *Maddox*'s navigational guidelines would irritate—possibly enrage—the North Vietnamese. They were presumed to claim 12 miles of territorial water, and *Maddox* would patrol just a few miles from land, loitering near defensive facilities at a time when the North Vietnamese coast was being subjected to increasing penetration and violence. Hanoi later complained that *Maddox* made the longest and deepest intrusions of any American ship. At least one officer of the ship was under the same impression, although at the 1968 hearing Secretary McNamara said the track was "almost identical" to that of the previous two patrols.

Back in Washington, the Joint Chiefs of Staff realized that the *Maddox*'s patrol would be risky, and they warned CINCPACFLT about the growing sensitivity of the Tonkin Gulf. Yet, at a minimum, the planned track was "almost identical" to that of previous patrols. Among their specific points of concern, the Joint Chiefs listed increased 34-A activity and the public talk of military action against North Vietnam (apparently referring to Premier Khanh's "To the North!" campaign). Again the voice of restraint went unheeded. *Maddox* entered the Gulf during or immediately after the unprecedented shelling of North Vietnam from the sea. The refueling destroyer actually was greeted by the raiders on their way home.

In Washington the subject of raiding gunboats was not taken very seriously. Publicly Secretary McNamara said he did not know of any such operations; to senators he said that the Navy was not involved with gunboat activities, "if there were any." Too late, the senators learned better. In 1968 McNamara had a new story. He then assured lawmakers that the headquarters of Admiral Moorer and General Westmoreland had been *coordinating* the destroyer and gunboat operations, to keep them *away* from each other. Someone should have asked the Defense Secretary why the coordination broke down on the morning of Friday, July 31. McNamara, however, repeatedly said that Commodore Herrick knew so little about 34-A operations that he could not tell a friendly gunboat from a Russian-built torpedo boat. That was incorrect, though, oddly, there seems to have been documentary evidence for McNamara's assertion.

Conceivably, the real purpose of *Maddox*'s patrol was to scout for 34-A, perhaps without anybody on board knowing it. The Defense Department would not have wanted to give that information to the Foreign Relations Committee.

But Sunday's scrap with torpedo boats precipitated one of the notable crises of the Cold War, and the Defense Department then faced a new ball game. The major purpose of *Maddox*'s patrol now *should* have been to show the flag. Nonetheless, CINCPACFLT and MACV arranged more gunboat raids, and again the so-called coordination broke down. Targets were designated farther north than they were supposed to be, and the destroyers, two of them now, steamed farther south than seems to have been anticipated. Evidently nobody conveyed to Commodore Herrick the importance of staying put. For sheer incompetence, Monday night just about takes the prize —unless the purpose of the coordination was not what Secretary McNamara said it was. In any case, the Defense Secretary's revised version of events becomes totally preposterous when one considers the plan for Tuesday night. CINCPACFLT and MACV again scheduled gunboat raids, and the President's flag-showing patrol was to help out by acting as a decoy. The admirals in Hawaii wanted the *Maddox* and *Turner Joy* to draw Communist patrol craft away from the area to be raided, that is, *toward the destroyers*. Such a maneuver risked a shooting incident—and war.

Even before the decoy plan went into effect, the situation in the Gulf had reached a hair-trigger degree of sensitivity. Commodore Herrick judged his assignment "not unlike war patrol," and he was prepared to open fire on any fast-moving radar contact that ventured within gun range. Admiral Johnson feared for the safety of the 34-A boats, thinking Herrick might shoot at *them*. But Admiral Johnson's plan to cancel the destroyer patrol was overruled. So was Commodore Herrick's demand for air reconnaissance at night.

In the face of documentary evidence, Secretary McNamara at the 1968 hearing denied that there had been any decoy plan. The purpose of the coordination, he insisted, was "to assure that there was less reason for anybody, including the North Vietnamese, to associate the two" (De Soto and 34-A operations). However, the North Vietnamese were given plenty of reason to associate the two; they did associate the two; and Commodore Herrick reported that they associated the two. It was the American people who were not given reason to associate the two. They were led to believe that the gunboat raids were just Communist propaganda.

In addition to being provocative, the destroyer patrol was more vulnerable than necessary. The quasi-intelligence ship *Maddox* entered the Tonkin Gulf alone, allegedly ignorant of what was happening there, and apprehensive about a prospective shortage of fuel. Later came warning of North Vietnamese hostility and possible attack. Commodore Herrick thought it wise to cancel the patrol, but his request was denied. As a concession to the apparent danger, someone ordered the *Ticonderoga* to prepare air support, and the carrier did make some half-hearted preparations. As she did so, *Maddox* lazed far up the North Vietnamese coast, drawing figure eights between two anchorages for Communist naval craft. Next the destroyer exchanged fire with three torpedo boats which apparently intended to make an attack. By means of her timely run to the southeast, the old short hull seems to have narrowly escaped destruction. The *Ticonderoga* had plenty of time in which to dispatch air support, but, for whatever reasons, she delayed in doing so. Four jets did arrive in time to chase the fleeing Communists. An hour or so passed before relief planes came on station.

Why, despite many hours of warning, were higher levels of command so unconcerned about the *Maddox*? It could be argued that higher command thought the commodore was excessively nervous. Admiral Moorer later said that the intelligence Herrick forwarded was "ambiguous." The commodore himself could have done more to get ready for battle.

In the public announcement everything got smoothed over nicely. A statement approved in Washington—but not released from there

—said the *Maddox* was patrolling routinely about 30 miles from shore when she suffered an unprovoked torpedo attack. The destroyer "answered" with gunfire, and she was defended by aircraft.

Following Sunday's battle, if not before, there was plenty of reason for concern. With some fanfare, President Johnson doubled the number of destroyers in the Gulf. Conveniently available was the *Turner Joy,* which had a nebulous mission near but not with the *Maddox.* We do not know where *Turner Joy* previously fitted into the chain of command. For that matter, it is not quite clear where *Maddox* fitted in, either. General Wheeler does not seem to have known. He told the senators that on August 2 *Maddox* was getting instructions from the *Ticonderoga.* She should have been getting instructions from Admiral MacPherson or maybe Admiral Moorer. The few instructions that came were from Admiral Johnson, commander of the Seventh Fleet.

The President told newsmen that he had ordered air support for the destroyer patrol, but the *Ticonderoga* continued to be less than generous. Did the daytime-only CAP comply with the President's directive? Admiral Sharp has indicated that it did. Supporting Sharp seems to be the Official Chronology prepared in Washington. Commodore Herrick, anyway, objected to the partial CAP. He wanted aircraft overhead at all times, controlled by the destroyers. Was this demand unreasonable? At the 1968 hearing, Secretary McNamara affirmed vigorously that a continuous CAP was needed. If so, why didn't McNamara provide it? Was this one of the problems that he somehow did not hear about? Even the promised 15-minute reaction time proved mythical. Tuesday's CAP was slower than Sunday's.

Peculiar, too, is the record of secrecy. The Congress and the people were kept ignorant of important information. So were Commodore Herrick and Secretary McNamara, who, like the Congress, were making decisions of great consequence. Herrick was supposed to be on an intelligence patrol of some kind, but he apparently knew less about the Tonkin Gulf than many a naval officer or "liaison man" who wasn't even there. Despite his twenty-five security clearances, the Defense Secretary seems to have known little about 34-A plans. Nor could McNamara influence those activities, which, nevertheless, were being coordinated by his subordinates. On Monday, August 3, McNamara told senators he thought the Gulf would quiet down. Almost as he spoke, 34-A boats again were shelling North Vietnamese defenses. It seems that CINCPACFLT and MACV were not doing what the Secretary of Defense expected them to do. Nevertheless, Admiral Moorer today is Chairman of the Joint Chiefs, and General Westmoreland is Army Chief of Staff.

On the night of August 4, the destroyers opened fire on some fast-moving radar contacts, and reported a truly incredible torpedo assault. Whether a North Vietnamese attack took place was (and remains) uncertain. Commodore Herrick urged caution. He wanted daylight reconnaissance and a complete evaluation to precede any action in reply. Secretary McNamara was mystified; it seems possible that he was becoming leery of inscrutable happenings in the Tonkin Gulf. But President Johnson and Admiral Sharp were prepared, even eager, to believe in the nocturnal attack. While McNamara and Herrick held back, the President rushed forward with plans for a dramatic telecast, plans for gathering congressional leaders, plans for securing passage of a blank check for war (prepared in advance of the crisis), and even plans for the hot line to Moscow. Lost in the shuffle were not only the complete evaluation but even the plans for the air raids, which the American people imagined to be uppermost in the President's mind. It could be argued that the administration's aim was to get everything settled by sun-up, and then, if necessary, excuse the lack of evidence for an attack by saying that it had been a very dark night.

When Secretary McNamara and General Wheeler met with lawmakers on August 6, to report on what had happened in the Tonkin Gulf, they still seem to have lacked an elementary knowledge of events there. McNamara still did not know about the gunboat raids (those of August 3, anyway), and one must suppose that he was also ignorant of Hawaii's decoy plan for the night of August 4. Lacking information on these subjects, the witnesses were unable to bring them to the lawmakers' attention. The Pentagon men do not even seem to have known who shot first in either of the two reported surface battles. Senators demanded precise information on that subject, but they did not get it. According to Senator Fulbright, the two Senate committees did not even find out that *Maddox* was on an intelligence patrol (though they should have, considering the warnings of Senator Morse). In short, the all-important briefings of August 6 were a mockery of the legislative process.

From the beginning, a miasma of doubletalk and deception

shrouded the naval action in the Gulf. Hanoi had most of the facts, but the Congress and the American people could not get them. Much more was concealed than could be excused on any reasonable grounds, to the extent of damaging seriously the democratic process. Security procedures ought to have as their object the nation's security. They ought not to subvert the Constitution by cloaking the nation's entry into war. Had the facts become known, senators would not have handled the Tonkin Gulf resolution so carelessly. They probably would not have handled it at all.

Basically, the Congress did not expect a naval incident to escalate into a major land war on the continent of Asia. Yet by what other means could that have happened? Following a Viet Cong attack on land, as at Bien Hoa, the Congress would have sensed the potential danger ahead. Lawmakers might have accepted retaliation against North Vietnam, if the President had made a strong case for it, but they would not have signed anything remotely resembling a blank check. Assuming, therefore, that someone intended to widen the war as a gamble toward winning it, an old-fashioned naval engagement perhaps offered the best opportunity. A history of fighting for freedom of the sea had conditioned the American people to responding vigorously when their ships were attacked. They would "remember Pearl Harbor"; they would "remember the *Maine*"; they would remember the War of 1812. They might even remember the Barbary Pirates and the legendary heroism of John Paul Jones. Such memories—traditions or symbols, if one prefers—galvanize the most powerful emotions in the body politic. They are not to be triggered lightly.

As the strategic background to these events, in 1964 the Johnson administration's view of the Vietnamese situation was very dark, much darker than admitted publicly. At the same time, it appeared to certain strategists that the war could yet be won if only a bigger effort were made, drawing directly on the limitless potential of American might. This notion fitted in with the attitude of President Johnson. For years Johnson had thought it necessary to do more in Vietnam and—most important—to make it clear that the United States was *prepared to do whatever might be required for victory*. As matters stood, the anti-Communists in Saigon barely survived, depending on a limited allowance from Washington that the enemy could match at will. Who was the enemy? He was, according to the strategists, a gang of master plotters based in Hanoi and Peking, chiefly in Peking. The real enemy was not the young South Vietnamese farmer who mauled the South Vietnamese army every week, fighting like a tiger, as if he resented sharecropping and were determined to elect his own village chief. Most farmers were neutral. What they wanted was stability. Stability and economic aid would lead the way to prosperity and—after the war—perhaps even to democracy. First, in order to achieve stability, Washington had to convince Hanoi and Peking that they were in the wrong league, that the game wasn't worth the candle, the way London and Paris ought to have convinced Berlin in 1938. Once the top Asian Communists got the message, the strategists reasoned, they would stop backing the Viet Cong, and the war would disappear. If, however, Vietnam succumbed to the manipulations of international communism, it would be followed by the rest of Southeast Asia, and there was no telling where that process might end. The Free World would have to hold the line at the 17th parallel, thus proving that Peking-inspired "wars of liberation" could not succeed.[1] Moreover, South Vietnamese territory then

---

[1] Somebody leaked the secret strategy to Kiplinger's *Washington Letter,* which published it on December 19, 1965. Some excerpts (dots and italics are Kiplinger's):

"What's at stake is not just Vietnam . . . Vietnam is a symbol."

"Red China is masterminding this war . . . so say our top officials. China is out to take over from Russia as leader in boosting communism and undermining capitalism. China says, do it by fomenting internal wars, revolutions, toppling governments; Russia says no, coexist with capitalism.

"China must try to keep the war going, and hope to wear us out. Any other result would be defeat, a loss of face in the communist world.

"We are out to show China it can not succeed with its tactics. If it did, WE would lose face, and embolden Reds to try the same game in many other countries of the world . . . In Asia, Africa, Latin America.

"Why don't our officials explain this? Well, it's delicate . . . it would sound as if we were making South Vietnam a pawn in a bigger game, and the Reds would seize on this fact to make propaganda against us. So our officials say we are defending South Vietnam against aggression. That's true, but not the WHOLE truth. Whole truth is soft-pedaled."

Kiplinger went on to warn that the conflict would get "MUCH" bigger. Later that month, the Dow Jones average hovered at 1000. The long bull market then plunged into a long bear market.

could serve as a base for "containing" Red China. (Secretary Rusk worried about a "billion Chinese armed with nuclear weapons," and he somehow identified that problem with the fate of South Vietnam, although, obviously, thrashing about in the jungles of Indochina would not—and did not—prevent the Chinese from building as many bombs and rockets as they were capable of building.)

It has been said that Lyndon Johnson, a Vietnam dove in the 1950s, formed a new attitude when, as a traveling Vice-President, he visited Saigon in the spring of 1961. In a two-day stopover, Johnson enjoyed a huge welcoming celebration (as did the Chinese Nationalists when they reached Hanoi in 1945). He learned from American officials that the guerrilla war was going badly, and that President Ngo Dinh Diem, being too remote from the people, was not an effective leader. The cheers that greeted Johnson he interpreted as a "hunger" for a more "human approach" in the South Vietnamese leadership.[2] As for what American policy should be, the Vice-President's solution was twofold: put up a big front and try harder. Publicly, Johnson hailed Diem as the "Winston Churchill of Asia" (explaining later, "Now, you know he's the only boy we got out there"). Privately, according to Diem, Johnson promised "total support" in South Vietnam's struggle for freedom. When he got back to Washington, the traveling Texan described Diem's 2000-year-old country as "young and unsophisticated," and he urged upon President Kennedy a "major effort" to save it. Time was running out, said Johnson; without prompt action, dominoes would be toppling all the way back to San Francisco.[3] Evidently these wobbly dominoes were to include the Philippines, Japan, and Hawaii— all of those inscrutable places beyond the Golden Gate.

If Diem got a promise of "total support," as he claimed he did, Johnson must have exceeded his instructions. Just a few days before the meeting in Saigon, President Kennedy reiterated his policy of limited support. South Vietnam could get American help, said he, but there was a "limit beyond which we cannot go." Perhaps Kennedy anticipated the effect of a well-planned, if unsophisticated, Saigon welcoming celebration.

[2] President Johnson's January 1, 1964, message to General Duong Van Minh.

[3] Arthur M. Schlesinger, Jr., *A Thousand Days* (Boston: Houghton Mifflin, 1965), pages 540–43.

In the fall of 1961 the South Vietnamese capital entertained some more distinguished visitors. Two of them were General Maxwell D. Taylor, military adviser to President Kennedy, and Professor Walt W. Rostow, a presidential assistant for "national security affairs." Rostow formerly was an economic historian at the Massachusetts Institute of Technology. General Taylor, formerly Army Chief of Staff, advocated a strong Army capable of fighting "brushfire wars"; he proposed a doctrine of "flexible response" to Communist aggression, as opposed to the theory of "massive retaliation" adopted by the Eisenhower administration. Publicly, General Taylor seemed to oppose direct American intervention in Vietnam. But he thought of the conflict there as a Communist brushfire, and upon his return to Washington, Taylor recommended privately the dispatch of 10,000 American troops as an emergency reserve. Even Professor Rostow came home with a military scheme. He wanted to establish a contingency plan of *gradual attack* on North Vietnam, which he regarded as the instigator of the trouble in South Vietnam.[4] Jokingly, the economist's proposal became known within the Kennedy administration as "Rostow Plan No. 6" because it came after SEATO Plan No. 5.

A Kennedy adviser who opposed American intervention in Vietnam was John K. Galbraith, the Harvard economist who was appointed Ambassador to India. After reading the Taylor-Rostow report, Galbraith noted, "It is a curious document. The recommendations are for vigorous action. The appendices say it cannot possibly succeed given the present Government in Saigon."[5] On his own initiative, Ambassador Galbraith made a brief visit to South Vietnam, and warned President Kennedy against any kind of combat involvement. Diem's government he diagnosed as inept and weak, liable to fall apart like a rotten log. Galbraith could not get over the fact that the Viet Cong were taking over the country with a ragtag army of 15,000 men, adept at vanishing when need be, while opposing them were 250,000 well-armed government troops. Perhaps the real war was not being fought with bullets. (Estimates of guerrilla numbers have been extremely variable, as have reports of *when*

---

[4] Schlesinger, pages 546–47.

[5] John K. Galbraith, *Ambassador's Journal* (Boston: Houghton Mifflin, 1969), page 254.

North Vietnamese regulars entered the war. After the large-scale deployment of U.S. ground troops, official estimates of Viet Cong strength shot up to 120,000 and 190,000. In 1969, as American troops began to withdraw, official estimates of Viet Cong strength were reduced to the more convenient numbers of 60,000 and 80,000.[6])

Like the Presidents before and after him, John F. Kennedy had to deal with wildly conflicting advice on Vietnam. Sometimes he wondered aloud whether the people offering this advice had visited the same country. In recent years there has been much discussion of which presidential advisers have been right on Vietnam and which have been wrong, but over a period of decades, some were bound to be right and others were bound to be wrong. (Most, in fact, were wrong. An equal number of astrologers might have done better.) A more important question is this: how was any President to distinguish a good adviser from a bad one? On the public record it does not appear that any key adviser really knew much about Vietnam or any other part of Southeast Asia. Not one, for example, was able to speak the Vietnamese language—not in a whole *generation* of involvement with Vietnam. I have watched scores of foreign policy advisers interviewed on television, and only one of them even took notice of the language problem. This man, supposedly qualified to predict North Vietnamese behavior, admitted that his capability was limited by not knowing the "North Vietnamese language"—as if there were such a thing. In short, our policy makers have been more inclined to burn villages than midnight oil. Neither has the academic community been blameless. It has contributed to the making of Vietnam policy the views of many scholars (sometimes correct), along with a barrage of criticism and moral indignation. But the academic community has contributed little in the way of authoritative advice based on Southeast Asian scholarship. As recently as June 8, 1970, the New York *Times* has reported academic experts on Vietnam to be "almost non-existent" in the United States. Not one American scholar devoted most of his time to current affairs in North Vietnam; not one university boasted a tenured professorship in Vietnamese studies. When the *Times* made this survey, financial support for

[6] For details of how such figures were arrived at, see Joseph Alsop's critique in morning newspapers of October 6, 1969.

Asian studies actually was dwindling. Nonetheless, with respect to other academic specialties, so many new Ph.Ds were walking the campuses that half or more could not find suitable employment.

Military men moved into the policy vacuum. They brought with them specific plans, impressive hardware, virtually unlimited funds, and a reputation for success. The Pentagon takes a lively interest in every part of the world.

In the early days of the Kennedy administration, Vietnam was thought to be an urgent problem, but, compared to other urgent problems, a relatively minor one. The President temporized and took the middle of the road. Partly to impress the Soviet Union, Kennedy wanted to look tough; at the same time, he wanted to avoid committing the nation to a land war in Asia. Therefore, Kennedy decided to send the troops that General Taylor wanted, but not as combat troops. He slipped them into the country as "military advisers" instead. The aim was to stiffen the South Vietnamese army rather than put in an American one. When Kennedy took office, some 685 American advisers were in South Vietnam, as permitted by the Geneva agreement. During 1961 the number of American advisers soared to 4000, while the State Department published a pamphlet that accused North Vietnam of guiding and supporting subversion in South Vietnam.[7] In 1962 the advisory force multiplied to 12,000, already 20 percent more than General Taylor originally thought necessary. Some of the men were Air Force pilots who secretly flew missions for the South Vietnamese. Most of them were Army men, and they, too, were armed. The advisers often got shot at, and, of course, they shot back. General Taylor returned to the Pentagon as Chairman of the Joint Chiefs. In that capacity he authorized Army advisers to wear the Combat Infantryman's Badge. In 1963 Taylor upped the total force to 17,000.

Whatever he did, President Kennedy did not sink into the conflict over his head. No American military unit marched into the war, parading its colors. Kennedy preserved the option of drawing back. When in 1963 Buddhist monks demonstrated against Ngo Dinh Diem, accusing the Catholic ruler of discriminating against Buddhists, Kennedy found himself in an embarrassing position. As the

[7] *A Threat to the Peace, North Viet-Nam's Effort to Conquer South Viet-Nam.* Department of State Publication 7308; December, 1961.

first Catholic President of the United States, he was vulnerable to criticism, and to show his displeasure with the Diem government, Kennedy reduced American aid. In a television interview of September 1, 1963, the American President again stated his policy of limited help. He said, "We can help them, give them equipment. We can send men out there as advisers, but they have to win it, the people of Vietnam, against the Communists."

Two months later, President Diem, having lost his influence in Washington, died in a military coup. The event took place just three weeks before President Kennedy, too, was shot and killed.

Despite the establishment of a new government in Saigon, President Kennedy at the time of his death intended to go through with a planned withdrawal of 1300 military advisers, who reportedly did leave Vietnam during the early weeks of the Johnson administration. At the time, the withdrawal very definitely seemed to reflect confidence in the progress of the war. The year 1963 was one of glowing promises. Body counts showed the Viet Cong dying like flies. Never numerous, the enemy was bound to disappear. (According to official figures, every Communist in South Vietnam *has* disappeared. As of December, 1969, some 300,000 had been killed; 100,000 had defected; and another 100,000 were in jail.[8]) Moreover, the rapidly increasing number of "fortified hamlets" (with sharpened stakes pointing inward as well as outward) proved that the South Vietnamese government was rapidly extending its control over the countryside. At this rate, U.S. officials said publicly, most of the American advisers would be home by Christmas of 1965. Privately, General Paul D. Harkins, head of MACV, estimated that most advisers would make it home in 1964. The withdrawal of 1300 was to be the first step in this encouraging process. The withdrawal did not prove that President Kennedy was changing his policy in Vietnam, although before his death, he ordered a full-scale review of American policy there. The withdrawal did prove that Kennedy wasn't writing any blank checks.

When Lyndon B. Johnson became President, only 141 Americans had died in Vietnam, and the U.S. commitment was de-escalating. But the new President was in for a shock. With Diem out of the way, American officials in Saigon no longer were obliged to praise him.

[8] Reuters dispatch of December 18, 1969.

They now opened their eyes and began to see how false their reports had been. The statistics were nonsense. Diem had been losing the war, not winning it. As for the new military rulers, they weren't doing any better as had been hoped. To the contrary, in the wake of Diem's downfall, peasants came streaming out of the fortified hamlets as if they didn't like living there (in what the critics called "concentration camps"); and the Viet Cong rapidly extended *their* control over the countryside. These events demonstrated the truth of what the younger American journalists in Saigon had been saying about the failure of American policy. President Kennedy once became so disturbed by adverse news reports that he tried to persuade the New York *Times* to replace its man in Saigon. (Kennedy's attempt to manage the news was scandalous in its day, but six years later it would seem mild in comparison with the Nixon administration's campaign to influence the New York *Times,* the Washington *Post,* and the television networks.)

President Johnson was the fifth American President to deal with problems in Vietnam, and like his predecessors, he discovered them to be hotter than officially advertised. Would he lose South Vietnam entirely, the way President Truman had lost China and President Eisenhower had lost Cuba? If not, would the conflict grow like a cancer throughout the whole Johnson administration—optimistically a period of five to nine years? The new President made it clear to his staff that he wanted a major effort and quick results.[9]

It didn't take the Johnson administration long to modify the Kennedy policy of limited help. Just before Christmas, 1963, Secretary McNamara made one of his two-day visits to Saigon and gave the generals an open-ended pledge of support. The New York *Times* reported: "The United States will back the war against Communist guerrillas as long as its help is needed and wanted, the Vietnamese leaders were told." Still the pledge was not unlimited as to the *degree* of support. But that was soon to come.

Secretary McNamara flew out to Saigon with an encouraging word but he flew back to Washington with a discouraging one. The war, in truth, was going badly. What to do about it? Professor Rostow and the military wanted to bomb North Vietnam. While

[9] Roger Hilsman, *To Move a Nation* (New York: Doubleday & Co., 1967), page 534.

McNamara did not yet favor bombing, he did recommend drawing up a list of targets. President Johnson decided to appoint a committee for that purpose.

In a further attempt to cheer up the junta, President Johnson personally signed a rather blank-looking check and mailed it to Saigon. This was a public New Year's message, virtually unreported at the time, which Johnson sent to General Duong Van Minh, then leader of the junta. The season's greeting included these reassuring words:

"The United States will continue to furnish you and your people with the fullest measure of support in this bitter fight. We shall maintain in Vietnam American personnel and material as needed to assist you in achieving victory."

The President seemed to lay only one requirement on General Minh. "The U. S. Government," said he, "shares the view of your government that 'neutralization' of South Vietnam is unacceptable." Apparently, in order to qualify for unlimited help, the junta had only to remain anti-Communist and at least go through the motions of fighting the Viet Cong.

Notwithstanding all of Washington's lavish encouragement, General Minh did not last out the month. In a bloodless coup, he was overthrown on January 30 by General Nguyen Khanh. Minh seems to have failed to live up to President Johnson's dictum. Khanh explained that his predecessor was conspiring with French agents to neutralize the country. General Harkins, head of MACV, was very pleased with the coup. He touted General Khanh as a much better, more aggressive military leader. President Johnson sent Khanh a message which said, "I am glad to know that we see eye to eye on the necessity of stepping up the pace of military operations against the Viet Cong."

In the last days of February, Johnson again turned his attention to Vietnam and boxed himself in still farther. On Friday, February 21, the President warned those who were supplying and directing the Viet Cong that they were engaged in a "deeply dangerous game." By official reports, the Viet Cong were getting most of their supplies in South Vietnam from the people and from the South Vietnamese army. But Johnson's statement amounted to an unmistakable warning, of some kind, to North Vietnam. On Monday, February 24, the administration had two more interesting announcements. It was appointing an inter-agency "Vietnam Task Force" to be chaired by a

State Department career man, William H. Sullivan. This committee was to plan the possible expansion of the war; it was the descendant of the committee appointed to select bombing targets. Monday's other announcement concerned Secretary McNamara. He was going to make another trip to South Vietnam, this time for a period of five days. McNamara, reporters learned later, would study proposals for carrying the war to North Vietnamese territory, and he would consider the possible effectiveness of bombing infiltration routes. On the day after these two announcements, Roger Hilsman, Assistant Secretary of State for the Far East, quit the State Department.

Roger Hilsman was not a career diplomat but a scholar and guerrilla warfare expert. His tenure as Assistant Secretary for the Far East reflected the Kennedy administration's counterinsurgency ("Win the hearts and minds of the people") strategy for Vietnam. For Hilsman to stay in that post did not necessarily make sense if the Johnson administration were switching to a more direct approach ("Get the people by the throats and their hearts and minds will follow") or if the administration were planning an assault on North Vietnam. In a book published in 1967, Hilsman said that his resignation followed a lengthy dispute concerning whether the war should be expanded, with Hilsman arguing against proposals to bomb North Vietnam. Bombing, he insisted, would accomplish nothing useful and probably would backfire. According to the best intelligence of the time, the Viet Cong needed no more than five or six tons of supply per day from outside South Vietnam. No amount of bombing, said Hilsman, could prevent that little dab of matériel from finding its way over a long, mountainous border covered with dense jungle (not to mention the long, tortuous coastline that the Navy thought important). Hilsman believed that the threat of bombing was worth more than the actual bombing could be. Once the aerial campaign started, said he, the North Vietnamese might as well go for broke, sending their regular army to the South.

The State Department's new Assistant Secretary for the Far East was a man from the Pentagon, William Bundy. Before his stint in the defense establishment, Bundy had worked ten years for the CIA.

Just after Roger Hilsman left the government, a few rumblings of subterranean debate stirred the surface of the news. *Newsweek* of March 9 surveyed official opinion on the situation in Vietnam.

Samples from the scene of battle indicated sentiment in favor of direct intervention:

". . . it is now an increasingly accepted view that the war against the Communists has reached a critical point. 'It will go down the drain like a leaf in a whirlpool,' said one American officer, 'unless radical measures are taken.' "

". . . Most Americans in Vietnam are convinced that the Viet Cong would wither in the south if even moderate reprisals were taken against the Communist north."

Washington too had its hawks. Said *Newsweek:*

". . . The leader of the 'hard-liners' is self-assured Walt W. Rostow, the former professor of economic history who now heads the State Department's policy-planning staff. With the support of some Pentagon officials, Rostow offers his 'Rostow Plan No. 6,' a scheme of graduated response to North Vietnam's meddling in the south. First would come a naval blockade of Haiphong—the effect of which would probably be more symbolic than practical. If that did not force Hanoi to call off its support of the South Vietnamese guerrillas, it would be followed, for example, by PT-boat raids on North Vietnamese coastal installations and then by strategic bombing raids flown by U.S. pilots under either the U.S. or South Vietnamese flag. (The bombs used would presumably be non-nuclear.)

"Rostow and his supporters are convinced that the situation in North Vietnam is so precarious and the Sino-Soviet split so deep that there is little danger of massive retaliation from the Communist bloc."

President Johnson, according to *Newsweek,* was determined that South Vietnam "simply cannot be lost."

In brief, officialdom perceived that a crisis had been reached and felt that something drastic had to be done. Otherwise, something drastic would happen. The departure of Roger Hilsman gave more leeway to the hard-liners, who calculated that North Vietnam could be attacked without fear of reprisal by China or Russia. Hanoi, they figured, was a house of cards. A good puff might blow it down.

The description of Rostow Plan No. 6 seems to have been accurate. The "symbolic" blockade of Haiphong never came off, but nearly everything else did, including a few bombing raids flown by South Vietnamese pilots.

Besides its failure to win the war, the plan attributed to Professor

Rostow had some other impractical features. American pilots could not fly many bombing missions with South Vietnamese markings on their wings. What would happen when a pilot, like Lieutenant Alvarez, was captured? He certainly would not pretend to be South Vietnamese. Therefore, if Americans were going to fly the bombers, in anything more than border raids, they would have to do so with American insignia. In that case, the U. S. Government would be committing an overt act of war—what modern crisis managers call an "undeniable" act of war. This helps to explain why William Bundy, as his first major task, began preparing in the early spring of 1964, an all-inclusive war authority to be presented to Congress at some appropriate time. Meanwhile, Nasty gunboats were shipped to South Vietnam, and preparations for a bombing campaign moved ahead.

Asked about rumors of action against North Vietnam, President Johnson cautioned that it would do no good to speculate about the strategy of the South Vietnamese. Senator Morse and Senator Gruening demanded that American military men get out of Vietnam. Secretary Rusk assailed the "quitters"; their remarks, he said, played into the hands of the nation's foes. Already the Johnson administration was trying to discourage both speculation and quitting.

In May Southeast Asia came to a slow boil. On May 2, as the reader will recall, Viet Cong saboteurs sank, briefly, the aircraft transport *Card*. Two days later Roger Hilsman's replacement, William Bundy, told lawmakers that the United States would drive the Communists out of South Vietnam even if it meant "attacking countries to the north" (including Red China?). This statement did not become public until late June; nevertheless, just a few days after Bundy made it, Ho Chi Minh personally issued a warning against attacking *his* country. Ho branded it "sheer stupidity" to talk of expanding the scope of the war when South Vietnamese forces could not control areas right around Saigon. American officials acknowledged that a "Red doughnut" or "arc of insurgency" presented a threat to the South Vietnamese capital. Another trouble spot was down south in the Mekong Delta, even farther from North Vietnam, but full of tenant farmers. Secretary McNamara called the Mekong Delta "the center of Viet Cong strength."[10]

[10] Statement on February 17, 1964, to the Defense Subcommittee of the House Appropriations Committee.

General Nguyen Khanh, of all people, stated his agreement with Ho Chi Minh. According to the New York *Times* of May 26, Khanh opposed carrying the war to the North because he already had his hands full in the South. The junta leader would not go along with attacking North Vietnam unless he could get "ironclad guarantees of United States protection and support, including the use of American combat troops if necessary . . ." The United States "is not believed to be willing to give such firm guarantees now," said the *Times*.

In May the energetic Secretary McNamara made a two-day visit to Saigon, again returning to Washington with a dismal report. This time lawmakers threw at the Defense Secretary charges of defective and obsolete equipment in use by American advisers. Helicopters in particular were notorious; they often crashed with Americans aboard. McNamara assured the men on Capitol Hill that MACV had a "blank check" on arms, manpower, and funds. The term "blank check" startled newsmen, but President Johnson vouched for the accuracy of McNamara's statement.

At the end of May, Congressman Laird dropped his hint about plans to move north. A few days later President Johnson poured cold water on it, reminding reporters that the Republican party had not yet captured the White House. When newsmen pressed for a more definite reply, Johnson, in a huff, said that *he* knew of no plans to carry the war to North Vietnam. The President thought he had answered that question before.

While the President chided reporters for listening to Melvin Laird, a huge conference at Honolulu mapped strategy for Southeast Asia. Present were such notables as Secretary Rusk, Secretary McNamara, General Taylor, CIA Director John A. McCone, Assistant Secretary of State Bundy, General Westmoreland (already scheduled to take over MACV, though not yet in command), and Ambassador Henry Cabot Lodge. The conclusions of the conference were not revealed. Afterward Ambassador Lodge resigned his post, explaining that he would help Governor William W. Scranton with his bid for the Republican presidential nomination. Upon leaving Saigon, Lodge reassured newsmen about the direction of American policy, saying it was "on the right track." General Westmoreland assumed command of MACV. Radio Hanoi attributed the departure of General Harkins to the failure of Washington's counterinsurgency strategy.

At this point war was chiefly a question of timing, according to a newspaper columnist, Ralph de Toledano, known for his intimacy with right wing sources. The Joint Chiefs of Staff wanted "instant action," said de Toledano, but the election campaign prevented that, although military preparations were going ahead. It was expected that air power and sea power could do the job; there would be no need for American ground forces.[11]

The new ambassador to Saigon turned out to be none other than General Taylor, who did not even have time to wind up his personal affairs before getting on the plane. For the Chairman of the Joint Chiefs to go rushing out to the Far East as a mere ambassador was a singular event. In Japan people were reminded of the soldier-diplomats that their government used to send abroad in the heyday of empire. All over the world U.S. officials took pains to assure people that Taylor's appointment signified no change in American policy. Newsmen heard that Taylor was one of those "Never Again" generals who since the Korean War had strongly opposed committing American ground forces to the continent of Asia. (Nobody mentioned a certain qualification to the Never Again thesis: many generals thought the Korean War would have gone better if they had been allowed to bomb the enemy's source of supply in Manchuria).

But if the job of the new ambassador were going to be the same as that of the old ambassador, why should the Chairman of the Joint Chiefs of Staff have been chosen for it? Inside dopesters revealed that Premier Khanh had been demanded "assurances." In order to provide these assurances, several high-ranking officials—including Secretary Rusk—had volunteered for the ambassadorship. One must infer that the assurances had something to do with American support, but what? A pull-out hardly seemed likely. President Johnson repeatedly said that that was out of the question; furthermore, the United States was known to be building a huge air base at Da Nang. In retrospect, the assurances must have had to do with South Vietnam's imminent collapse and/or the "ironclad guarantees" that General Khanh was demanding in May. Later events provided clues pointing in both of those directions.

Ambassador Taylor assumed his new duties on July 7. Evidently a first-rate diplomat, he managed to provide such excellent assurances that within two weeks Premier Khanh was acting like a new man. "To

[11] New Orleans *Times-Picayune*, June 22, 1964.

the North!" became his rallying cry. Not to be outdone, Air Commander Nguyen Cao Ky, the dapper pilot trained by the French, declared that he was ready to start bombing North Vietnam at any time. Ky boasted that secret raids—by air, land, and sea—already were being stepped up. During the spring and summer, as the reader will recall, Radio Hanoi increasingly complained of such irritations.

Ambassador Taylor thought the local junta talked too much. On July 23, the day after Ky's outburst, Taylor met with Ky and Premier Khanh, reportedly to put a muzzle on Ky and straighten out any policy differences. Khanh assured Taylor that American and South Vietnamese policy were the same; the only differences, he said, centered on timing and what to say publicly.[12]

These colorful developments in Saigon received little attention in the United States, where the big news about Vietnam was President Charles de Gaulle's demand for a new Geneva conference. De Gaulle spoke against any expansion of the war, and suggested that the big powers try to cool off Southeast Asia by guaranteeing the area's neutrality. President Johnson rejected the French proposal. He regarded it as a sell-out and as a device to "ratify terror." On July 27 the President underlined his determination by letting it be known that an extra 5000 advisers were going to South Vietnam. The new total, in excess of 20,000, would be an all-time high.

The sudden announcement of a major increase in "advisory" strength mystified certain commentators. What was the reason for it? The Khanh government was shaky, but in recent weeks rumors of a coup had been abating. The only obvious change in the Vietnamese situation had to do with American leadership. Besides Ambassador Taylor, recent appointees included General Westmoreland as head of MACV, Admiral Sharp as CINCPAC, and Admiral Moorer as CINCPACFLT. The Lodge-Harkins team had been preoccupied with problems of the Buddhists and how to get the Vietnamese to do more for themselves. The Taylor-Westmoreland team, one read in the newspapers, would put less emphasis on "politics" and more on "winning the war."

Was additional "advisory" strength needed to deal with some crisis? The summer rainy season always helped the Viet Cong,

---

[12] New York *Times*, July 24, 1964. Radio Hanoi attributed a similar report to United Press International.

whose operations were not mechanized. Other than that seasonal phenomenon, outwardly the war seemed to go on about the same: South Vietnamese "victories" followed by increased American help. But secretly MACV was eying that leaf in the whirlpool. The Viet Cong were thought to be getting strong enough to mount big unit attacks, as the Communists had done at Dien Bien Phu. A CIA study warned that even with greatly increased American aid, the war was liable to result in a prolonged stalemate. CIA Director McCone, an ex-shipbuilder, had such a grasp of Asian affairs that he seriously wished to land a Chinese Nationalist army in Vietnam.[13]

Despite evidence to the contrary, top officials of the Johnson administration in later years talked as if their first big Vietnamese crisis came along in 1965 rather than 1964. At the 1968 Tonkin Gulf hearing, for example, Secretary McNamara refused to admit that there had been any crisis in mid-1964. Senator Fulbright directed his very first questions to that subject:

"Mr. Secretary, is it true that the government of General Khanh which overthrew the Minh junta in January 1964 was in serious trouble by the spring and early summer of 1964?"

McNamara: "I think there was considerable dissension among the members of the government, Mr. Chairman, and there was then and later a series of changes in the government as a result of that dissension."

Fulbright: "Did you not say recently on 'Meet the Press,' and I quote: 'Three and a half years ago the South Vietnamese forces were on the verge of defeat. The North Vietnamese and Viet Cong forces were on the verge of victory.' Is that accurate?"

McNamara: "Mr. Chairman, if I said that, I misestimated the date. What I was talking about—I think later in that same broadcast I specifically referred to it, was July 1965."

McNamara's first version reappeared, under new sponsorship, a few months after President Johnson left the White House. In the book *Report on the War in Vietnam*, General Westmoreland titled one of his chapters, "Year of Crisis—1964." Things got so bad, recalled Westmoreland, that Saigon itself almost went down the

[13] Edward Weintal and Charles Bartlett, *Facing the Brink* (New York: Scribner's, 1967), page 72. According to Radio Hanoi, the CIA in 1963 tried to sneak Chinese guerrillas into North Vietnam.

drain. Now writing as Army Chief of Staff, the former head of MACV told of how he saved the capital city:

"By late summer it was also evident that the Viet Cong posed an immediate threat to Saigon. They were extremely active in the critical provinces around the capital city and had even penetrated in strength into Gia Dinh Province, which constitutes the immediate environs of Saigon. It was obvious to all of us that the seat of government had to be held at all costs.

"Political instability in the Saigon government notwithstanding, we urged upon the South Vietnamese government a coordinated political-military pacification effort radiating outward from Saigon."

A broad array of government ministries planned the operation, named Hop Tac, which belatedly got underway in September. South Vietnamese officials were not eager to cooperate. Evidently unimpressed by the danger, some of them objected to the drive as "American-dominated." Westmoreland concluded that the concept was sound, the execution weak, but Hop Tac "probably saved Saigon from enemy control."

Westmoreland noticed the threat to Saigon in "late summer," he said. But there are indications that he thought the situation shaky as early as June when he took over MACV. According to press accounts of the time, Westmoreland on June 23 obtained special authority in the provinces around Saigon. By July 10 elements of two South Vietnamese divisions were combing the area, and similar operations followed. In short, the new head of MACV, concerned about the Red doughnut, began attacking it first with infantry sweeps, which could be mounted quickly, and then with a coordinated political-military campaign, which took longer to launch. Admiral Sharp was more explicit about the timing. In his part of *Report on the War in Vietnam,* the admiral said that "by August" Communist forces held the military initiative and "appeared to be building up to a final push against the largely demoralized armed forces and unstable government" (of South Vietnam).

Thus it appears that the Tonkin Gulf incidents coincided with a desperate situation in South Vietnam—or, at least, with what the new men, Sharp and Westmoreland, believed to be a desperate situation.

Every summer was worrisome. The Viet Cong always were expected to make trouble during the rainy season, and every year they grew stronger. Saigon was, of course, holding blank checks on Washington, and the presence of Ambassador Taylor was reassuring. But with all of the peace talk back home, would these blank checks be honored in a pinch? The Tonkin Gulf affair gave "everyone" a big boost. Said Westmoreland:

"The psychological impact of these events upon everyone was tremendous. It gave us clear indication of the aggressive intentions of Hanoi; it crystallized allied determination and resolve; and it provided *solid evidence of our resolute support* [italics mine] to the South Vietnamese."

A Washington official put it even more strongly: ". . . Tonkin saved the war for us. It was a life raft that kept us afloat from the summer of '64 through the election, when Mr. Johnson felt the political freedom to make the decisions that had to be made."[14]

Three years after the Tonkin Gulf incidents, President Johnson admitted that as early as May of 1964 he began to think about how to deal with the Congress on Vietnam. He recalled in a press conference (of August 18, 1967):

"Back in May and June, 1964, before the Tonkin Gulf, we considered what we should do in order to keep the Congress informed, to keep them in place, and to keep them in agreement with what our action should be there in case of contingencies. There was a very active debate in the government, as I remember it, back as far as May and June of that year. Then we had the Tonkin Gulf."

The President scorned those senators who, not knowing their place, objected to his using the resolution as authority for war: "I believe that every congressman and most of the senators knew what that resolution said. That resolution authorizes the President—and expressed the Congress's willingness to go along with the President —to do whatever was necessary to deter aggression."

(The President's remark about keeping the Congress "in place" and his using the resolution as authority for war impelled Senator Eugene J. McCarthy to seek the Democratic nomination for President in 1968. McCarthy's anti-war campaign then led to Johnson's retirement.)

President Johnson always knew what was in the Tonkin Gulf resolution even if the Congress did not. It has been reported that Johnson

14 Goulden, page 20.

carried the text around in his pocket for weeks "waiting for the right moment" to get it passed.[15]

Probably if the leaders of any other country had done what American officials now are known to have done in 1964, many Americans would be quick to label their actions as part of an obvious plot. In 1964 Red China was accused of dark machinations without any evidence at all.

Conceivably, however, the naval incidents themselves might have represented no more than a "confused bungle," as some Pentagon official wrote anonymously to the Foreign Relations Committee. The administration then might have taken advantage of the bungle, which happened to come along at the opportune time.

But what about the largely secret military build-up of 1964? There was nothing accidental or fortuitous about that. The build-up resulted from many conscious decisions taken at the highest level. What was its purpose? Surely the purpose was not to improve the anti-Communist negotiating position. President Johnson did not favor neutralization or compromise, and there was nothing else to negotiate. Certain lawmakers and expert observers hoped that after the election Johnson would "get down to business" and arrange some kind of settlement, but this hope proved illusory. Most probably, the build-up was meant to intimidate Hanoi and, if that failed, to facilitate direct action.

In 1964 the official rhetoric was such that, despite the large number of clues on every hand, most expert observers could not divine the administration's attitude toward Vietnam. Former Vice-President Richard Nixon, while campaigning for Senator Goldwater, even accused President Johnson of planning to pull out of Vietnam after the elections were over. Some of Johnson's statements illustrate why it was difficult to arrive at a true assessment of his policy:

August 12 (just two days after signing the Tonkin Gulf resolution) —"Some others are eager to enlarge the conflict. They call upon us to supply American boys to do the job that Asian boys should do. They ask us to take reckless action which might risk the lives of millions and engulf much of Asia and certainly threaten the peace of the entire

[15] Tom Wicker, "Lyndon Johnson vs. the Ghost of Jack Kennedy," *Esquire* (November 1965).

world. Moreover, such action would offer no solution at all to the real problem of Vietnam."

August 29—"I have had advice to load our planes with bombs and to drop them on certain areas that I think would enlarge the war . . . and result in our committing a good many American boys to fighting a war that I think ought to be fought by the boys of Asia . . . I haven't chosen to enlarge the war."

September 25—"There are those that say we ought to go north and drop bombs . . . We don't want our American boys to do the fighting for Asian boys. We don't want to get involved in a nation with 700 million people and get tied down in a land war in Asia."

September 28—"What I have been trying to do, with the situation that I found, was to get the boys in Vietnam to do their own fighting with our advice and equipment. So we are not going north and drop bombs at this stage of the game, and we are not going south and run out and leave it for the Communists to take over."

October 21—"Sometimes our folks get a little impatient. Sometimes they rattle their rockets some, and they bluff about our bombs. But we are not about to send American boys nine or ten thousand miles away from home to do what Asian boys ought to be doing for themselves."

The reader might have noticed a change of nuance on September 28. The President then said that we were not going north and drop bombs "at this stage of the game." A month later, on October 21, he said that we were not "about" to send American boys to Vietnam. Those statements left the possibility (a very ambiguous one on October 21) of taking military action if, as William Bundy said in Tokyo, such action were "forced upon us." When did President Johnson decide to go through with the bombing plan? In October of 1964, according to what he later told Charles Roberts of *Newsweek*.[16] Tom Wicker dismissed as "bombast" what Johnson told Roberts. But Wicker reported that, according to what he heard from Johnson, the bombing targets were selected by October, 1964, on a contingency basis.[17]

[16] Charles Roberts, *LBJ's Inner Circle* (New York: Delacorte Press, 1965), page 20.

[17] Tom Wicker, *JFK and LBJ* (New York: William Morrow and Company, 1968), page 232.

In his book Admiral Sharp disclosed that there were two contingency plans for bombing North Vietnam: Flaming Dart and Rolling Thunder. Flaming Dart raids were to be carried out in response to specific provocation. Rolling Thunder was to be a regular campaign.

On February 4, 1965, two weeks after President Johnson's second inaugural, the President remarked in a press conference that American policy in Vietnam was *"to the general effect* [italics mine] that we would help the people of Vietnam to help themselves." Three days later the Viet Cong fired mortar shells into a U. S. Air Force base at Pleiku, South Vietnam. U.S. officials said that the attack was instigated by Hanoi; and, within hours of the Pleiku attack, the first Flaming Dart raid hit North Vietnam. Presidential adviser McGeorge Bundy was in Saigon at the time. He later remarked to a newsman: "Pleikus are streetcars"—meaning that if one waits for a provocation, it will come along.[18]

No fewer than three aircraft carriers launched the first of the Flaming Dart raids. Admiral Sharp has provided an interesting explanation for this unusual concentration of naval power. In his book Sharp mentioned the carriers in connection with a destroyer patrol scheduled for the Tonkin Gulf. The patrol was to begin on February 7, the day of the Pleiku attack. "However," said the admiral, "it developed that this was the date of a state visit by Soviet Premier Alexei N. Kosygin to Hanoi and the patrol was cancelled in order to avoid any incident that might worsen United States-Soviet relations." When the patrol was cancelled, two carriers were ordered to "stand down from a fully ready condition and on the morning of the seventh the two ships turned eastward for Subic Bay, leaving only the aircraft carrier *Ranger* in the Gulf of Tonkin." But within hours Viet Cong shells pelted Pleiku, and the departing carriers, *Coral Sea* and *Hancock,* swiftly came about. In the words of Admiral Sharp:

"After this [the Pleiku] attack our forces resumed promptly the operational readiness posture so recently relaxed."

CINCPAC informed the Joint Chiefs that he was ready to execute the Flaming Dart plan. The Joint Chiefs responded promptly: "Execute."

[18] Townsend Hoopes, *The Limits of Intervention* (New York: David McKay, 1969), page 30.

A one-word order released aircraft that were poised to strike pre-selected targets just north of the Demilitarized Zone.

Admiral Sharp did not reveal the purpose of the destroyer patrol that would have risked an incident. But it all sounds familiar. One or two destroyers (Sharp didn't say how many) would nose along the North Vietnamese coast. The carrier force at Yankee Station was augmented. The airmen prepared for bombing operations, this time with specific North Vietnamese targets in mind. Recently Hanoi had been complaining about various provocations from air and sea, similar to those of the summer of 1964. If Pleiku had not reported a Communist attack, such tidings might well have come from the Tonkin Gulf.

The air raid definitely worsened United States-Soviet relations. There had been speculation that Premier Kosygin, relatively pro-American for a Russian leader, would mediate between Washington and Hanoi. Instead, Kosygin went home vowing strong support for his comrades in North Vietnam.

Within a month Flaming Dart merged into Rolling Thunder. Authorities disagree on exactly when one series stopped and the new one began.

It was barely noticed at the time, but American airmen commenced overt operations in South Vietnam.

The still-secret war in Laos quickened. Now serving as ambassador there was William Sullivan, formerly chairman of the Vietnam Task Force, who from Vientiane personally supervised the bombing of his host country. Increasingly, the Laotian campaign was directed not at the Pathet Lao guerrillas but at Vietnamese sneaking through the jungle toward South Vietnam. The role of the American ambassador was even stranger if one considers that, as chairman of the Vietnam Task Force, Sullivan had *opposed* the bombing strategy. He favored instead the invasion of North Vietnam.[19] In 1968, following the suspension of bombing in North Vietnam, the air campaign in Laos ran up to 600 and 700 sorties per day.

Was there any good reason to expect air power to win the war?

---

[19] U. S. Congress, Senate, Committee on Foreign Relations; *United States Security Agreements and Commitments Abroad;* Hearing, 91st Congress, 1st Session (Washington: Government Printing Office, 1970), Part 2, page 403. See the remarks of Senator Stuart Symington, Democrat of Missouri.

In Washington North Vietnam's tyrannical regime was thought to be unsteady. Its people had worked hard to build a few factories, which they did not want to see destroyed. Food production was low, and the partial collectivization of land caused unrest. Add to these current problems the horror of bombing, and the people of North Vietnam might rise up and overthrow their detested, incompetent Communist masters. Before that could happen, the authorities in Hanoi probably would abandon their venture in South Vietnam, that is, stop aiding and directing the Viet Cong. Washington would have spoken more loudly than Peking. The Viet Cong, demoralized, would wither away. Did that sort of optimism penetrate the highest levels of the U. S. Government? Apparently so.

When the bombing clearly had failed, ground forces were ordered to take up the slack. Here was a contingency that had not been so well prepared for. The troops began operations with a severe shortage of helicopters—because in 1964 the Army had not been permitted to order the big increase in production that it wanted.[20] The blank check that McNamara and Johnson talked about in the spring of 1964 seems not to have been good for whirlybirds after all. The Johnson administration planned for a short war. Thus shortages, surpluses, and enormous waste occurred in the supply line from 1965 through 1968, while General Westmoreland rushed troops into the field without adequate logistical preparation.[21] Students of government procedure will be interested to note that many—if not most—officials at the "working level" anticipated a long war. Their conviction, like the CIA study, was not accepted by men at the top.

It appears that President Johnson was a secret Goldwater man. Goldwater, too, favored bombing; Goldwater, too, hoped to avoid the use of ground forces. As comedian Jack Paar said of the defeated candidate: "His trouble was that he discussed the issues."

Whatever its intentions during 1964, the Johnson administration

[20] " 'Whiz Kid' Says He Regrets Copter Decision," AP story in Washington *Evening Star* of November 27, 1967.

[21] *Logistic Support in the Vietnam Era, A Report by the Joint Logistics Review Board;* published in three volumes by the U. S. Defense Department in 1970. On the expectation of a short war, see page 281 of Volume 2. See also "Huge Waste Laid to U.S. in Vietnam," New York *Times*, October 9, 1970; "Military Hits LBJ on Viet War," Washington *Post*, November 6, 1970.

during the early months of 1965 vigorously engineered consent to a set of military plans. Members of Congress were invited to the White House for sessions of briefing, cajolery, and arm-twisting. Dealt with individually and in small groups, only a few lawmakers could not be won over. Some feared reprisals if they did not cooperate. As for the press and public, they were swept along by events, buoyed by the natural optimism of action as opposed to the natural pessimism of thought.

But objections mounted, domestically and internationally; and President Johnson, though riding high, at least had to give a nod in the direction of the unreconstructed doves. In a speech of April 7 he offered Hanoi "unconditional discussions," and promised for Southeast Asia, perhaps including North Vietnam, a "billion-dollar American investment." It is difficult to guess how serious the President was about this initiative for peace. The speech followed an intensification of bombing. Two days later bombs fell again, without waiting for Hanoi's reply. Yet even Roger Hilsman was surprised to see the offer turned down. On April 12 the North Vietnamese rejected Johnson's package deal as the "bait of a stupid pirate."

The bombing campaign welded the North Vietnamese people into a solid unit behind their government, as the Pearl Harbor attack unified Americans in 1941. Nor did Rolling Thunder stop or even reduce the flow of men and material to the south. To the contrary, Hanoi's regular army joined the parade, and when President Johnson called off the bombing in 1968, North Vietnamese troops were still in South Vietnam. The threat of bombing had been more valuable than the actual bombing, as Roger Hilsman argued until his sudden exit from the State Department. When the Paris peace talks failed to make progress, the bombing was not resumed; and U.S. officials explained that the *lack* of it fostered disunity in North Vietnam. By that time the American people had heard a bewildering variety of reasons for the aerial campaign, such as hitting Viet Cong sanctuaries, reducing infiltration, and even raising South Vietnamese morale. In his definitive explanation, published in 1967, General Taylor said that the "first reason" for bombing was to improve South Vietnamese morale; the "second reason" was to restrain infiltration.[22] The reader

[22] General Maxwell D. Taylor, *Responsibility and Response* (New York: Harper and Row, 1967), pages 26 and 27.

will have his own opinion as to whether improving South Vietnamese morale was worth the cost. In any case, what persuaded General Taylor that bombing North Vietnam would bring happiness to South Vietnam? When Taylor was in Saigon as ambassador, the raids of August 5, 1964, made General Westmoreland happy; they also gave enormous pleasure to General Khanh and his military colleagues. But what about those South Vietnamese who did not speak English or hang around the American Embassy? An American intelligence agent who went eavesdropping on Vietnamese conversations found only doubtful support for the raids.[23] Out of twenty-five South Vietnamese whom he overheard, not one expressed disapproval of the reported North Vietnamese attacks on American ships. A number spoke against the retaliatory raids because Americans now were killing Vietnamese, instead of merely helping the Vietnamese to kill Vietnamese.

However one looks at it, the bombing was a "crazy idea"—just as the voters thought it was in 1964.

As for the commitment of ground troops—which the voters also disapproved—was this necessary to "keep our word" as Johnson and Rusk were prone to say? Evidently not. In the ever-astounding *Report on the War in Vietnam,* General Westmoreland told of how it was "my judgment" that South Vietnam could not be saved without American ground forces. "With the concurrence of Ambassador Taylor, I so recommended," wrote the former head of MACV. In his part of the book, Admiral Sharp said that the South Vietnamese government requested American soldiers. But the State Department has no record of such a request, as Senator Fulbright discovered a few months after the Sharp-Westmoreland book was published. More recently, the irrepressible General Ky, who was the South Vietnamese Premier in 1965, has declared: "American policy was wrong in the past when the U.S. wanted to pour in troops to win the guerrilla war. I told them they should modernize and train our army and not send in large amounts of U.S. troops."[24]

On its own initiative, the Johnson administration decided to expand and escalate the war. It did so as the alternative to what it saw

[23] Henry Brandon, *Anatomy of Error* (Boston: Gambit, Inc., 1969), pages 34 and 35.
[24] Associated Press story quoted in *Parade* magazine (February 1, 1970).

as the eventual defeat of the South Vietnamese government. The aim was to win and win fast. The President and his advisers compared Vietnam to Hungary and Czechoslovakia where, if one could only keep the Russians out, everything would be fine. Thus the Johnson administration, like those before it, underestimated the amount of South Vietnamese support for the Communist guerrillas. In 1965 General Taylor, in strictest confidence, advised a few senators that North Vietnamese supply lines already were overextended with an estimated infiltration rate of 1500 men per month.[25] But a year later the official estimate of infiltration was up to 7000 men per month, and the enemy was getting food and whatever he needed from somewhere. Similarly, General Taylor thought that the number of American troops would never reach 175,000. The number actually climbed to 550,000, and in 1968 General Westmoreland wanted another 206,000.

Like many another historical blunder, the Vietnamese intervention was planned in secret, far from the light of public discussion. Decisions then were justified by citing the unanimous views of military experts at the Pentagon. Private critics were told to "get on the team." Their irresponsible statements, officials pointed out, were not based on the secret information available to government planners. Among the most secret of that information concerned South Vietnamese public opinion. The Executive Branch consistently has refused to give the Foreign Relations Committee access to the public opinion polls taken in South Vietnam, but in 1970 the American Broadcasting Company got hold of a poll and made it public. It showed that 65 percent of the South Vietnamese people wanted all Americans out of the country; that 30 percent had no opinion (or would not express it); and that only 5 percent—mostly in Saigon—wanted the Americans to stay.[26]

The official theory of the war, nonetheless, still postulates a small clique of fanatics in Hanoi (and perhaps in Peking) manipulating a vast number of the Vietnamese people through propaganda and ter-

---

[25] General Taylor gave these classified estimates to a few skeptical senators in 1965. The information was not made public until 1968 when the question of sending more troops was hotly debated. See the remarks of Senators Nelson, McCarthy, and Hartke in the *Congressional Record* of March 7, 1968; pages 5650 and 5652.

[26] Senator Stephen Young, *Congressional Record*, July 24, 1970.

ror. Ironically, the New Left peaceniks have come to see their own country in the same way, although on principle they would not accept that view of Vietnam. The more typical American dove questions the right of any country to help put down a rebellion, especially when the government under attack shows the earmarks of dictatorship. That is a traditional American attitude. The typical hawk, on the other hand, tends to accept the Johnsonian concept of invasion from the north, and he compares the war in Indochina to helping the South Koreans throw back the North Koreans. Sympathy for the underdog, too, is a traditional American attitude. In a real sense, the war represents a conflict between American traditions—a conflict engendered by disagreement on the *facts* of what is happening. This is the first war that the American people have had to fight without being able to agree on who the enemy is, where he lives, and what he is doing.

Such questions ought to have been thoroughly aired before the nation went to war. The Congress ought to have decided by vote whether South Vietnam was the victim of aggression and, if so, whether Americans should fight in South Vietnam's defense. One of the chief effects of the Tonkin Gulf resolution was to prevent such a debate and such a vote. Inadvertently the Congress made war possible. Later it debated the merits of the conflict. By that time the biggest argument for continuing the war was, "We're already in it!" The solution: "Win it!" National pride and the tradition of victory threaten to tear the nation apart rather than permit the confession of error or defeat.

The Tonkin Gulf not only confused the war; it also confused the U. S. Constitution. The action of Congress made war possible—a political accomplishment—but it did not necessarily make the war legal. The Supreme Court, had it chosen to accept a legal challenge, could have found grounds on which to declare the resolution null and void. Senator Fulbright claims that the resolution was obtained under false pretenses, and that argument surely carries some weight. Senator Nelson points out that using the resolution as authority for war violated the intent with which it was passed. Probably most people would agree with that if they read the congressional debate of the time, especially that of the Lower House. Finally, as Senator Morse declaimed in 1964, the resolution was unconstitutional. It supposedly transferred the war power from the Congress to the

President for the latter to use at his discretion, and that is exactly what the writers of the Constitution meant to avoid.

Because of the Tonkin Gulf resolution and the trend which it represents, the nature of the government's authority to make war has become controversial and extremely confused. Many citizens continued to believe, as they were taught in school, that for a war to be legal it must be declared by the Congress. But a very different view is held by many experts on public affairs, including officials of the Executive Branch, probably most political scientists, and even a few senators. They insist that the President, as Commander-in-Chief of the armed forces, can fight an undeclared war on his own authority without *any* authorization from Congress. According to this view, the Tonkin Gulf resolution merely confirmed a power that the President already had. (The text, in fact, can be read in that way; the word "authorize" never appears.) Having no real power of its own, the Congress then should "declare" the war if it wants to or shut up.

If we look back to the eighteenth century, there can be no doubt concerning the intent of the men who wrote the Constitution and pleaded for its adoption. The Founding Fathers viewed with abhorrence the idea that one man should have the power to make war. A major purpose of the Revolutionary War was to escape that kind of situation: the English kings were always fighting somebody, and the colonies were dragged into the conflict against their will. In his "Federalist Paper No. 6," Alexander Hamilton referred to the problem of one-man rule, recalling how King Henry VIII stepped into a perilous conflict merely to improve Cardinal Wolsey's chances of becoming Pope—a ploy that failed. As for elected leaders, Hamilton did not trust them, either. He alleged that Pericles, the great Athenian statesman, once made war at the behest of a prostitute. With such precedents in mind, writers of the Constitution determined to give Congress, not the President, the authority to declare war—by which they meant the power to initiate war. Both Houses of Congress would have to debate the proposed war, vote on it, and appropriate money for it. With extended discussion the conflict might be avoided entirely.

Delegates to the Constitutional Convention considered giving Congress the power to "make" war rather than to "declare" war. But the term "make" was too broad. What if the nation were attacked while the Congress was not in session. Before shooting back, the armed forces could not wait for lawmakers to come galloping on horseback all the way from remote places like Georgia and New Hampshire. For that reason, the Convention settled upon the word "declare." The intention of the delegates was for the President, as Commander-in-Chief of the armed forces, to repel attack instantly and for him to seek congressional authority for war as soon as possible. It was not meant for the President to initiate any fighting. Today, those who want the President to have complete control over the war power often argue that the congressional authority is "old-fashioned" because the armed forces, if attacked by modern weapons, "can't wait" to make their reply. But the armed forces never were intended to wait, and they never have. That is why military commanders are given rules of engagement.

In the eighteenth century some Americans doubted the wisdom of letting the President be Commander-in-Chief of the armed forces, and among them was the great American naval hero, Commodore John Paul Jones. In a letter to the Marquis de Lafayette, Jones said: ". . . General Washington might be safely trusted with such tempting power, as the chief command of the Fleet and Army, yet, depend on it, in some other hands it could not fail to overset the liberties of America. The President should be only the first civil Magistrate . . ."[27]

As matters turned out, the very first war fought by the newly formed United States was an undeclared naval conflict with France, and the men who headed the government were largely the same ones who invented it. Thus the little known Quasi War of 1798–1801 provides an example of how the Constitution ought to work in the case of a limited, undeclared war.

On the American side, the aim was to stop French warships and French-authorized privateers (legal pirates) from raiding American merchant vessels. To put an end to these depredations, the Congress established a Navy Department and authorized President John Adams to protect American commerce by force. Adams did so, and the stern Puritan never exceeded the authority given to him. Indeed, when he made peace with France, most of the Congress was far from pleased. Adams rejected the urgings of his party to seize French-

[27] Quoted by Lincoln Lorenz, *John Paul Jones* (Annapolis, Maryland: U. S. Naval Institute, 1943).

controlled territories in the New World. Ironically, such urgings came from Alexander Hamilton, who had succumbed to dreams of Napoleonic conquest.

At first glance, the hawkishness of Adams's Congress might seem to be at odds with the theory of the Constitution. However, except for not declaring the war, the important events bore out the expectations of delegates to the Constitutional Convention. They not only had anticipated the Congress's slowness to make war (in this case the authorization took years); they also had anticipated the Congress's slowness to make peace. Hence the writers of the Constitution left the peace-making job to the President, who, relatively nimble and secretive, could work behind the scenes to bring about the unpopular compromises that usually are needed to stop the fighting.

In sum, the Constitution was designed to "clog" the process of going to war and to "facilitate" the process of making peace. To those ends, the writers of the Constitution took the "singular" step of dividing the peace-making power from the war-making power, giving one to the President and the other to the Congress.[28]

With respect to the authority for initiating war, the intent of the Constitution remained clear enough throughout the last years of the eighteenth century and the entire nineteenth century, even though during that time the nation undertook six foreign conflicts: the Quasi War, the War with Tripoli, the War of 1812, the War with Barbary Pirates, the Mexican War, and the Spanish-American War. During the twentieth century, however, there has been a swift and steady erosion of the congressional prerogative. Little by little, Presidents have increased their power to make war, though not necessarily their legal authority to do so.[29]

The trend began in 1900. President William McKinley, during the Boxer Rebellion, ordered several thousand American troops to China where they, with an international force, helped to rescue the foreign

[28] James Madison's journal for August 17, 1787, as published in *The Records of the Federal Convention*, edited by Max Farrand (New Haven, Connecticut: Yale University Press, 1927), pages 318 and 319.

[29] As background for the resolution on National Commitments, the Foreign Relations Committee discussed this subject with Professor Ruhl J. Bartlett of the Fletcher School of Law and Diplomacy, Tufts University, and with other authorities. See the hearing text: *U. S. Commitments to Foreign Powers;* 90th Congress, 1st Session (Washington: Government Printing Office, 1967).

legations under siege at Peking. McKinley acted in time of emergency, and the Congress was not in session. As was customary in those days, the Congress did not reconvene for several months; when it did, the lawmakers were concerned with other matters that seemed more important than a formal reassertion of their rights. Besides, McKinley took the position that the United States was not at war with China—a diplomatic fiction that helped to settle the conflict. Roughly, and on a big scale, McKinley's dispatch of troops followed nineteenth century precedents for using military force to protect American citizens in lawless areas. It is important to note that at the turn of the century an international force of only 20,000 men was able to march into Peking and impose its will on the whole Chinese Empire. The ease with which this was done helps to explain the habit of military intervention acquired by the industrial nations; it also helps to explain the later triumph in China of the anti-foreign, pro-industrial Communist movement led by Mao Tse-tung.

In 1903 President Theodore Roosevelt definitely overstepped his authority—but secretly—when he ordered the U. S. Navy to help Colombian rebels to set up the independent state of Panama. The impatient Roosevelt wanted to "make the dirt fly" and get the canal rights for less than Colombia's asking price. The aggrieved Central American nation later picked up a large sum in hush money.[30]

It was President Woodrow Wilson, a former professor of political science, who really unlocked the floodgates. During the civil wars in Mexico, Wilson twice invaded that country without a valid congressional authorization. The first invasion followed an extremely minor naval incident. A few American sailors in a small boat landed in Tampico, a combat zone, and were detained 1½ hours. The Mexican dictator, General Victoriano Huerta, apologized; President Wilson, nevertheless, avenged this insult to the flag by ordering the U. S. Navy to seize Vera Cruz, a port 200 miles south of Tampico—where General Huerta was expecting a shipment of arms. It was Wilson's policy to help the Constitutionalist rebels being led by General Venustiano Carranza. As President Wilson rescued constitutional gov-

[30] For a brief discussion, see Samuel Eliot Morison's *Oxford History of the United States* (London: Oxford University Press, 1927), II. Basic sources: *Senate Documents*, 58th Congress, 2nd Session, No. 53; *House Documents*, 58th Congress, 1st Session, No. 8.

ernment in Mexico, the U. S. Constitution fell afoul of congressional bumbling at home. Each House of Congress passed a bill in support of Wilson's action, but the bills differed in wording and failed to become law.

The second time President Wilson invaded Mexico he was goaded into it by the victorious General Carranza's former ally, Pancho Villa, who attacked the town of Columbus, New Mexico. Villa hoped that a new American invasion would unite the Mexican people behind him in a nationalistic rage. Wilson's second invasion did anger the Mexican people, as did the first one, but not enough to topple Carranza.

Meanwhile, President Wilson found time to occupy the Dominican Republic. Through the U. S. Navy he also administered Haiti.

The U. S. Congress retained enough of its constitutional authority to declare the American participation in World War I and World War II, though, it must be noted, the latter was thrust upon it by events. World War II greatly increased the power of the President, and it contributed to the Congress's growing sense of inferiority. Congress had been the home of the now-discredited isolationism. (Lawmakers had favored defensive *preparedness,* appropriating record naval budgets, but they had not seen the need for a strong initiative in foreign affairs.) Following World War II, the drift toward presidential power was accelerated by the complex and perpetual emergency known as the Cold War. Congress agreed to the NATO alliance, and that led to stationing troops in Europe as a "trip wire" defense. If the American garrison were attacked, there could be no doubt of the American response. This took the decision for war out of congressional hands, but lawmakers chose to wink at the new arrangement. They hoped to prevent war by establishing a deterrent of maximum credibility.

The U. S. Government made no alliance with South Korea, and no trip wire was installed there, either. But in 1950 President Harry S Truman undertook a major war in Korea, and he did so without any congressional authorization. American public opinion strongly favored throwing back the Communist invaders, and, time being short, the peppery Truman acted on his own. This was not a war, said he. It was a "police action" against a "bunch of bandits." In effect, Truman compared his action to Woodrow Wilson's pursuit of Pancho Villa. After the military situation improved, the President still neglected to ask Congress for proper authority. Then the Chinese intervened, and, after another seesaw, the battle line stabilized near the original boundary of the two Koreas. (A fact that tends to be forgotten is that the Communist side actually lost about 1500 square miles.) Truman's intervention preserved the independence of South Korea; but, since it failed to dislodge permanently the Communist government in North Korea, it did not reunify the country as part of the Free World. Republican critics, disgusted by the "stalemate," called the war a war and needled the President for getting into it without a proper legal authorization. (The memory of that criticism, said President Johnson in 1967, prompted him to seek a resolution concerning Vietnam.)

Neither Democratic nor Republican lawmakers were satisfied by the results of the so-called Korean Conflict. Nevertheless, the men on Capitol Hill proceeded even more rapidly to dismantle their power to initiate war. During the Eisenhower and Kennedy administrations, the Executive and Legislative branches, working together, papered the Free World with defense treaties and area resolutions. If the resolutions were very much like blank checks, the treaties became even more so, wherever large numbers of troops were stationed. Behind this great effort lay not only the Congress's desire for Executive leadership in foreign affairs, but the conviction that the frustrating, bloody conflict in Korea could have been avoided if only the American determination to protect South Korea had been made known in advance.

Ironically, however, what obscured the American willingness to fight for South Korea was neither congressional ineptitude nor some musty provision of the eighteenth-century Constitution. Rather, it was the freshly minted observations of supposedly expert officials of the Executive Branch of government. On two occasions high ranking officials went out of their way to indicate that the United States would not defend South Korea. In 1949 General Douglas MacArthur, Commander-in-Chief in the Far East, told the press that his defensive line ran from the Philippines to Japan and thence to the Aleutian Islands. MacArthur left out South Korea (also Taiwan, Thailand, Vietnam, and other places later deemed vital to American security). Early in 1950 the Secretary of State, Dean Acheson, repeated MacArthur's words in a speech to the National Press Club. Six months later the American people found themselves in an undeclared war. Many conservative critics have ignored MacArthur's blunder in order to focus blame for the Korean War on Secretary Acheson, allegedly a soft, pinkish diplomat. However, the MacArthur-Acheson position on South Korea was based on the Defense Department's analysis of the military situation in the Far East. Erroneously, the Defense Department believed that South Korea was militarily stronger than North Korea, and thus well able to take care of itself.

At the one extreme of post-World War II policy, the U. S. Government advertised its unwillingness to defend a large portion of the globe; at the other extreme, the same government now advertises its readiness to fight in at least forty-two countries. Moreover, it appears that the Congress need not ratify a decision for war. The President can shuffle a few documents and declare that, added together, these give him plenty of authority. He can refer to similar decisions made by his recent predecessors; if he wishes, the President can obtain agreement from the National Security Council, Secretary of State, and other high authorities—all appointed by himself. In whatever number desired, distinguished officials will appear on television and explain why it is proper and necessary to support the Commander-in-Chief in this hour of crisis.

In certain respects the concentration of power has gone farther in the United States than in the Soviet Union, where an eleven-man Politburo seems to make the biggest decisions. On a question of war, the American President might consult as many as eleven men or he might not. President Nixon reportedly consulted about half that many on his decision to invade Cambodia. Furthermore, those consulted will probably be the President's own appointees, and, among them, perhaps the most agreeable instead of the most qualified. With respect to the Cambodian invasion, the Secretary of State is said to have opposed the plan while the Attorney General favored it—though the latter, John N. Mitchell, denies having been consulted. On a later occasion (when asked why he did not step in with some timely advice when President Nixon publicly declared guilty a man undergoing trial for murder), the Attorney General remarked, "It is not the proper posture for anybody to correct the President of the United States."

The post-Stalin USSR has been struggling away from the "cult of the personality" while, to an alarming degree, the United States has been drifting into it. The change became evident several years ago when Premier Kosygin visited the United States and met with President Johnson at Glassboro, New Jersey. Hearing that the encounter was a cordial and friendly one, crowds outside the meeting place went wild with enthusiasm. The scene on television was unforgettable as the two Cold War leaders, smiling, walked outside into a hurricane of public approval. Immediately, journalists and government officials warned everybody not to expect much in the way of practical results from the Glassboro meeting. The Soviet Premier, they explained, did not have the *authority* to commit his country that President Johnson did.[31]

A series of Presidents, aided by the permanent bureaucracy, have found ways to increase their power in foreign affairs, as they have in domestic matters; and regardless of who is in the White House the same tendency continues. Power is gathered most easily in times of emergency, but the process can go on even during times of tranquility. One technique is to re-interpret existing treaties. The SEATO treaty, for example, requires the United States to act "in accordance with its constitutional processes," and when the treaty was ratified this phrase was understood to mean with the consent of Congress. Since then, two Presidents, Eisenhower and Johnson, have announced—using identical words—that they would "instantly repel" an attack on the Philippine signatory. Obviously, this careful choice of language was meant to cut Congress out of the picture. Furthermore, the Philippines do not seem at all threatened except by their own citizens—or "internal dissident groups," to use the Pentagon term.

Although treaties have helped to expand Executive power, Presidents now try to avoid making them. Such formal agreements require two-thirds approval in the Senate, and, as a further inconvenience, their contents become public knowledge—hence anyone is free to say what he likes about them. The Executive Branch now finds it more convenient to bring about informal understandings, secret or public, without reference to the Senate. Initially, such understandings may be termed "executive agreements," "communiqués," "joint declarations," or "contingency plans." In time of crisis, the same under-

---

[31] Senator Karl E. Mundt, Republican of South Dakota, called these remarks to the attention of the Foreign Relations Committee. See page 34 of *U. S. Commitments to Foreign Powers.*

standing can be styled a "national commitment," and it allegedly will have been in existence many years, upheld by successive Presidents. In justifying the war in Vietnam, President Johnson repeatedly asserted that the American commitment began with a letter about "aid" that President Eisenhower sent to Ngo Dinh Diem.

Such informal methods of putting American power and prestige on the line can not only bypass the Senate but the State Department, which is supposed to do the negotiating. In 1968 representatives of the Defense Department made some arrangements with Spain that, until they became known, tended to commit the United States to Spanish defense. From where might the Spanish be attacked? From Algeria, it was thought, or possibly within the Spanish colonies in Africa. (Coincidentally or not, it was in the same year, 1968, that guerrilla attacks in Portuguese Guinea first required strong forces to suppress.) The U. S. Defense Department, to oblige General Francisco Franco, averred that the mere presence of American bases on Spanish soil constituted a more significant guarantee of help than would a written agreement. Such negotiations were undertaken by General Wheeler and by General Burchinal—the Air Force officer who in 1964 "confirmed" the August 4 attack in the Tonkin Gulf. As the President strays farther and farther from the Constitution, not only the Senate and the State Department, but the President himself could drop out of the picture.

Congress was not greatly disturbed by the hyperbolic increase in presidential power so long as the Chief Executive seemed to know what he was doing—and even sometimes when he obviously did not. But the calamity in Indochina was too big and too drawn-out. Prodded by men like Senator Fulbright, the nation's lawmakers began taking a new look at recent arrangements. Commentators marked the 1968 Tonkin Gulf hearing as the most important congressional action of that year, and as the probable end of unquestioned White House supremacy in foreign affairs. The commentators were right. Slowly a reassertion of congressional authority began to get underway. In 1969 the Senate resolved by a vote of 70–16 that any "national commitment" must have its consent. As Senator Fulbright observed, this is what the Constitution intended when it gave the Senate power to advise and consent on treaties; yet the very mild National Commitments resolution evoked the vigorous opposition of the Nixon administration. As 1969 drew to a close, both Houses of Congress voted to limit the war in Indochina. An appropriations amendment sponsored by Senator Church prohibited the sending of U.S. ground troops into Laos or Thailand. The amendment did not include Cambodia; consequently, its supporters were greatly chagrined when President Nixon later sent troops into *that* country. Along with Senator Cooper, Senator Church then introduced a measure restricting the use of American troops in Cambodia. By the time the "Cooper-Church amendment" got through the hawkish Lower House and became law, opinions differed as to whether its language would permit another "limited" invasion of Cambodia.

True to its deceptive character, the Tonkin Gulf resolution suffered a highly publicized but fictitious demise in the middle of 1970. The Senate twice voted overwhelmingly for its repeal, in two different bills; and the news media began referring to the resolution as null and void—without noting that action by the Lower House was needed. In the closing hours of the 91st Congress, the two Houses finally got together on repeal, slipping it into the Foreign Military Sales Act. President Nixon affixed his signature on January 14, 1971. Here was the bona fide end of the Tonkin Gulf resolution—little noted by press or public. But, in the absence of congressional authority, how was the Indochina War to proceed? The Nixon administration already had made the necessary psychological preparations.

In the early days of his administration, President Nixon wanted to keep the Tonkin Gulf resolution, saying that it had consequences for Southeast Asia that went beyond Vietnam. Whatever the President meant by that, the literal truth of his assertion became evident when American troops crossed the Vietnamese border into Cambodia. Vice-President Spiro T. Agnew, appearing on television, cited the Tonkin resolution as legal authority. Next, as an outraged Senate debated how best to limit the President's war-making power, the Nixon administration, unable to beat 'em, decided to join 'em. The administration sponsored a repeal of its own through Senator Robert J. Dole, Republican of Kansas. Dole and others declared that the Tonkin Gulf resolution no longer was needed to justify American policy in Southeast Asia. The Democrats, they explained, had used the resolution to put American troops *into* Vietnam, but President Nixon's policy was to take American troops *out* of Vietnam; in fact, he already was reducing their number. Merely to withdraw troops— on honorable terms, of course—did not require any congressional authority. What about the Cambodian venture? The purpose of that was to protect the withdrawal of Americans from Vietnam, where they were threatened by Vietnamese Communists making use of Cambodian sanctuaries. As Commander-in-Chief, the President could do whatever was necessary—and should do whatever was necessary—to insure the safety of American troops, wherever they might be.

This argument persuaded Senator Fulbright to oppose repeal of the Tonkin Gulf resolution as sponsored by Senator Dole. The circumstances, said Fulbright, seemed to confer unlimited authority on the President as Commander-in-Chief of the armed forces. Fulbright pressed for repeal by "concurrent resolution," a means specified in the resolution itself and a means which would not require the President's approval. This kind of measure passed the Senate by an overwhelming vote but was rejected by the Lower House. Finally, in voice votes, both Houses accepted the Dole amendment to the Foreign Military Sales bill.[32] On January 2, 1971, when the Senate took action on the conference agreement, Senator Fulbright presented objections to other parts of the bill but said nothing at all about the amendment repealing the Tonkin Gulf resolution. Senator Dole took the floor to restate his opinion that the resolution was "superfluous" in the light of "today's realities in Southeast Asia"; Dole expressed a hope that getting rid of the resolution would clear away "some of the distrust" that grew out of its "original interpretation."

Many scholarly and experienced observers doubt that the Congress can regain its constitutional authority over the power to make war. Most lawmakers, especially in the Lower House, have come to prefer letting the President make the hard decisions in foreign affairs. As long as he works in harmony with the Pentagon and the CIA, the President is assumed to have available to him the necessary facts, the necessary skill, and the necessary experience. That, of course, is one of history's well-worn paths toward empire. The Roman Senate fell so far behind in the struggle for power that even its murder of one Chief Executive, Julius Caesar, failed to preserve the

[32] The text of the amendment:
"Sec. 12. The joint resolution entitled 'Joint resolution to promote the maintenance of International peace and security in Southeast Asia', approved August 10, 1964 (78 Stat. 384; Public Law 88-408), is terminated effective upon the day that the second session of the Ninety-first Congress is last adjourned."

Republic. The troubles Rome then had have filled such massive works of history as Edward Gibbon's *The Decline and Fall of the Roman Empire*. Modern times, too, have abounded in catastrophe caused—or certainly *not prevented*—by one-man rule. In the twentieth century, both World Wars generally have been blamed on the decisions of absolute rulers and the ambitious, militaristic cliques that tend to form around them. In the case of World War I, the responsibility for this conflict most often has been placed squarely on Kaiser Wilhem and a blank check that he gave to the Austro-Hungarian Empire, during her Balkan quarrel.

It is not possible in the space available here to discuss the steps needed to rejuvenate the U. S. Congress so that it can resume its proper constitutional role. In connection with the Tonkin Gulf, however, we must at least consider the problem of official secrecy and one or two things that might be done about that.

Against secrecy the first line of defense is the news media. This is almost as true for the Congress as it is for the people. Yet the Executive Branch frequently is able to deceive the media when it wants to. This is particularly true during a crisis when, as the first chapters of this book demonstrate, the media will grab for any scrap of information, even if the official providing it insists on being nameless—as he usually does. Again and again the media are fooled in this way. Critics of journalism (except for government officials) call for more skepticism and "investigative reporting." No doubt the methods of journalism could be improved. But in 1964 even the best reporters were fooled; in addition, many of the best reporters are lured away from journalism by the higher salaries in public relations, governmental or private. It is necessary, therefore, to think of ways in which the reporting problem can be simplified.

In 1964 President Johnson came up with an interesting suggestion: that reporters ask Communist officials in Hanoi about their motives. Johnson neglected to add that the U. S. Government had made this very difficult. Since the U. S. Government did not recognize North Vietnam, American reporters could not be stationed there. Nor did the North Vietnamese, for that matter, make it easy for Americans to visit their country; Harrison Salisbury waited eighteen months for the controversial visit that he made in 1966 to inspect the bombing damage. There can be little doubt, however, that the

American people would have learned more about the Tonkin Gulf incidents and their circumstances if American reporters had been residing in North Vietnam. It is important to realize that not recognizing certain countries not only prevents normal diplomatic relations with them but also normal press relations. The policy of non-recognition thus blacks out portions of the globe and becomes a powerful tool for managing the news. Since 1945 the United States has been at war with North Korea, Red China, and North Vietnam. All are countries that the United States would not recognize. All are countries that the American people still know very little about except that, according to official sources, they are the new "bad guys"—scarcely human, it sometimes would appear.

The Congress, too, has a responsibility to provide information, and available for this purpose is the vast amount of information that is turned up by the congressional committees. Much of that information does appear in published form. The investigative effort now should be expanded to include swift and expert inquiry into international incidents and sudden crises that involve American interests. Furthermore, the investigation must be *automatic*. If it is not, the question of whether to have an investigation at all will become a political football, impugning the patriotism of individual lawmakers and the integrity of the administration. Experience has already proved abundantly that investigation is needed. Adequate information cannot be obtained merely by having a short talk—or even a long talk—with a few high-ranking representatives of the Executive Branch, whose duty is to defend the bureaucracy and all of its far-ranging interests. Moreover, it is possible, as in 1964, that none of the representatives dispatched by the Executive Branch will speak with special knowledge of the armed service involved (or of the CIA as the case may be). When, for example, there is a naval incident, naval men should be questioned about it; and among those questioned should be many of the actual participants. It would not be necessary to transport several hundred sailors to Washington, D.C. A few congressional investigators could fly to where not only the actual participants but the original records could be examined, along with the actual equipment used. Had such an investigation been held in 1964, it might have changed the course of history.

The certainty of on-the-spot, automatic inquiry would insure far more accurate reporting by the Executive Branch. In turn, this would

increase public confidence in the Government—now at a low ebb—
and allay the suspicion of conspiracy, a growing problem in modern
affairs. The certainty of inquiry might even prevent some of the carelessness that, in the past, seems to have brought about certain
disasters. I refer particularly to the ill-timed flight of the CIA's reconnaissance plane in 1960, the misplacing of the USS *Liberty* in
1967, and the reckless cruise of the USS *Pueblo* in 1968.

In view of everything the nation has been through in the last dec-
ade, one might expect the Congress to become a little wary of international incidents and what they might presage. But congressional
complacency was barely disturbed in the spring of 1970 when the
Columbia Eagle, an American munitions vessel, reportedly was hi-
jacked by two young "hippies" and taken to Cambodia. The perpetra-
tors of this feat, aged twenty and twenty-five, denied that they were
hippies, but said that they were carrying out an "SDS [Students for a
Democratic Society] plot," the first in a series of hijackings by youths
of the New Left opposed to the war in Vietnam. (No further hijackings actually were attempted.) The *Columbia Eagle*'s hijackers asserted that the ship was carrying napalm. Communist sources, on the
other hand, called the hijacking a "CIA plot," and they alleged that
the ship was filled with small arms for the Cambodian army. Whatever was in the ship could not be determined by unbiased observers;
the *Columbia Eagle* was guarded so carefully by the Cambodian navy
that not even the Sihanoukville harbor master could get on board.
Two days after the ship's arrival, the Cambodian army overthrew the
neutralist government of Prince Sihanouk. Taking power was General Lon Nol, who favored strong action against the Vietnamese
Communists making use of eastern Cambodia—the border areas soon
to be invaded by American and South Vietnamese troops.

The pro-American Lon Nol freed the *Columbia Eagle,* and, according to U.S. officials, the ship left Sihanoukville with her cargo.
In fact, the ship seems to have been unloaded in Cambodia. An Associated Press photograph showed her waterline high and dry; even
the rudder protruded over a churning wake. Nor did the wayward
vessel proceed to her original destination, even though the Lon Nol
government placed no restrictions on where she could go. Light as a
cork, the *Columbia Eagle* floated off to Subic Bay.

The story of the *Columbia Eagle* ought to have piqued the curiosity
of the most lethargic lawmaker. Yet the Cambodian uproar did not

begin on Capitol Hill until President Nixon suddenly ordered ground troops into the country, chasing Vietnamese Communists and trying to bolster the shaky government of General Lon Nol. Despite foreign help—or because of it—Lon Nol soon abandoned most of his country to the Communists, who had been pushed westward by the advance of American and South Vietnamese forces. By that time the *Columbia Eagle* was forgotten.

APPENDIX I

DEFENSE DEPARTMENT PRESS RELEASE

August 2, 1964

The following was released by CINCPAC at 1015 EDT today:

While on routine patrol in international waters at 020808 GCT (1608 local time), the U.S. destroyer MADDOX underwent an unprovoked attack by three PT-type boats in latitude 19–40 North; longitude 106–34 East; in the Tonkin Gulf.

The attacking boats launched three torpedoes and used 37 millimeter gunfire. The MADDOX answered with five-inch gunfire. Shortly thereafter four F-8 (Crusader) aircraft from the USS TICONDEROGA joined in the defense of MADDOX, using ZUNI rockets and 20 millimeter strafing attacks. The PT boats were driven off, with one seen to be badly damaged and not moving and the other two damaged and retreating slowly.

No casualties or damage were sustained by MADDOX or the aircraft.

APPENDIX II

DEFENSE DEPARTMENT PRESS RELEASE

FOR THE PRESS   August 3, 1964   NO. 566-64
                                               OXford 75131 (Info)
                                               OXford 73189 (Copies)

The following is a chronology of the incident concerning the USS MADDOX (DD-731) on August 2, 1964:

(All times are Eastern Daylight Time)

11:00 P.M., August 1:
MADDOX reported observing an estimated 75 junks near her assigned patrol area off the North Viet Nam coast. She reported changing her course in order to avoid the junk concentration and indicated that there was no evidence of any hostility.

1:30 A.M., August 2:
MADDOX reported that three torpedo boats were on a southerly course heading toward the ship at extreme range (over 10 miles). The MADDOX at this point was about 30 miles from the coast.

3:40 A.M., August 2:
MADDOX reported she was being approached by the high speed (estimated 45 to 50 knots) craft whose apparent intention was to conduct a torpedo attack and that she intended to open fire in self-defense if necessary.

4:08 A.M., August 2:
MADDOX reported she was being attacked by the three PT craft. She opened fire with her five-inch battery after three warning shots failed to slow down the attackers.

4:08 A.M., August 2:
The PT's continued their closing maneuvers and two of the PT's closed to 5000 yards, each firing one torpedo. The MADDOX changed course in

an evasive move and the two torpedoes passed close aboard on the starboard side (100 to 200 yards).

USS TICONDEROGA (CVA-14) advised she was sending four already airborne F-8E's (CRUSADERS) with rockets and 20 mm. ammunition to provide air cover for MADDOX. The pilots were instructed not to fire unless MADDOX or the aircraft were fired upon.

4:21 A.M., August 2:
The third PT moved up to the beam of the MADDOX and received a direct hit by a five-inch round, and at the same time dropped a torpedo into the water which was not seen to run. Machine gun fire from the PT's was directed at the MADDOX. However, there was no damage or injury to personnel. The MADDOX continued in a southerly direction to join with the C. TURNER JOY (DD-951) as TICONDEROGA aircraft commenced attacking the PT's. ZUNI rocket runs and 20 mm strafing attacks were directed against two of the PT's and they were damaged. The third PT remained dead in the water after the direct hit by the MADDOX. At 4:29 A.M., the aircraft broke off the engagement and escorted the MADDOX towards South Viet Nam waters.

The C. TURNER JOY has joined with the MADDOX and they are continuing patrols in the area in international waters. Aircraft from the TICONDEROGA are providing protective coverage.

Index

Turner Joy (cont'd)
joins with the *Maddox* to form Task Group in Tonkin Gulf patrol, 162–63, 298; Com. Herrick's greeting to, in Tonkin Gulf patrol, 163; as Navy's latest type of DD, 164; near-destruction of, by the *Maddox*, 207–8; report of, on August 4 Tonkin Gulf battle, 217–18; end of patrol of, in the Gulf, 246; visit of investigative party to, 252–54; return of, to Long Beach, Cal., 255. *See also* August 4, 1964; Task Group in Tonkin Gulf

United Nations, 17–18, 24, 32, 35, 135, 249, 250, 254
U. S. Intelligence Board, 63*n*
U. S. Naval Institute Proceedings, 132
United States Naval Operations: Korea (Field), 133*n*
United States-Soviet relations, and air raids over North Vietnam, 321
Urban, Com. Henry, 232, 236
U-2 flight of 1960, 82, 340
U-2 photographs of North Vietnamese territory, 239, 240

Vance, Cyrus R., 48, 90, 214
Viet Cong in South Vietnam, 27, 29, 36–37, 38, 154–55, 239, 303–4, 306, 307, 308, 309, 315, 316; bombing of USNS *Card* by, 154–55, 311; attack of, on U.S. secret base of air bombers, 241–42; rocket and mortar attacks of, 263; attack of, on U. S. Air Force base at Pleiku, 320
Vietnamese situation: in 1964, attitude of Johnson and his administration toward, 300–1; and the Kennedy administration, 302–6; language situation in, 304–5; and early days of Johnson's presidency, 306–8; year of 1963 as one of glowing promise, 306; March 9, 1964 *Newsweek* survey of official opinion on, 309–10; change in, with new leadership of Taylor-Westmoreland team and emphasis on "winning the war," 314; in 1964, and the Tonkin Gulf incidents, 316–17; and Tonkin Gulf resolution, 317; actions of American officials in 1964 could be labeled as part of obvious plot, 318; military build-up of 1964, largely secret, 318; difficulty of divining administration's attitude toward (1964), 318–19; commitment of ground troops, 322, 324;

supply line, and shortages, and waste, 322; long war or short war, differences in plans and expectations for, 322; Johnson administration's maneuverings in early 1965 for consent to set military plans, 322–23; Johnson's offer (April 1965) of "unconditional discussions: to Hanoi, 323; expansion and escalation of the war by Johnson administration, 324–25; and South Vietnamese public opinion, 325; error of planning intervention in secret, 325
Vietnam issue as 1964 election asset for President Johnson, 25, 47
Vietnam Task Force, 308–9, 321
Vietnam War: U.S. Shuffling into, with President Johnson calling the tune, 35–39; commitment of U.S. ground troops in, and Congress, 37–38; President Johnson's television announcement of, July 28, 1965, 38–39; military victory as President Johnson's aim in, 41, 325; hearings of Foreign Relations Committee on, 41–42, 46, 50; beginning of hawk and dove confrontation on, 42; determining who the real enemy in Vietnam was, 300–1, 326; official theory of, 325–26; typical views of doves and hawks on, 326
Villa, Pancho, of Mexico, 331
Visual sightings as evidence in August 4 battle, 270–81
Visual signals: use of, by Navy in communicating, 140–43; failure of the *Maddox* to use, 141, 142, 143

Warning shots: fired by *Maddox* in August 2 battle in Tonkin Gulf, 120, 121, 128, 136, 139, 144, 161, 255; in naval tactics, 139–40, 149
Wars of U.S. made by Presidents without congressional authorization, 329–31, 331–32
Watchdog Station, radar picket duty at, 160–62
Weems, John E., 1*n*
Weintal, Edward, 315*n*
Westmoreland, Gen. William C., 31*n*, 37, 170, 258, 296, 312, 314, 315, 316, 322, 324, 325
Wheeler, Gen. Earle G., 9–10, 18, 101, 139, 150, 151, 161, 170, 183, 193, 214, 226, 237, 258, 298, 299, 335
White, Lt. John W., 49–50, 100
Whitmore, Lt. Wayne, of the *Turner Joy*, 199, 274
Wicker, Tom, 318*n*, 319